The Earl & the Fairy

Story & Art by Ayuko
Original Concept by Mizue Tani

From Cobalt Series *Hakushaku to Yosei Aitsu Wa Yuga Na Daiakuto* (The Earl and the Fairy: He Is an Elegant Scoundrel)

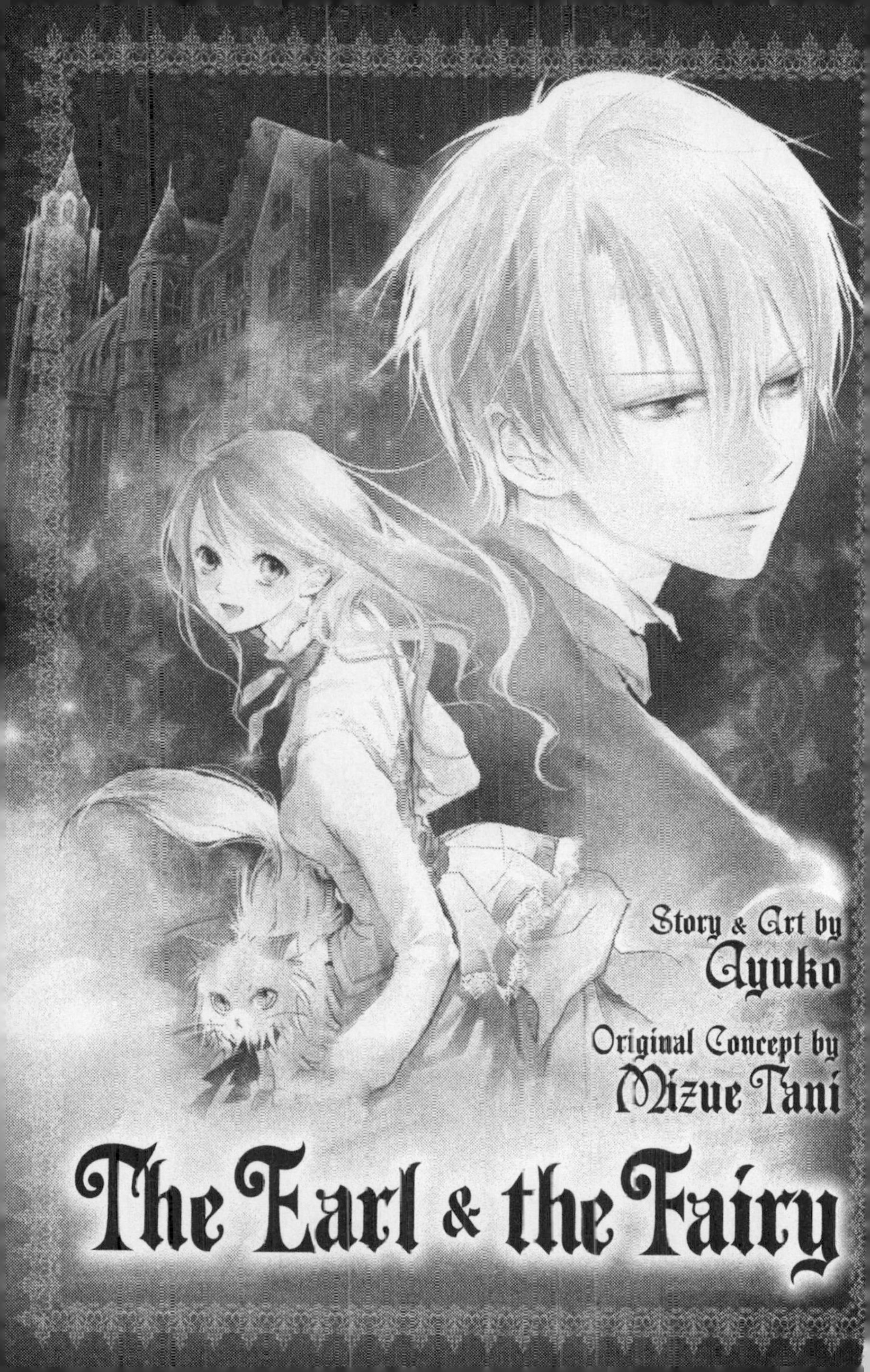
Story & Art by
Ayuko
Original Concept by
Mizue Tani
The Earl & the Fairy

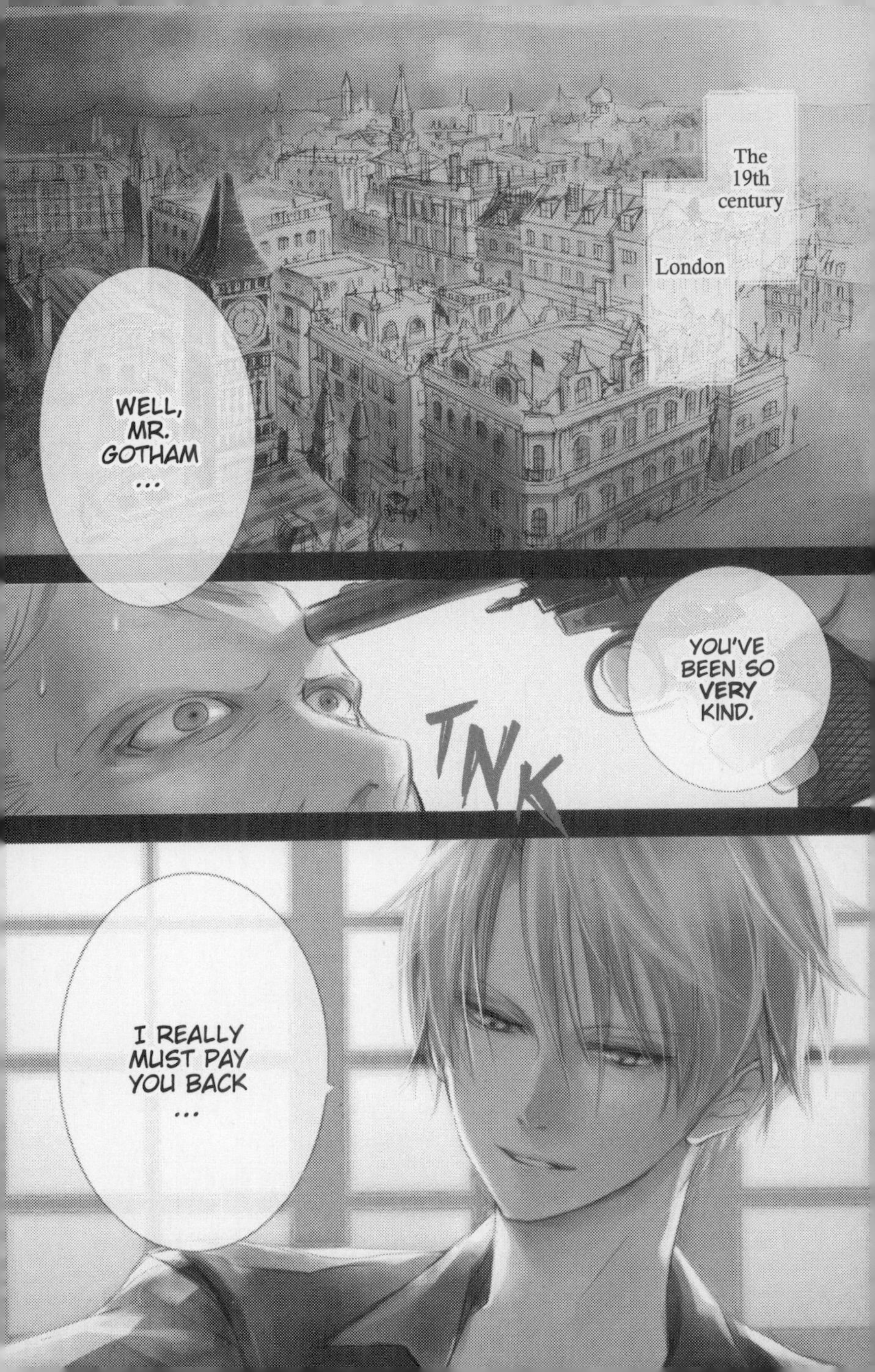
The 19th century
London
WELL, MR. GOTHAM ...
YOU'VE BEEN SO VERY KIND.
TNK
I REALLY MUST PAY YOU BACK ...

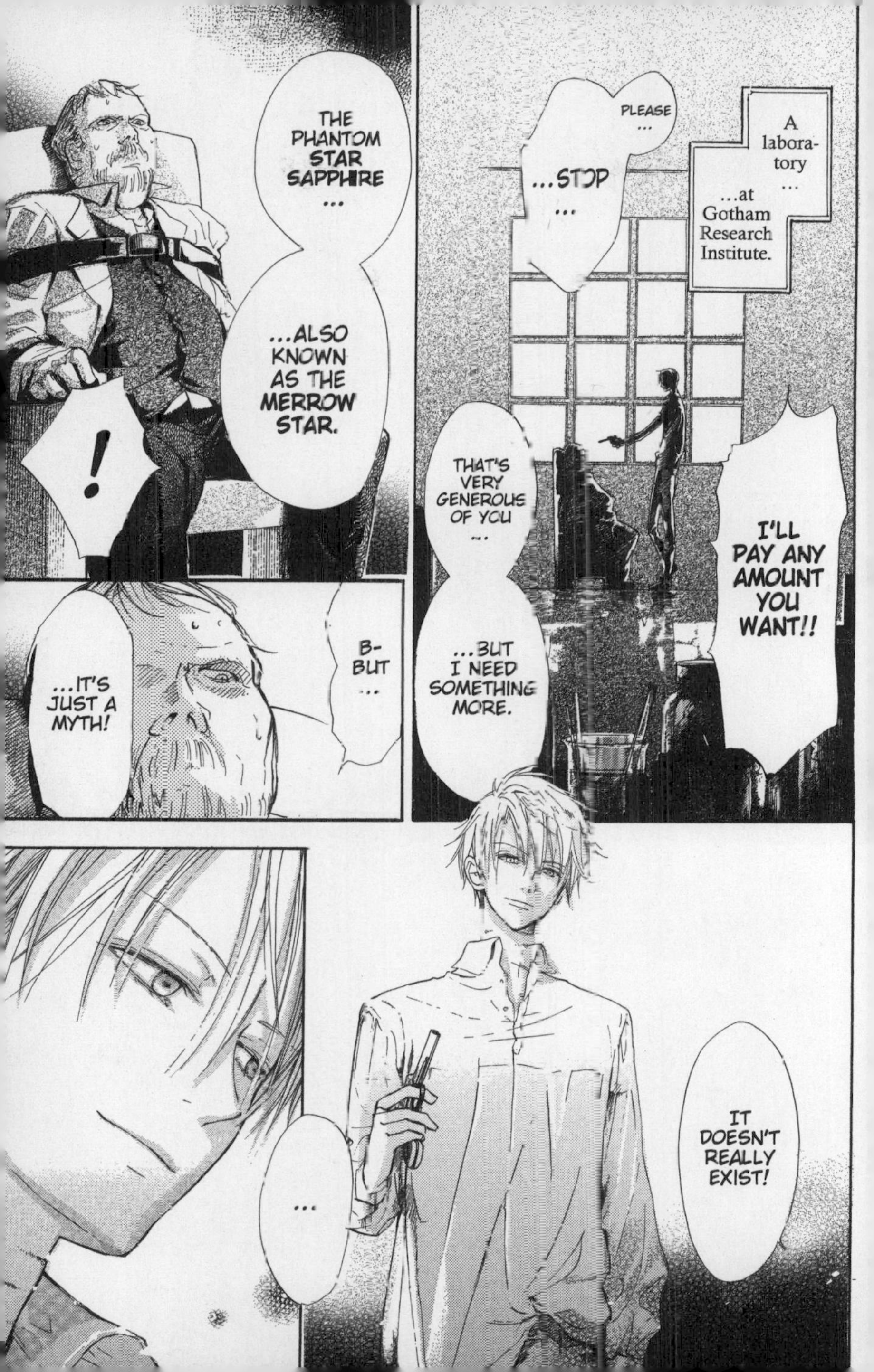
A laboratory ...
...at Gotham Research Institute.
PLEASE ...
...STOP ...
I'LL PAY ANY AMOUNT YOU WANT!!
THAT'S VERY GENEROUS OF YOU ...
...BUT I NEED SOMETHING MORE.
THE PHANTOM STAR SAPPHIRE ...
...ALSO KNOWN AS THE MERROW STAR.
!
B-BUT ...
...IT'S JUST A MYTH!
IT DOESN'T REALLY EXIST!
...

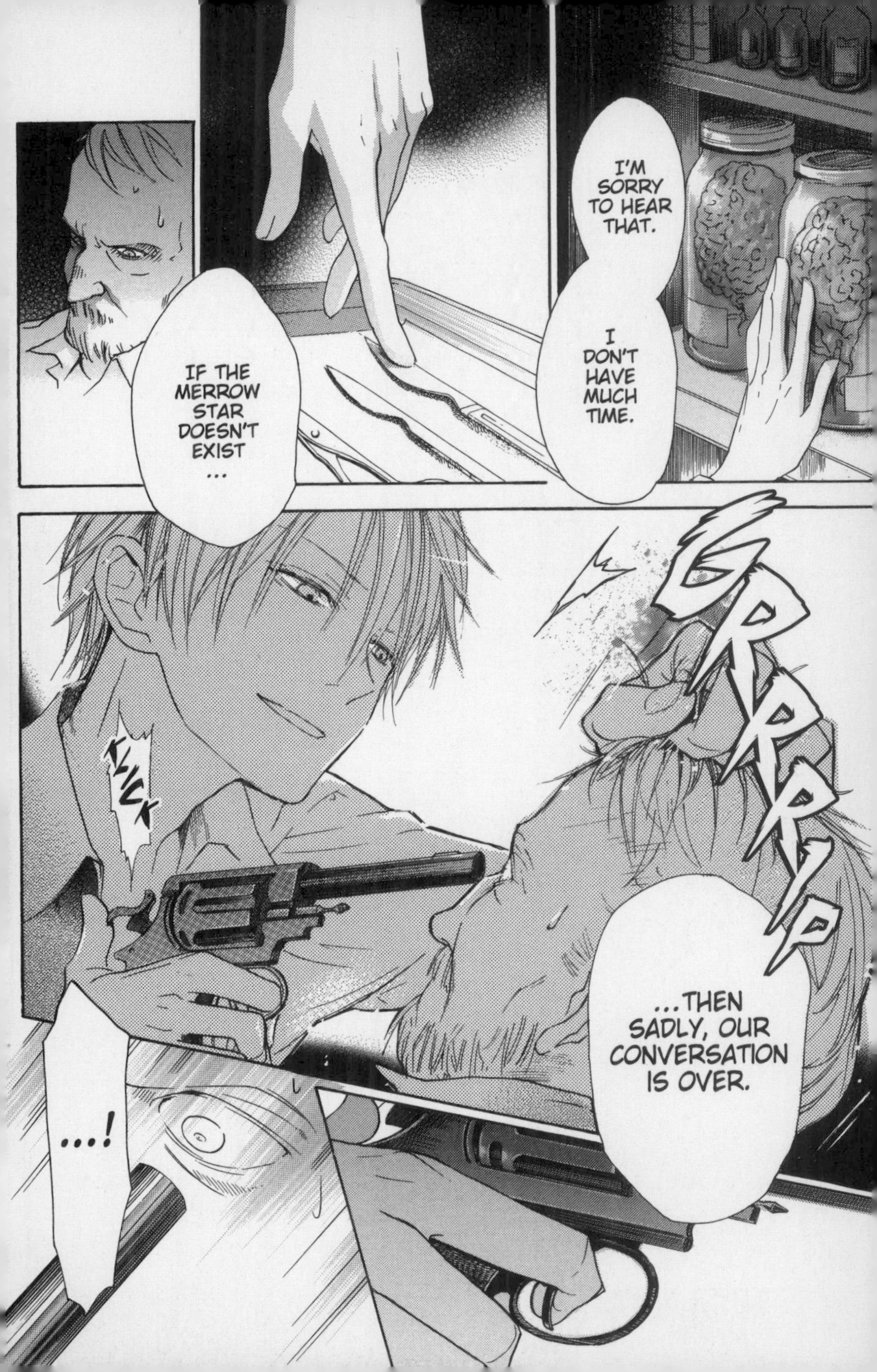
I'M SORRY TO HEAR THAT.
I DON'T HAVE MUCH TIME.
IF THE MERROW STAR DOESN'T EXIST ...
GRRRIP
KLICK
...THEN SADLY, OUR CONVERSATION IS OVER.
...!

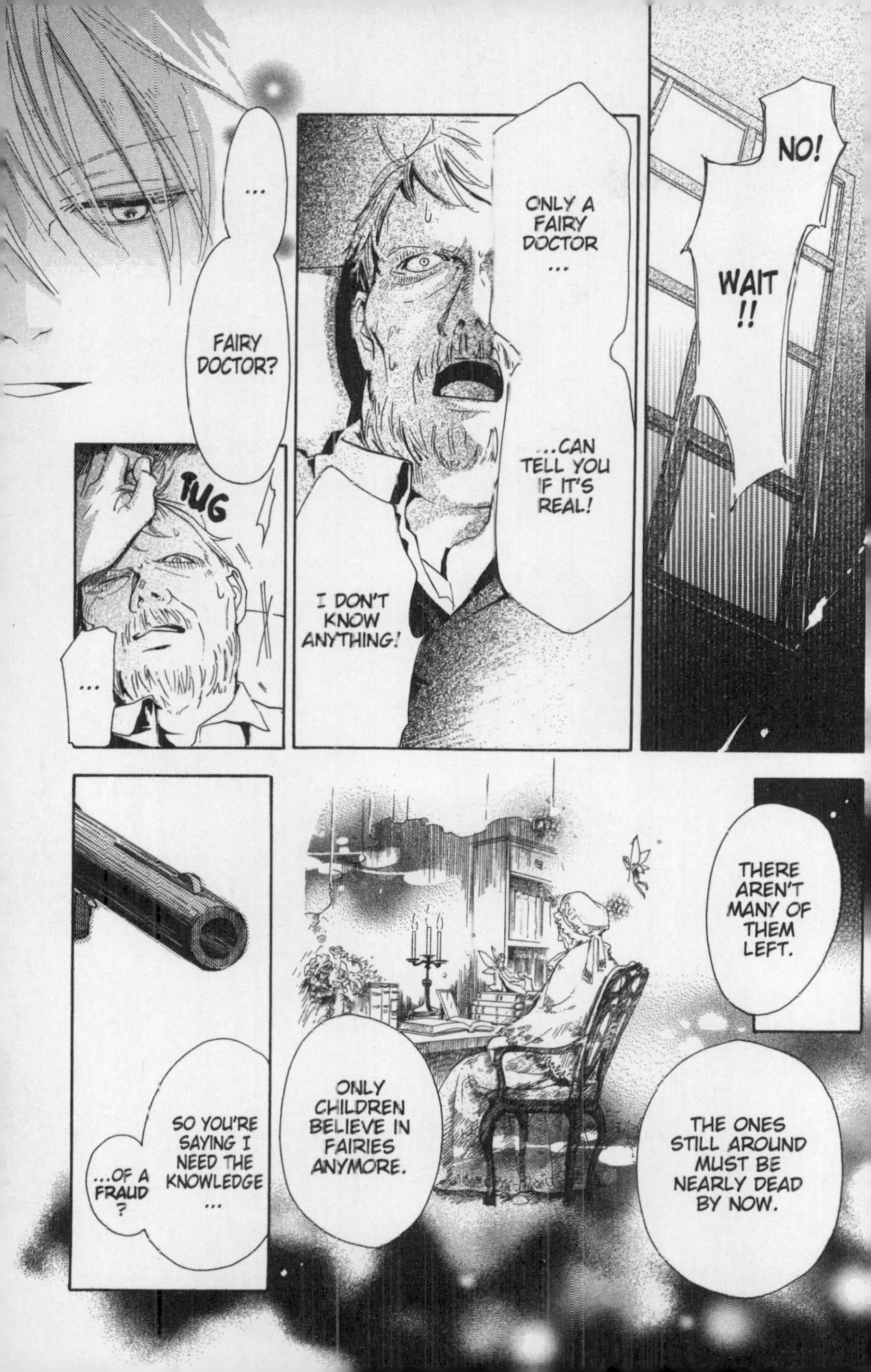
NO!
WAIT !!
ONLY A FAIRY DOCTOR ...
...CAN TELL YOU IF IT'S REAL!
I DON'T KNOW ANYTHING!
...
FAIRY DOCTOR?
TUG
...
THERE AREN'T MANY OF THEM LEFT.
THE ONES STILL AROUND MUST BE NEARLY DEAD BY NOW.
ONLY CHILDREN BELIEVE IN FAIRIES ANYMORE.
SO YOU'RE SAYING I NEED THE KNOWLEDGE ...
...OF A FRAUD ?

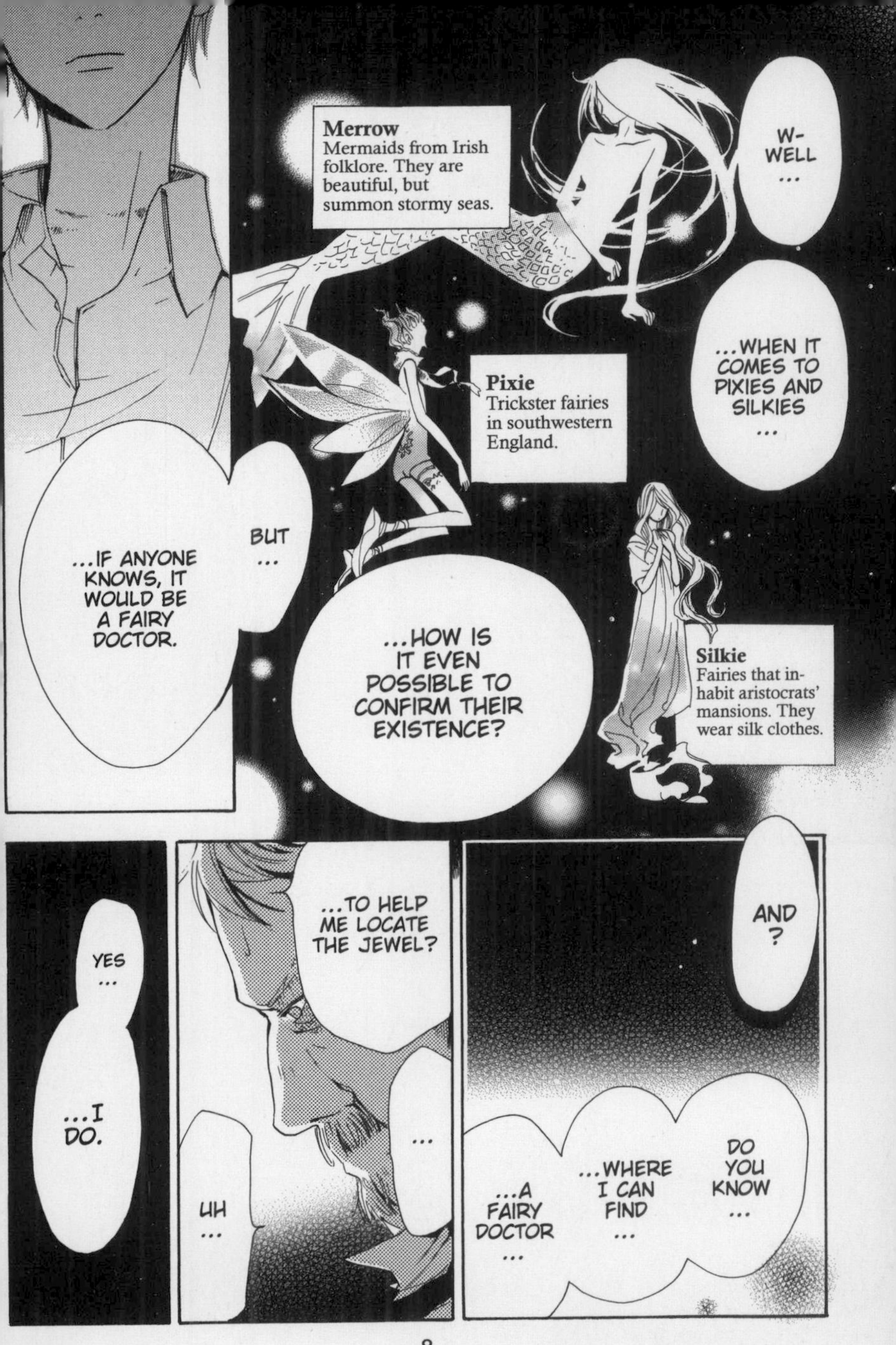
W-WELL ...
Merrow
Mermaids from Irish folklore. They are beautiful, but summon stormy seas.
...WHEN IT COMES TO PIXIES AND SILKIES ...
Pixie
Trickster fairies in southwestern England.
Silkie
Fairies that inhabit aristocrats' mansions. They wear silk clothes.
...HOW IS IT EVEN POSSIBLE TO CONFIRM THEIR EXISTENCE?
BUT ...
...IF ANYONE KNOWS, IT WOULD BE A FAIRY DOCTOR.
AND ?
DO YOU KNOW ...
...WHERE I CAN FIND ...
...A FAIRY DOCTOR ...
...TO HELP ME LOCATE THE JEWEL?
...
UH ...
YES ...
...I DO.

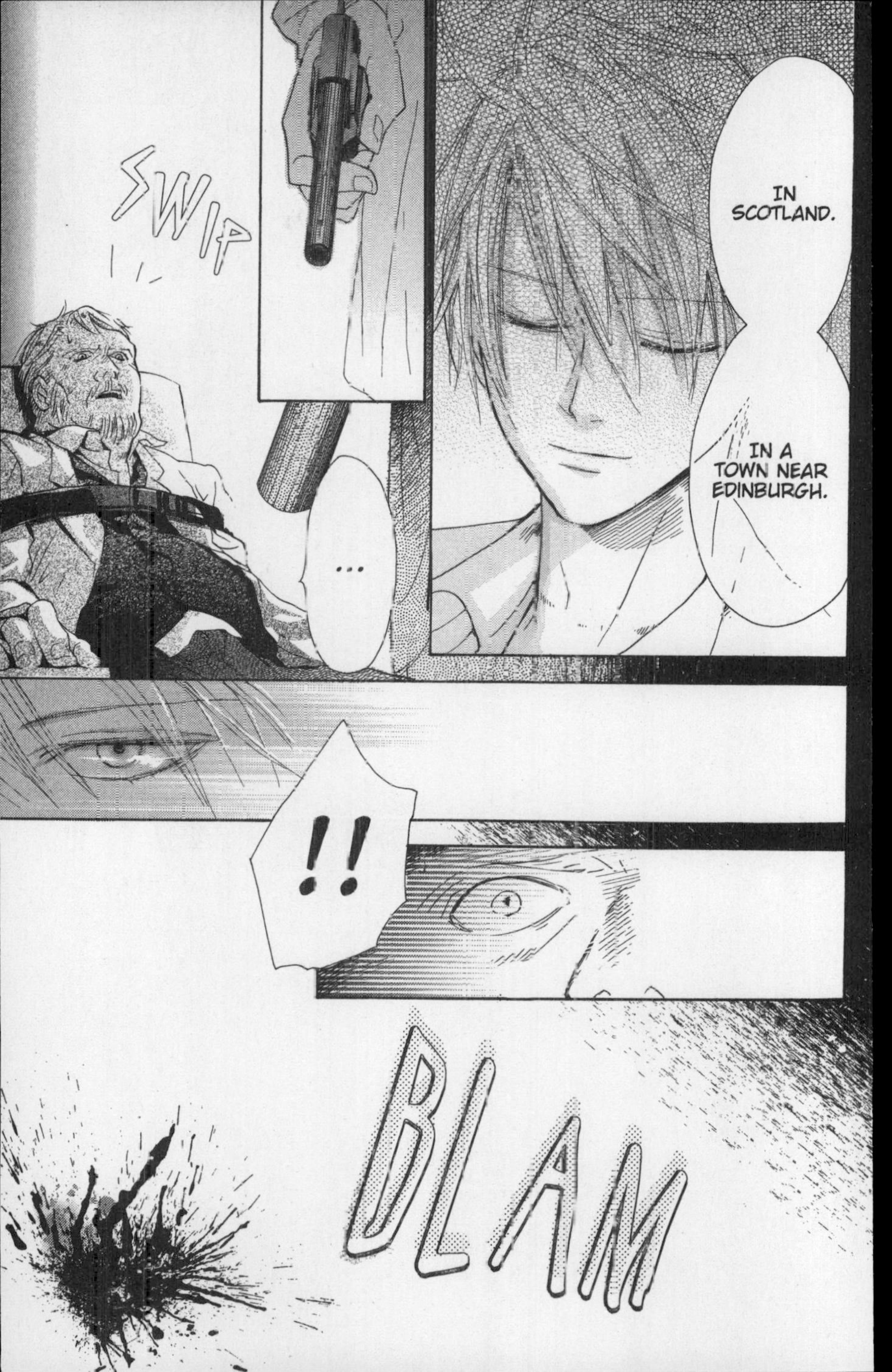
IN SCOTLAND.
IN A TOWN NEAR EDINBURGH.
SWIP
...
!!
BLAM

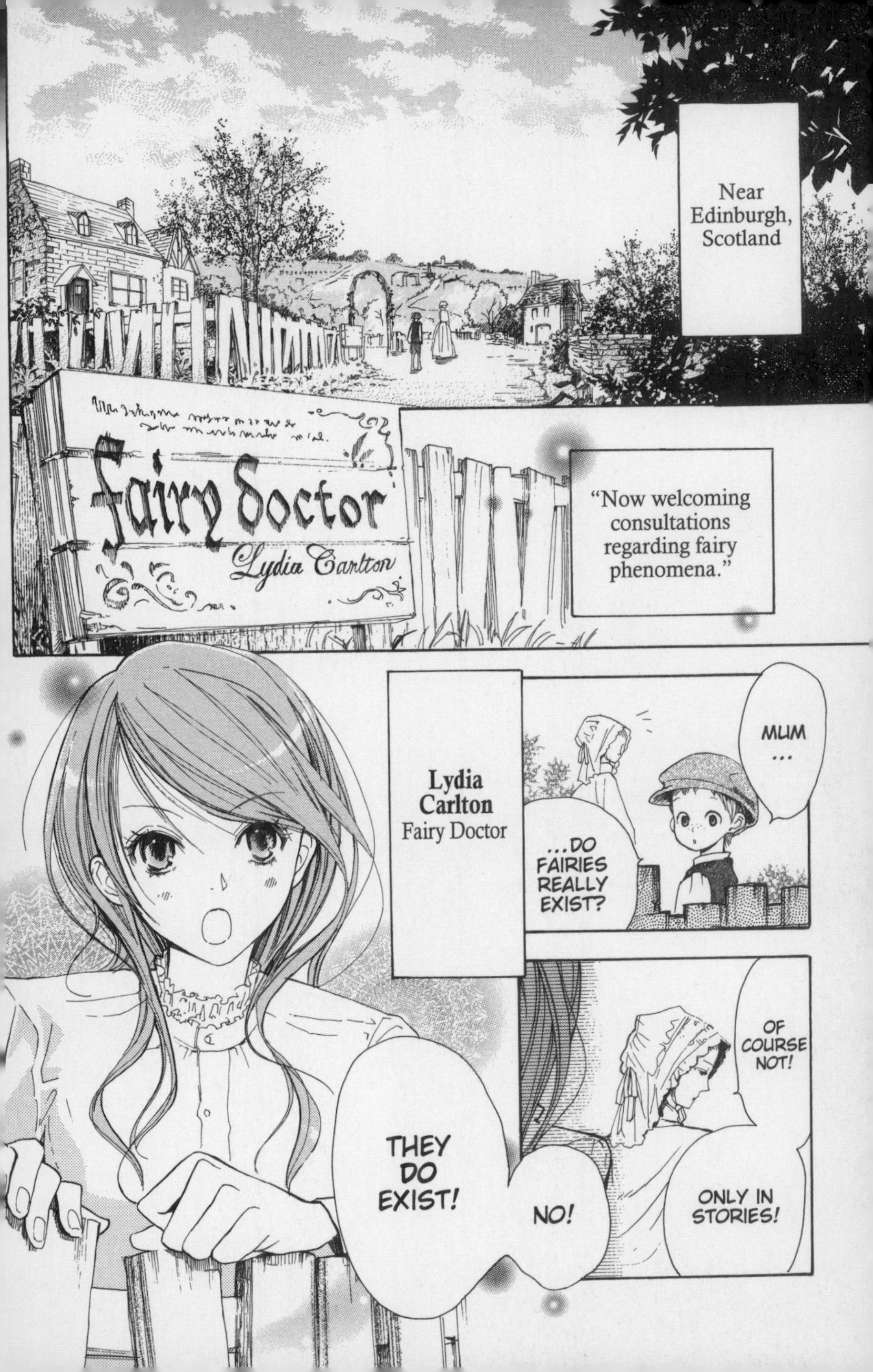
Near Edinburgh, Scotland
"Now welcoming consultations regarding fairy phenomena."
Fairy Doctor
Lydia Carlton
MUM ...
...DO FAIRIES REALLY EXIST?
OF COURSE NOT!
ONLY IN STORIES!
Lydia Carlton
Fairy Doctor
NO!
THEY DO EXIST!

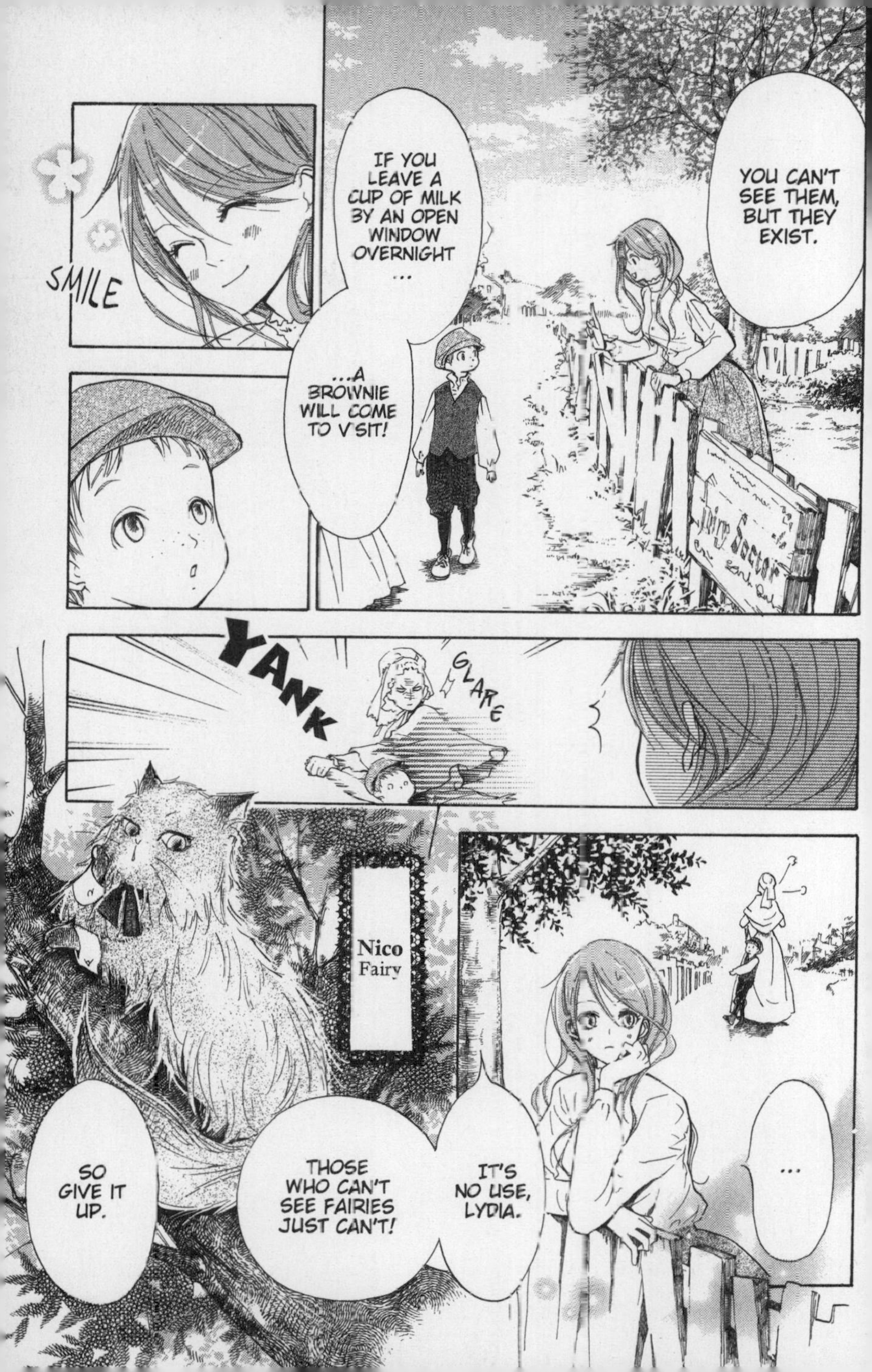
YOU CAN'T SEE THEM, BUT THEY EXIST.
IF YOU LEAVE A CUP OF MILK BY AN OPEN WINDOW OVERNIGHT...
...A BROWNIE WILL COME TO VISIT!
SMILE
YANK
GLARE
...
IT'S NO USE, LYDIA.
THOSE WHO CAN'T SEE FAIRIES JUST CAN'T!
SO GIVE IT UP.
Nico
Fairy

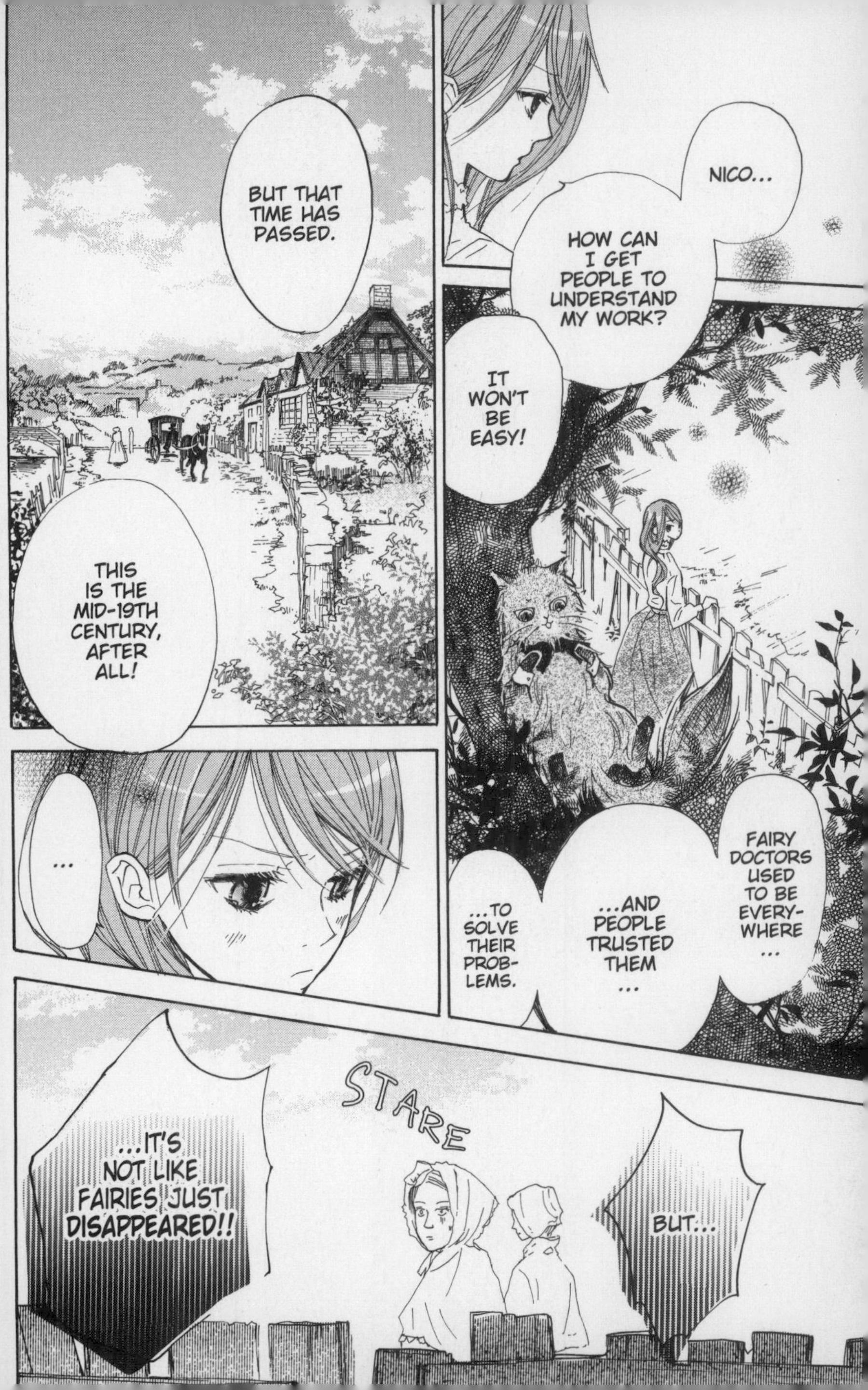
NICO...
HOW CAN I GET PEOPLE TO UNDERSTAND MY WORK?
IT WON'T BE EASY!
FAIRY DOCTORS USED TO BE EVERY-WHERE...
...AND PEOPLE TRUSTED THEM...
...TO SOLVE THEIR PROB-LEMS.
BUT THAT TIME HAS PASSED.
THIS IS THE MID-19TH CENTURY, AFTER ALL!
...
BUT...
STARE
...IT'S NOT LIKE FAIRIES JUST DISAPPEARED!!

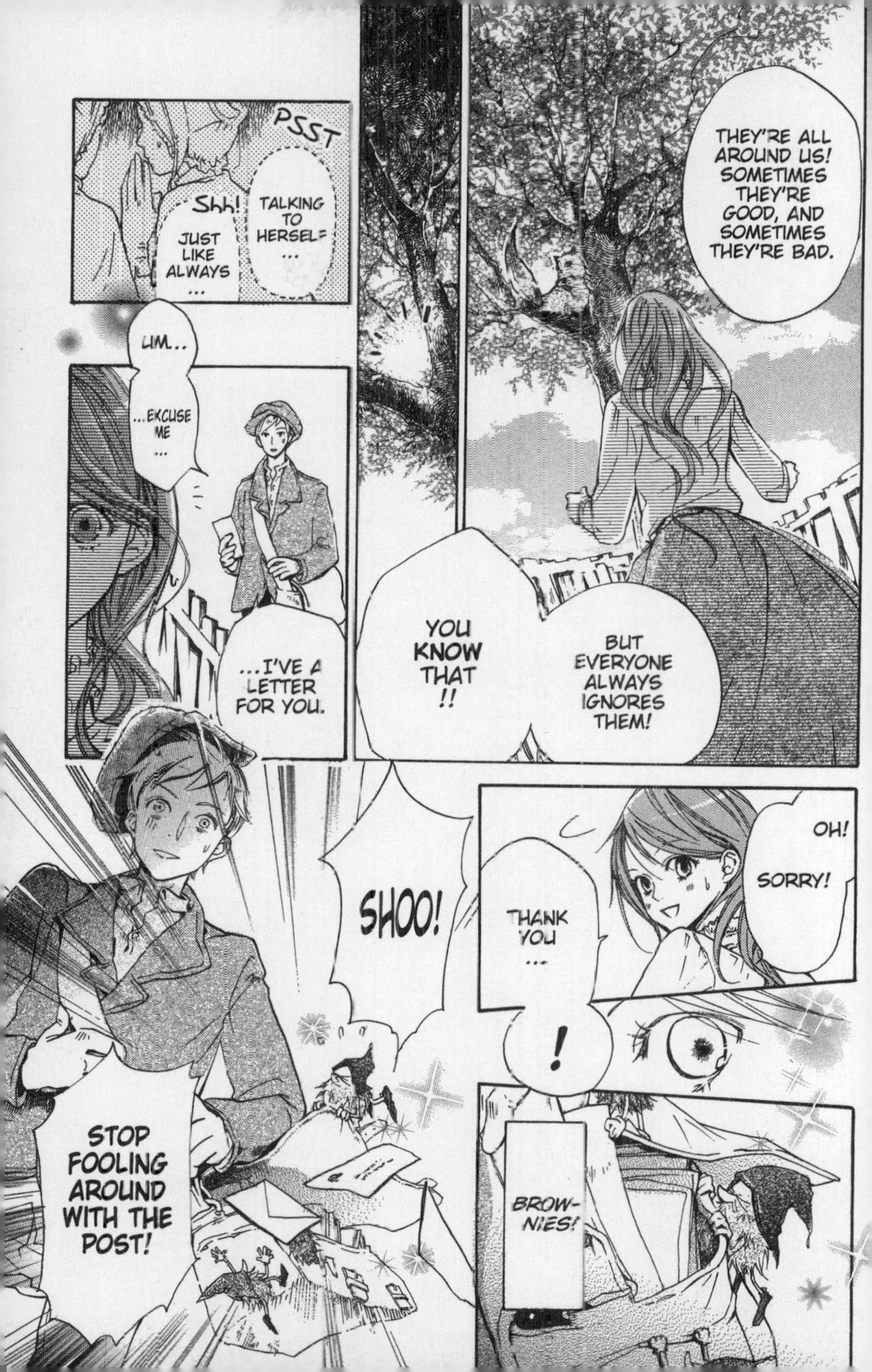
THEY'RE ALL AROUND US! SOMETIMES THEY'RE GOOD, AND SOMETIMES THEY'RE BAD.
BUT EVERYONE ALWAYS IGNORES THEM!
YOU KNOW THAT!!
PSST
TALKING TO HERSELF...
Shh!
JUST LIKE ALWAYS...
UM...
...EXCUSE ME...
...I'VE A LETTER FOR YOU.
OH!
SORRY!
THANK YOU...
!
BROWNIES!
SHOO!
STOP FOOLING AROUND WITH THE POST!

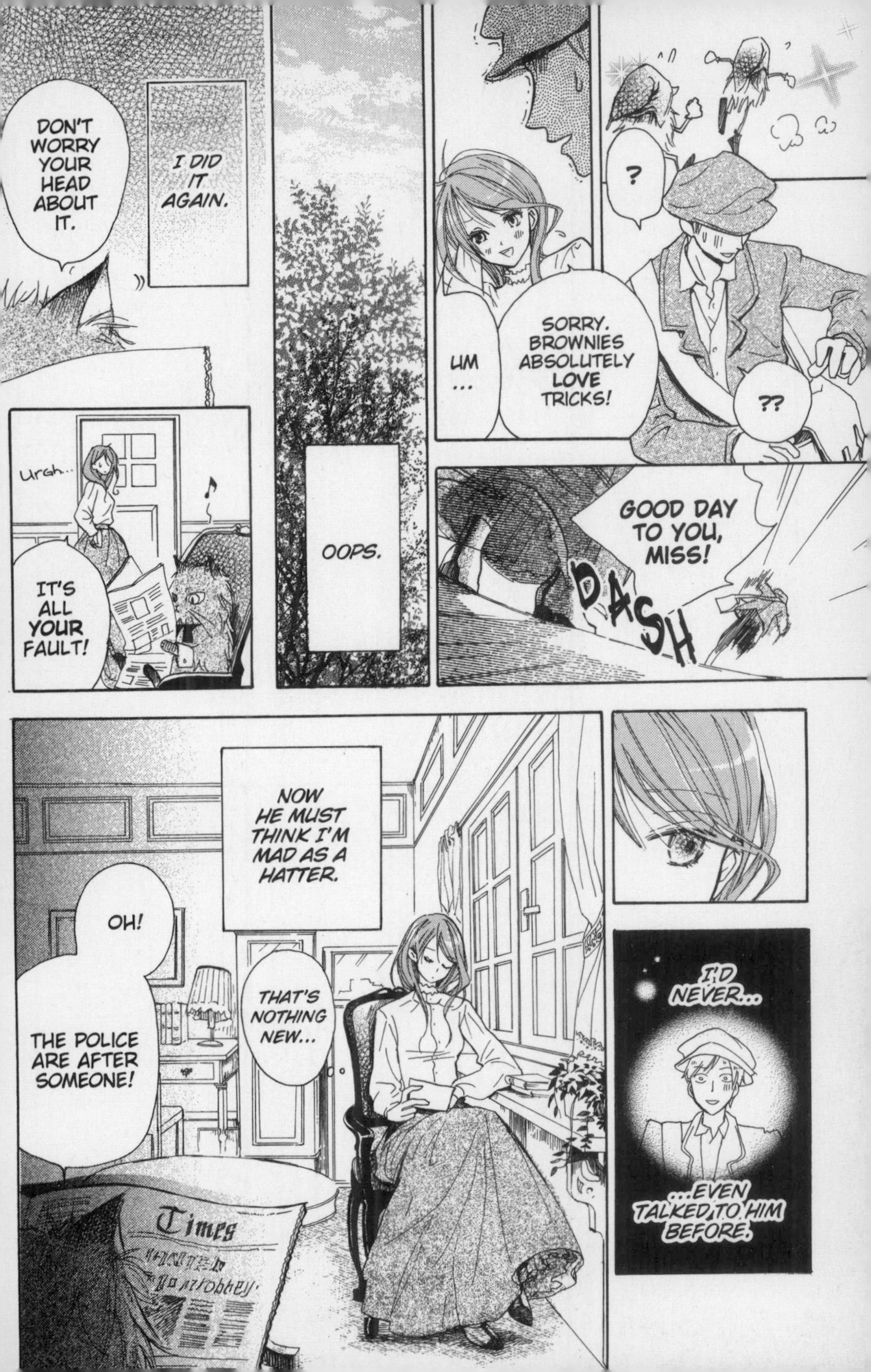
?
??
SORRY. BROWNIES ABSOLUTELY LOVE TRICKS!
UM...
GOOD DAY TO YOU, MISS!
DASH
OOPS.
I DID IT AGAIN.
DON'T WORRY YOUR HEAD ABOUT IT.
Urgh...
IT'S ALL YOUR FAULT!
I'D NEVER...
...EVEN TALKED TO HIM BEFORE.
NOW HE MUST THINK I'M MAD AS A HATTER.
THAT'S NOTHING NEW...
OH!
THE POLICE ARE AFTER SOMEONE!
Times

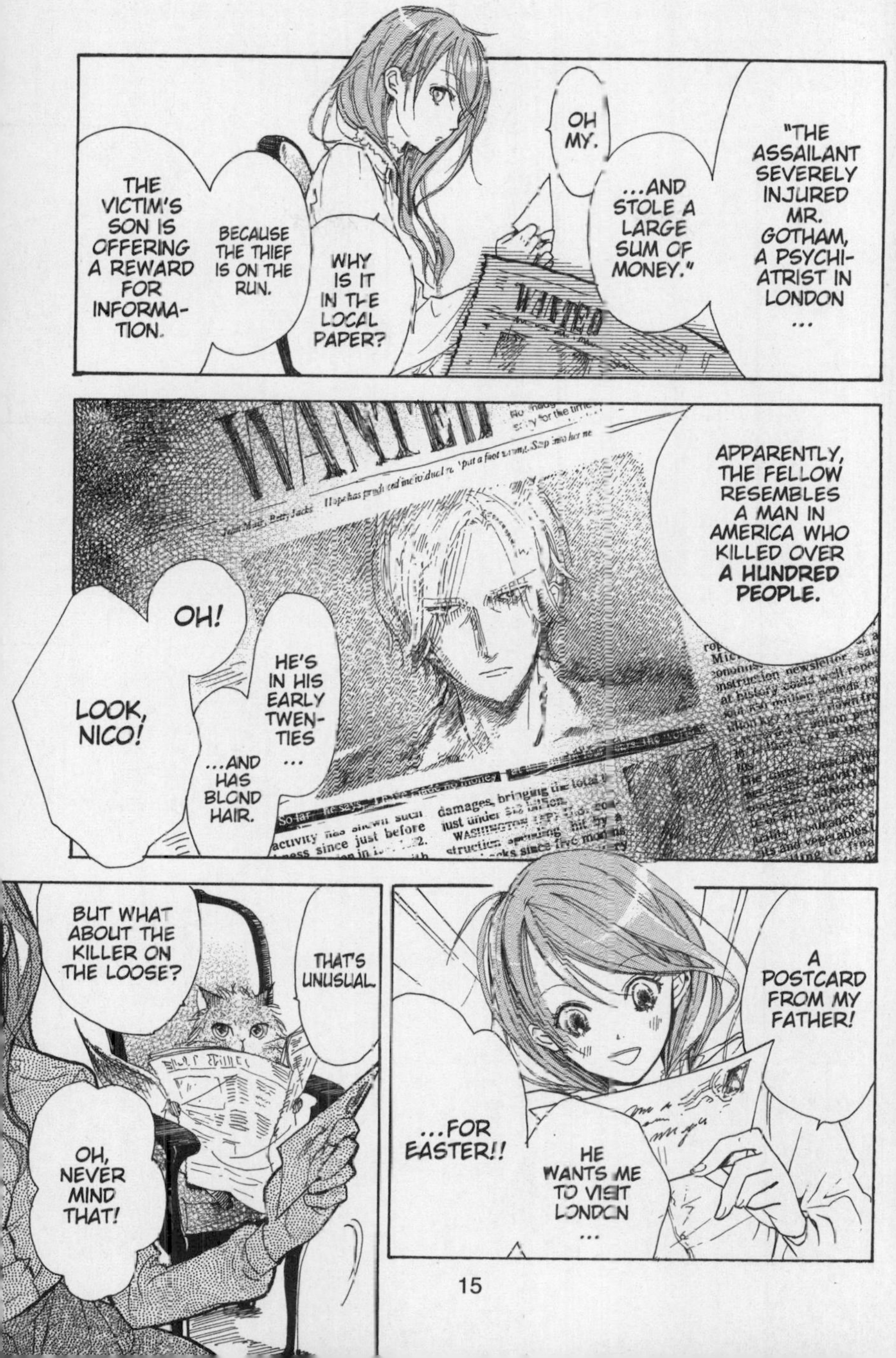
"THE ASSAILANT SEVERELY INJURED MR. GOTHAM, A PSYCHIATRIST IN LONDON ...
...AND STOLE A LARGE SUM OF MONEY."
OH MY.
WHY IS IT IN THE LOCAL PAPER?
BECAUSE THE THIEF IS ON THE RUN.
THE VICTIM'S SON IS OFFERING A REWARD FOR INFORMATION.
WANTED
APPARENTLY, THE FELLOW RESEMBLES A MAN IN AMERICA WHO KILLED OVER A HUNDRED PEOPLE.
HE'S IN HIS EARLY TWENTIES ...
...AND HAS BLOND HAIR.
OH!
LOOK, NICO!
A POSTCARD FROM MY FATHER!
HE WANTS ME TO VISIT LONDON ...
...FOR EASTER!!
THAT'S UNUSUAL.
BUT WHAT ABOUT THE KILLER ON THE LOOSE?
OH, NEVER MIND THAT!

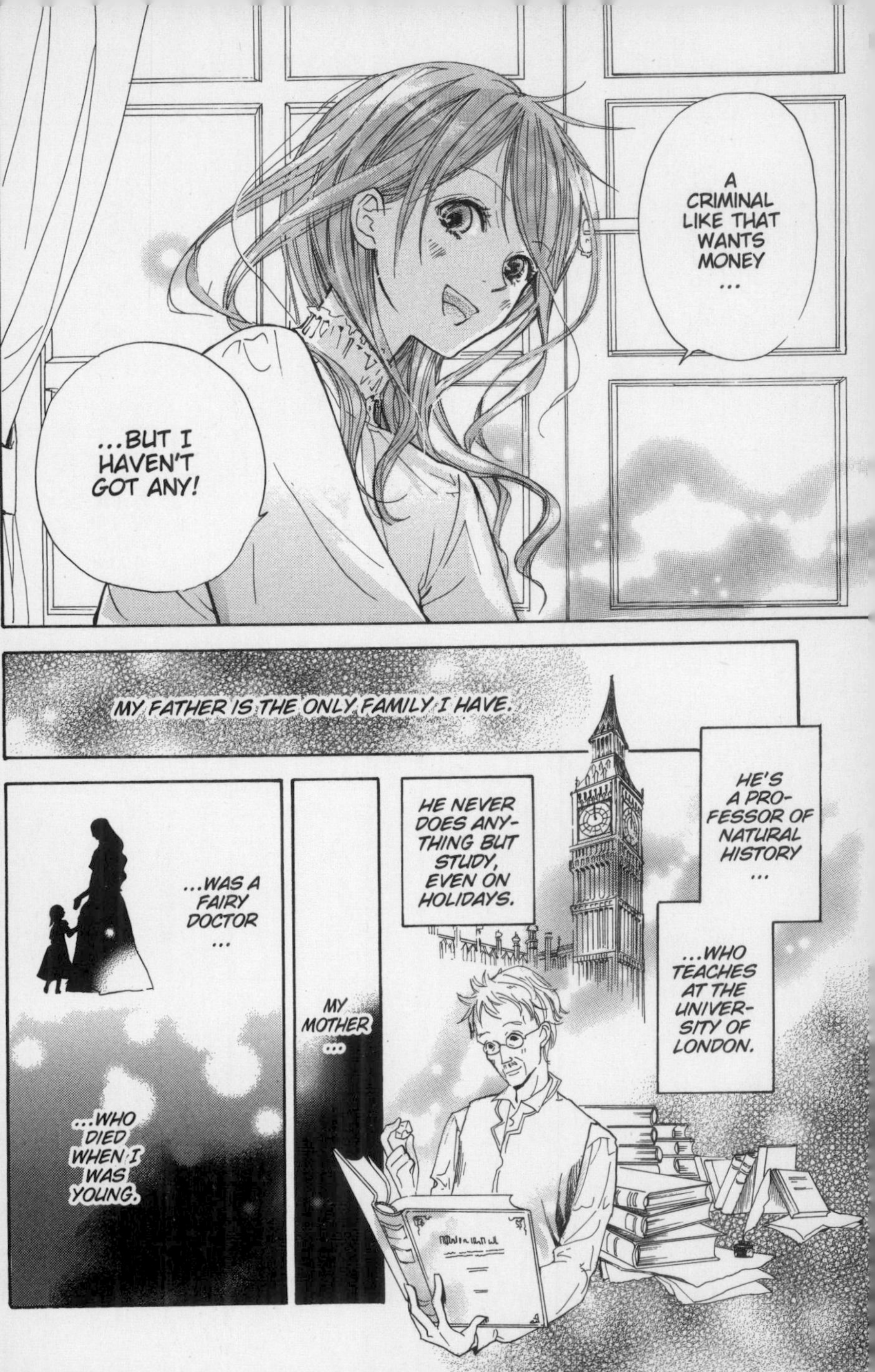
A CRIMINAL LIKE THAT WANTS MONEY ...
...BUT I HAVEN'T GOT ANY!
MY FATHER IS THE ONLY FAMILY I HAVE.
HE'S A PROFESSOR OF NATURAL HISTORY ...
...WHO TEACHES AT THE UNIVERSITY OF LONDON.
HE NEVER DOES ANYTHING BUT STUDY, EVEN ON HOLIDAYS.
MY MOTHER ...
...WAS A FAIRY DOCTOR ...
...WHO DIED WHEN I WAS YOUNG.

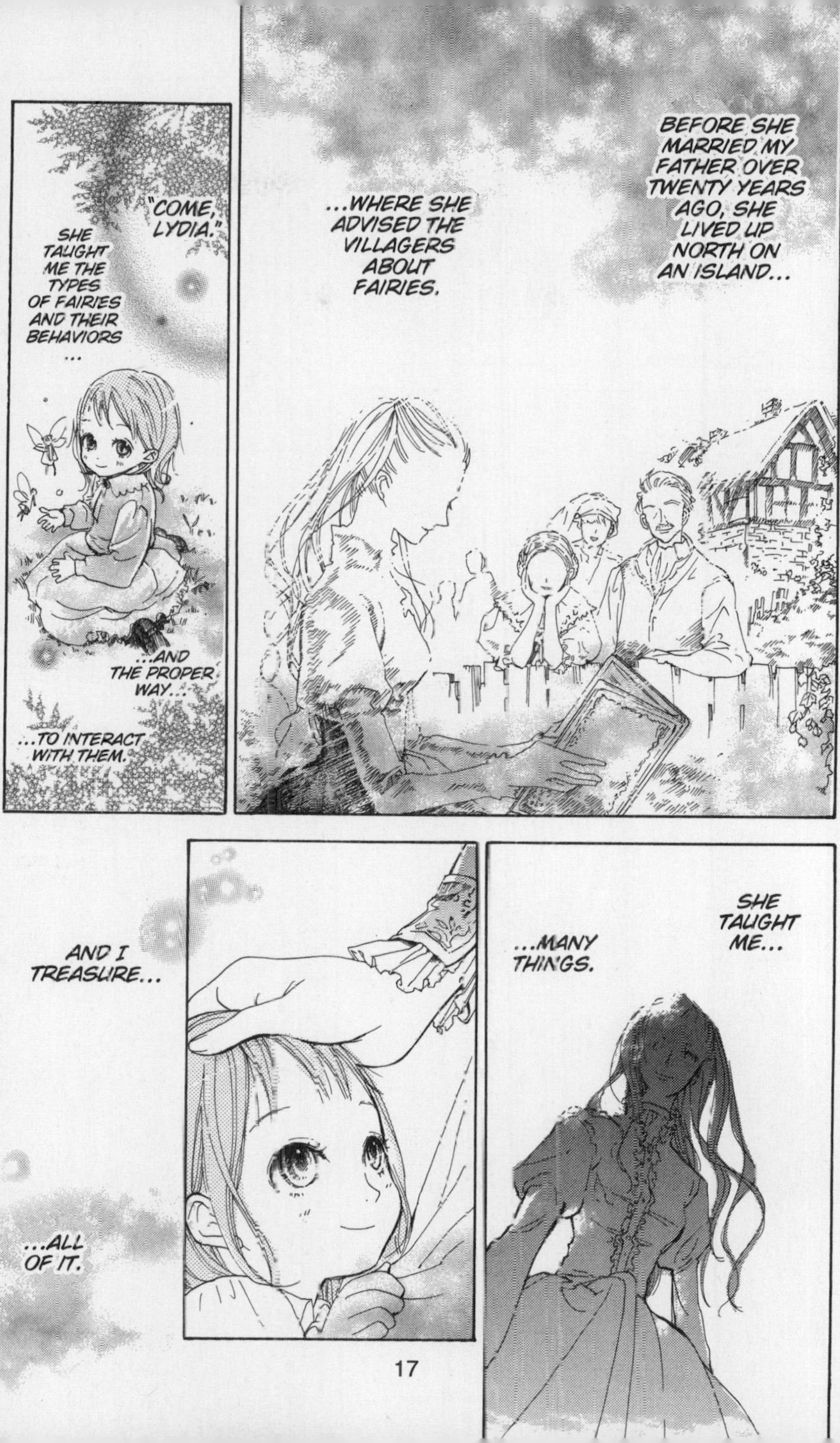
BEFORE SHE MARRIED MY FATHER OVER TWENTY YEARS AGO, SHE LIVED UP NORTH ON AN ISLAND...
...WHERE SHE ADVISED THE VILLAGERS ABOUT FAIRIES.
"COME, LYDIA."
SHE TAUGHT ME THE TYPES OF FAIRIES AND THEIR BEHAVIORS...
...AND THE PROPER WAY...
...TO INTERACT WITH THEM.
SHE TAUGHT ME...
...MANY THINGS.
AND I TREASURE...
...ALL OF IT.

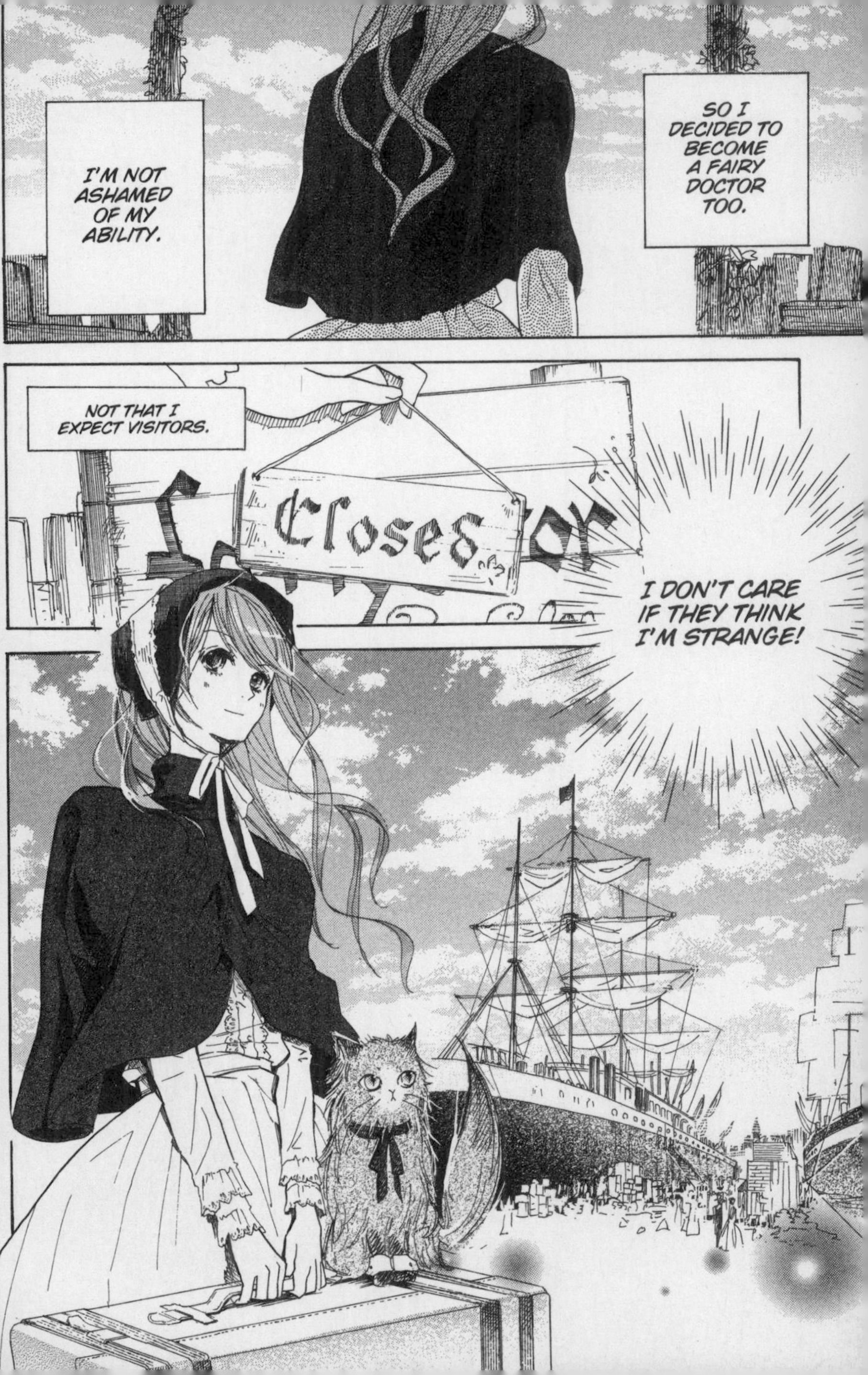
SO I DECIDED TO BECOME A FAIRY DOCTOR TOO.
I'M NOT ASHAMED OF MY ABILITY.
NOT THAT I EXPECT VISITORS.
Closed
I DON'T CARE IF THEY THINK I'M STRANGE!

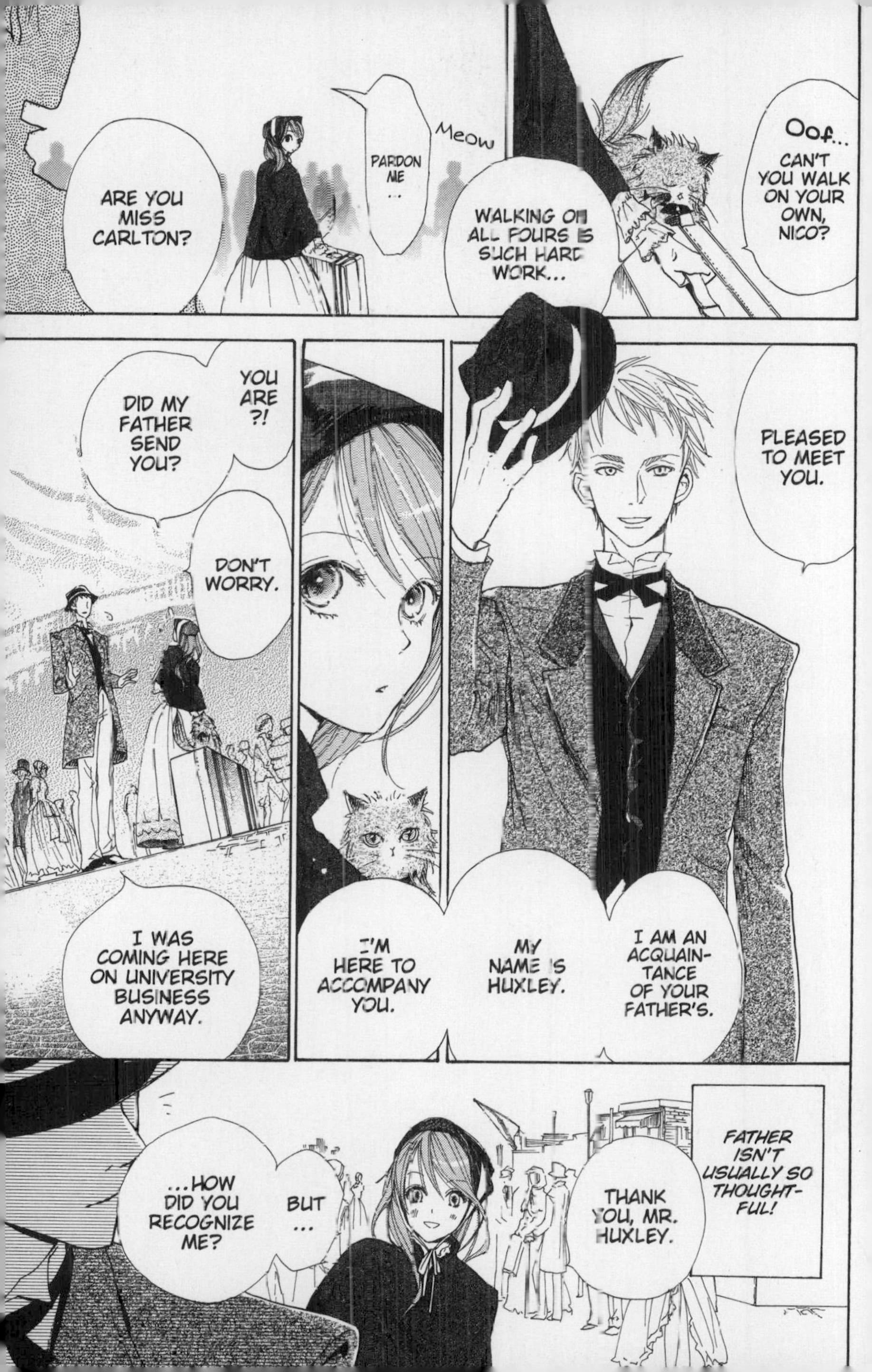
Oof...
CAN'T YOU WALK ON YOUR OWN, NICO?
WALKING ON ALL FOURS IS SUCH HARD WORK...
Meow
PARDON ME...
ARE YOU MISS CARLTON?
PLEASED TO MEET YOU.
I AM AN ACQUAINTANCE OF YOUR FATHER'S.
MY NAME IS HUXLEY.
I'M HERE TO ACCOMPANY YOU.
YOU ARE?!
DID MY FATHER SEND YOU?
DON'T WORRY.
I WAS COMING HERE ON UNIVERSITY BUSINESS ANYWAY.
FATHER ISN'T USUALLY SO THOUGHTFUL!
THANK YOU, MR. HUXLEY.
BUT...
...HOW DID YOU RECOGNIZE ME?

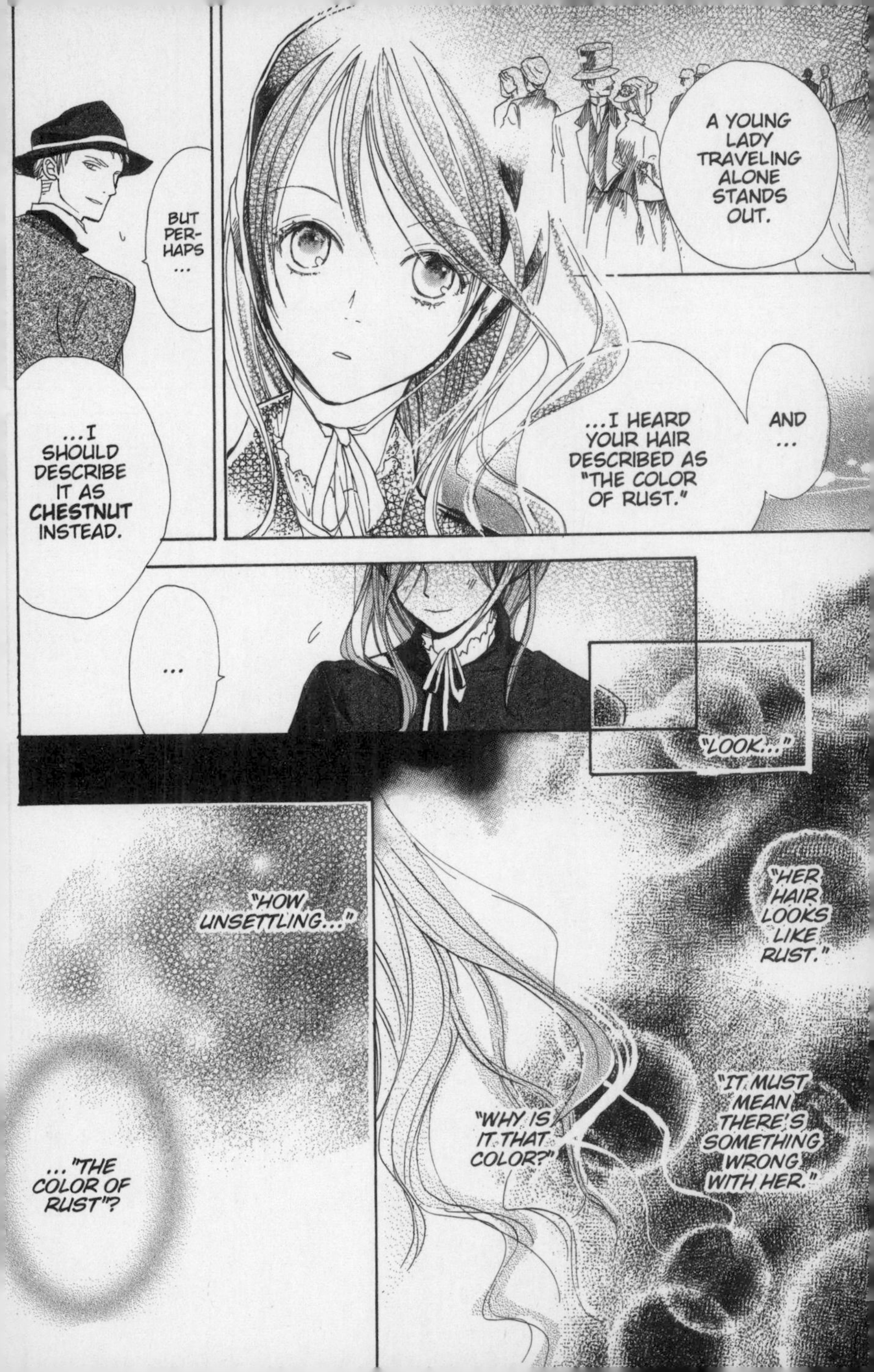
A YOUNG LADY TRAVELING ALONE STANDS OUT.
AND...
...I HEARD YOUR HAIR DESCRIBED AS "THE COLOR OF RUST."
BUT PER-HAPS...
...I SHOULD DESCRIBE IT AS CHESTNUT INSTEAD.
...
"LOOK..."
"HER HAIR LOOKS LIKE RUST."
"IT MUST MEAN THERE'S SOMETHING WRONG WITH HER."
"WHY IS IT THAT COLOR?"
"HOW UNSETTLING..."
..."THE COLOR OF RUST"?

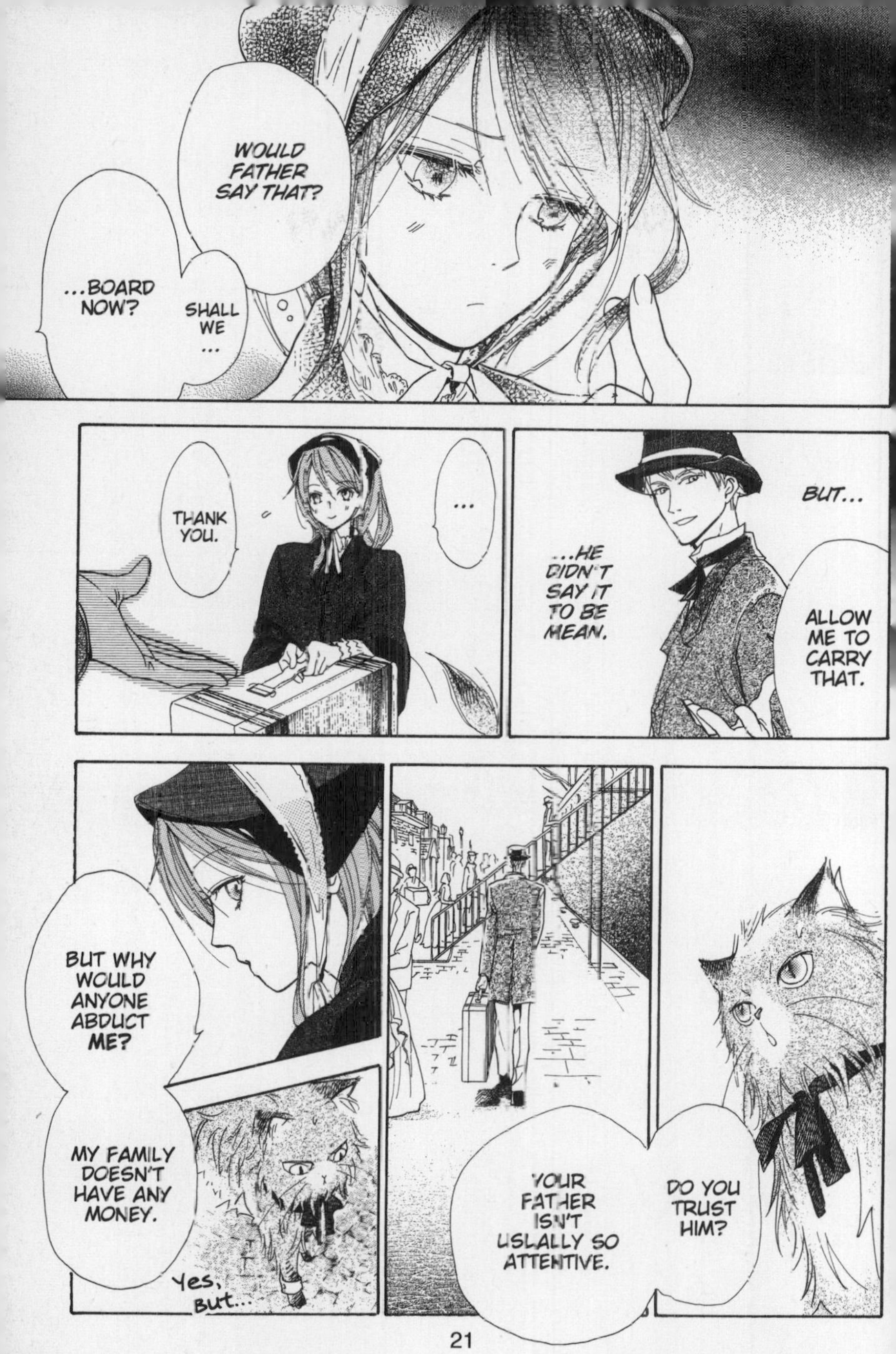
WOULD FATHER SAY THAT?
SHALL WE ...
...BOARD NOW?
BUT...
...HE DIDN'T SAY IT TO BE MEAN.
ALLOW ME TO CARRY THAT.
...
THANK YOU.
DO YOU TRUST HIM?
YOUR FATHER ISN'T USUALLY SO ATTENTIVE.
BUT WHY WOULD ANYONE ABDUCT ME?
MY FAMILY DOESN'T HAVE ANY MONEY.
Yes, but...

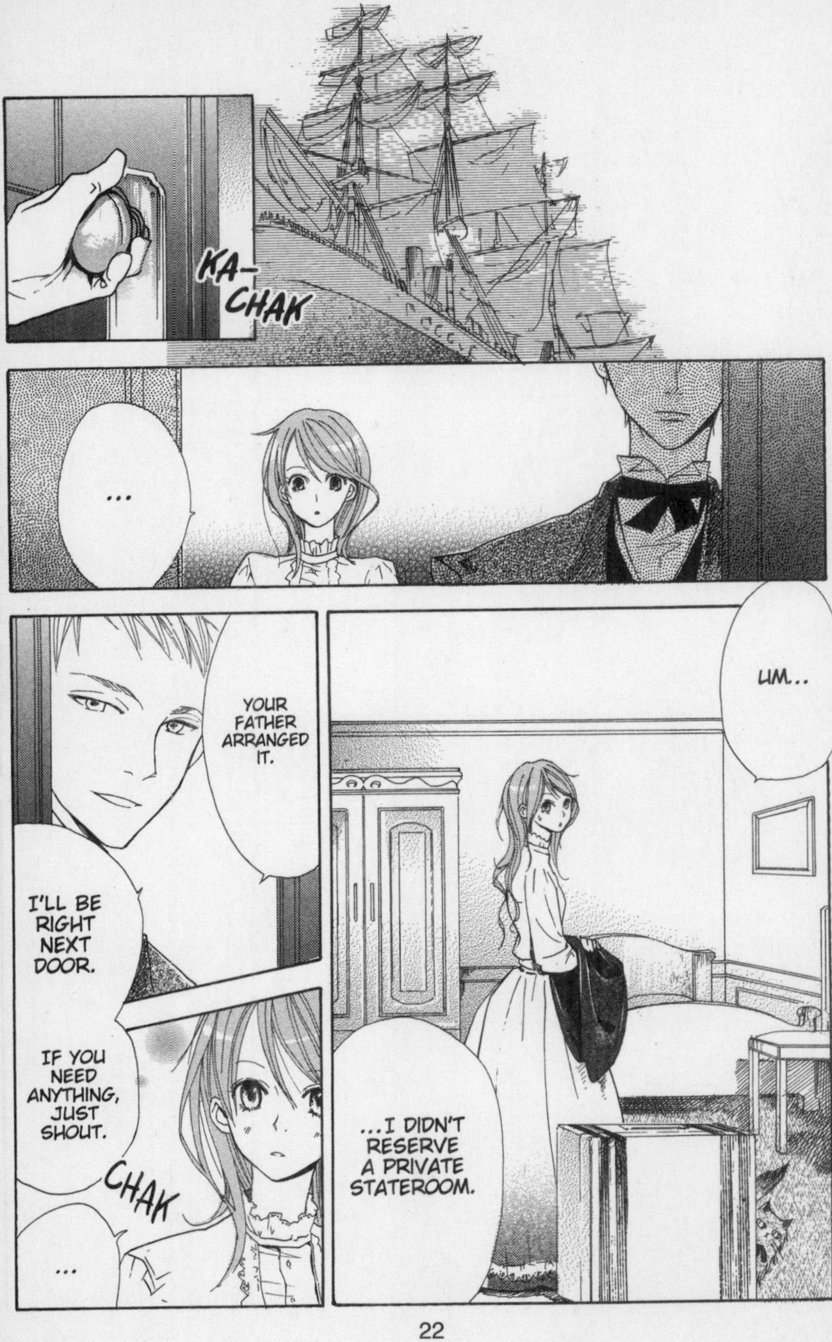
KA-CHAK
...
UM...
...I DIDN'T RESERVE A PRIVATE STATEROOM.
YOUR FATHER ARRANGED IT.
I'LL BE RIGHT NEXT DOOR.
IF YOU NEED ANYTHING, JUST SHOUT.
CHAK
...

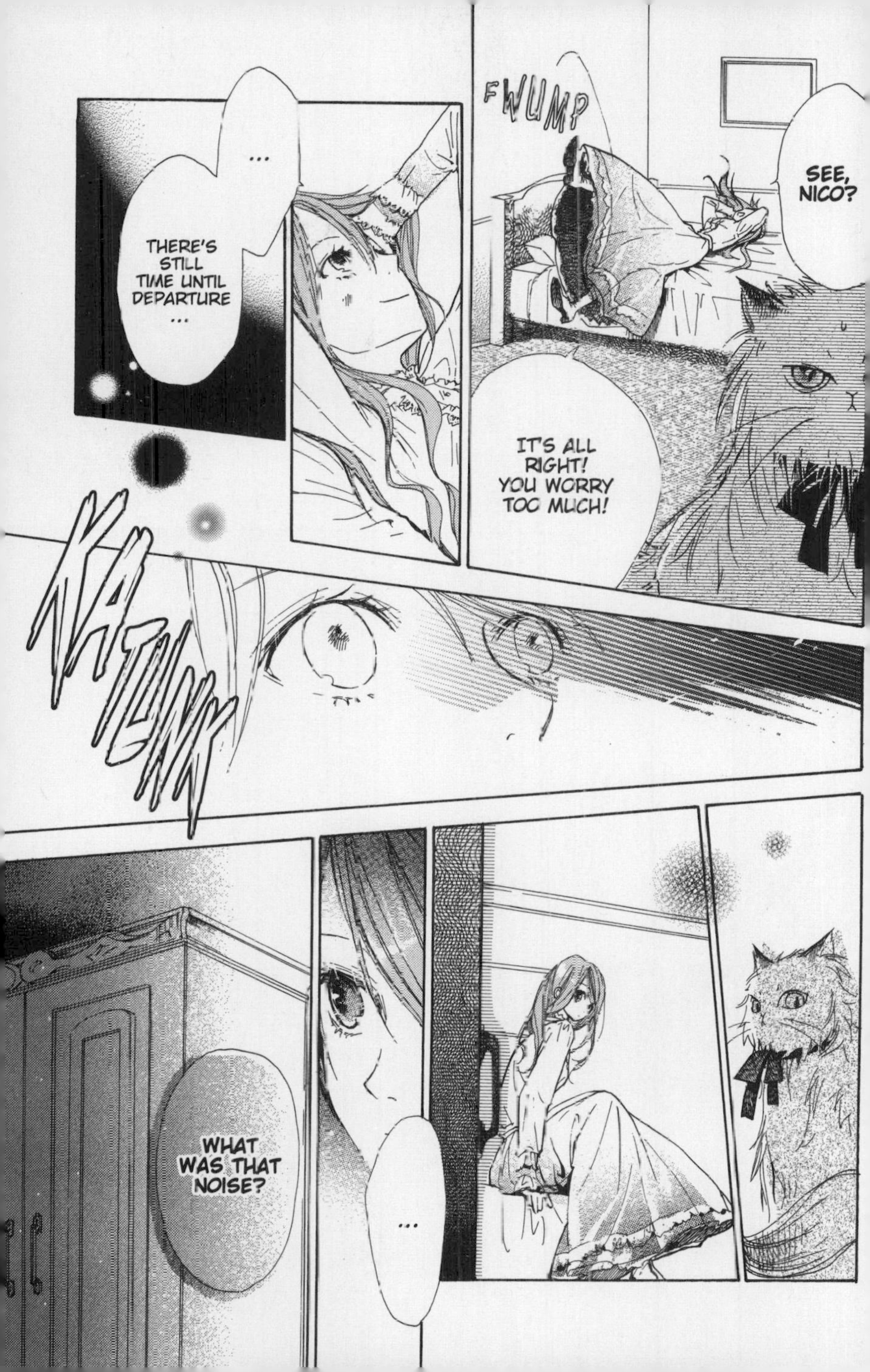
FWUMP
SEE, NICO?
IT'S ALL RIGHT! YOU WORRY TOO MUCH!
...
THERE'S STILL TIME UNTIL DEPARTURE ...
KA-TUNK
...
WHAT WAS THAT NOISE?

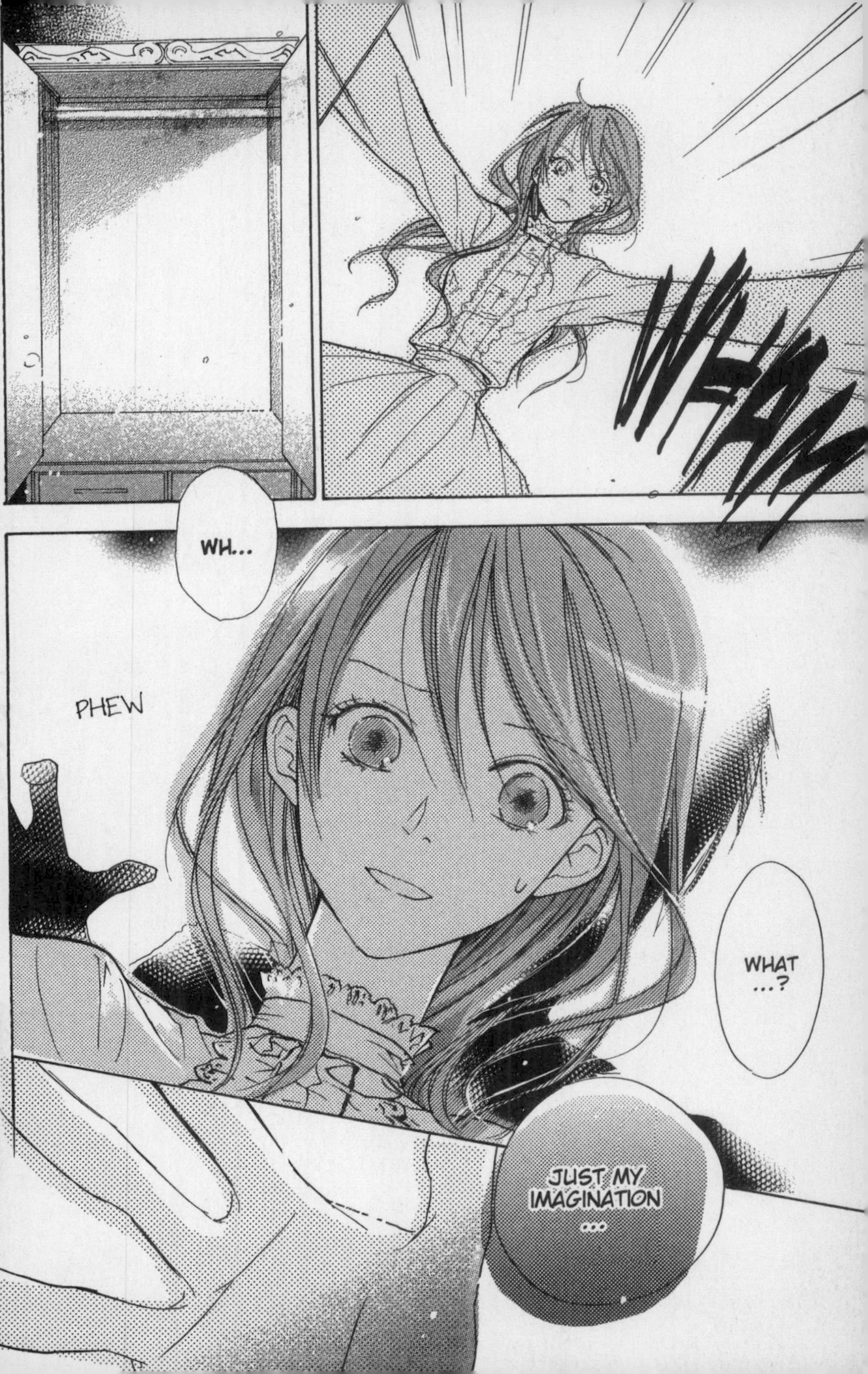
WHAM
WH...
WHAT ...?
PHEW
JUST MY IMAGINATION ...

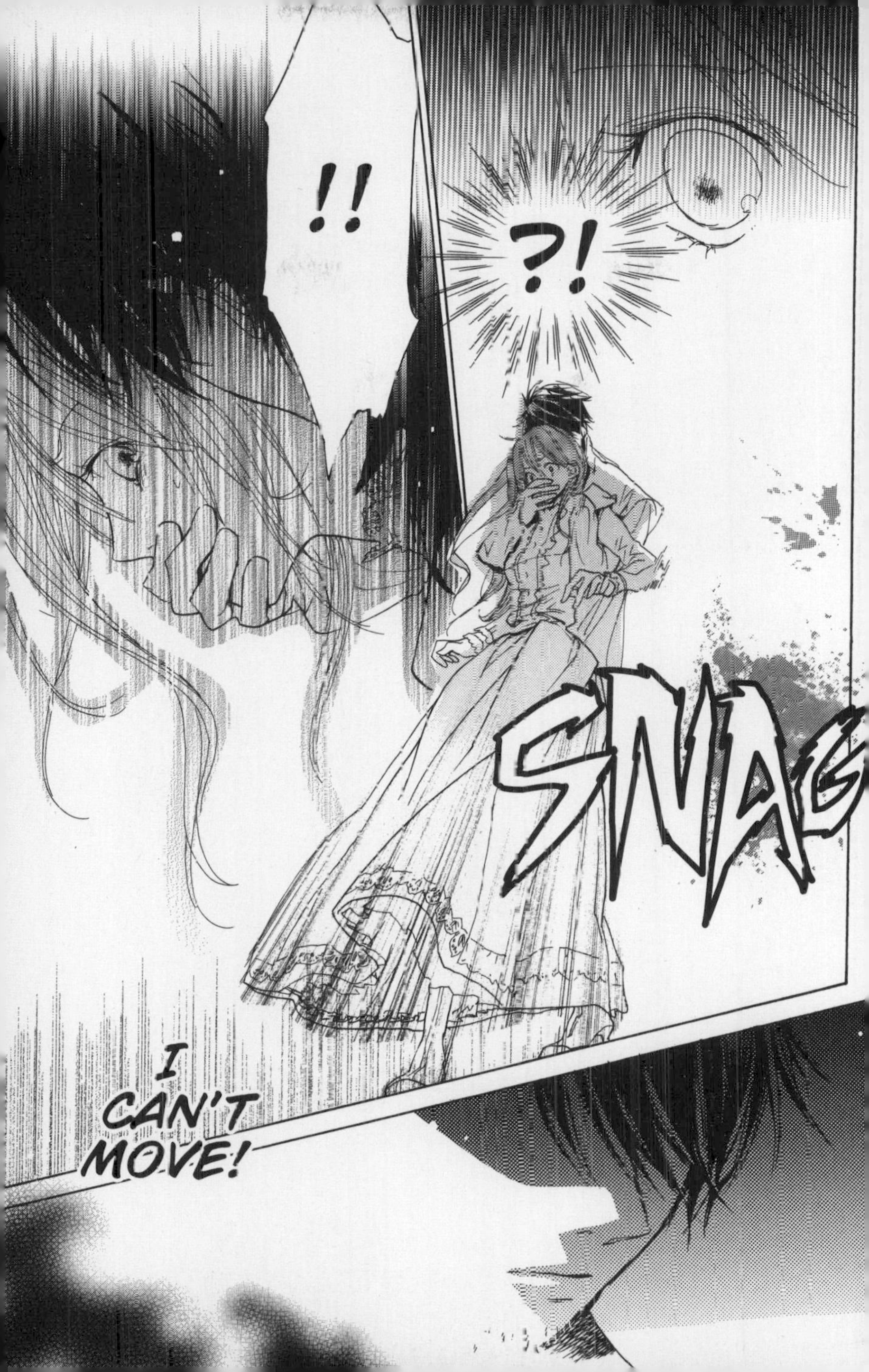
?!
SNAG
!!
I CAN'T MOVE!

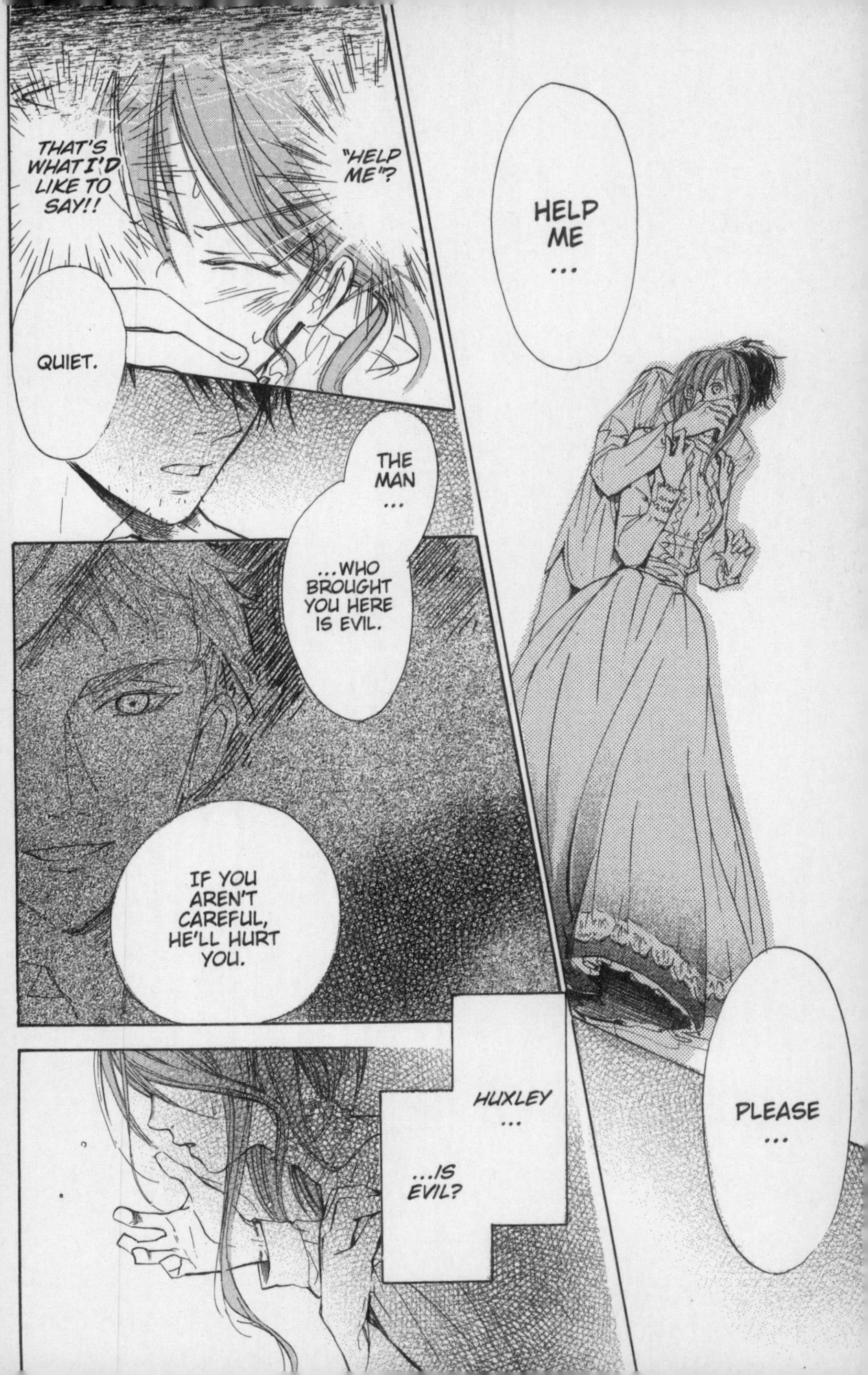

HELP ME ...
PLEASE ...
"HELP ME"?
THAT'S WHAT I'D LIKE TO SAY!!
QUIET.
THE MAN ...
...WHO BROUGHT YOU HERE IS EVIL.
IF YOU AREN'T CAREFUL, HE'LL HURT YOU.
HUXLEY ...
...IS EVIL?

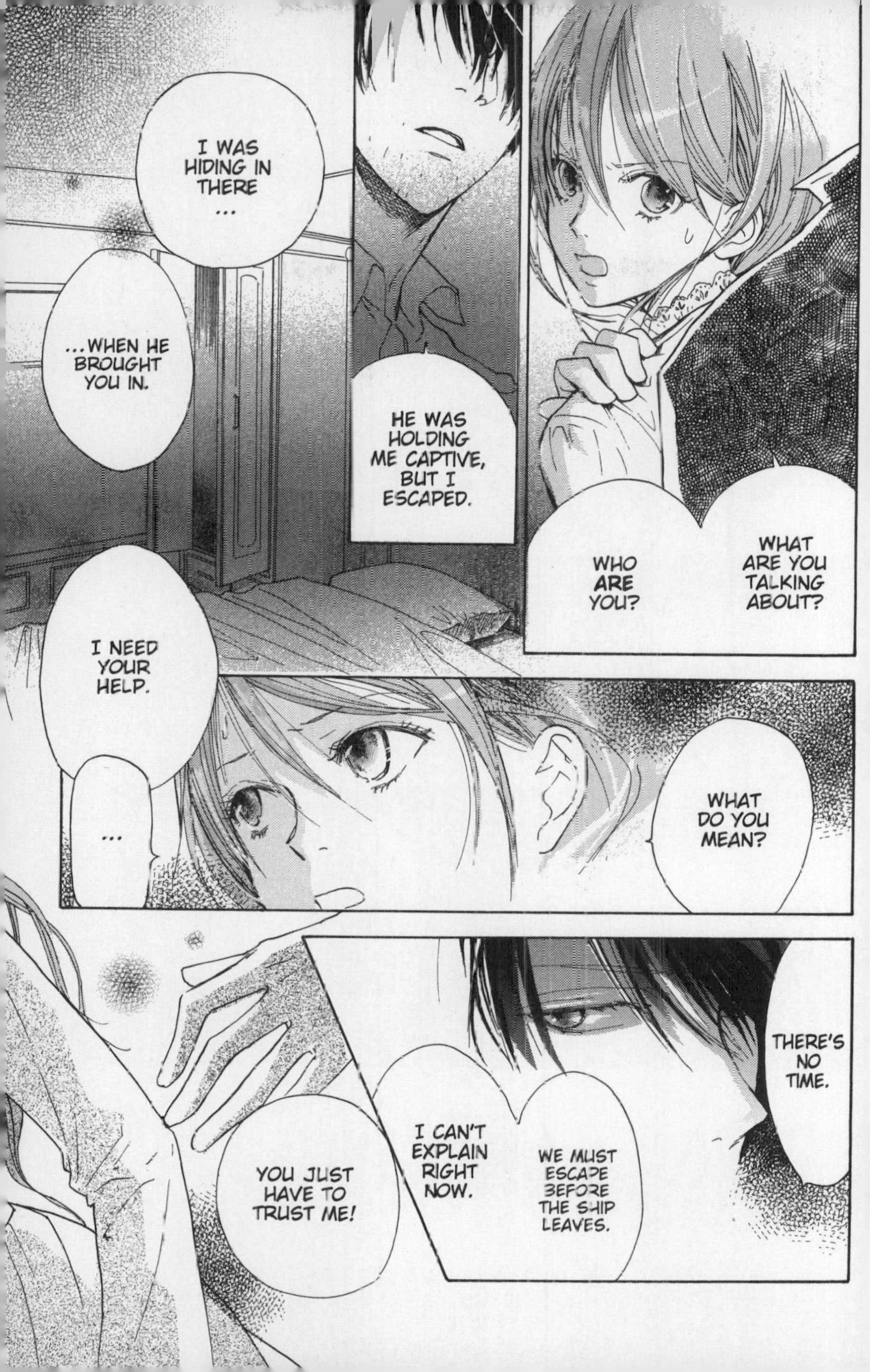
WHAT ARE YOU TALKING ABOUT?
WHO ARE YOU?
HE WAS HOLDING ME CAPTIVE, BUT I ESCAPED.
I WAS HIDING IN THERE ...
...WHEN HE BROUGHT YOU IN.
I NEED YOUR HELP.
WHAT DO YOU MEAN?
...
THERE'S NO TIME.
WE MUST ESCAPE BEFORE THE SHIP LEAVES.
I CAN'T EXPLAIN RIGHT NOW.
YOU JUST HAVE TO TRUST ME!

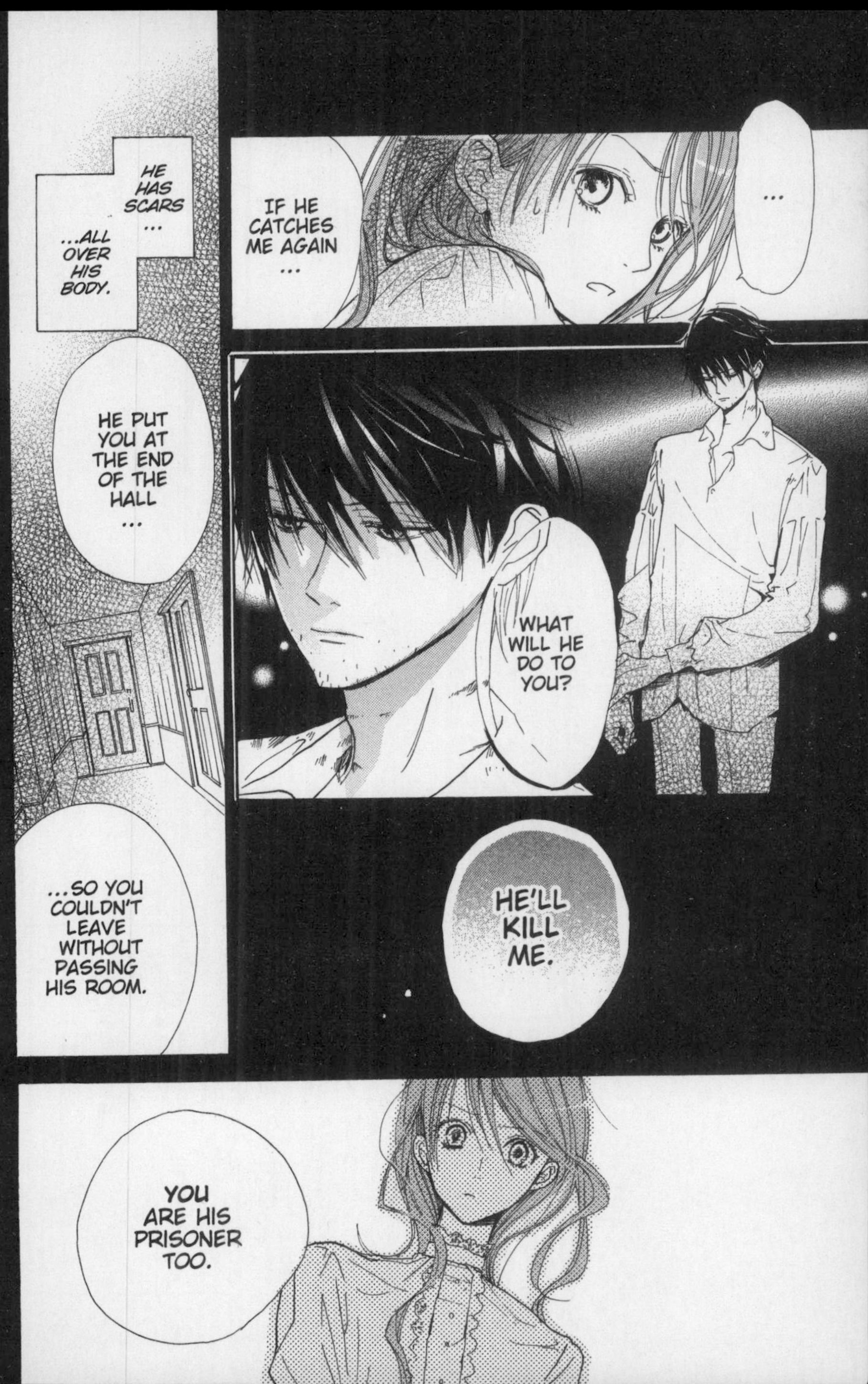
...
IF HE CATCHES ME AGAIN...
WHAT WILL HE DO TO YOU?
HE'LL KILL ME.
HE HAS SCARS... ...ALL OVER HIS BODY.
HE PUT YOU AT THE END OF THE HALL...
...SO YOU COULDN'T LEAVE WITHOUT PASSING HIS ROOM.
YOU ARE HIS PRISONER TOO.

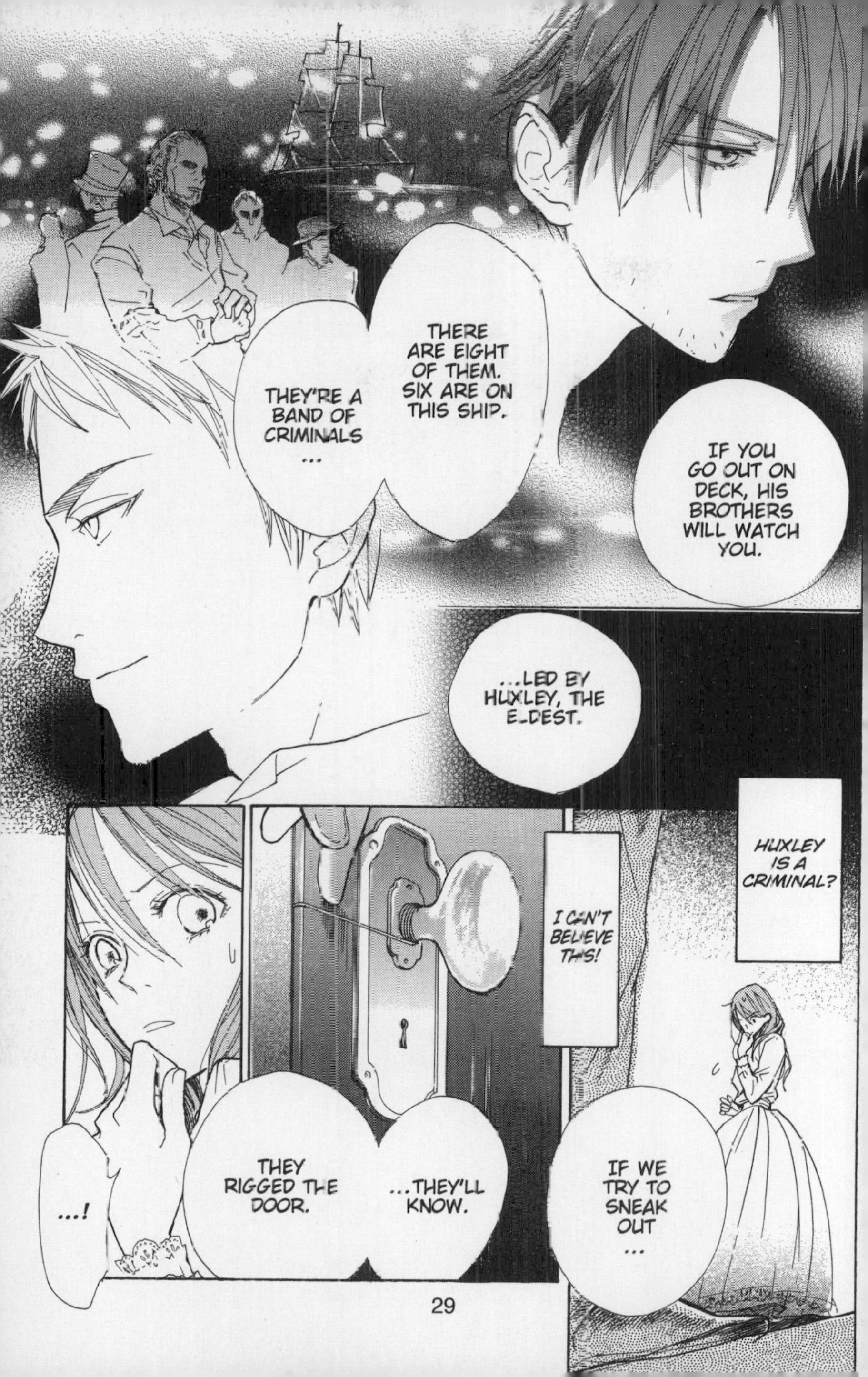
THEY'RE A BAND OF CRIMINALS ...
...LED BY HUXLEY, THE ELDEST.
THERE ARE EIGHT OF THEM. SIX ARE ON THIS SHIP.
IF YOU GO OUT ON DECK, HIS BROTHERS WILL WATCH YOU.
HUXLEY IS A CRIMINAL?
I CAN'T BELIEVE THIS!
IF WE TRY TO SNEAK OUT ...
...THEY'LL KNOW.
THEY RIGGED THE DOOR.
...!

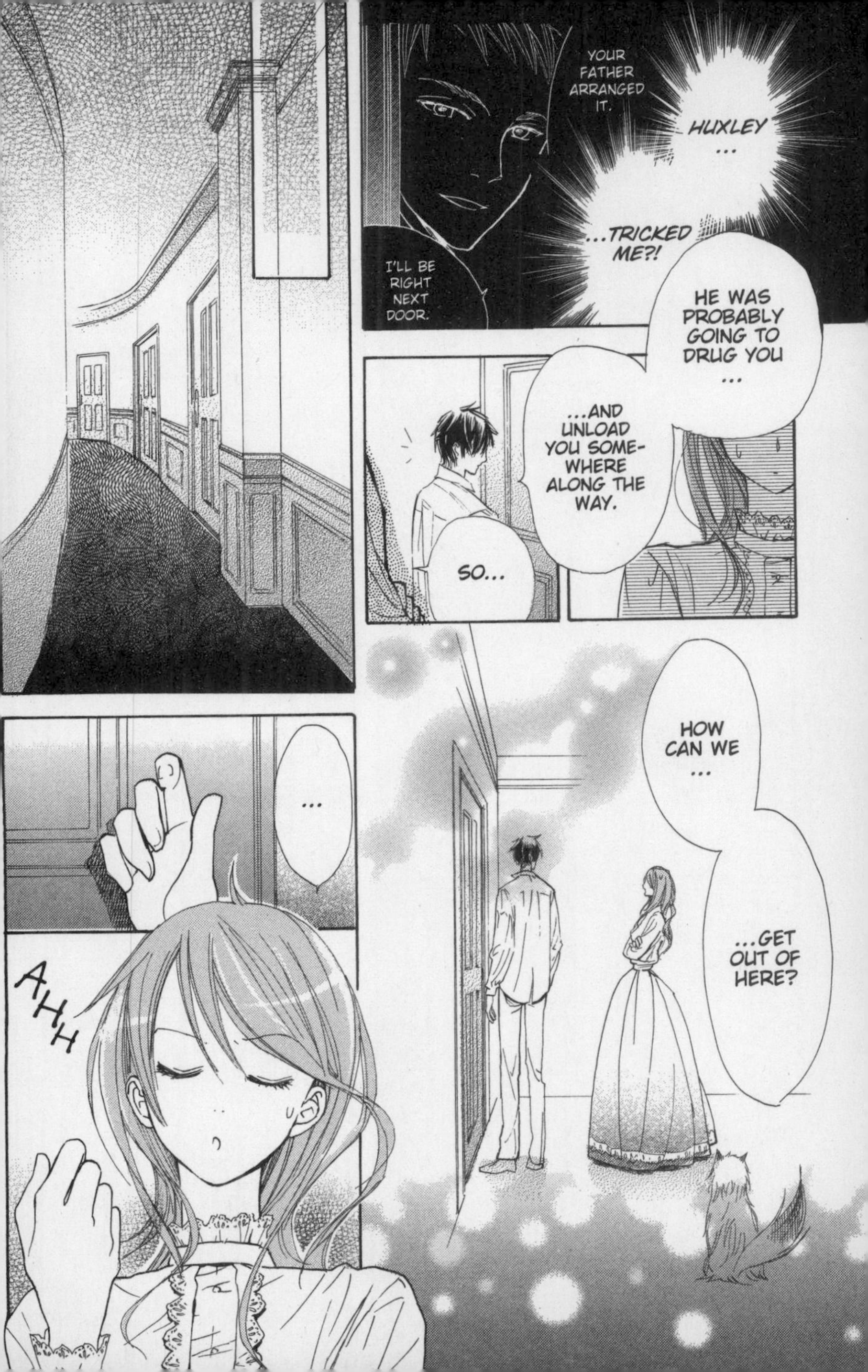
YOUR FATHER ARRANGED IT.
HUXLEY ...
...TRICKED ME?!
I'LL BE RIGHT NEXT DOOR.
HE WAS PROBABLY GOING TO DRUG YOU ...
...AND UNLOAD YOU SOME-WHERE ALONG THE WAY.
SO...
HOW CAN WE ...
...GET OUT OF HERE?
...
AHH

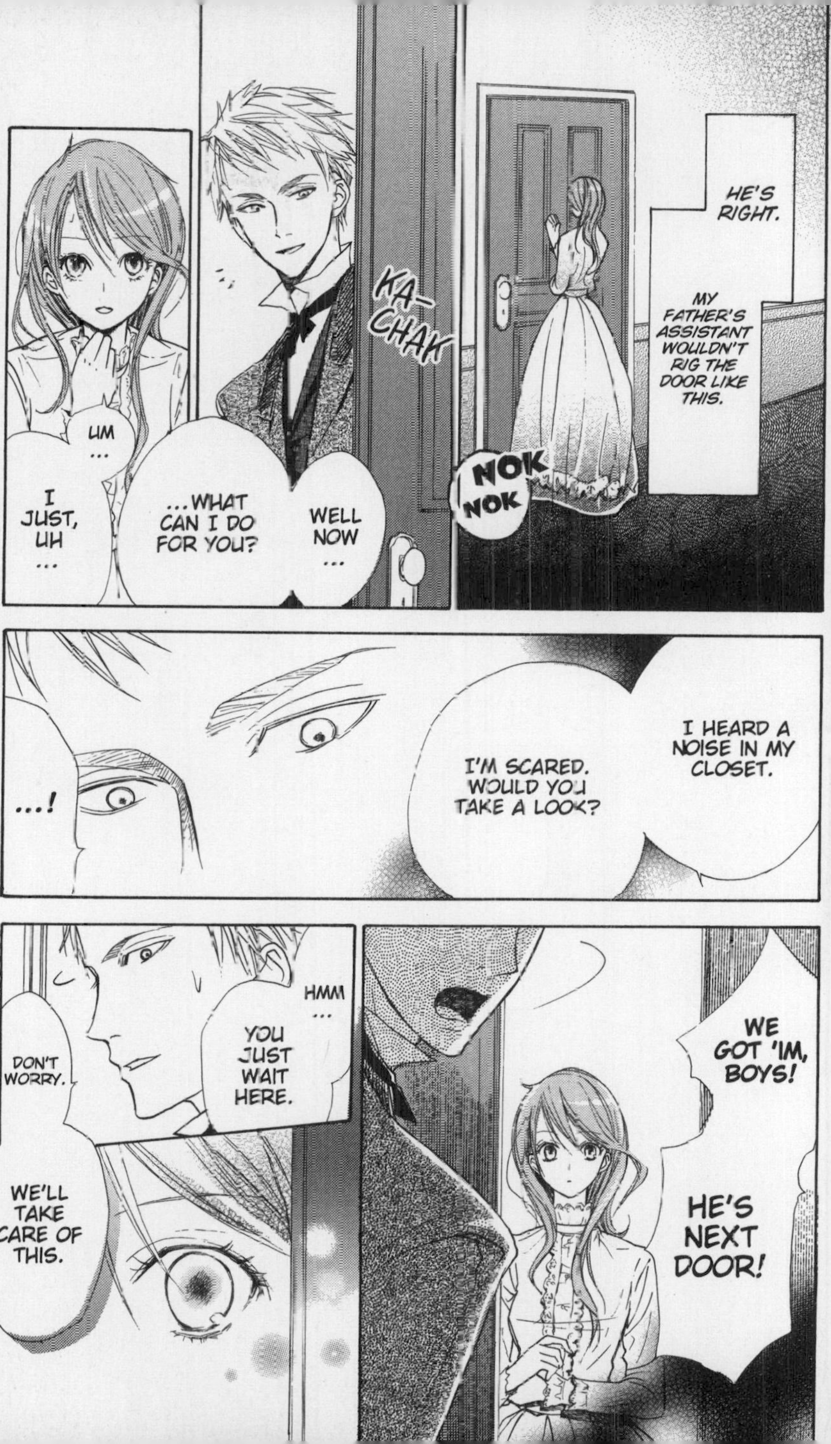
HE'S RIGHT.
MY FATHER'S ASSISTANT WOULDN'T RIG THE DOOR LIKE THIS.
NOK NOK
KA-CHAK
WELL NOW ...
...WHAT CAN I DO FOR YOU?
UM ...
I JUST, UH ...
I HEARD A NOISE IN MY CLOSET.
I'M SCARED. WOULD YOU TAKE A LOOK?
...!
WE GOT 'IM, BOYS!
HE'S NEXT DOOR!
HMM ...
YOU JUST WAIT HERE.
DON'T WORRY.
WE'LL TAKE CARE OF THIS.

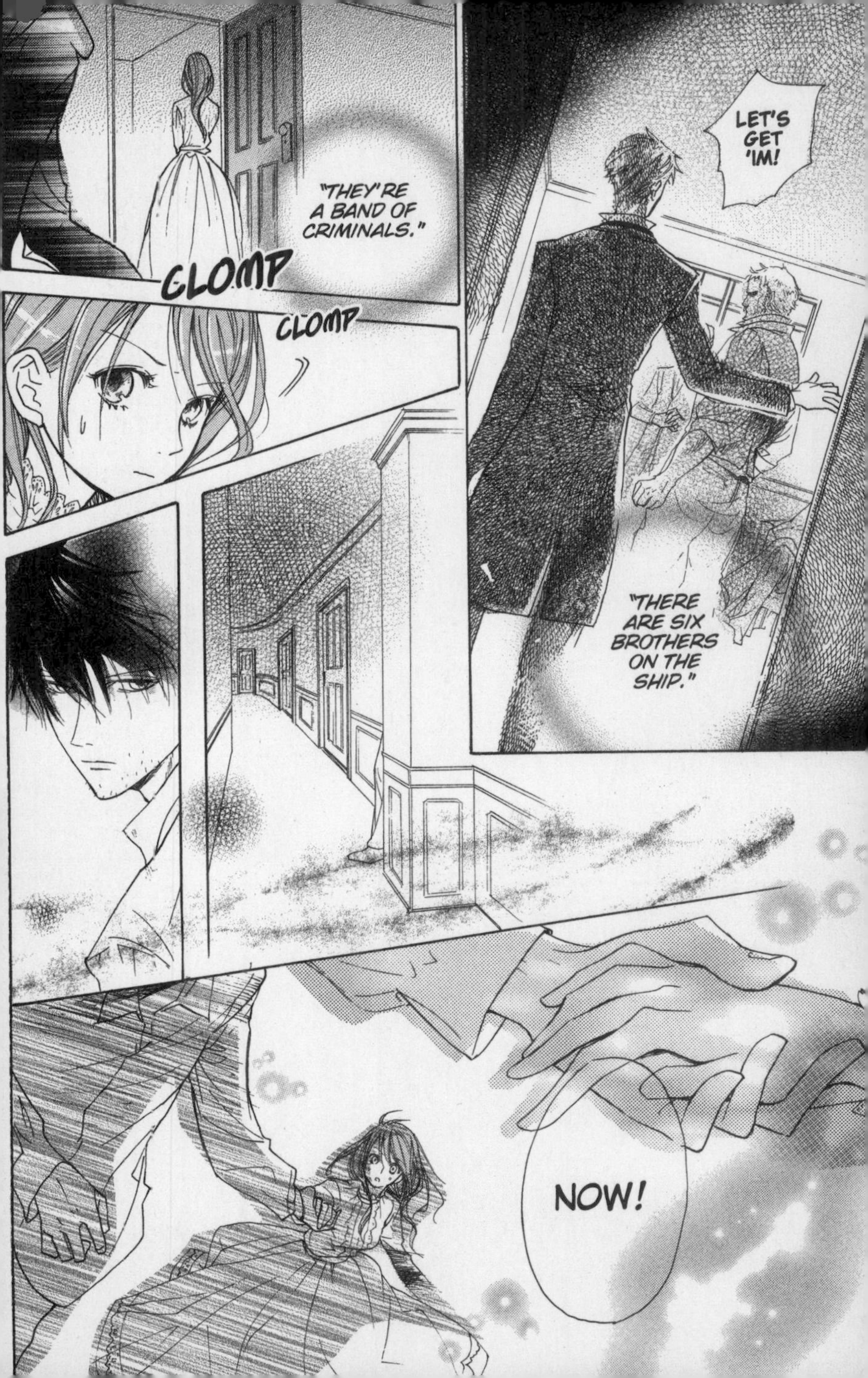
LET'S GET 'IM!
"THERE ARE SIX BROTHERS ON THE SHIP."
"THEY'RE A BAND OF CRIMINALS."
CLOMP
CLOMP
NOW!

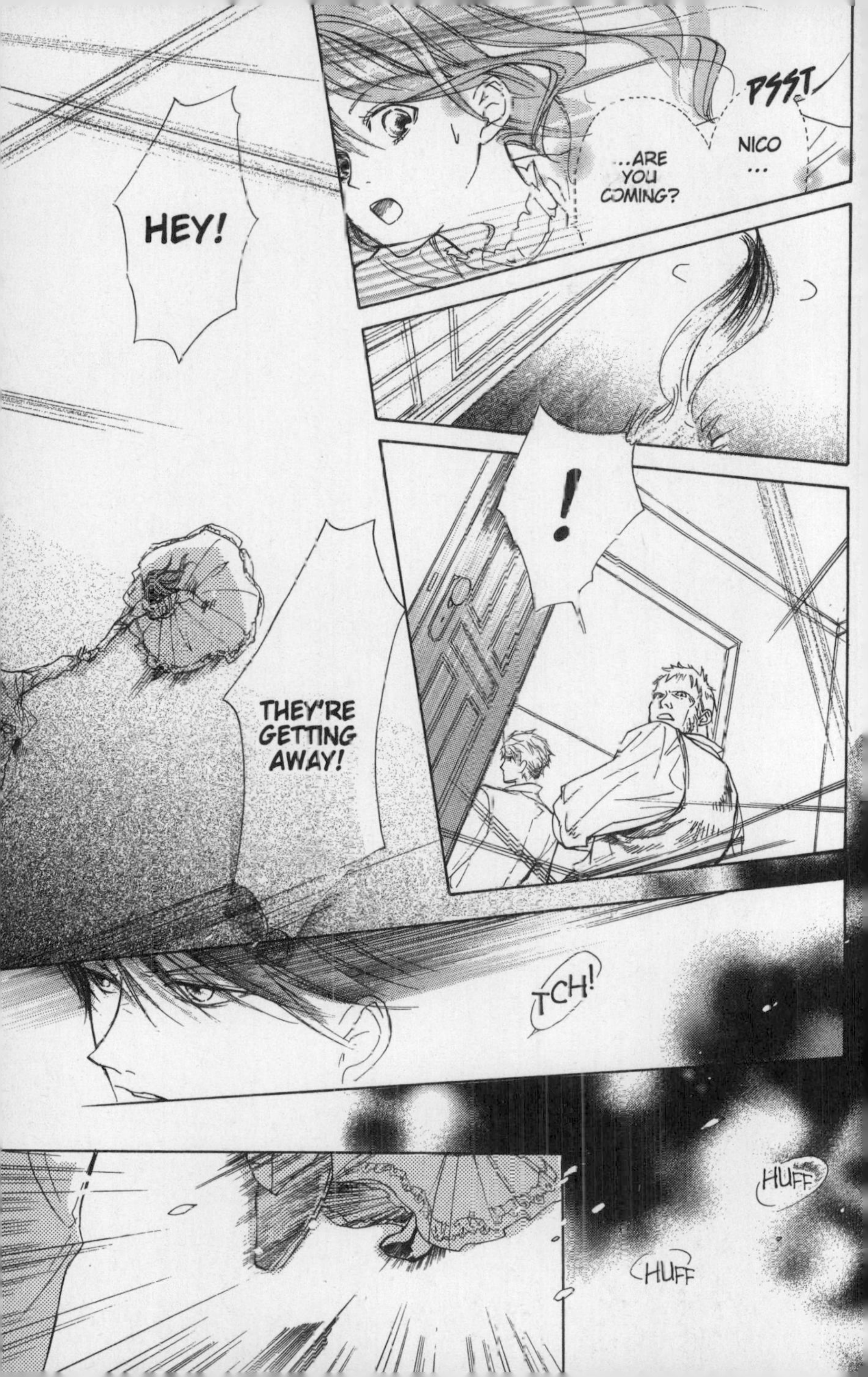
PSST
NICO ...
...ARE YOU COMING?
HEY!
!
THEY'RE GETTING AWAY!
TCH!
HUFF
HUFF

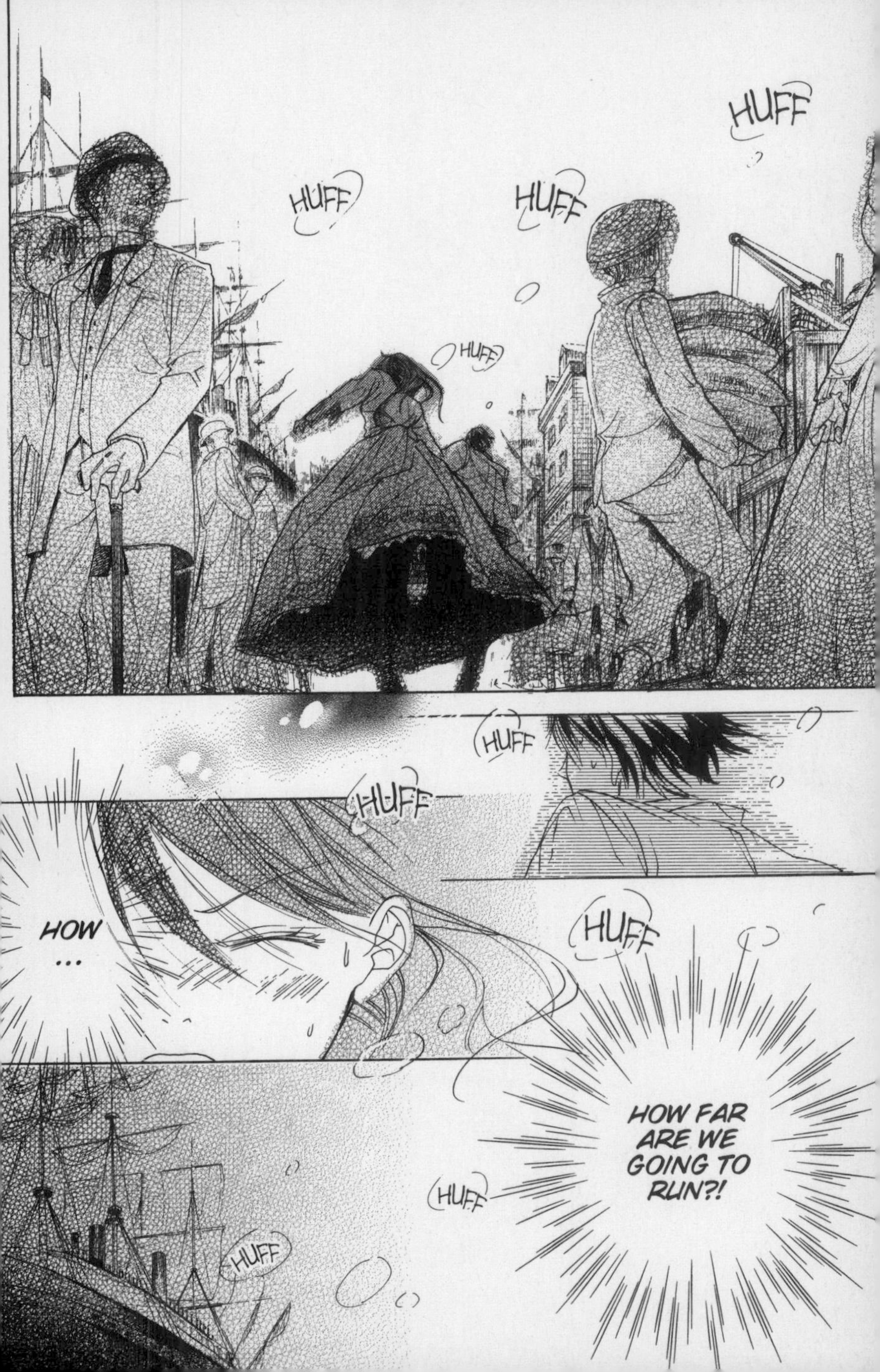
HUFF
HUFF
HUFF
HUFF
HUFF
HUFF
HUFF
HOW ...
HOW FAR ARE WE GOING TO RUN?!
HUFF
HUFF

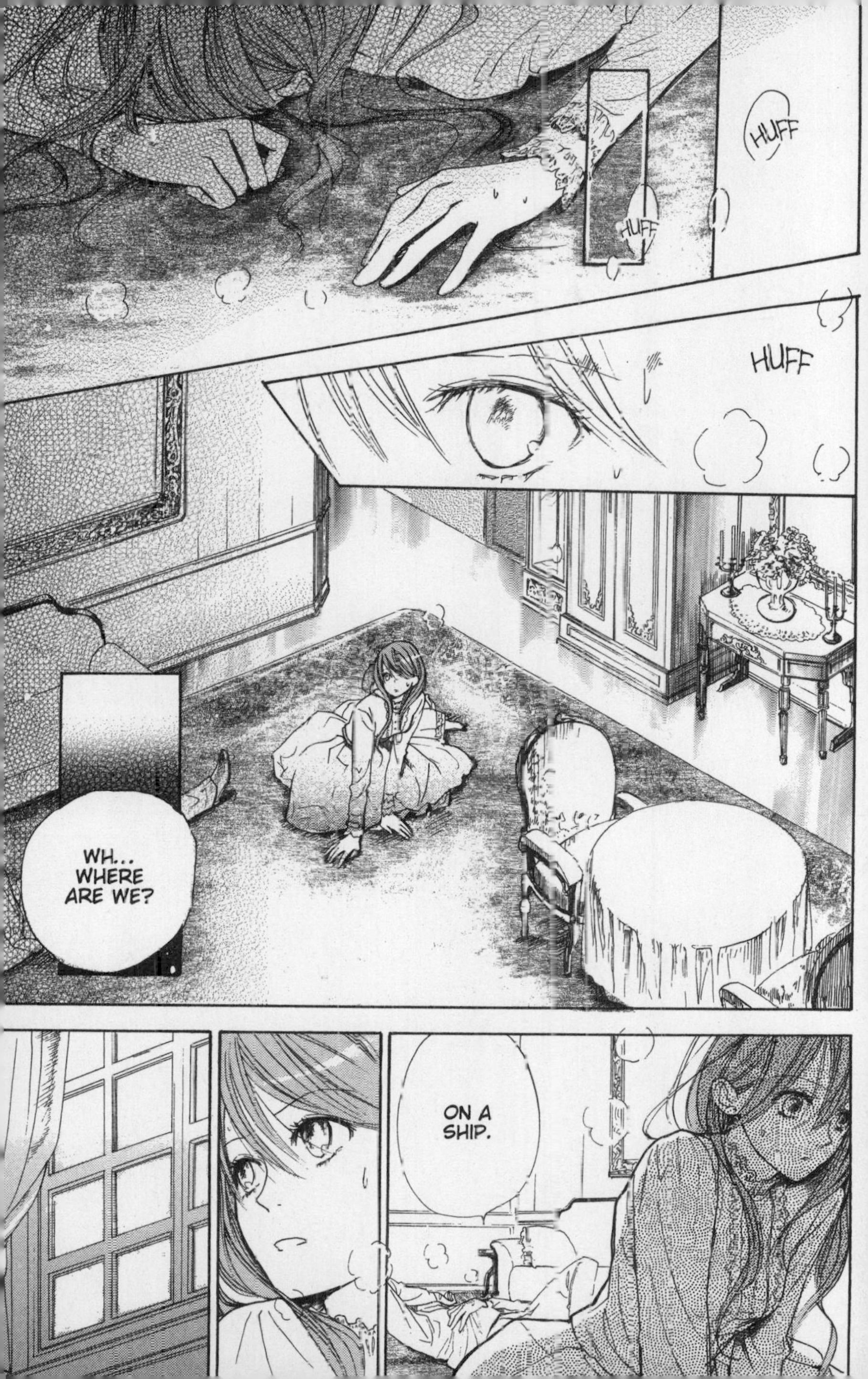
HUFF
HUFF
HUFF
WH... WHERE ARE WE?
ON A SHIP.

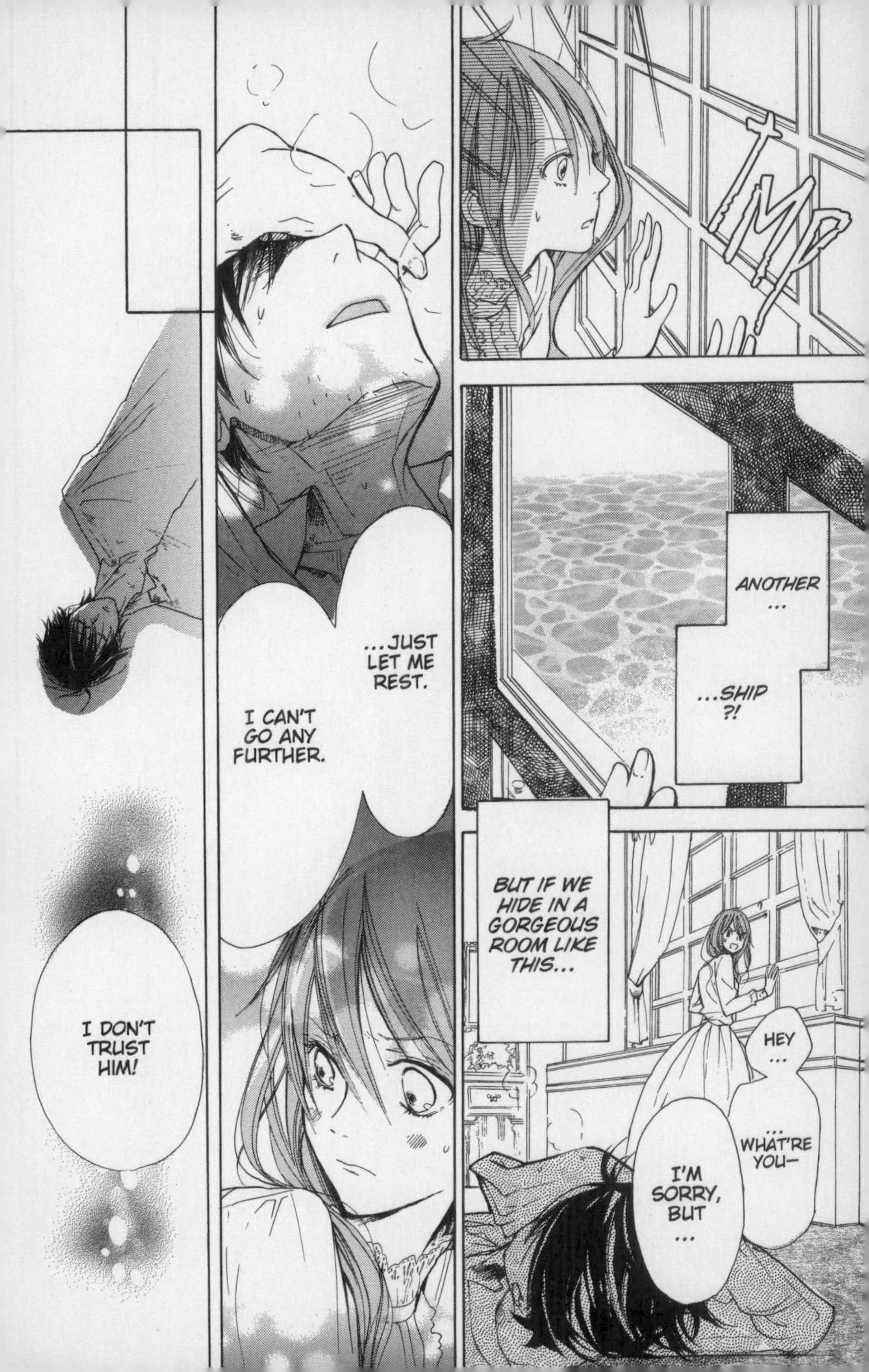
TMP
ANOTHER...
...SHIP?!
BUT IF WE HIDE IN A GORGEOUS ROOM LIKE THIS...
HEY...
...WHAT'RE YOU—
I'M SORRY, BUT...
...JUST LET ME REST.
I CAN'T GO ANY FURTHER.
I DON'T TRUST HIM!

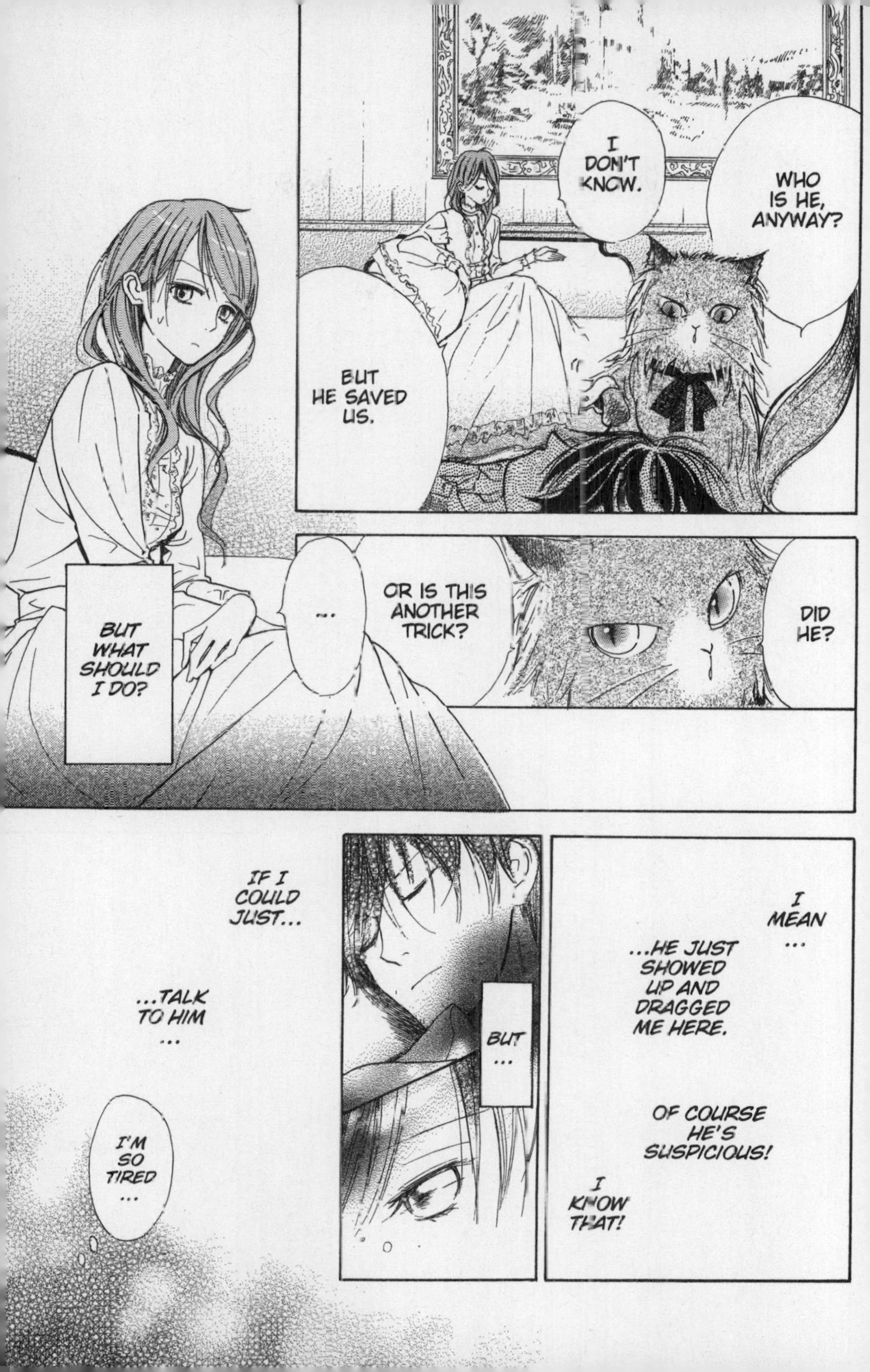
WHO IS HE, ANYWAY?
I DON'T KNOW.
BUT HE SAVED US.
DID HE?
OR IS THIS ANOTHER TRICK?
...
BUT WHAT SHOULD I DO?
I MEAN ...
...HE JUST SHOWED UP AND DRAGGED ME HERE.
OF COURSE HE'S SUSPICIOUS!
I KNOW THAT!
BUT ...
IF I COULD JUST...
...TALK TO HIM ...
I'M SO TIRED ...

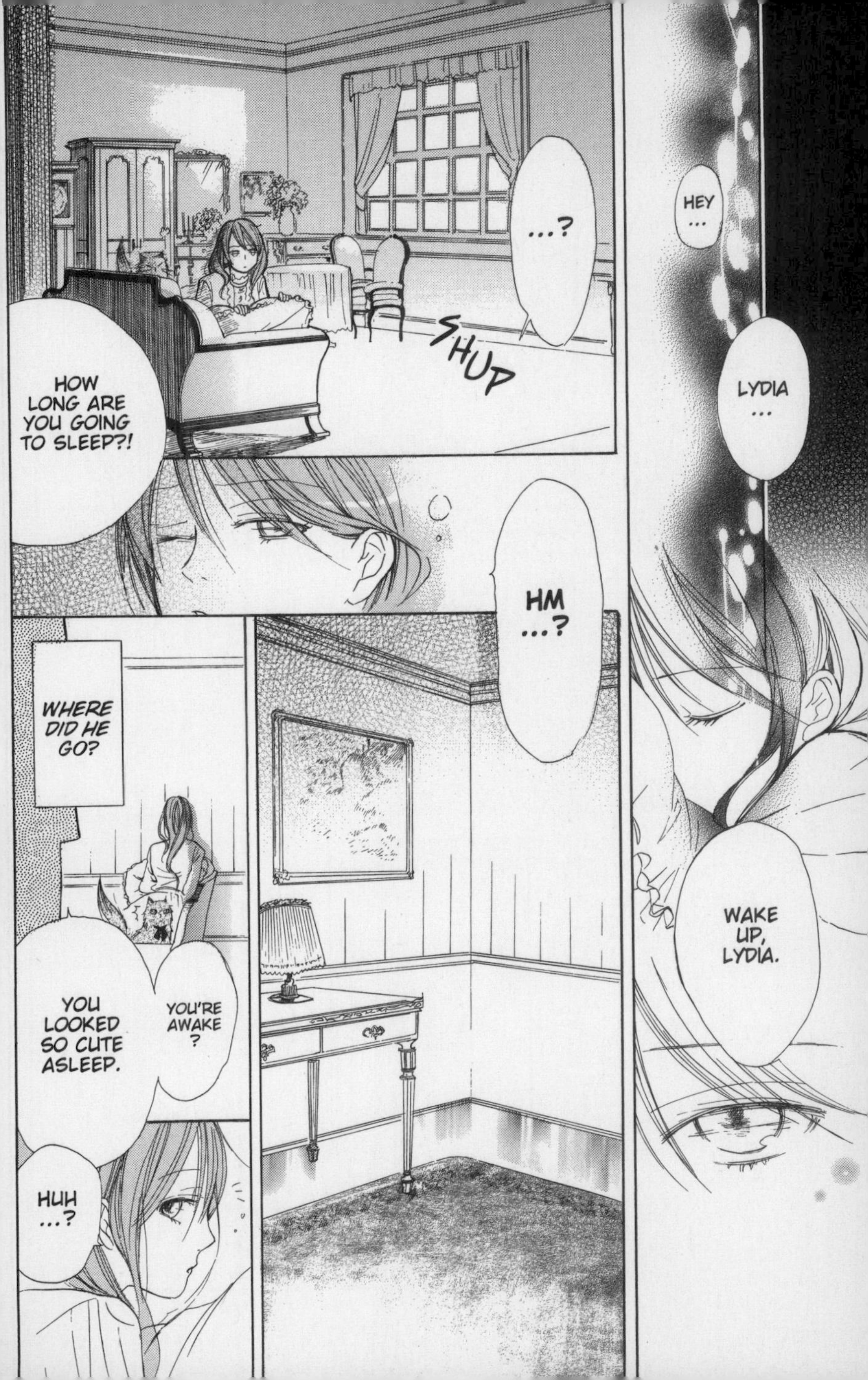
HEY ...
LYDIA ...
WAKE UP, LYDIA.
...?
SHUP
HOW LONG ARE YOU GOING TO SLEEP?!
HM ...?
WHERE DID HE GO?
YOU'RE AWAKE?
YOU LOOKED SO CUTE ASLEEP.
HUH ...?

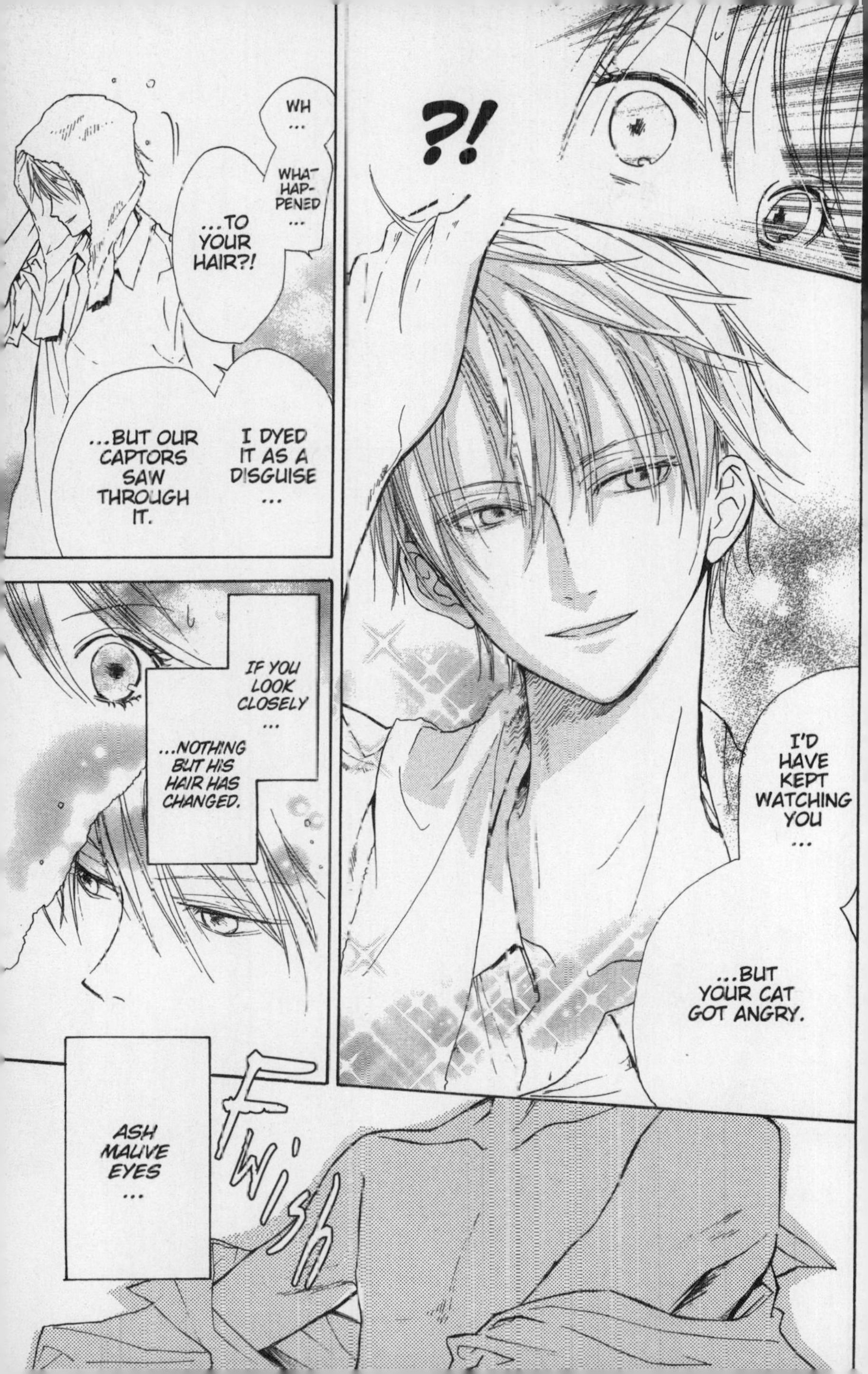
?!
I'D HAVE KEPT WATCHING YOU ...
...BUT YOUR CAT GOT ANGRY.
WH ...
WHAT HAPPENED ...
...TO YOUR HAIR?!
I DYED IT AS A DISGUISE ...
...BUT OUR CAPTORS SAW THROUGH IT.
IF YOU LOOK CLOSELY ...
...NOTHING BUT HIS HAIR HAS CHANGED.
FWISH
ASH MAUVE EYES ...

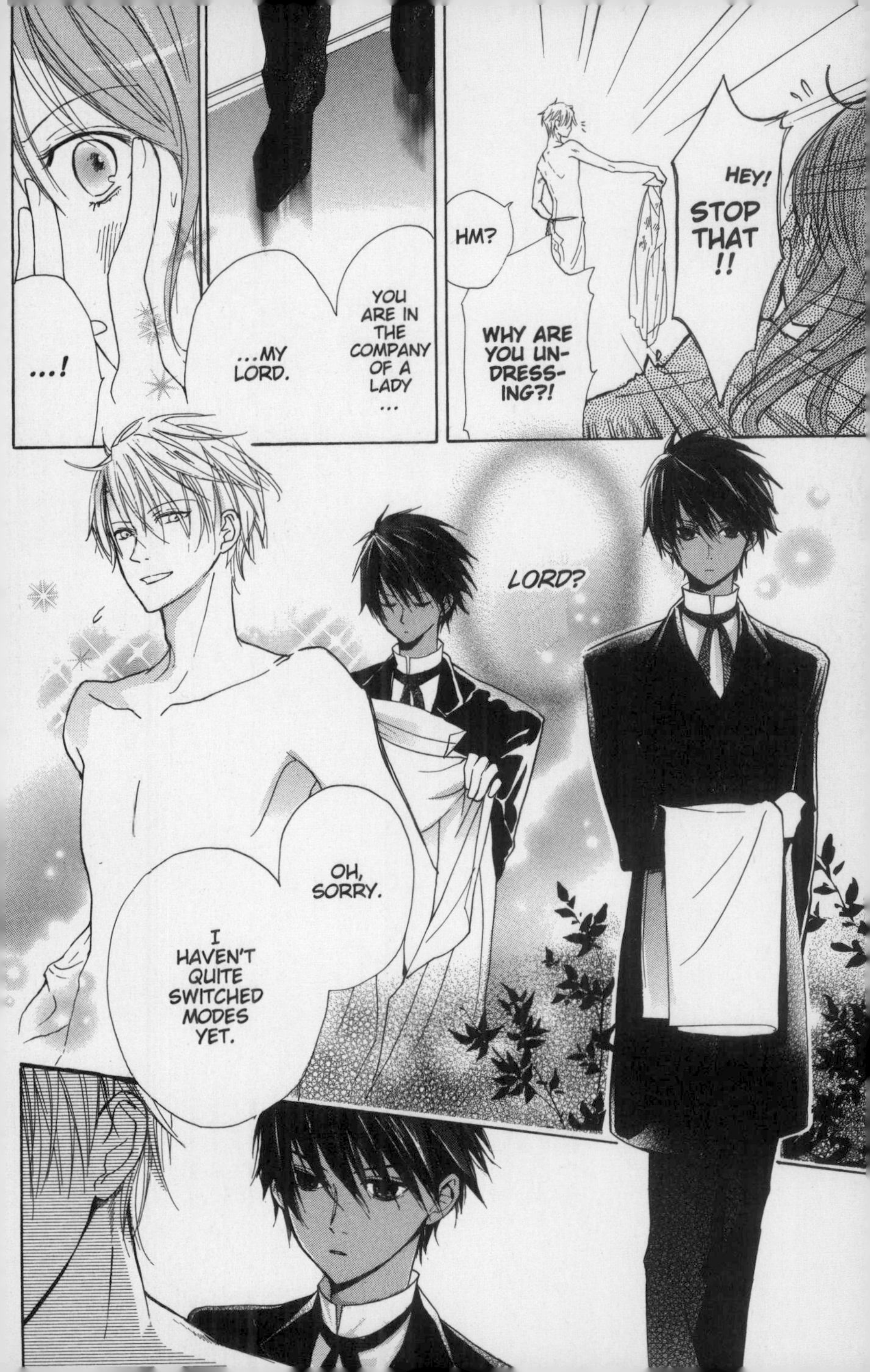
HEY!
STOP THAT!!
HM?
WHY ARE YOU UN-DRESS-ING?!
YOU ARE IN THE COMPANY OF A LADY ...
...MY LORD.
...!
LORD?
OH, SORRY.
I HAVEN'T QUITE SWITCHED MODES YET.

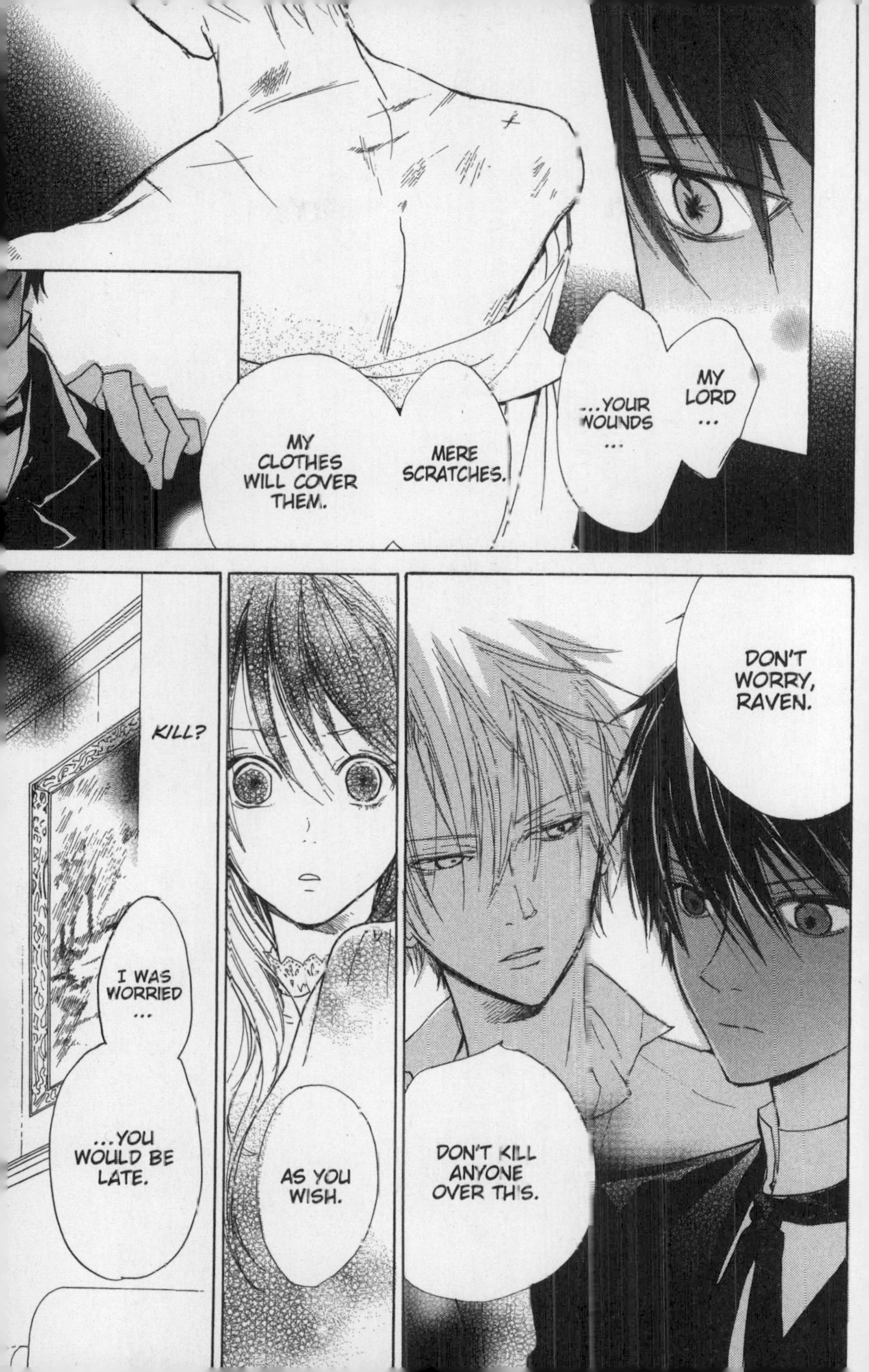
MY LORD ...
...YOUR WOUNDS ...
MERE SCRATCHES.
MY CLOTHES WILL COVER THEM.
DON'T WORRY, RAVEN.
DON'T KILL ANYONE OVER THIS.
AS YOU WISH.
KILL?
I WAS WORRIED ...
...YOU WOULD BE LATE.

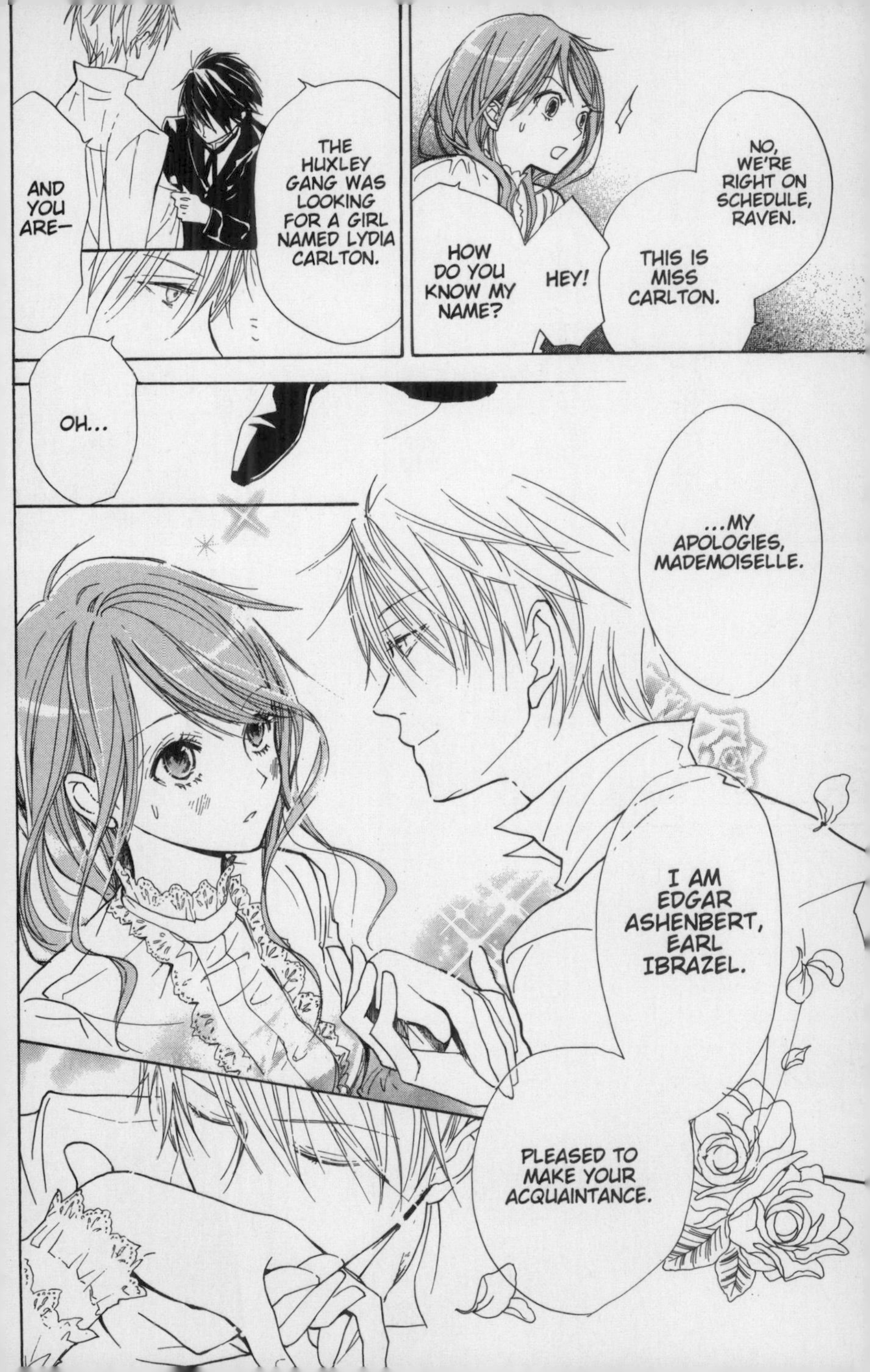
NO, WE'RE RIGHT ON SCHEDULE, RAVEN.
THIS IS MISS CARLTON.
HEY!
HOW DO YOU KNOW MY NAME?
THE HUXLEY GANG WAS LOOKING FOR A GIRL NAMED LYDIA CARLTON.
AND YOU ARE—
OH...
...MY APOLOGIES, MADEMOISELLE.
I AM EDGAR ASHENBERT, EARL IBRAZEL.
PLEASED TO MAKE YOUR ACQUAINTANCE.

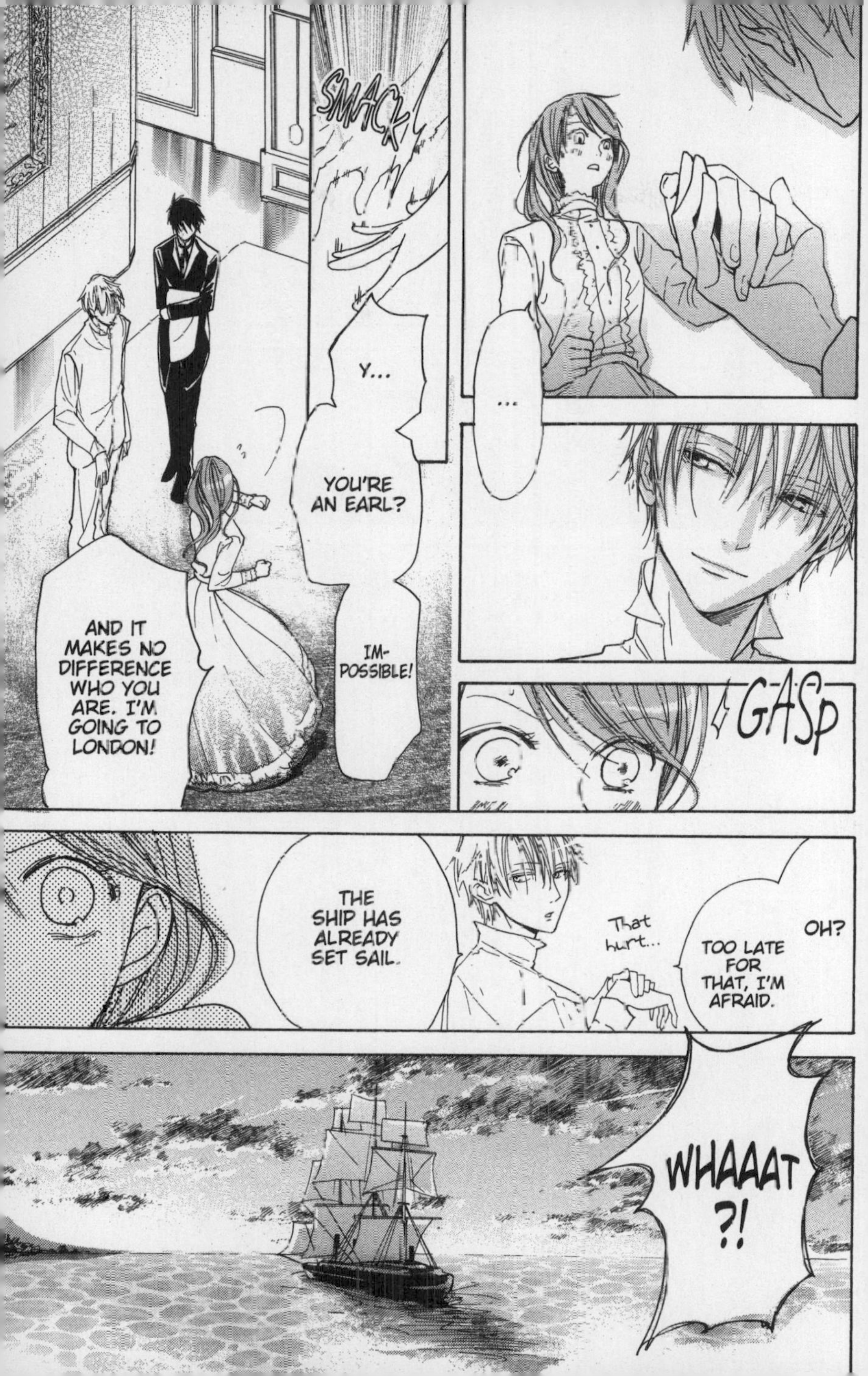
...
GASp
SMACK
Y...
YOU'RE AN EARL?
IM-POSSIBLE!
AND IT MAKES NO DIFFERENCE WHO YOU ARE. I'M GOING TO LONDON!
OH?
TOO LATE FOR THAT, I'M AFRAID.
That hurt...
THE SHIP HAS ALREADY SET SAIL.
WHAAAT?!

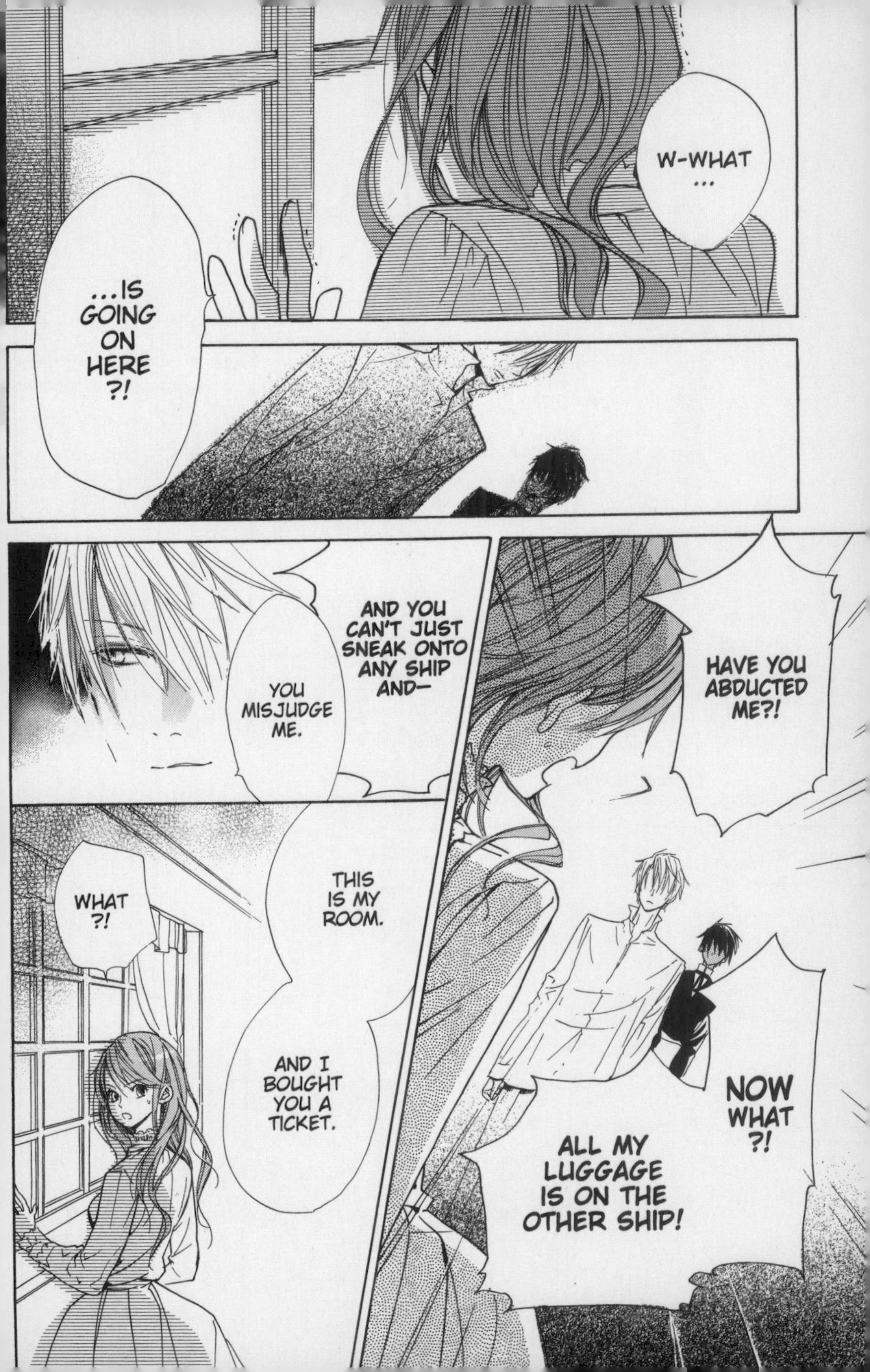
W-WHAT ...
...IS GOING ON HERE?!
HAVE YOU ABDUCTED ME?!
AND YOU CAN'T JUST SNEAK ONTO ANY SHIP AND—
YOU MISJUDGE ME.
THIS IS MY ROOM.
AND I BOUGHT YOU A TICKET.
WHAT?!
NOW WHAT?!
ALL MY LUGGAGE IS ON THE OTHER SHIP!

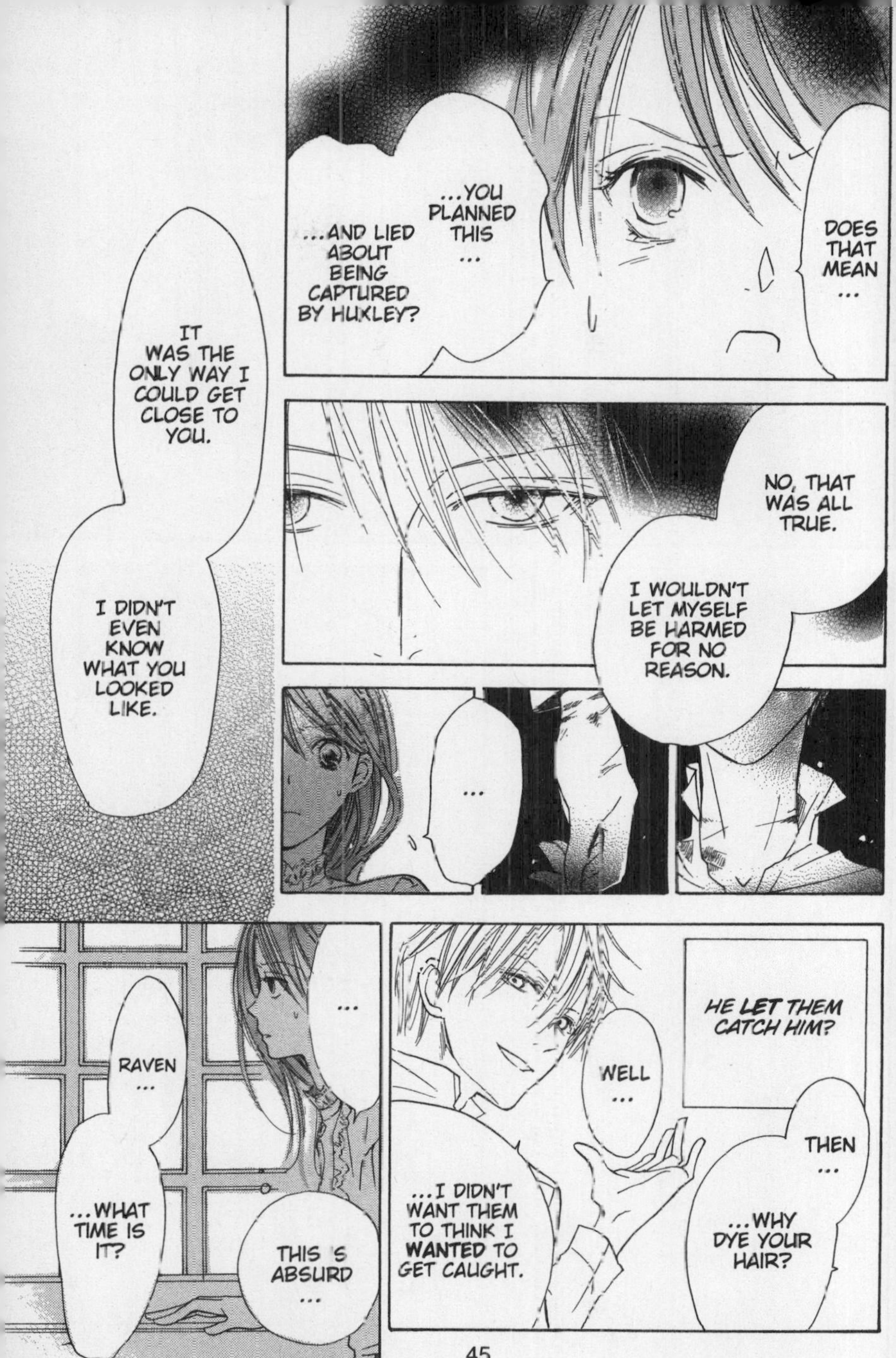
DOES THAT MEAN...
...YOU PLANNED THIS...
...AND LIED ABOUT BEING CAPTURED BY HUXLEY?
NO, THAT WAS ALL TRUE.
I WOULDN'T LET MYSELF BE HARMED FOR NO REASON.
...
IT WAS THE ONLY WAY I COULD GET CLOSE TO YOU.
I DIDN'T EVEN KNOW WHAT YOU LOOKED LIKE.
*HE **LET** THEM CATCH HIM?*
THEN...
...WHY DYE YOUR HAIR?
WELL...
...I DIDN'T WANT THEM TO THINK I **WANTED** TO GET CAUGHT.
...
THIS IS ABSURD...
RAVEN...
...WHAT TIME IS IT?

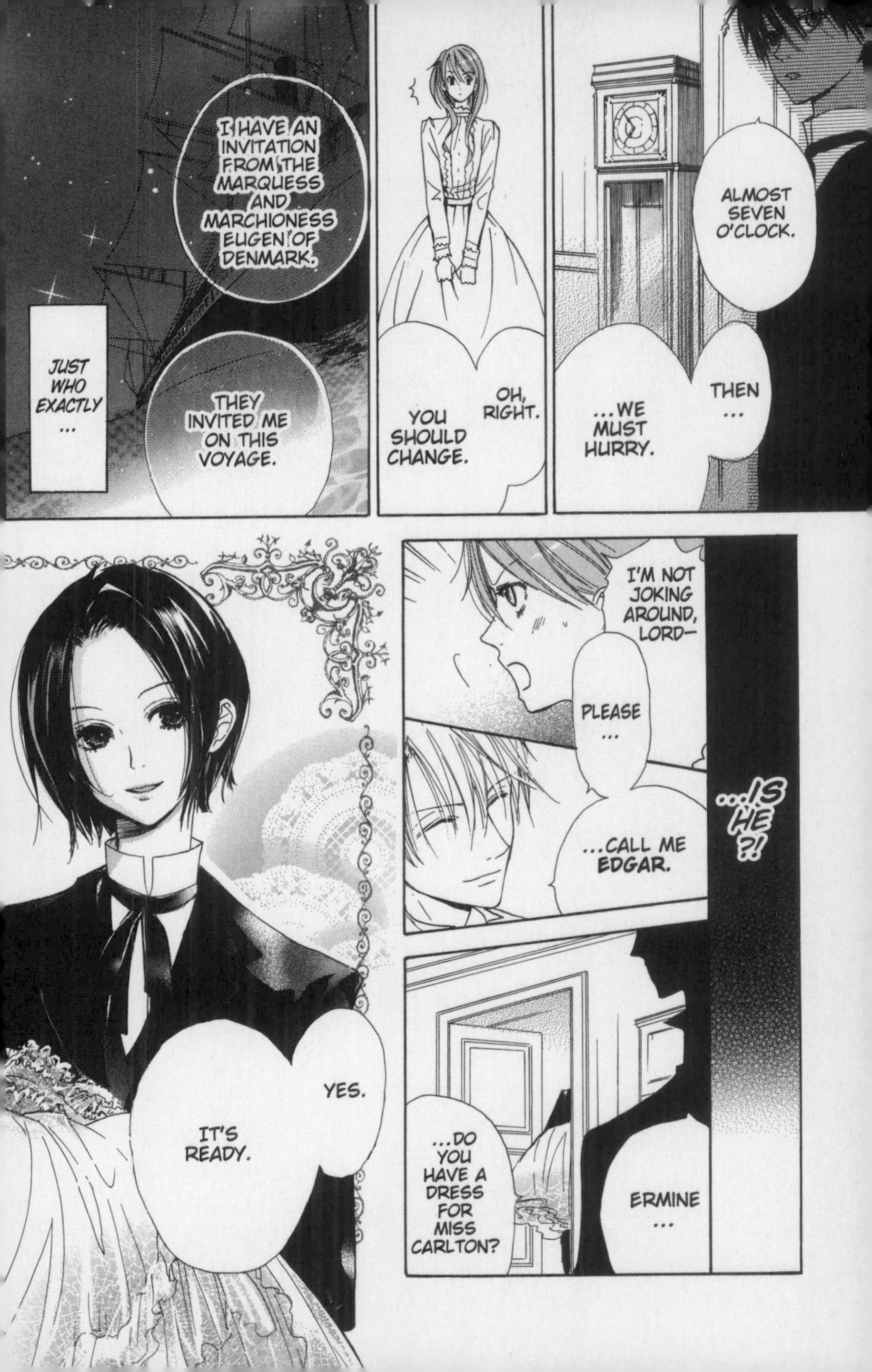
ALMOST SEVEN O'CLOCK.
THEN ...
...WE MUST HURRY.
OH, RIGHT.
YOU SHOULD CHANGE.
I HAVE AN INVITATION FROM THE MARQUESS AND MARCHIONESS EUGEN OF DENMARK.
THEY INVITED ME ON THIS VOYAGE.
JUST WHO EXACTLY ...
I'M NOT JOKING AROUND, LORD—
PLEASE ...
...CALL ME EDGAR.
...IS HE ?!
ERMINE ...
...DO YOU HAVE A DRESS FOR MISS CARLTON?
YES.
IT'S READY.

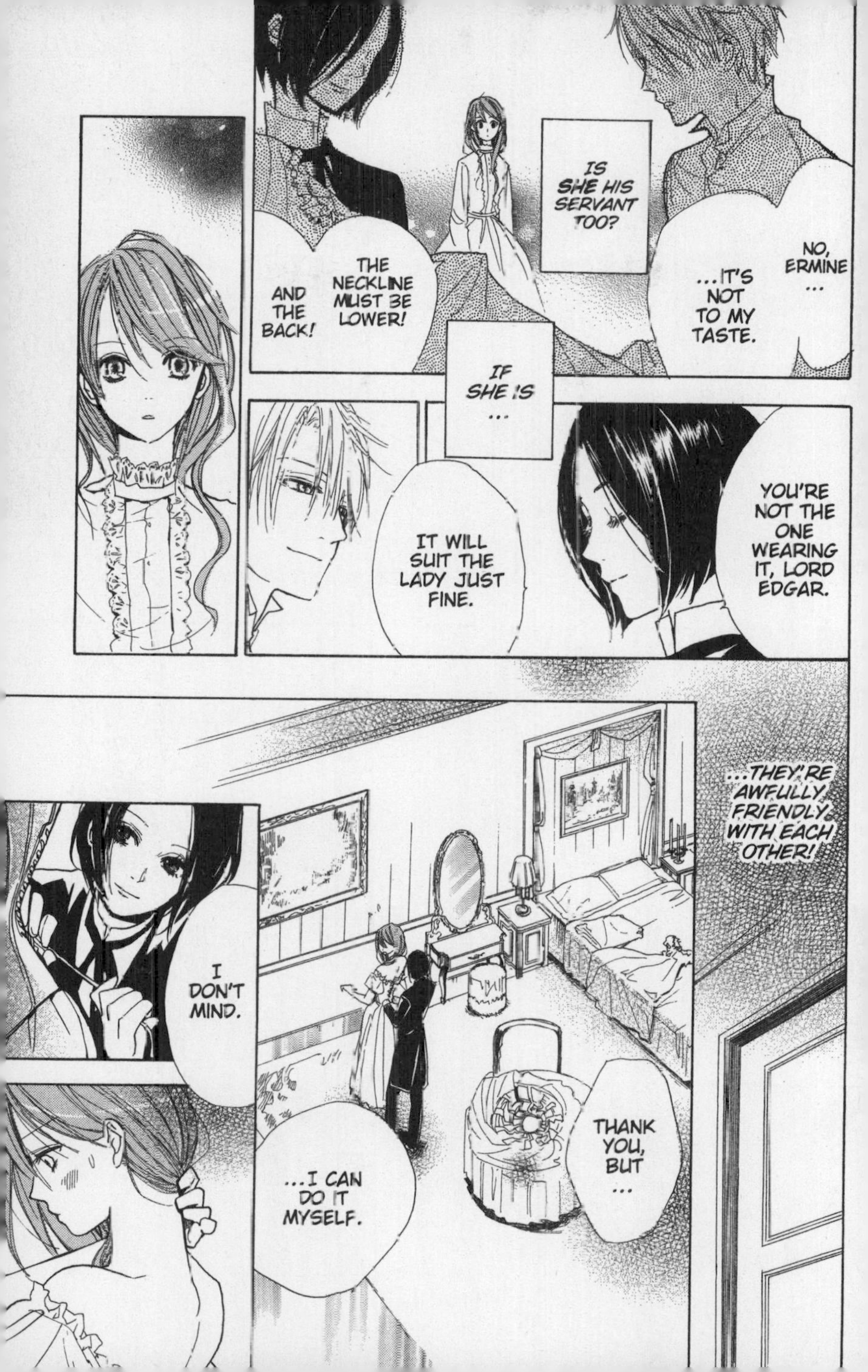
IS SHE HIS SERVANT TOO?
NO, ERMINE ...
... IT'S NOT TO MY TASTE.
THE NECKLINE MUST BE LOWER!
AND THE BACK!
YOU'RE NOT THE ONE WEARING IT, LORD EDGAR.
IF SHE IS ...
IT WILL SUIT THE LADY JUST FINE.
... THEY'RE AWFULLY FRIENDLY WITH EACH OTHER!
THANK YOU, BUT ...
... I CAN DO IT MYSELF.
I DON'T MIND.

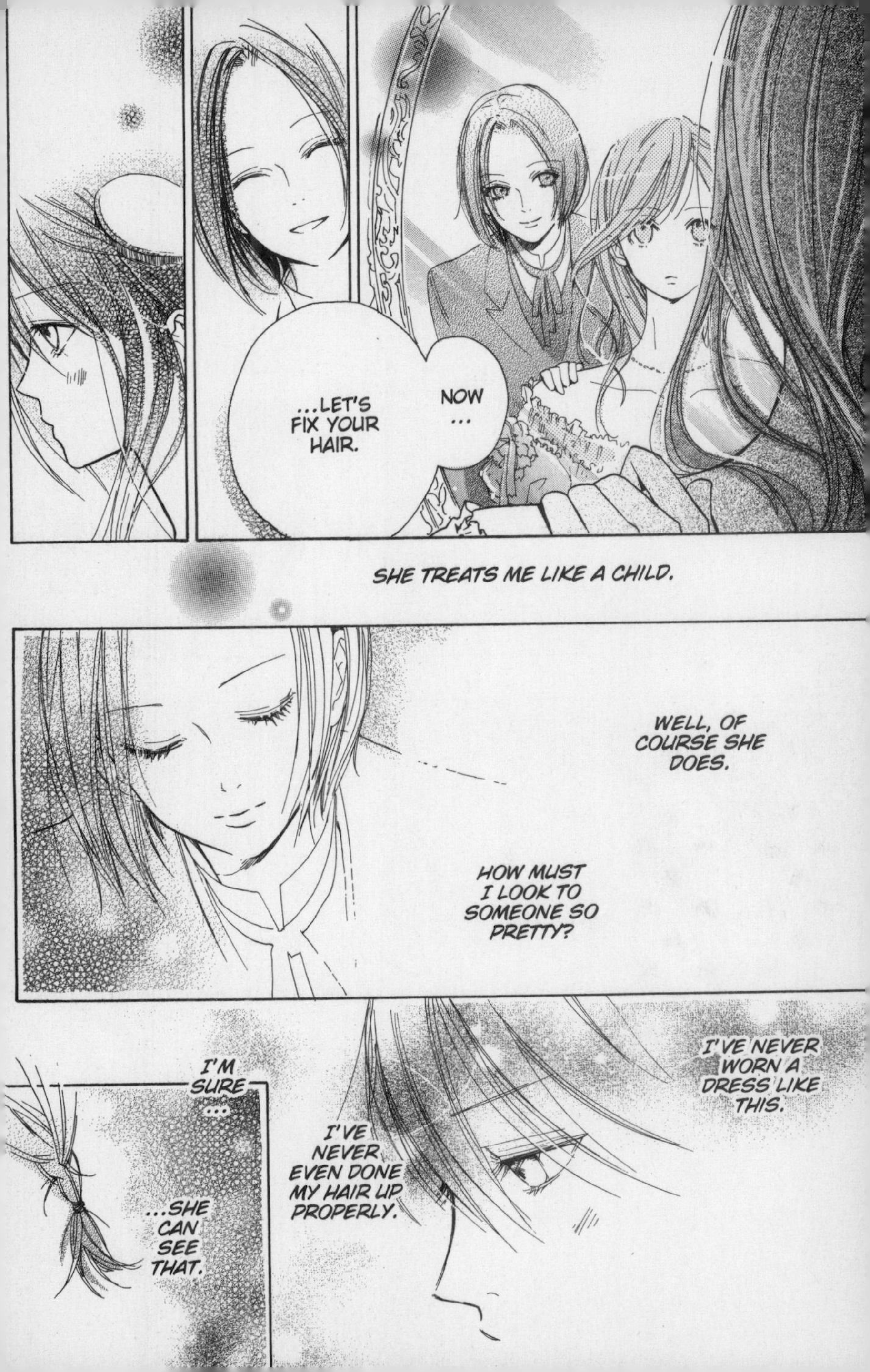
NOW ...
...LET'S FIX YOUR HAIR.
SHE TREATS ME LIKE A CHILD.
WELL, OF COURSE SHE DOES.
HOW MUST I LOOK TO SOMEONE SO PRETTY?
I'VE NEVER WORN A DRESS LIKE THIS.
I'VE NEVER EVEN DONE MY HAIR UP PROPERLY.
I'M SURE ...
...SHE CAN SEE THAT.

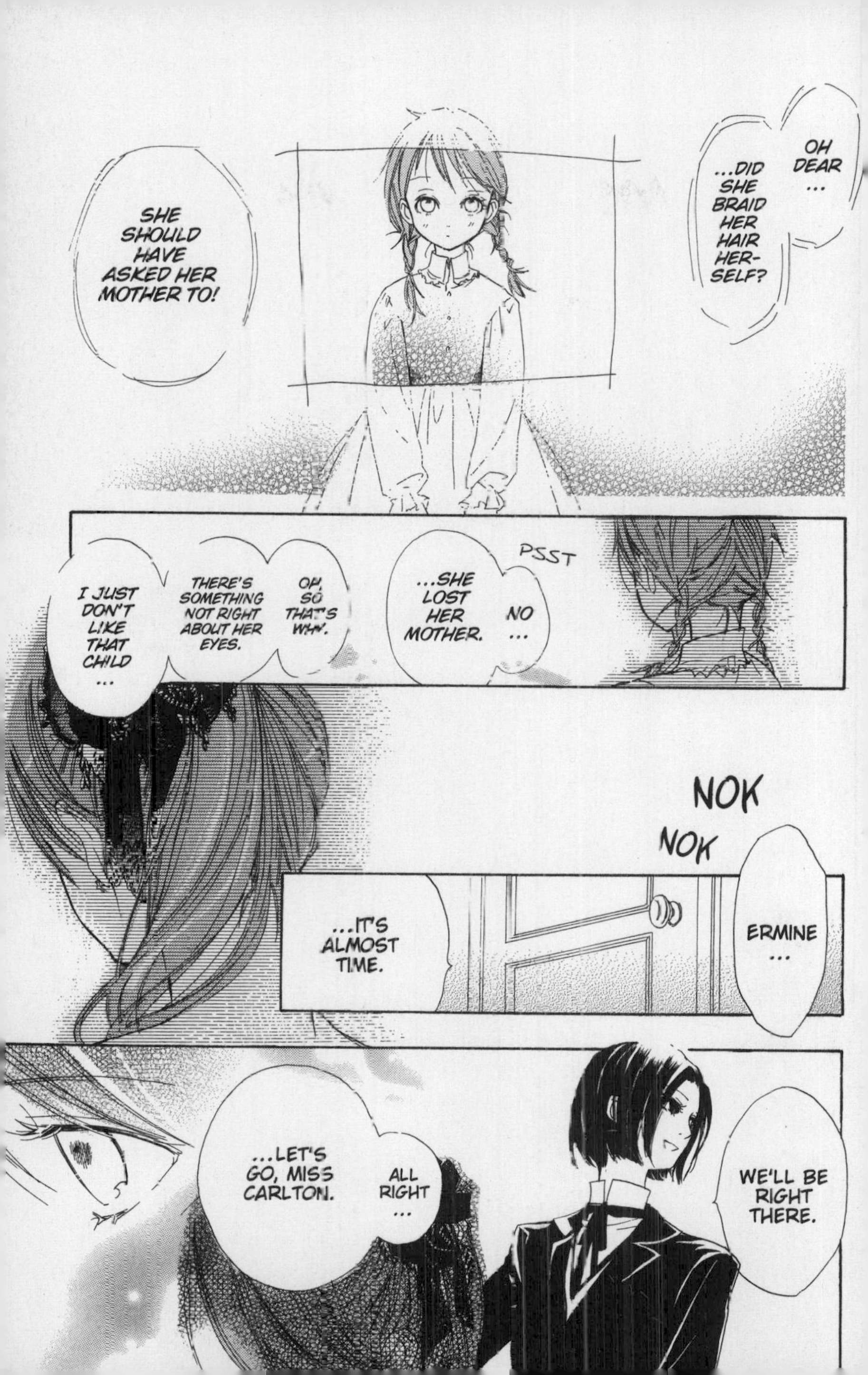
OH DEAR ...
...DID SHE BRAID HER HAIR HER-SELF?
SHE SHOULD HAVE ASKED HER MOTHER TO!
PSST
NO ...
...SHE LOST HER MOTHER.
OH, SO THAT'S WHY.
THERE'S SOMETHING NOT RIGHT ABOUT HER EYES.
I JUST DON'T LIKE THAT CHILD ...
NOK
NOK
ERMINE ...
...IT'S ALMOST TIME.
WE'LL BE RIGHT THERE.
ALL RIGHT ...
...LET'S GO, MISS CARLTON.

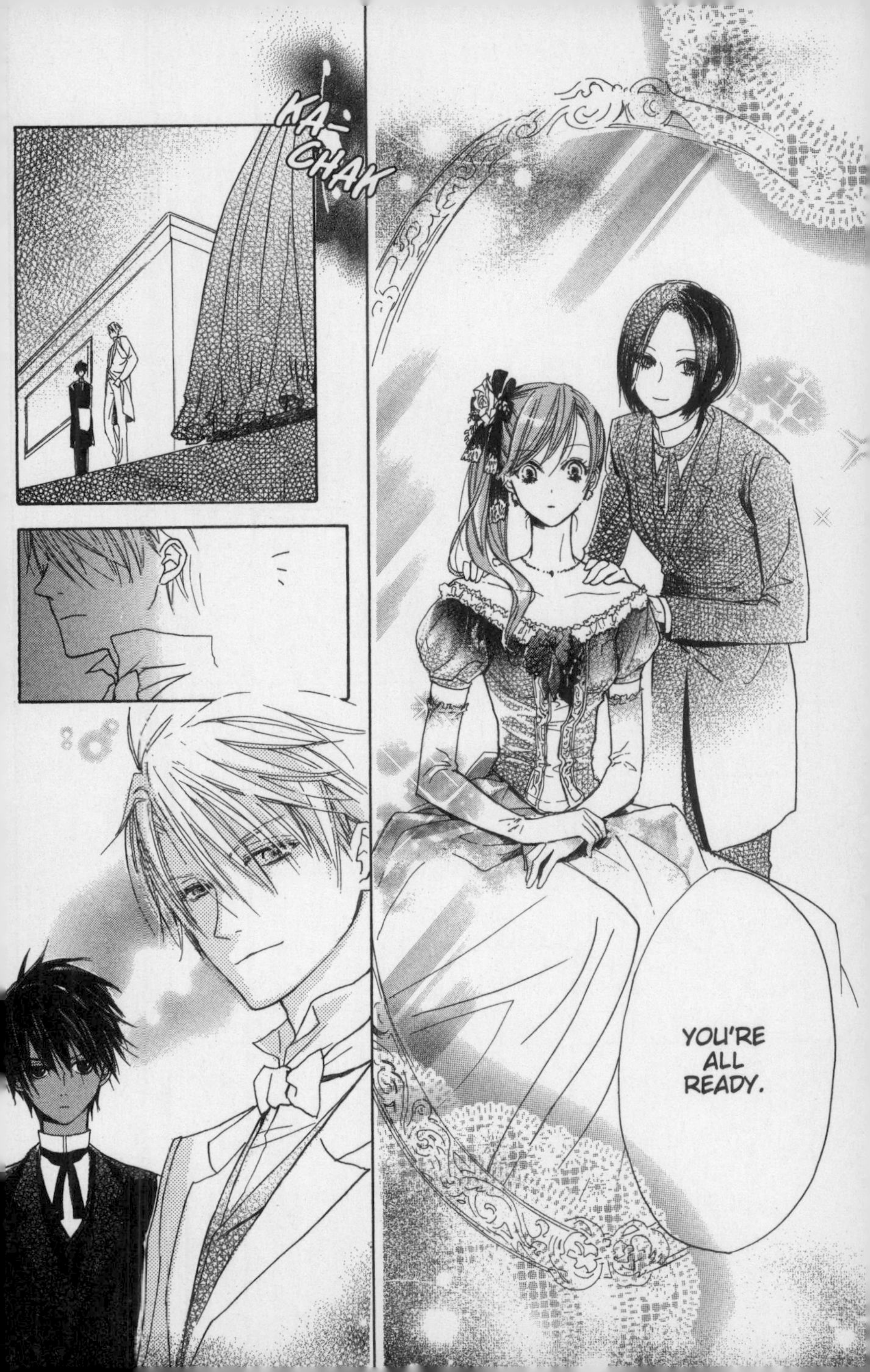
YOU'RE ALL READY.
KA-CHAK

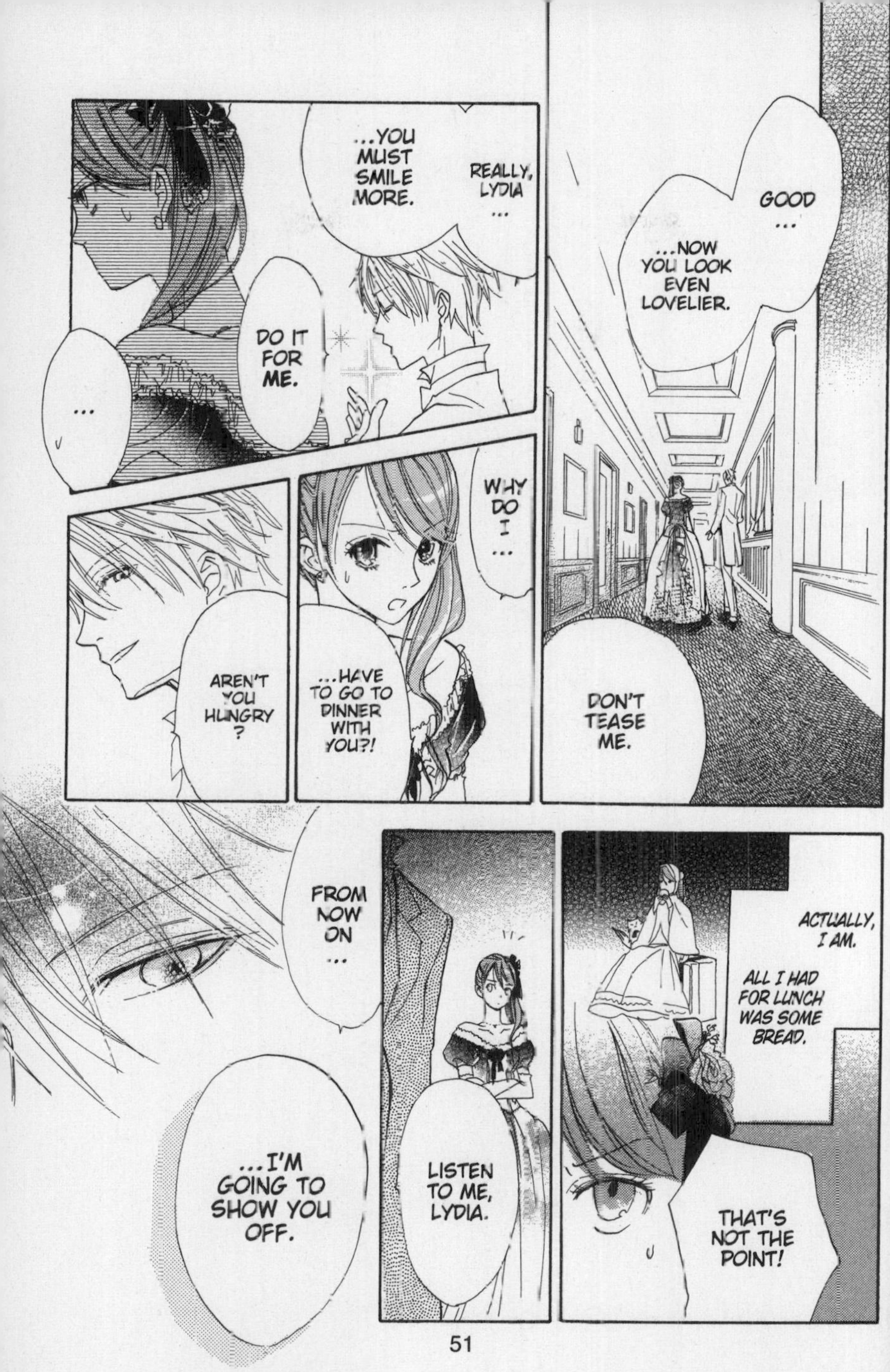
GOOD ...
...NOW YOU LOOK EVEN LOVELIER.
DON'T TEASE ME.
REALLY, LYDIA ...
...YOU MUST SMILE MORE.
DO IT FOR ME.
...
WHY DO I ...
...HAVE TO GO TO DINNER WITH YOU?!
AREN'T YOU HUNGRY?
ACTUALLY, I AM.
ALL I HAD FOR LUNCH WAS SOME BREAD.
THAT'S NOT THE POINT!
LISTEN TO ME, LYDIA.
FROM NOW ON ...
...I'M GOING TO SHOW YOU OFF.

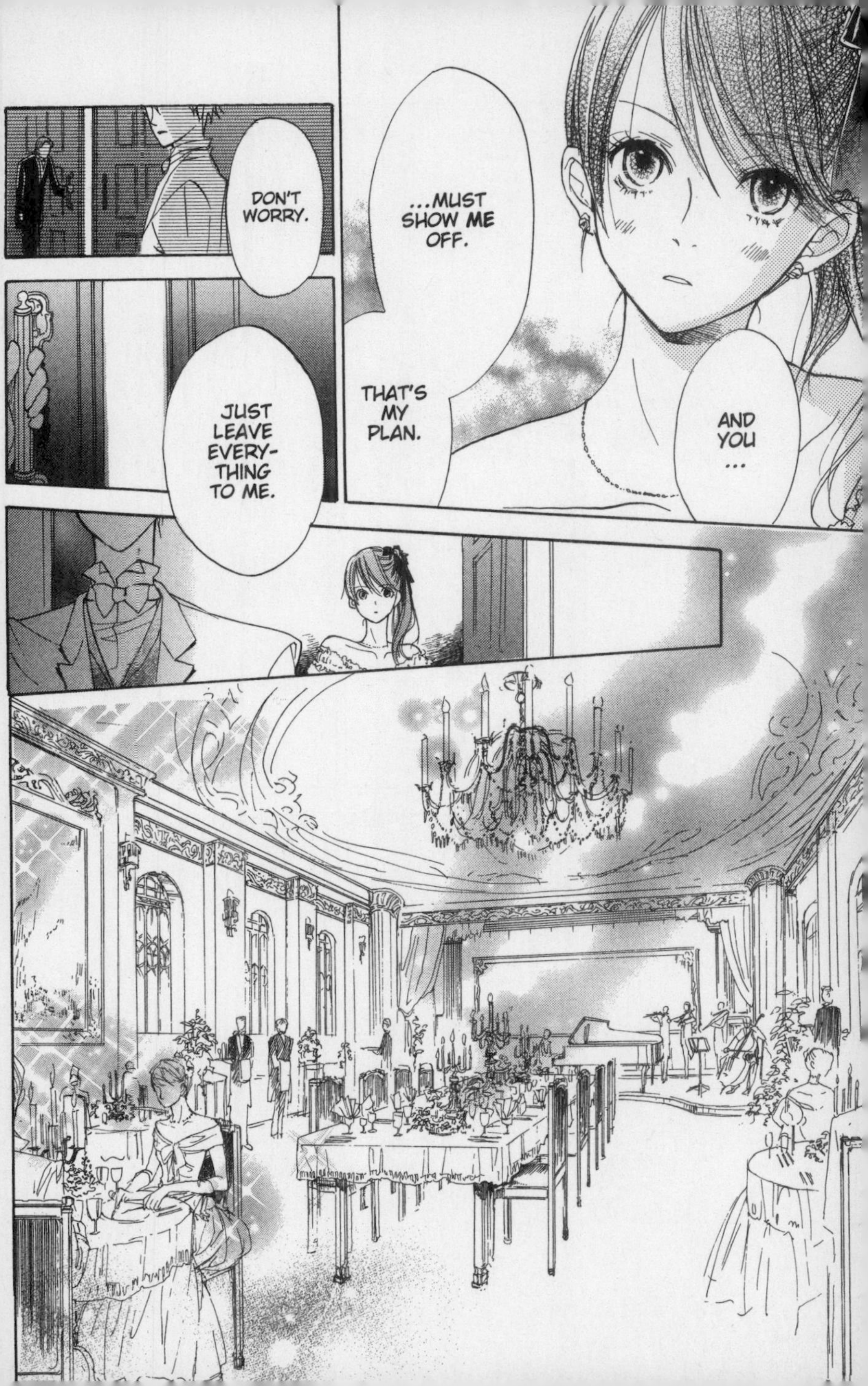
AND YOU ...
...MUST SHOW ME OFF.
THAT'S MY PLAN.
DON'T WORRY.
JUST LEAVE EVERY-THING TO ME.

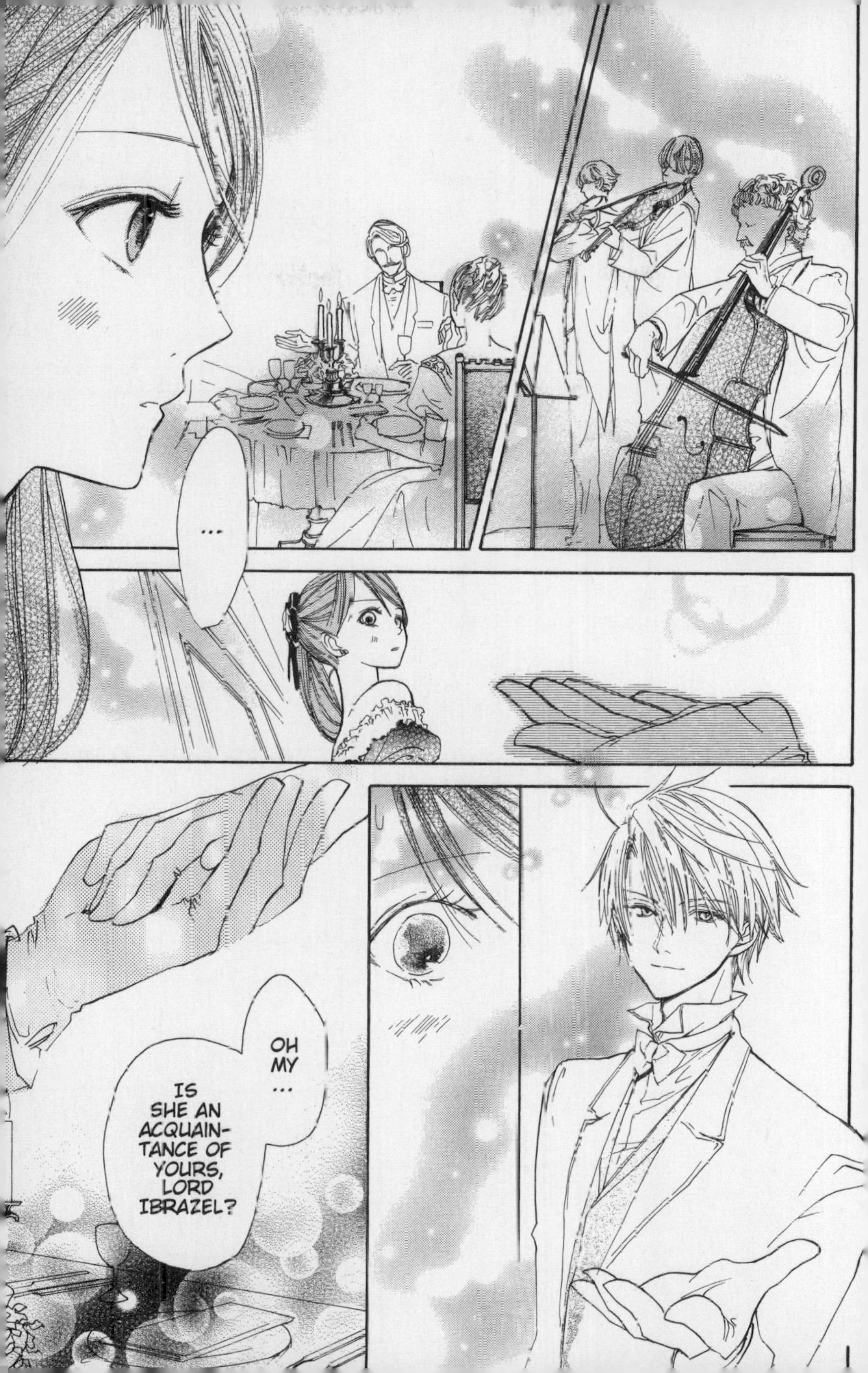
...
OH MY ...
IS SHE AN ACQUAINTANCE OF YOURS, LORD IBRAZEL?

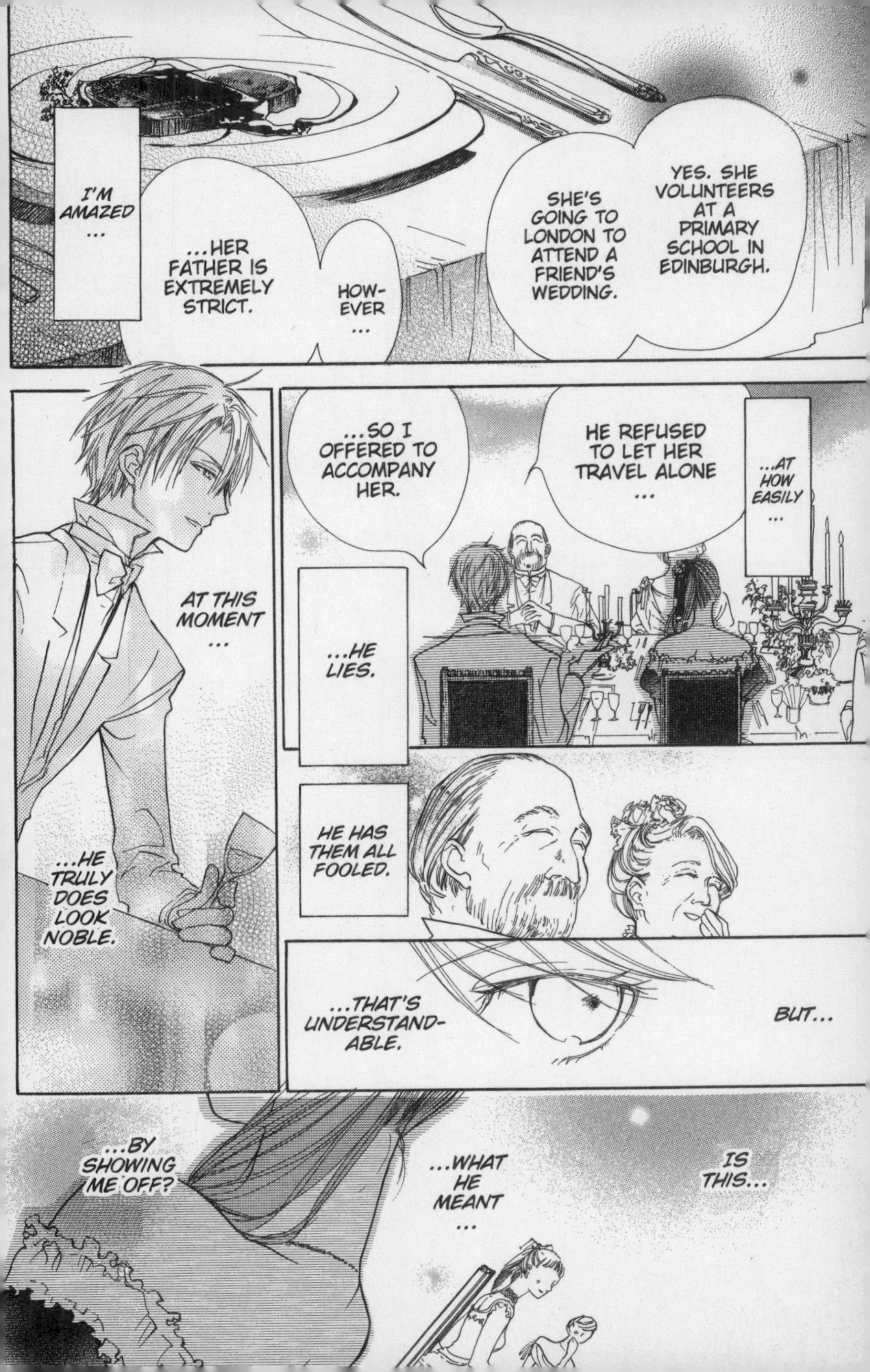
YES. SHE VOLUNTEERS AT A PRIMARY SCHOOL IN EDINBURGH.
SHE'S GOING TO LONDON TO ATTEND A FRIEND'S WEDDING.
HOW-EVER...
...HER FATHER IS EXTREMELY STRICT.
I'M AMAZED...
...AT HOW EASILY...
HE REFUSED TO LET HER TRAVEL ALONE...
...SO I OFFERED TO ACCOMPANY HER.
...HE LIES.
HE HAS THEM ALL FOOLED.
BUT...
...THAT'S UNDERSTAND-ABLE.
AT THIS MOMENT...
...HE TRULY DOES LOOK NOBLE.
IS THIS...
...WHAT HE MEANT...
...BY SHOWING ME OFF?

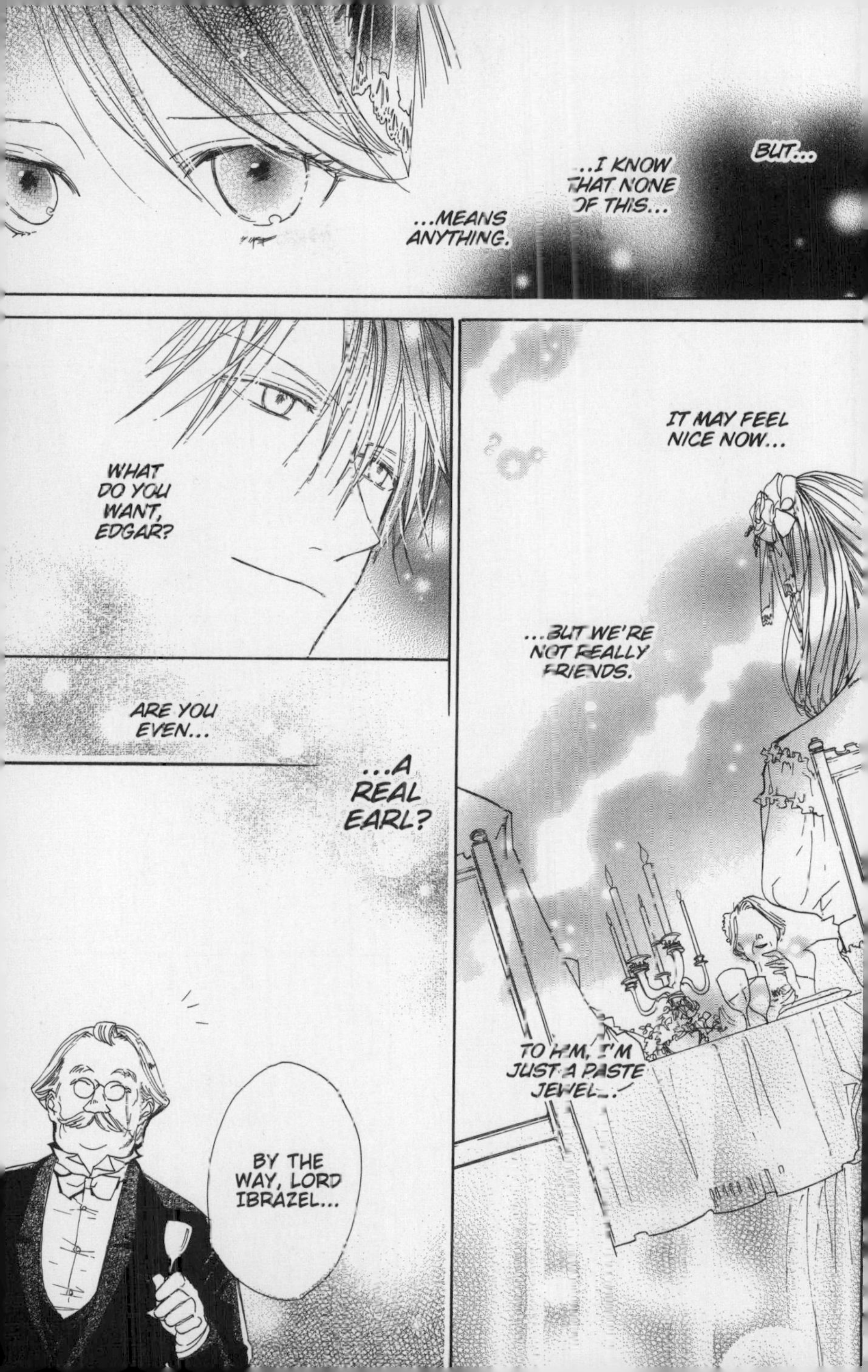
BUT...
...I KNOW THAT NONE OF THIS...
...MEANS ANYTHING.
IT MAY FEEL NICE NOW...
...BUT WE'RE NOT REALLY FRIENDS.
TO HIM, I'M JUST A PASTE JEWEL...
WHAT DO YOU WANT, EDGAR?
ARE YOU EVEN...
...A REAL EARL?
BY THE WAY, LORD IBRAZEL...

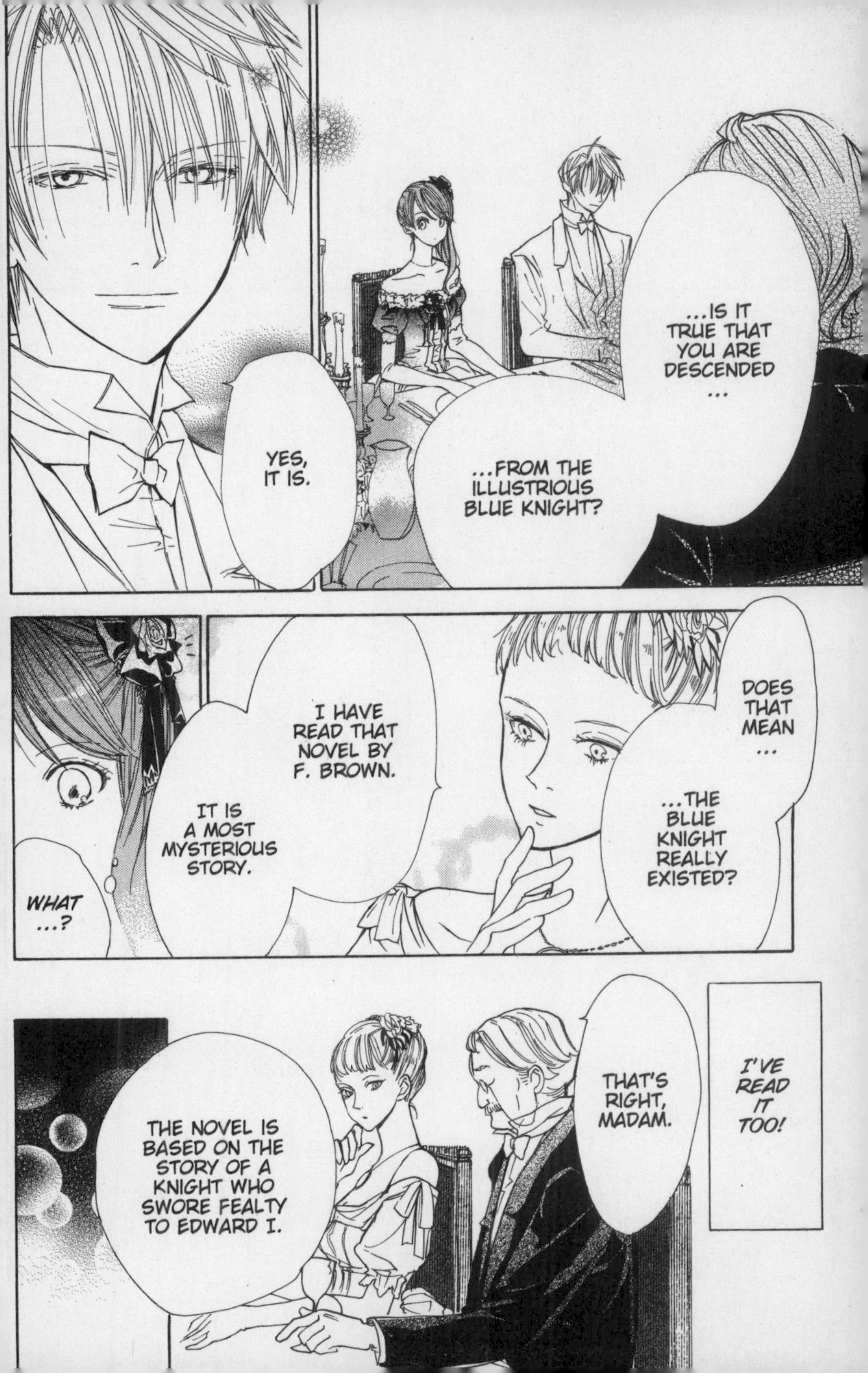
...IS IT TRUE THAT YOU ARE DESCENDED ...
...FROM THE ILLUSTRIOUS BLUE KNIGHT?
YES, IT IS.
DOES THAT MEAN ...
...THE BLUE KNIGHT REALLY EXISTED?
I HAVE READ THAT NOVEL BY F. BROWN.
IT IS A MOST MYSTERIOUS STORY.
WHAT ...?
I'VE READ IT TOO!
THAT'S RIGHT, MADAM.
THE NOVEL IS BASED ON THE STORY OF A KNIGHT WHO SWORE FEALTY TO EDWARD I.

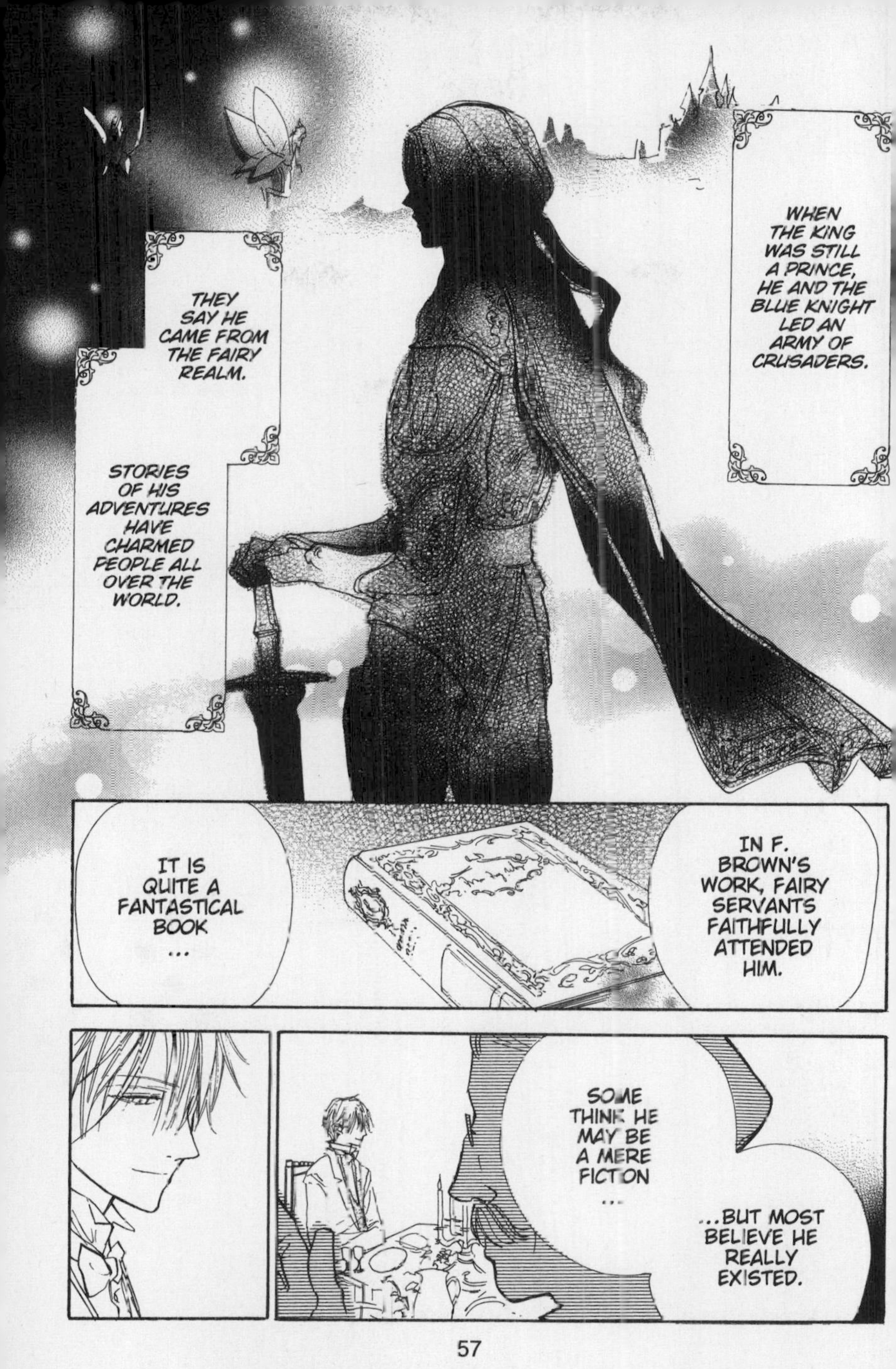
WHEN THE KING WAS STILL A PRINCE, HE AND THE BLUE KNIGHT LED AN ARMY OF CRUSADERS.
THEY SAY HE CAME FROM THE FAIRY REALM.
STORIES OF HIS ADVENTURES HAVE CHARMED PEOPLE ALL OVER THE WORLD.
IN F. BROWN'S WORK, FAIRY SERVANTS FAITHFULLY ATTENDED HIM.
IT IS QUITE A FANTASTICAL BOOK ...
SOME THINK HE MAY BE A MERE FICTION ...
...BUT MOST BELIEVE HE REALLY EXISTED.

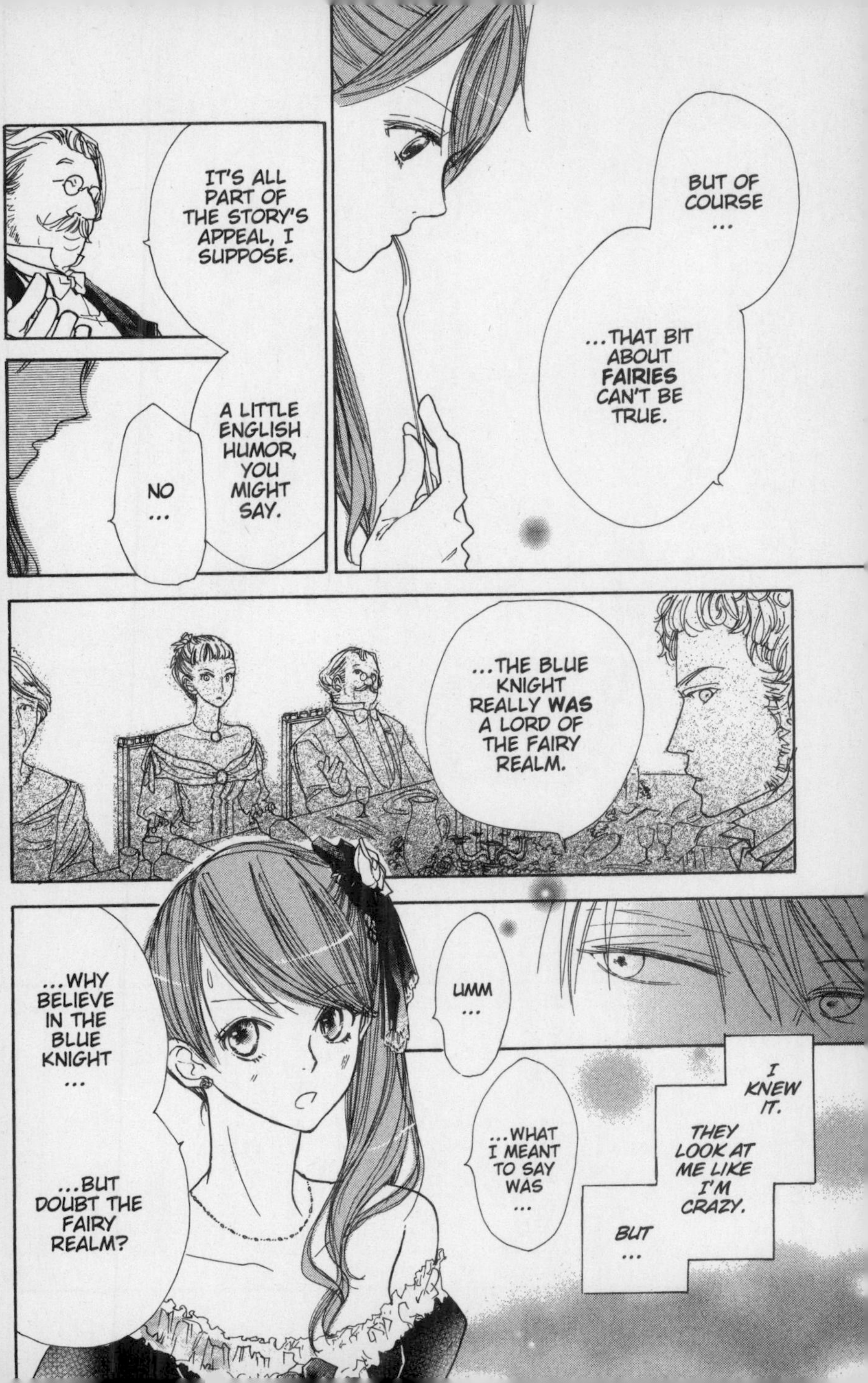
BUT OF COURSE ...
...THAT BIT ABOUT FAIRIES CAN'T BE TRUE.
IT'S ALL PART OF THE STORY'S APPEAL, I SUPPOSE.
A LITTLE ENGLISH HUMOR, YOU MIGHT SAY.
NO ...
...THE BLUE KNIGHT REALLY WAS A LORD OF THE FAIRY REALM.
UMM ...
I KNEW IT.
THEY LOOK AT ME LIKE I'M CRAZY.
BUT ...
...WHAT I MEANT TO SAY WAS ...
...WHY BELIEVE IN THE BLUE KNIGHT ...
...BUT DOUBT THE FAIRY REALM?

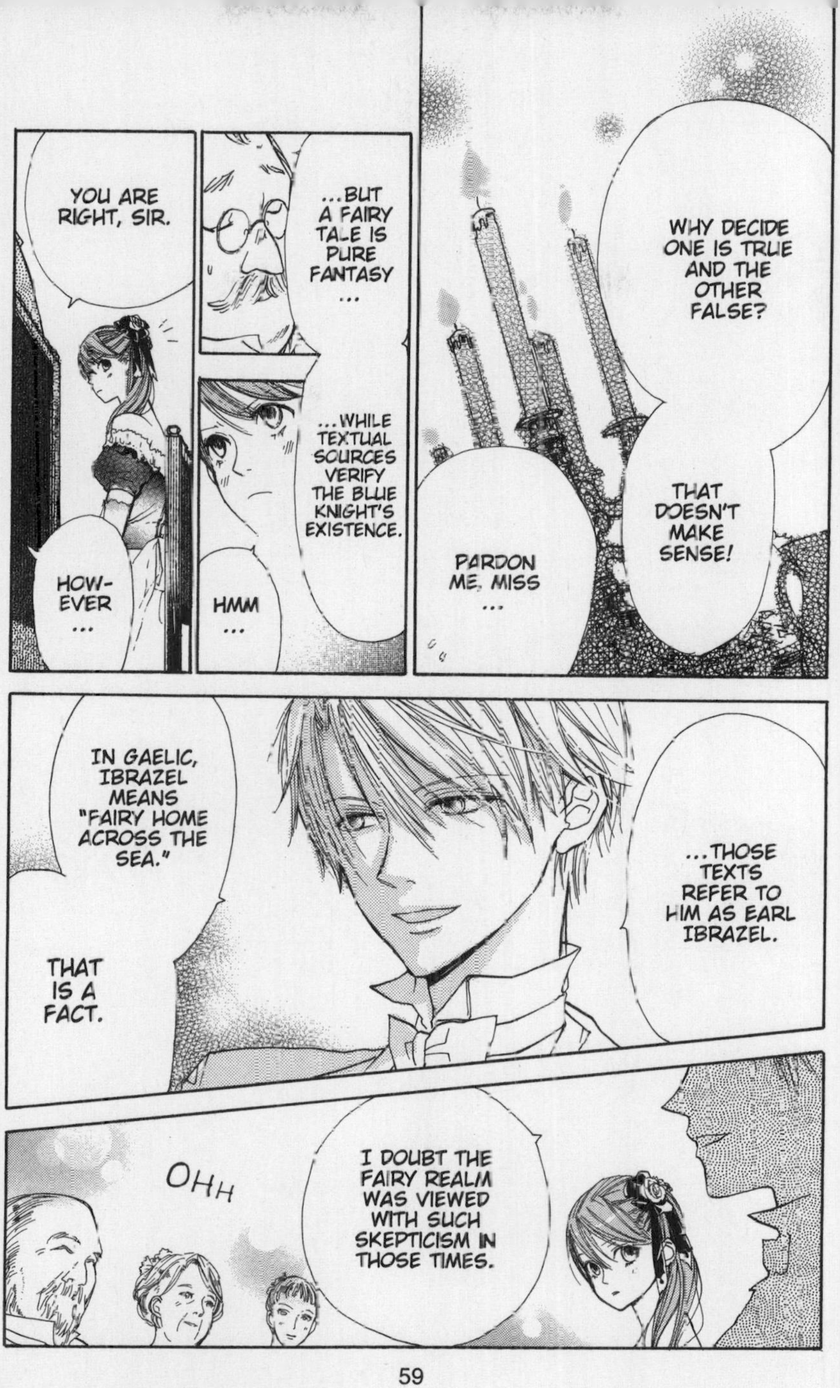
WHY DECIDE ONE IS TRUE AND THE OTHER FALSE?
THAT DOESN'T MAKE SENSE!
PARDON ME, MISS...
...BUT A FAIRY TALE IS PURE FANTASY...
...WHILE TEXTUAL SOURCES VERIFY THE BLUE KNIGHT'S EXISTENCE.
HMM...
YOU ARE RIGHT, SIR.
HOW-EVER...
...THOSE TEXTS REFER TO HIM AS EARL IBRAZEL.
IN GAELIC, IBRAZEL MEANS "FAIRY HOME ACROSS THE SEA."
THAT IS A FACT.
I DOUBT THE FAIRY REALM WAS VIEWED WITH SUCH SKEPTICISM IN THOSE TIMES.
OHH

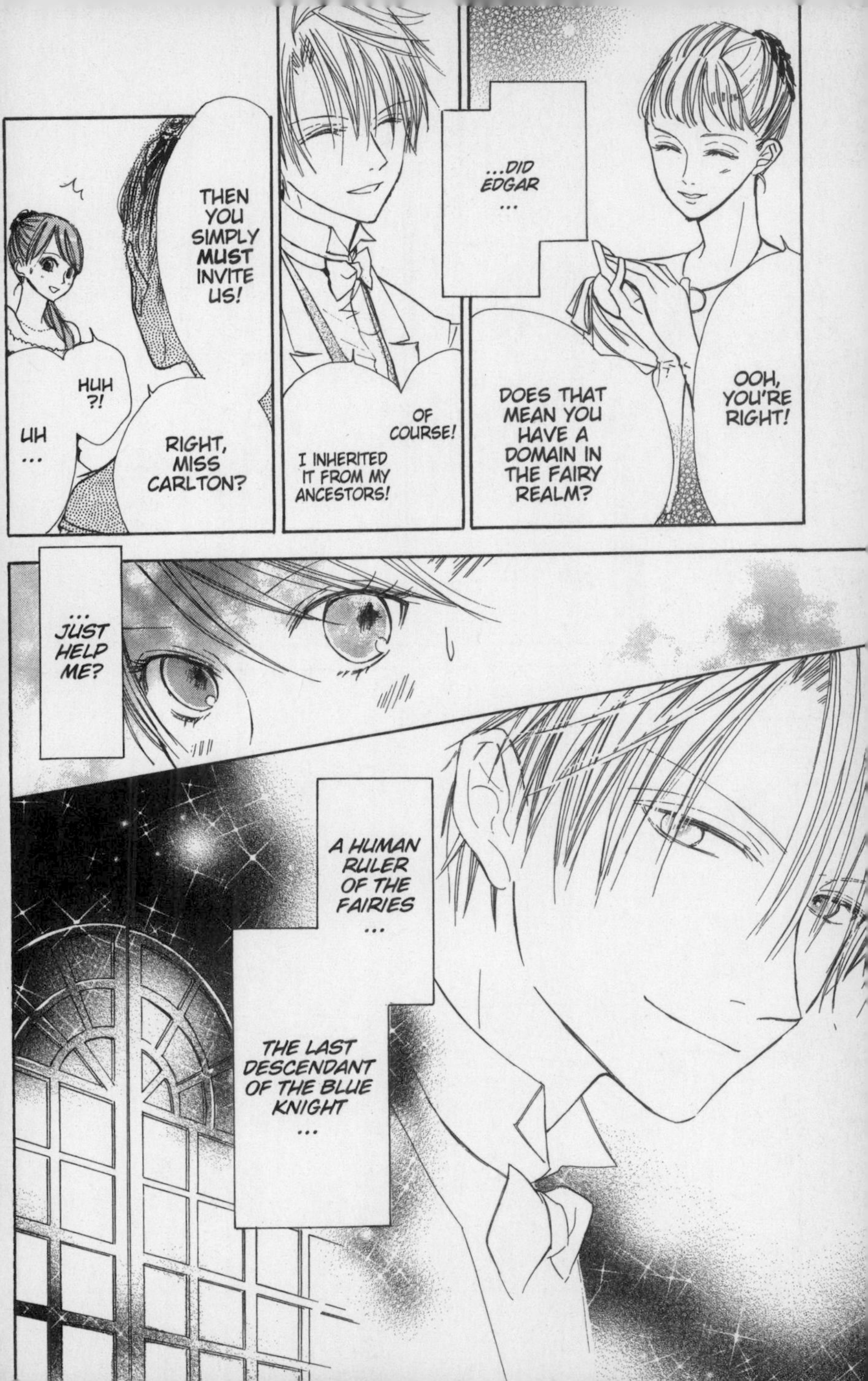
OOH, YOU'RE RIGHT!
DOES THAT MEAN YOU HAVE A DOMAIN IN THE FAIRY REALM?
...DID EDGAR ...
OF COURSE!
I INHERITED IT FROM MY ANCESTORS!
THEN YOU SIMPLY MUST INVITE US!
RIGHT, MISS CARLTON?
HUH ?!
UH ...
... JUST HELP ME?
A HUMAN RULER OF THE FAIRIES ...
THE LAST DESCENDANT OF THE BLUE KNIGHT ...

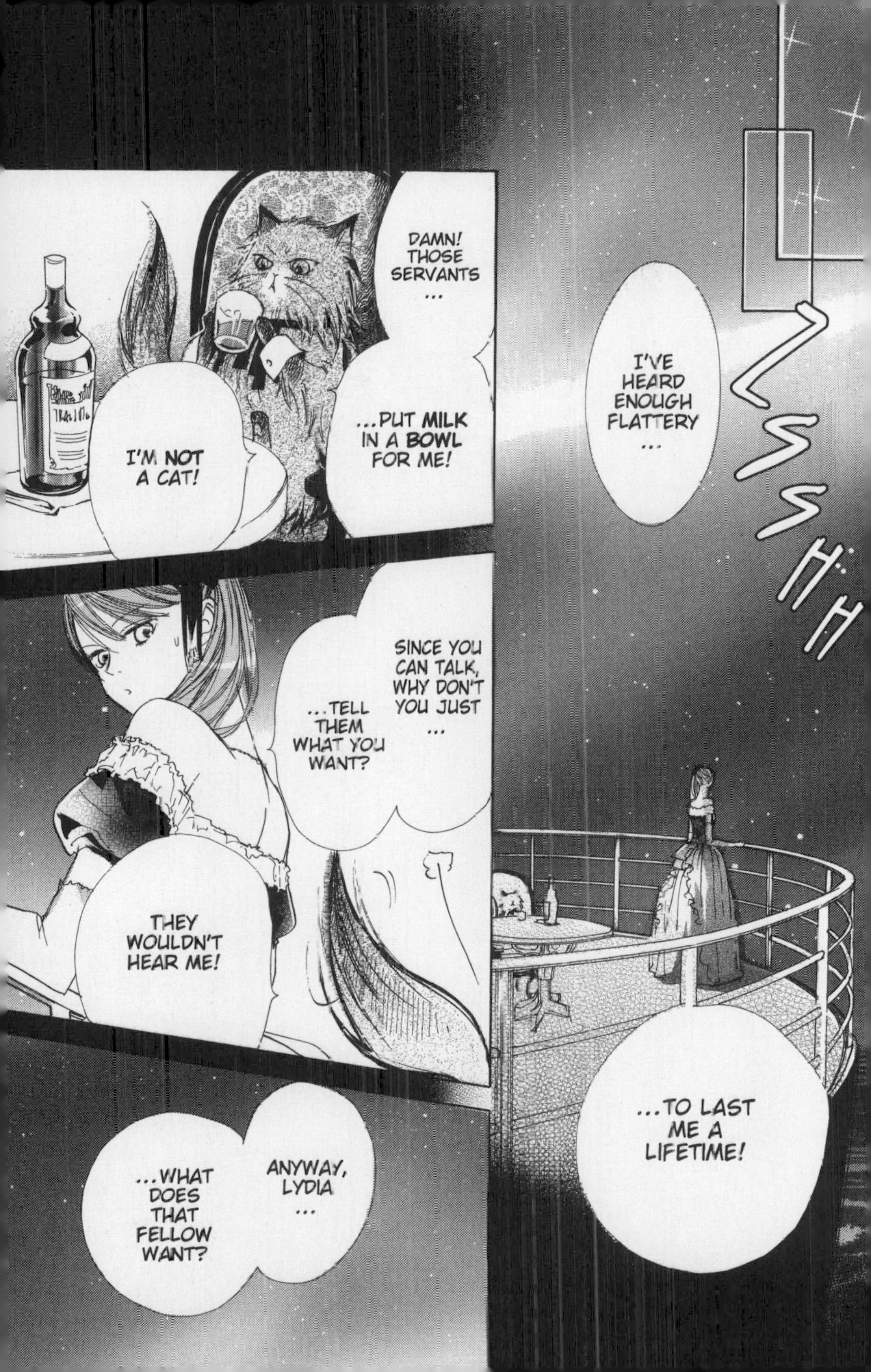
I'VE HEARD ENOUGH FLATTERY ...
...TO LAST ME A LIFETIME!
DAMN! THOSE SERVANTS ...
...PUT MILK IN A BOWL FOR ME!
I'M NOT A CAT!
SINCE YOU CAN TALK, WHY DON'T YOU JUST ...
...TELL THEM WHAT YOU WANT?
THEY WOULDN'T HEAR ME!
ANYWAY, LYDIA ...
...WHAT DOES THAT FELLOW WANT?

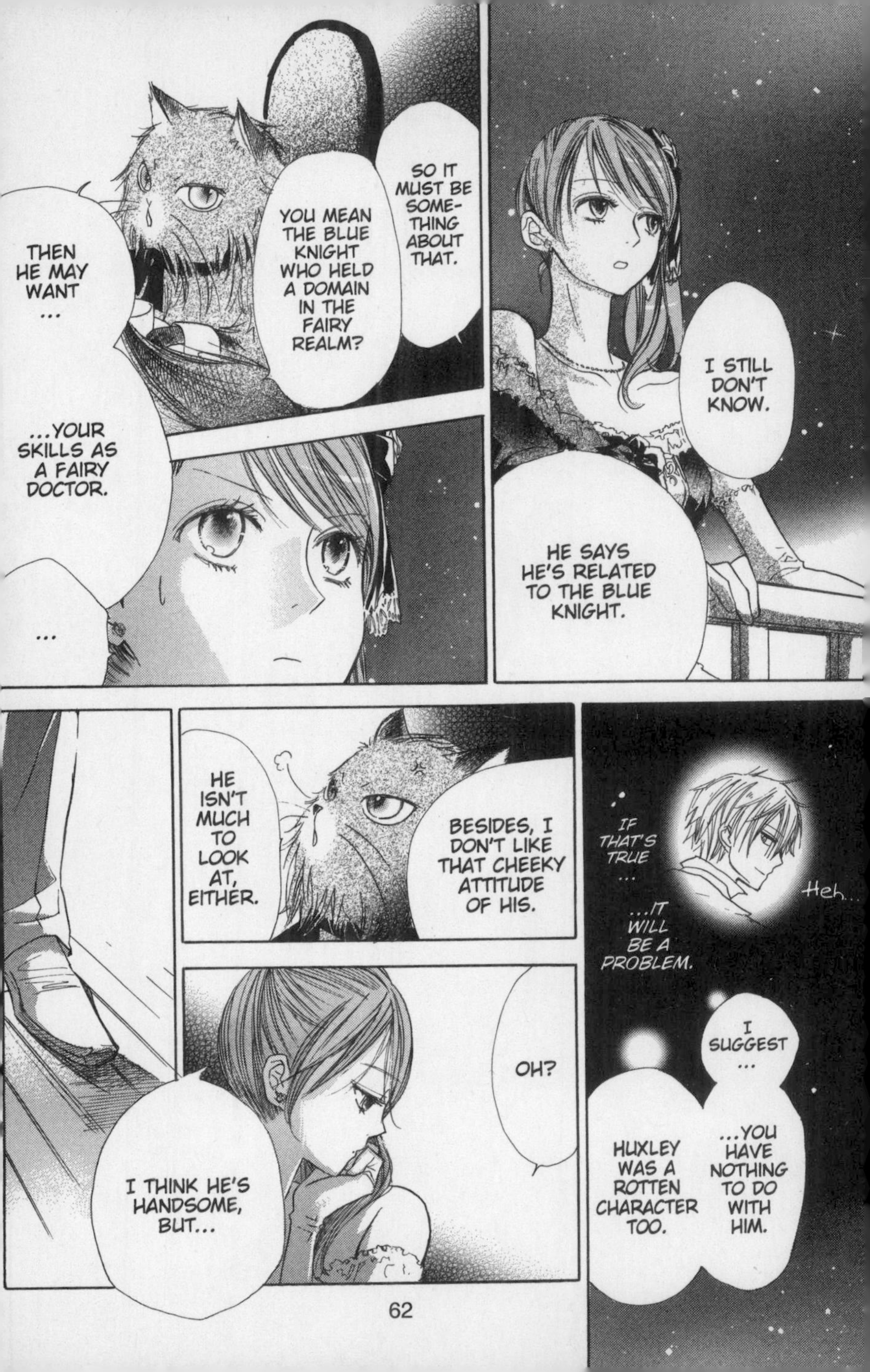
I STILL DON'T KNOW.
HE SAYS HE'S RELATED TO THE BLUE KNIGHT.
SO IT MUST BE SOME-THING ABOUT THAT.
YOU MEAN THE BLUE KNIGHT WHO HELD A DOMAIN IN THE FAIRY REALM?
THEN HE MAY WANT ...
...YOUR SKILLS AS A FAIRY DOCTOR.
...
IF THAT'S TRUE ...
...IT WILL BE A PROBLEM.
Heh...
I SUGGEST ...
...YOU HAVE NOTHING TO DO WITH HIM.
HUXLEY WAS A ROTTEN CHARACTER TOO.
BESIDES, I DON'T LIKE THAT CHEEKY ATTITUDE OF HIS.
HE ISN'T MUCH TO LOOK AT, EITHER.
OH?
I THINK HE'S HANDSOME, BUT...

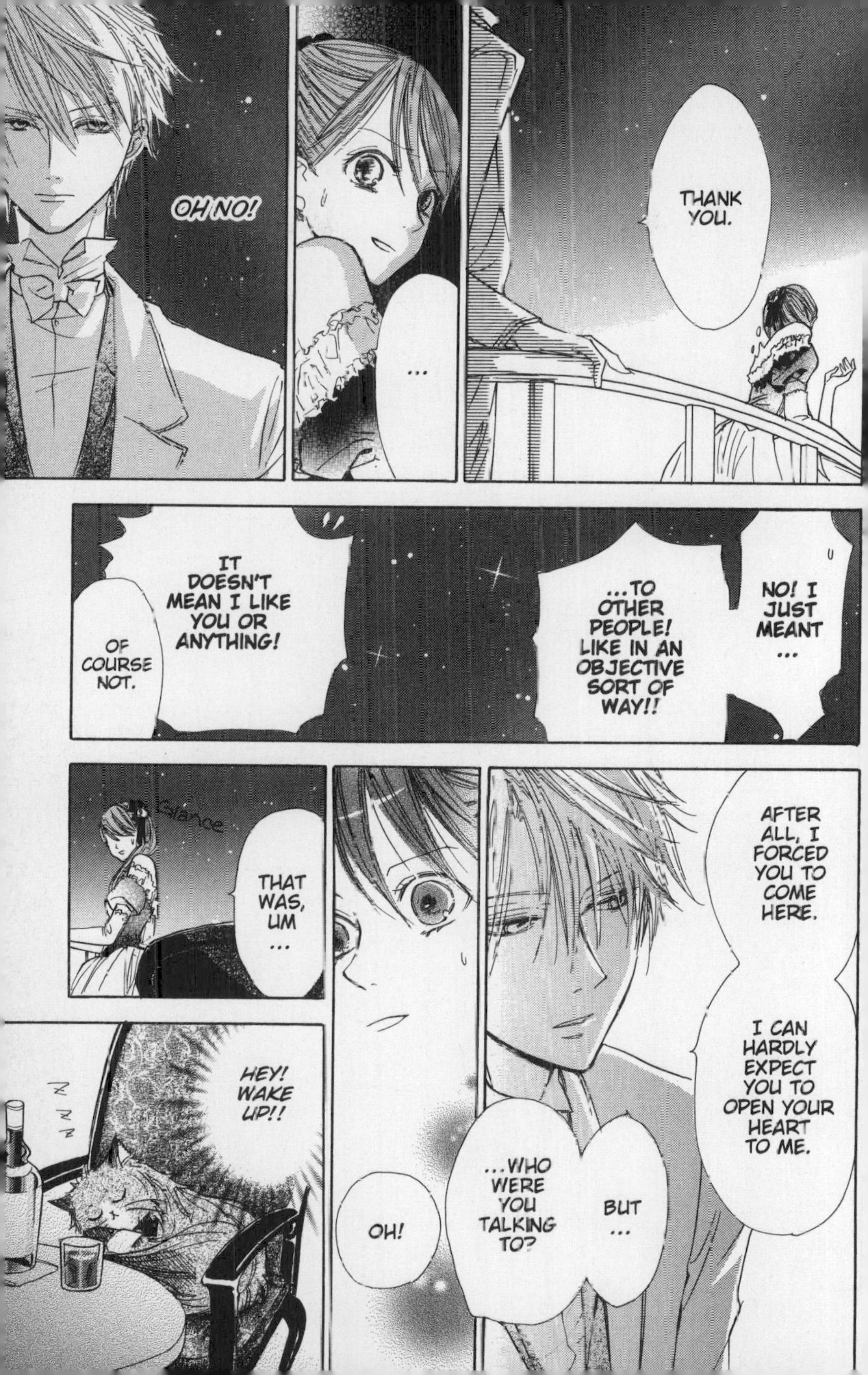
THANK YOU.
...
OH NO!
NO! I JUST MEANT...
...TO OTHER PEOPLE! LIKE IN AN OBJECTIVE SORT OF WAY!!
IT DOESN'T MEAN I LIKE YOU OR ANYTHING!
OF COURSE NOT.
AFTER ALL, I FORCED YOU TO COME HERE.
I CAN HARDLY EXPECT YOU TO OPEN YOUR HEART TO ME.
BUT...
...WHO WERE YOU TALKING TO?
OH!
Glance
THAT WAS, UM...
HEY! WAKE UP!!
Z Z Z

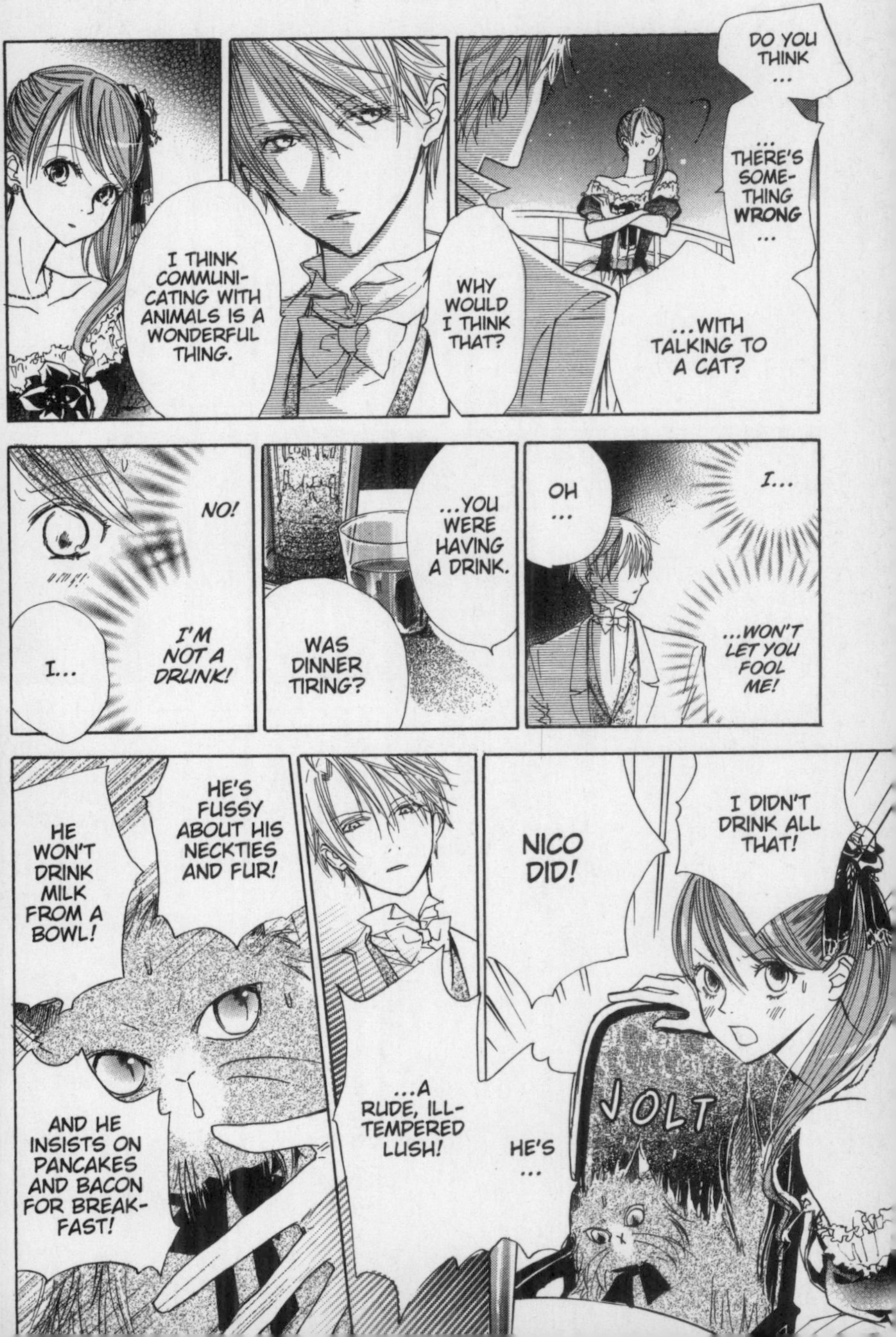
DO YOU THINK ...
... THERE'S SOMETHING WRONG ...
...WITH TALKING TO A CAT?
WHY WOULD I THINK THAT?
I THINK COMMUNICATING WITH ANIMALS IS A WONDERFUL THING.
I...
OH ...
...WON'T LET YOU FOOL ME!
...YOU WERE HAVING A DRINK.
WAS DINNER TIRING?
NO!
I'M NOT A DRUNK!
I...
I DIDN'T DRINK ALL THAT!
NICO DID!
JOLT
HE'S ...
...A RUDE, ILL-TEMPERED LUSH!
HE'S FUSSY ABOUT HIS NECKTIES AND FUR!
HE WON'T DRINK MILK FROM A BOWL!
AND HE INSISTS ON PANCAKES AND BACON FOR BREAKFAST!

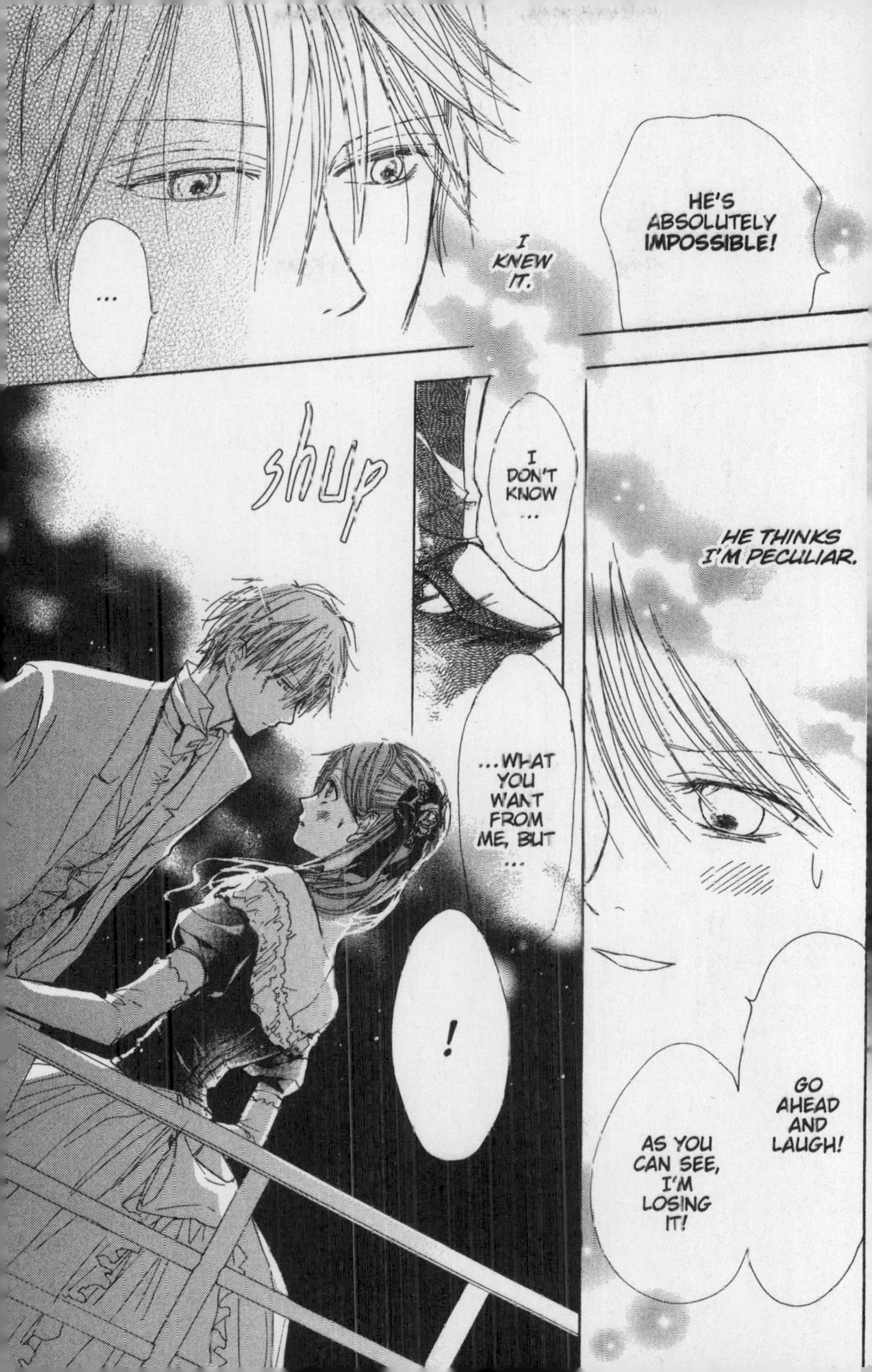
HE'S ABSOLUTELY IMPOSSIBLE!
I KNEW IT.
...
HE THINKS I'M PECULIAR.
GO AHEAD AND LAUGH!
AS YOU CAN SEE, I'M LOSING IT!
I DON'T KNOW...
...WHAT YOU WANT FROM ME, BUT...
shup
!

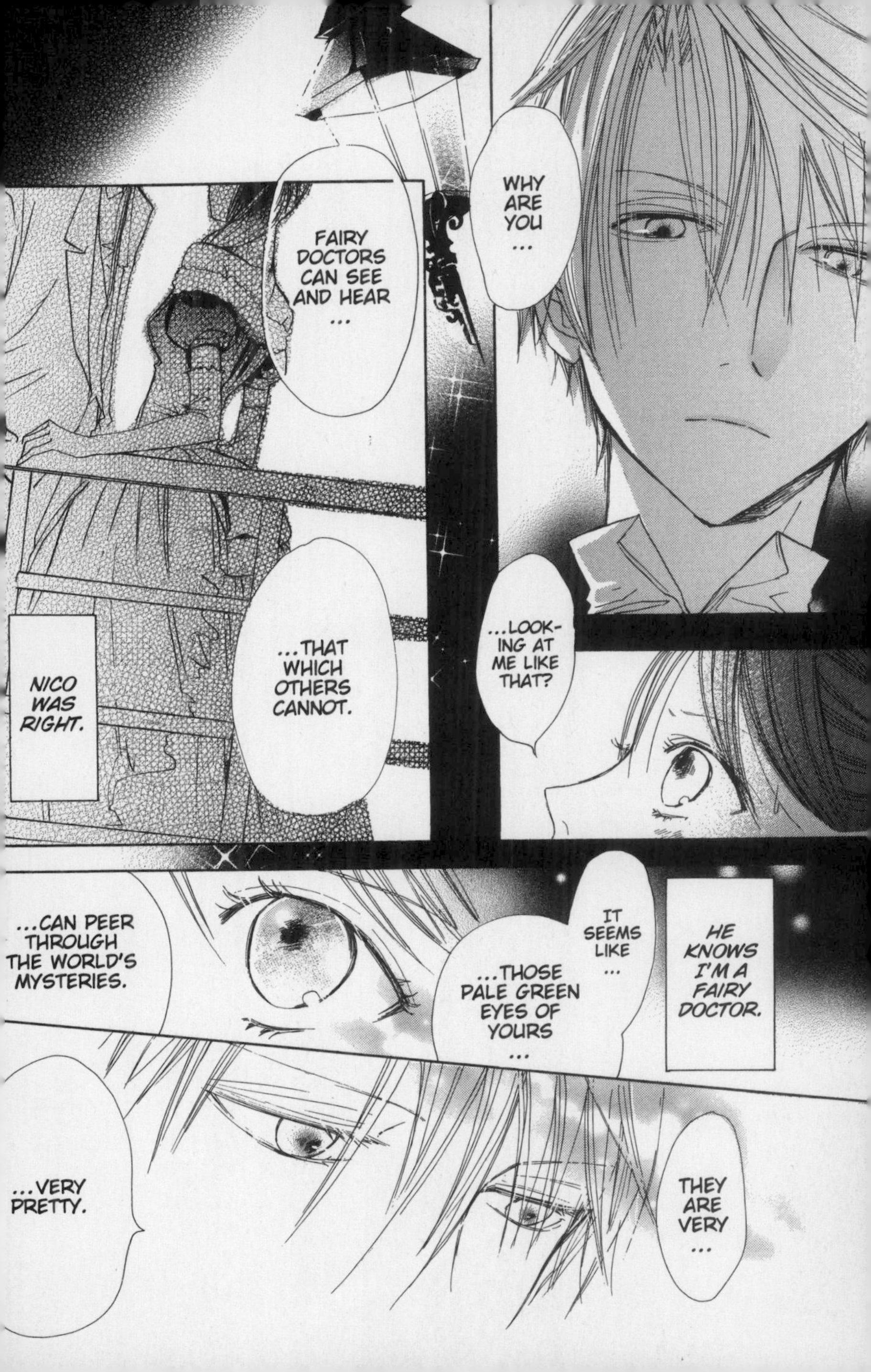
WHY ARE YOU ...
...LOOKING AT ME LIKE THAT?
FAIRY DOCTORS CAN SEE AND HEAR ...
...THAT WHICH OTHERS CANNOT.
NICO WAS RIGHT.
HE KNOWS I'M A FAIRY DOCTOR.
IT SEEMS LIKE ...
...THOSE PALE GREEN EYES OF YOURS ...
...CAN PEER THROUGH THE WORLD'S MYSTERIES.
THEY ARE VERY ...
...VERY PRETTY.

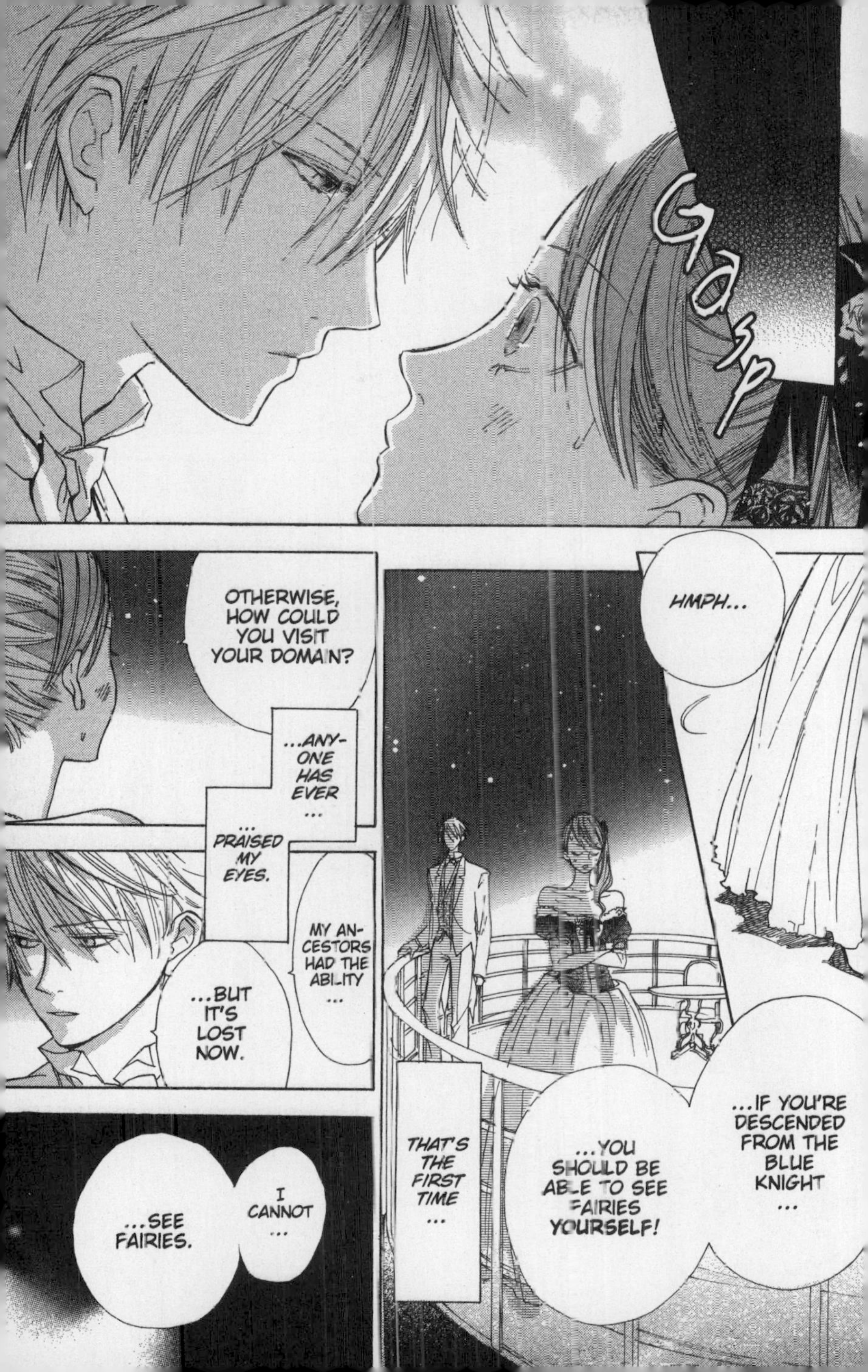
Gasp
HMPH...
...IF YOU'RE DESCENDED FROM THE BLUE KNIGHT...
...YOU SHOULD BE ABLE TO SEE FAIRIES YOURSELF!
THAT'S THE FIRST TIME...
OTHERWISE, HOW COULD YOU VISIT YOUR DOMAIN?
...ANYONE HAS EVER...
...PRAISED MY EYES.
MY ANCESTORS HAD THE ABILITY...
...BUT IT'S LOST NOW.
I CANNOT...
...SEE FAIRIES.

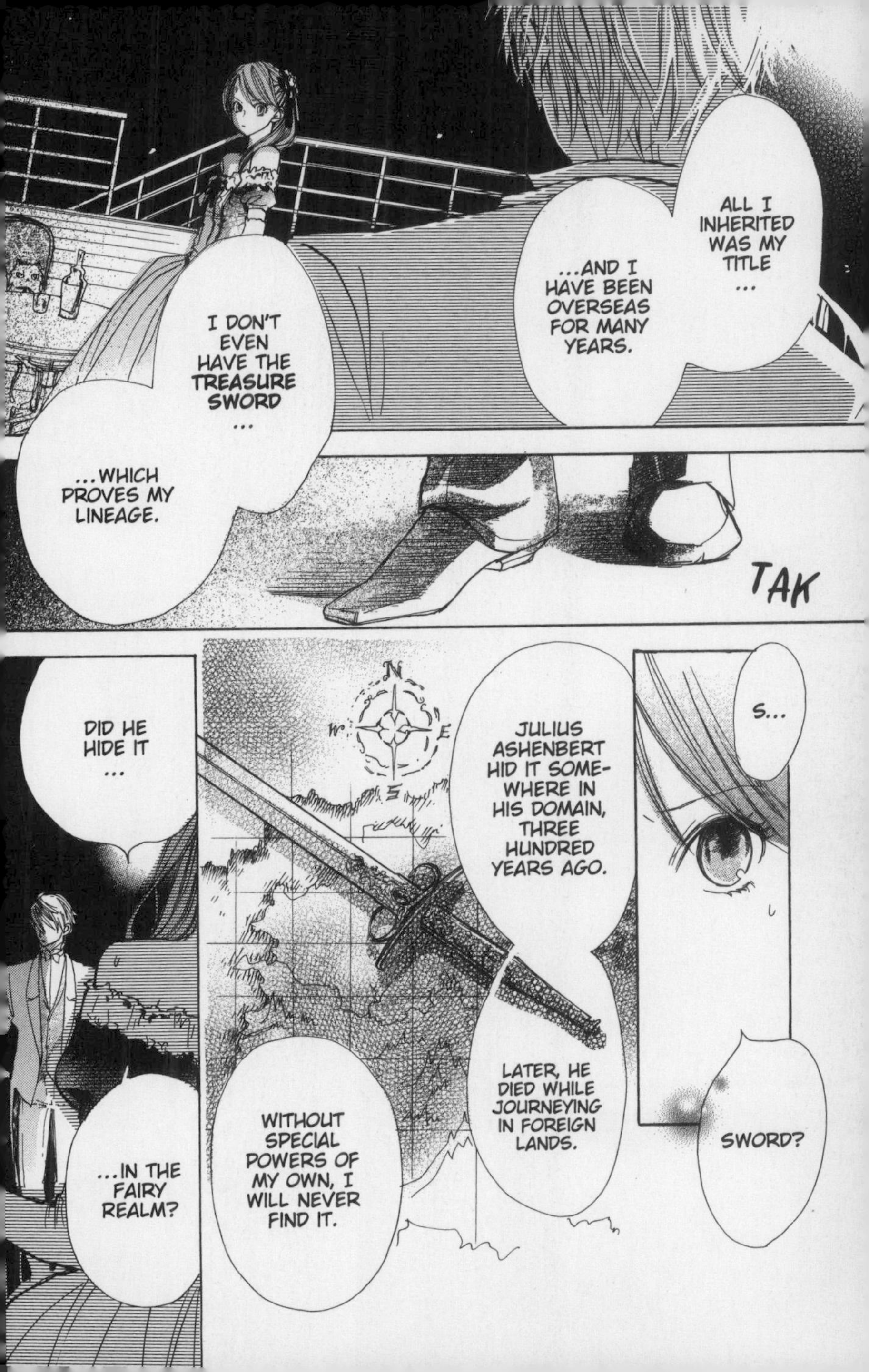
ALL I INHERITED WAS MY TITLE ...
...AND I HAVE BEEN OVERSEAS FOR MANY YEARS.
I DON'T EVEN HAVE THE TREASURE SWORD ...
...WHICH PROVES MY LINEAGE.
TAK
S...
SWORD?
N
W
E
S
JULIUS ASHENBERT HID IT SOME-WHERE IN HIS DOMAIN, THREE HUNDRED YEARS AGO.
LATER, HE DIED WHILE JOURNEYING IN FOREIGN LANDS.
WITHOUT SPECIAL POWERS OF MY OWN, I WILL NEVER FIND IT.
DID HE HIDE IT ...
...IN THE FAIRY REALM?

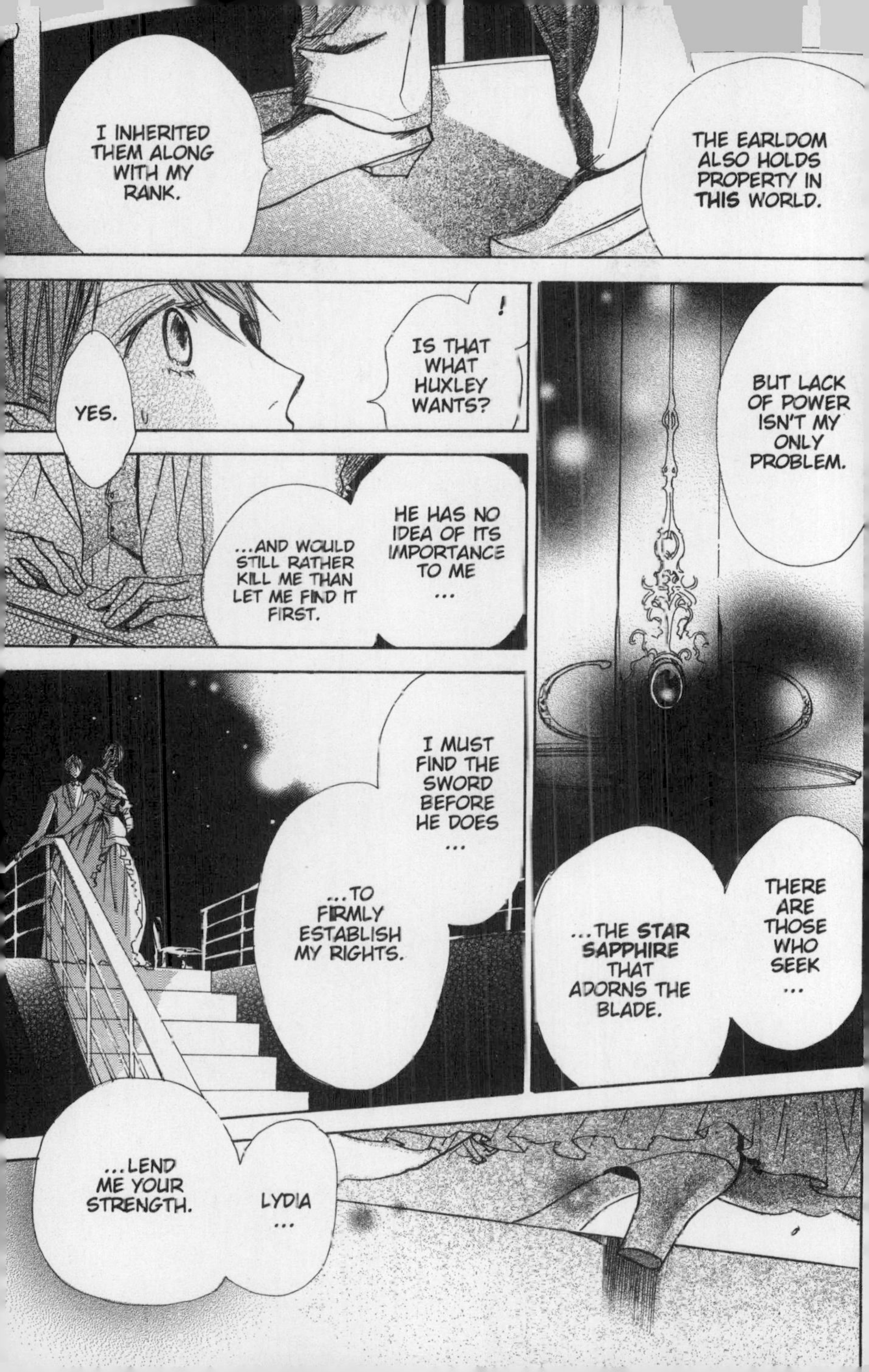
THE EARLDOM ALSO HOLDS PROPERTY IN THIS WORLD.
I INHERITED THEM ALONG WITH MY RANK.
BUT LACK OF POWER ISN'T MY ONLY PROBLEM.
THERE ARE THOSE WHO SEEK ...
...THE STAR SAPPHIRE THAT ADORNS THE BLADE.
!
IS THAT WHAT HUXLEY WANTS?
YES.
HE HAS NO IDEA OF ITS IMPORTANCE TO ME ...
...AND WOULD STILL RATHER KILL ME THAN LET ME FIND IT FIRST.
I MUST FIND THE SWORD BEFORE HE DOES ...
...TO FIRMLY ESTABLISH MY RIGHTS.
LYDIA ...
...LEND ME YOUR STRENGTH.

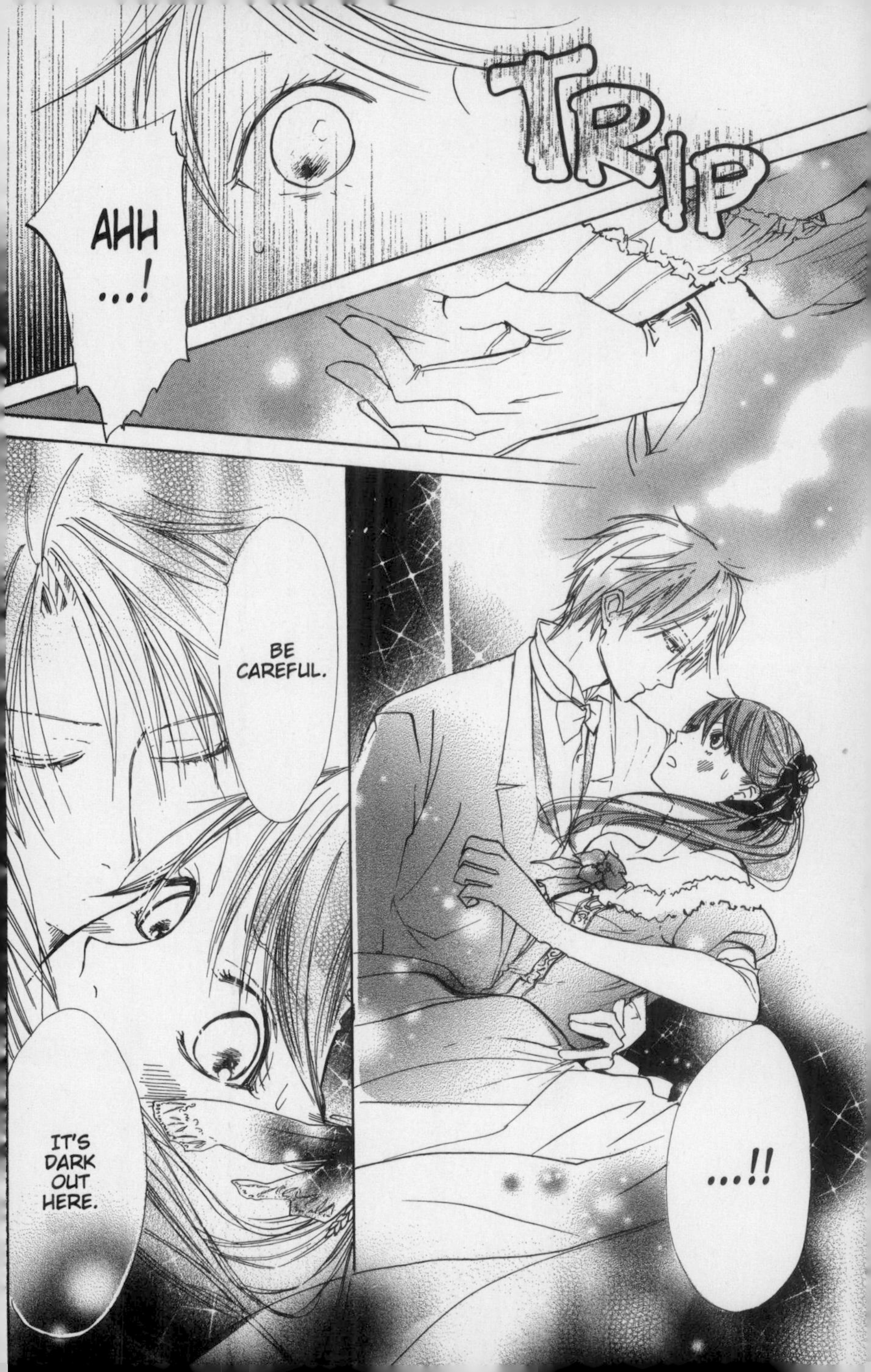
TRIP
AHH ...!
...!!
BE CAREFUL.
IT'S DARK OUT HERE.

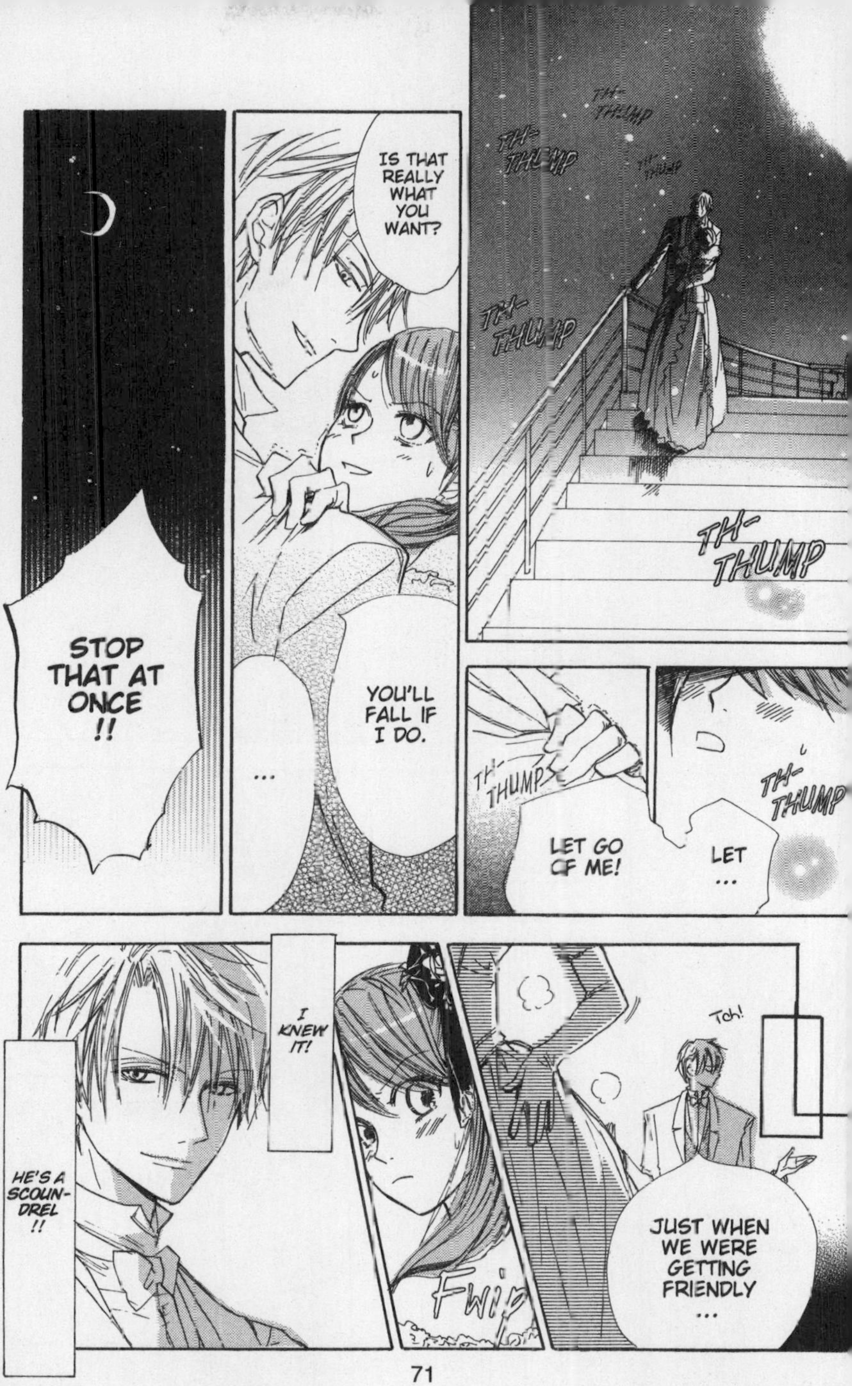
TH-THUMP
TH-THUMP
TH-THUMP
TH-THUMP
TH-THUMP
TH-THUMP
LET ...
TH-THUMP
LET GO OF ME!
IS THAT REALLY WHAT YOU WANT?
YOU'LL FALL IF I DO.
...
STOP THAT AT ONCE !!
Tch!
JUST WHEN WE WERE GETTING FRIENDLY ...
I KNEW IT!
Fwip
HE'S A SCOUNDREL !!

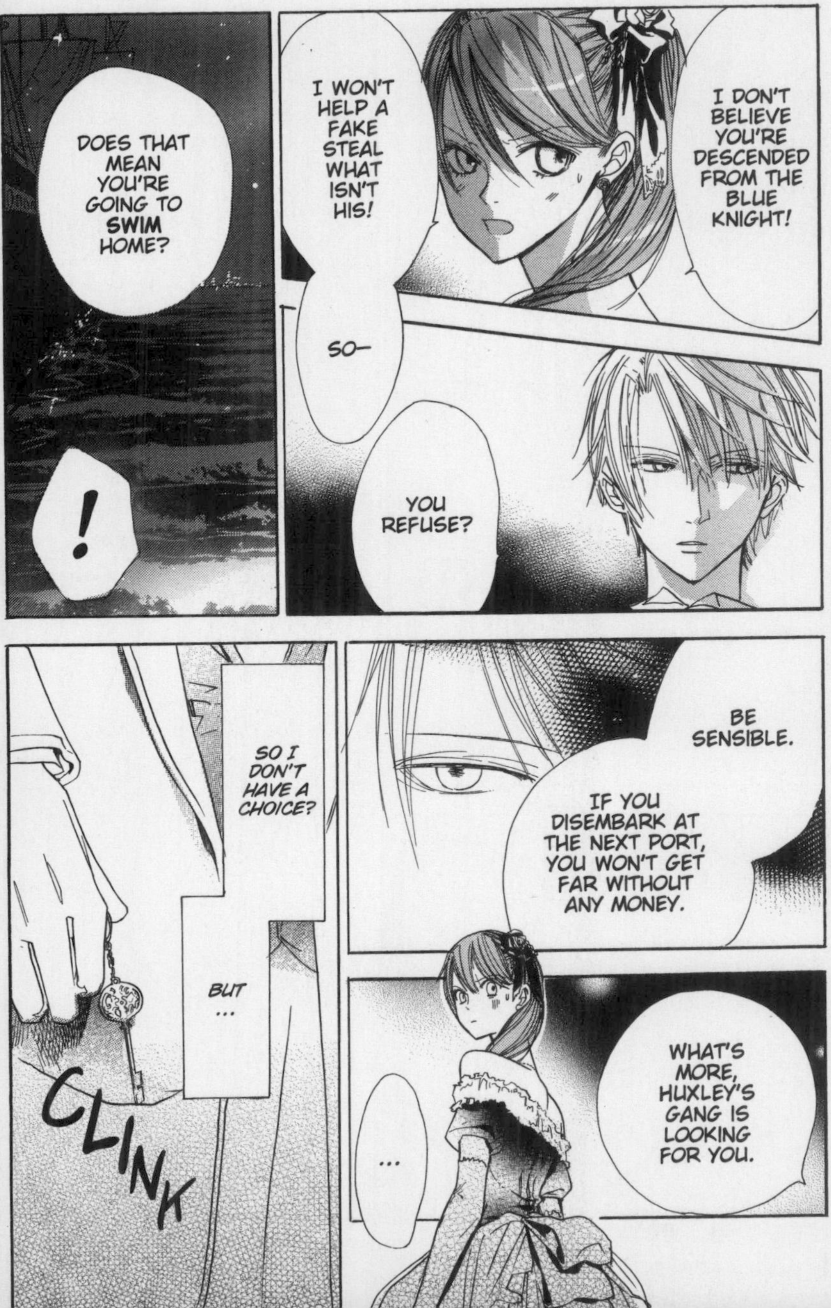
I DON'T BELIEVE YOU'RE DESCENDED FROM THE BLUE KNIGHT!
I WON'T HELP A FAKE STEAL WHAT ISN'T HIS!
SO—
YOU REFUSE?
DOES THAT MEAN YOU'RE GOING TO SWIM HOME?
!
BE SENSIBLE.
IF YOU DISEMBARK AT THE NEXT PORT, YOU WON'T GET FAR WITHOUT ANY MONEY.
WHAT'S MORE, HUXLEY'S GANG IS LOOKING FOR YOU.
...
SO I DON'T HAVE A CHOICE?
BUT ...
CLINK

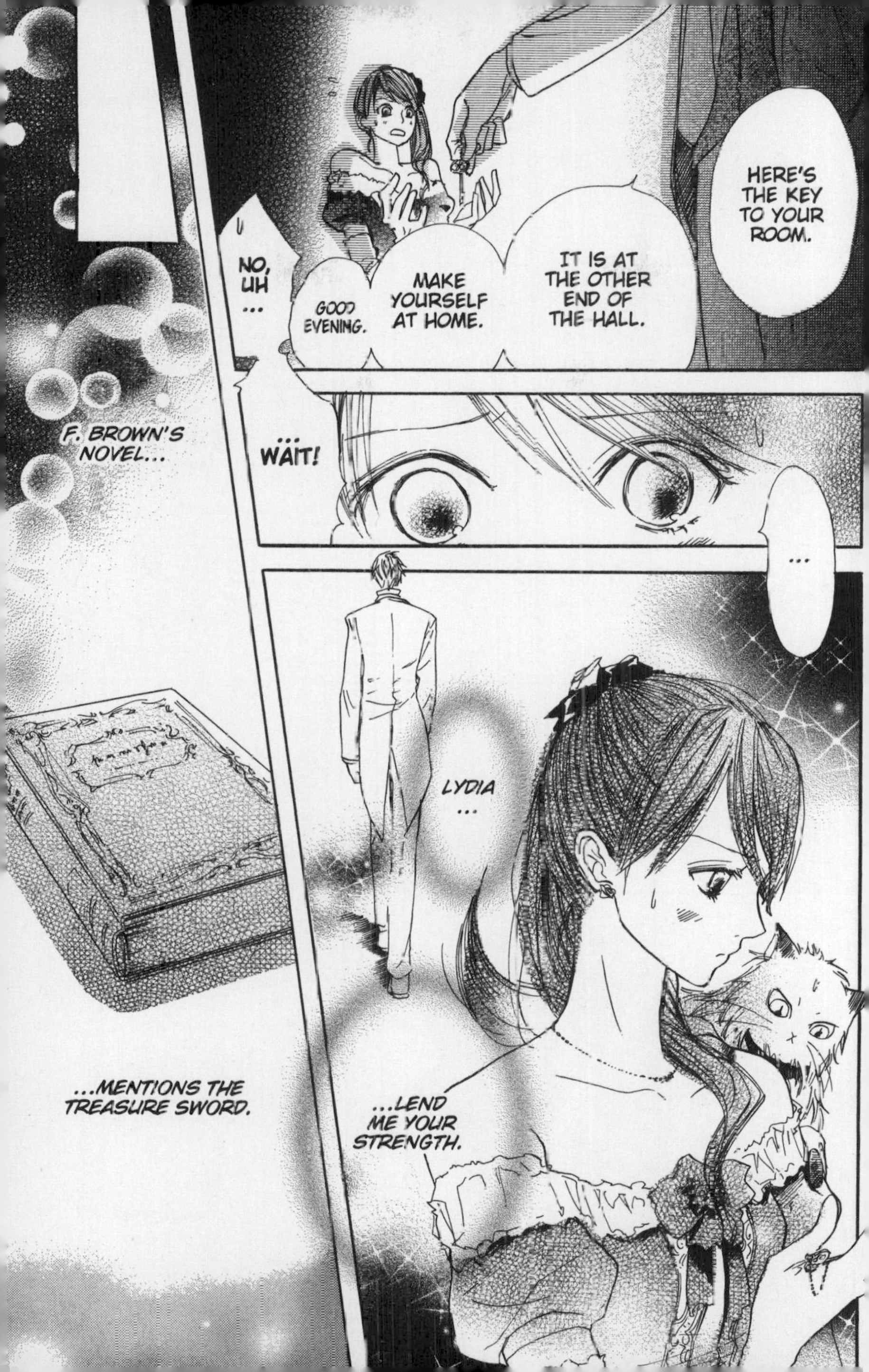
HERE'S THE KEY TO YOUR ROOM.
IT IS AT THE OTHER END OF THE HALL.
MAKE YOURSELF AT HOME.
GOOD EVENING.
NO, UH ...
...WAIT!
...
LYDIA ...
...LEND ME YOUR STRENGTH.
F. BROWN'S NOVEL...
...MENTIONS THE TREASURE SWORD.

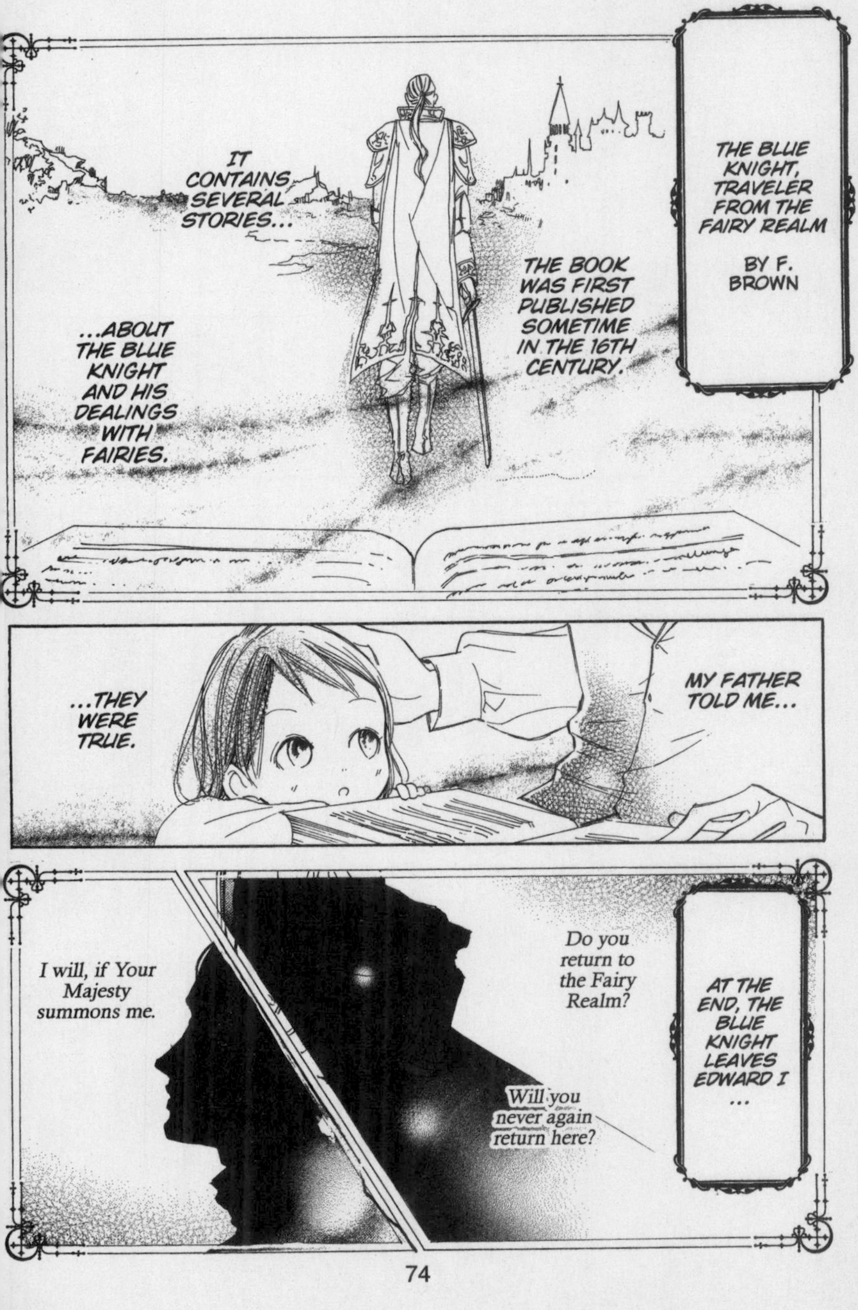
THE BLUE KNIGHT, TRAVELER FROM THE FAIRY REALM
BY F. BROWN
THE BOOK WAS FIRST PUBLISHED SOMETIME IN THE 16TH CENTURY.
IT CONTAINS SEVERAL STORIES...
...ABOUT THE BLUE KNIGHT AND HIS DEALINGS WITH FAIRIES.
MY FATHER TOLD ME...
...THEY WERE TRUE.
AT THE END, THE BLUE KNIGHT LEAVES EDWARD I ...
Do you return to the Fairy Realm?
Will you never again return here?
I will, if Your Majesty summons me.

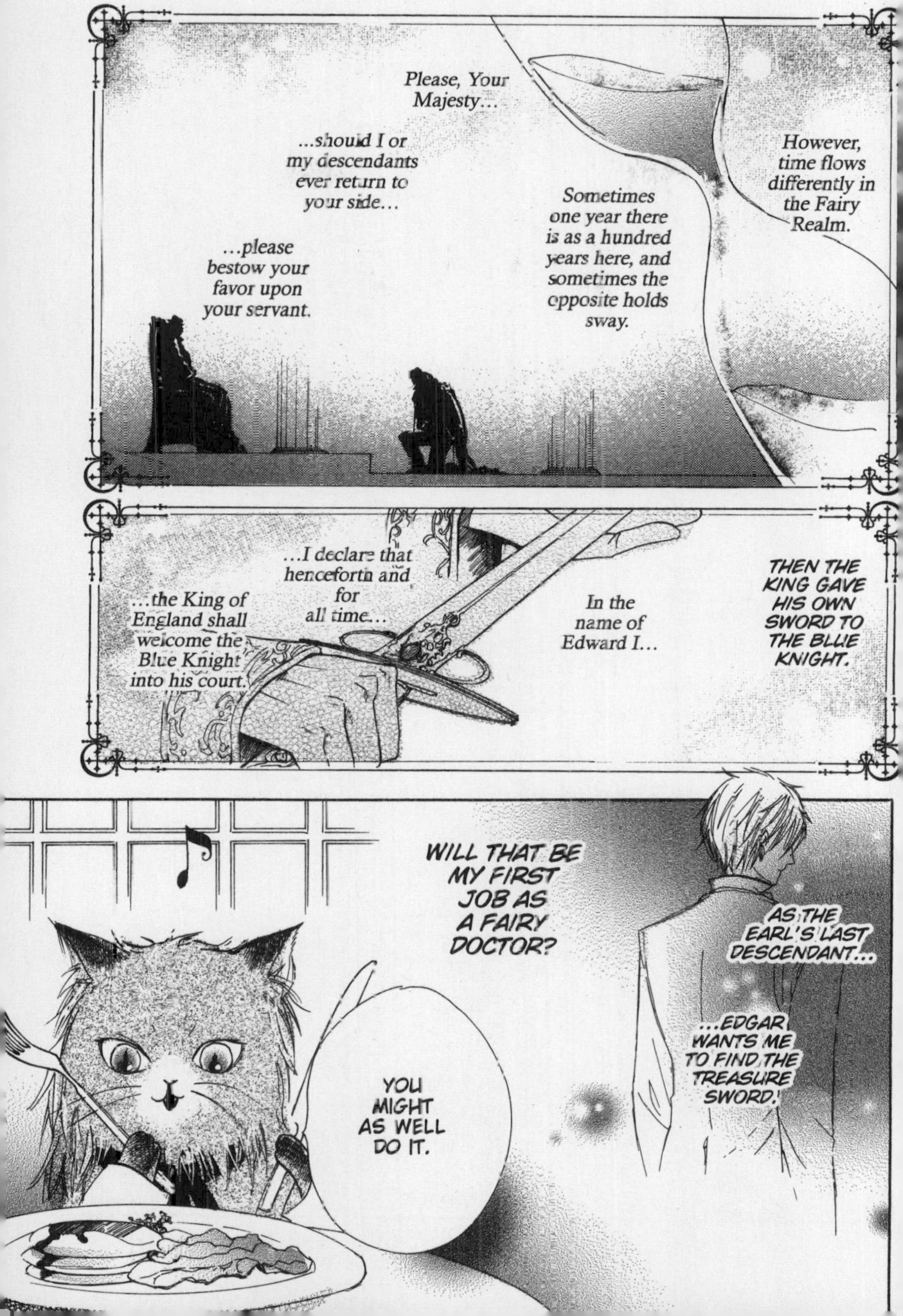
However, time flows differently in the Fairy Realm.
Sometimes one year there is as a hundred years here, and sometimes the opposite holds sway.
Please, Your Majesty...
...should I or my descendants ever return to your side...
...please bestow your favor upon your servant.
THEN THE KING GAVE HIS OWN SWORD TO THE BLUE KNIGHT.
In the name of Edward I...
...I declare that henceforth and for all time...
...the King of England shall welcome the Blue Knight into his court.
AS THE EARL'S LAST DESCENDANT...
...EDGAR WANTS ME TO FIND THE TREASURE SWORD.
WILL THAT BE MY FIRST JOB AS A FAIRY DOCTOR?
YOU MIGHT AS WELL DO IT.

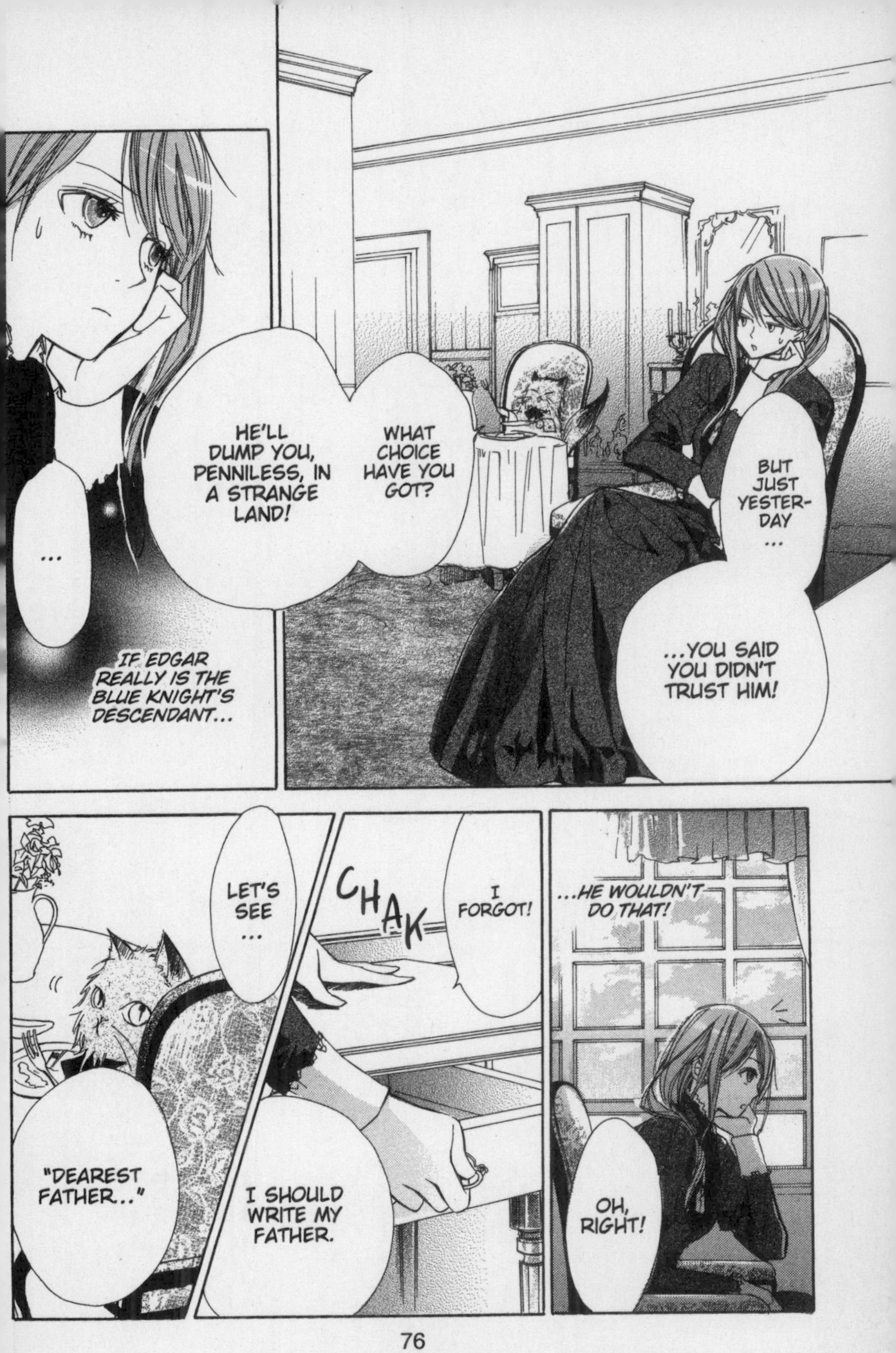
BUT JUST YESTER-DAY...
...YOU SAID YOU DIDN'T TRUST HIM!
WHAT CHOICE HAVE YOU GOT?
HE'LL DUMP YOU, PENNILESS, IN A STRANGE LAND!
...
IF EDGAR REALLY IS THE BLUE KNIGHT'S DESCENDANT...
...HE WOULDN'T DO THAT!
OH, RIGHT!
I FORGOT!
CHAK
I SHOULD WRITE MY FATHER.
LET'S SEE...
"DEAREST FATHER..."

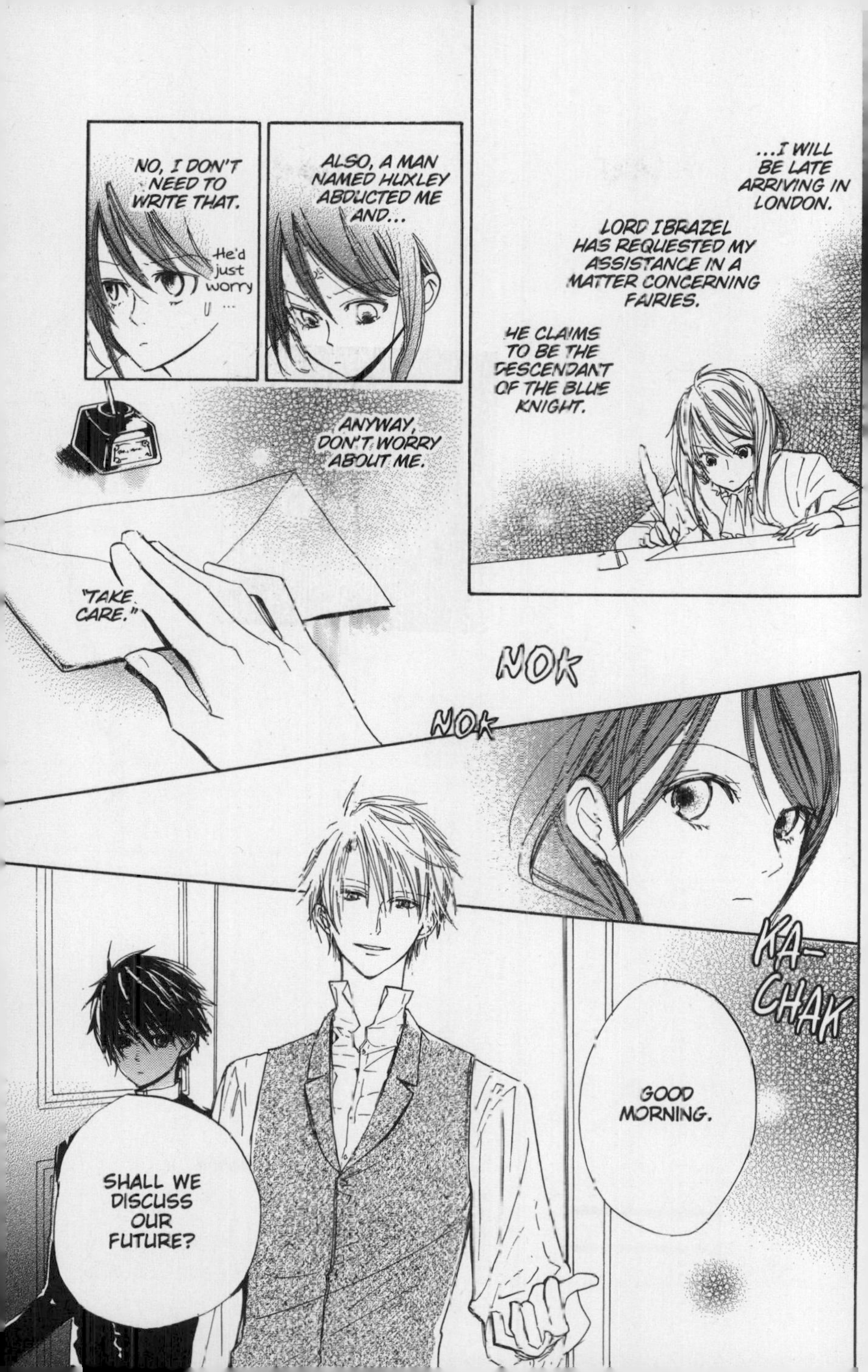
...I WILL BE LATE ARRIVING IN LONDON.
LORD IBRAZEL HAS REQUESTED MY ASSISTANCE IN A MATTER CONCERNING FAIRIES.
HE CLAIMS TO BE THE DESCENDANT OF THE BLUE KNIGHT.
ALSO, A MAN NAMED HUXLEY ABDUCTED ME AND...
NO, I DON'T NEED TO WRITE THAT.
He'd just worry...
ANYWAY, DON'T WORRY ABOUT ME.
"TAKE CARE."
NOK
NOK
KA-CHAK
GOOD MORNING.
SHALL WE DISCUSS OUR FUTURE?

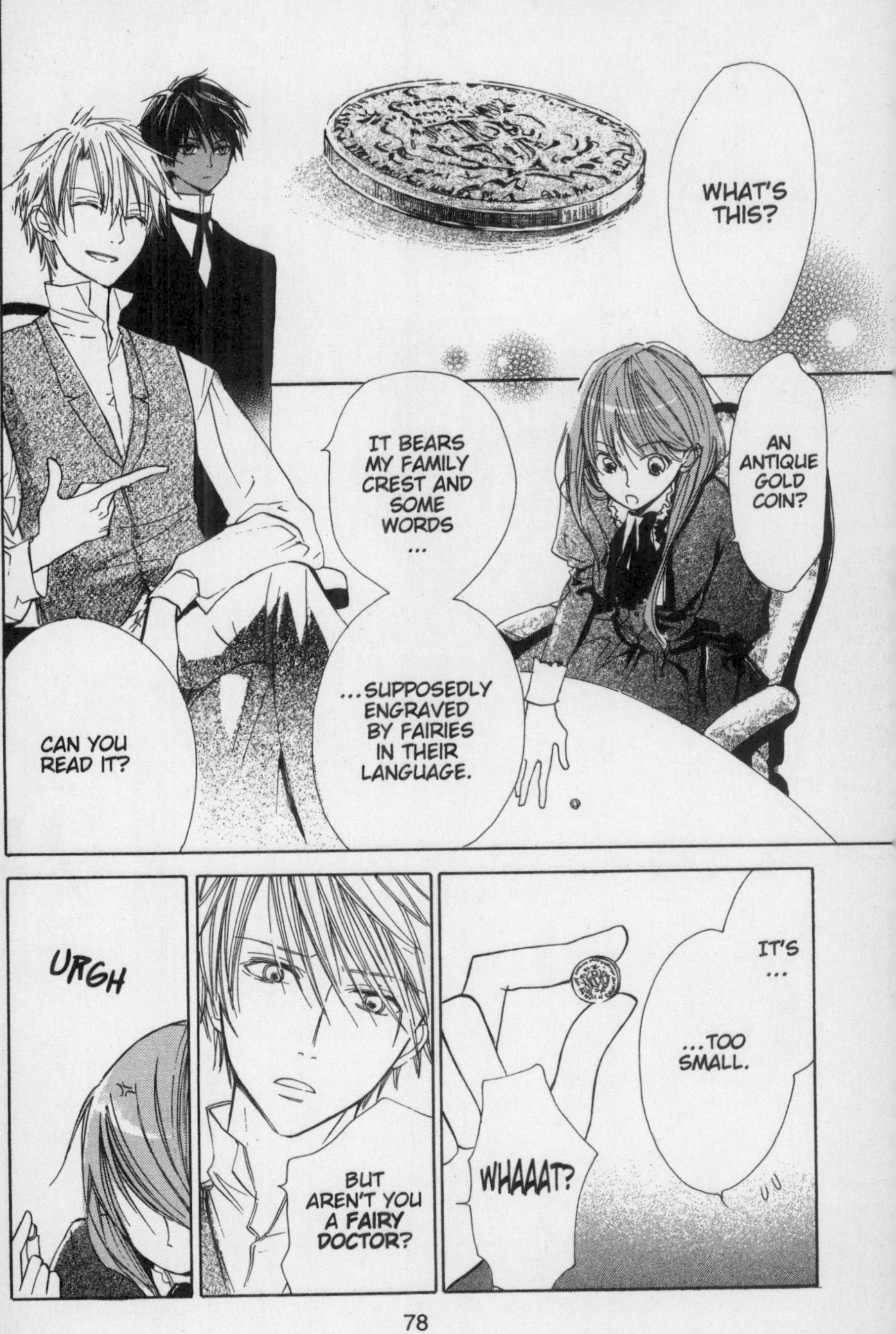
WHAT'S THIS?
AN ANTIQUE GOLD COIN?
IT BEARS MY FAMILY CREST AND SOME WORDS ...
...SUPPOSEDLY ENGRAVED BY FAIRIES IN THEIR LANGUAGE.
CAN YOU READ IT?
IT'S ...
...TOO SMALL.
WHAAAT?
BUT AREN'T YOU A FAIRY DOCTOR?
URGH

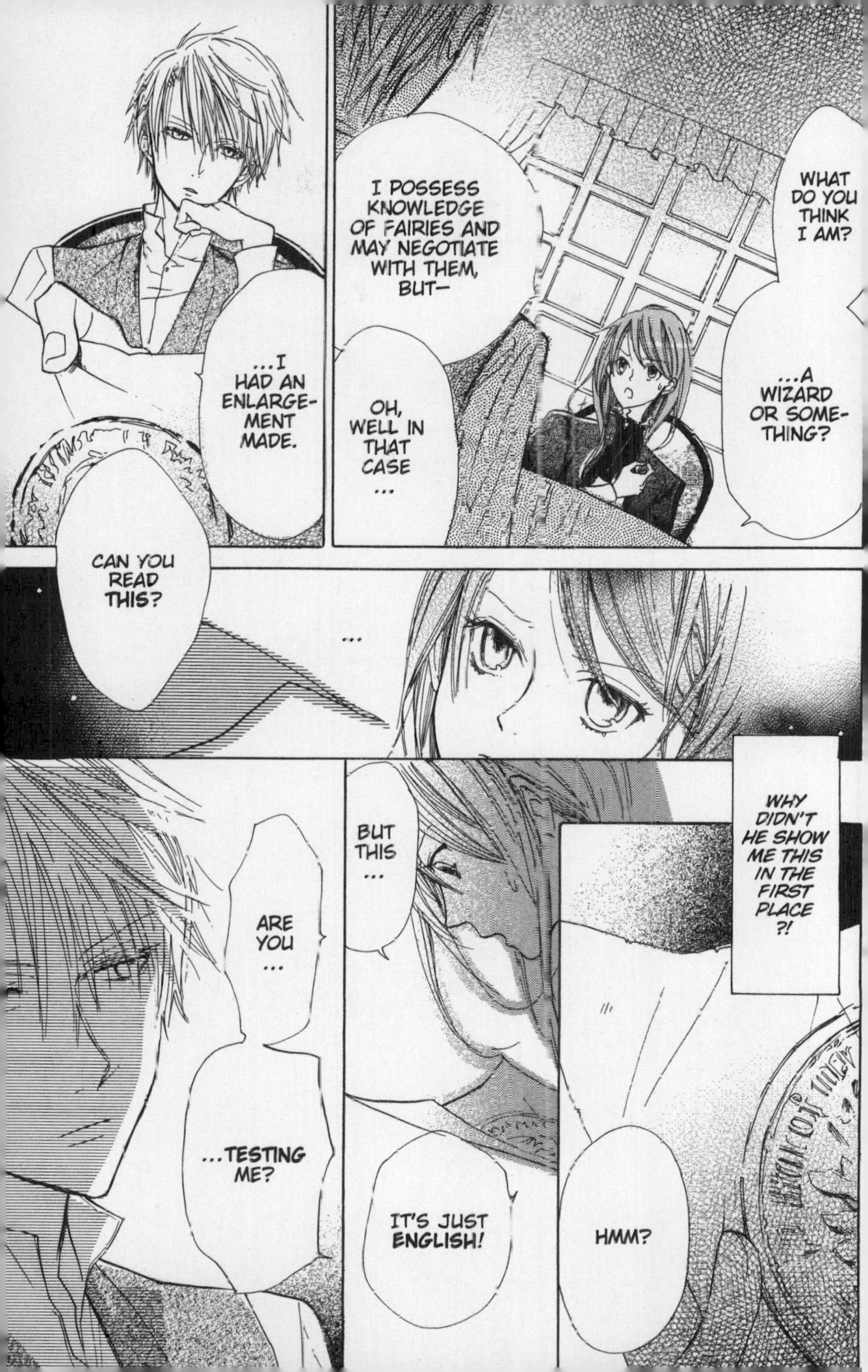
WHAT DO YOU THINK I AM?
...A WIZARD OR SOME-THING?
I POSSESS KNOWLEDGE OF FAIRIES AND MAY NEGOTIATE WITH THEM, BUT—
OH, WELL IN THAT CASE ...
...I HAD AN ENLARGE-MENT MADE.
CAN YOU READ THIS?
...
WHY DIDN'T HE SHOW ME THIS IN THE FIRST PLACE?!
HMM?
BUT THIS ...
IT'S JUST ENGLISH!
ARE YOU ...
...TESTING ME?

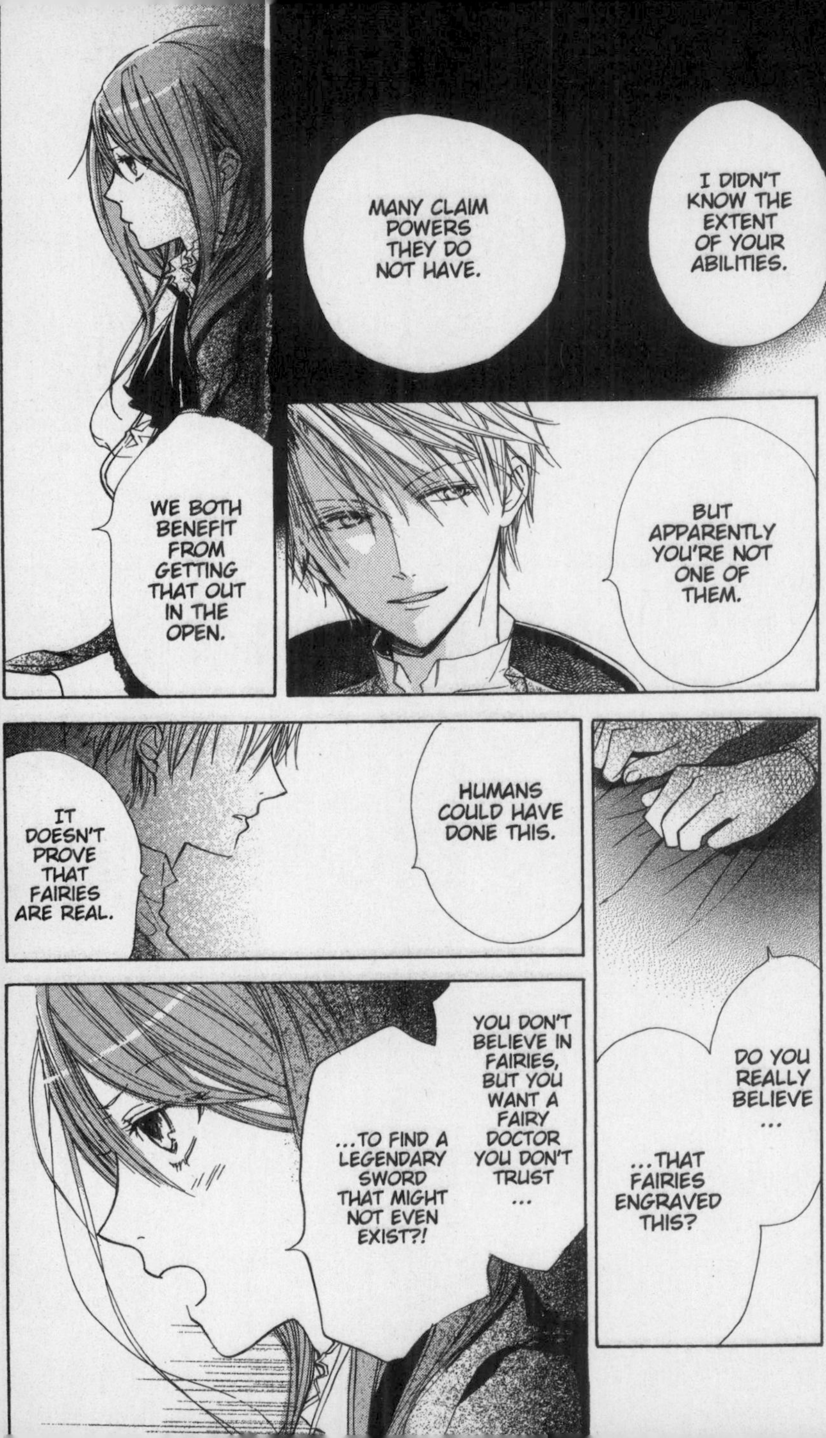
I DIDN'T KNOW THE EXTENT OF YOUR ABILITIES.
MANY CLAIM POWERS THEY DO NOT HAVE.
BUT APPARENTLY YOU'RE NOT ONE OF THEM.
WE BOTH BENEFIT FROM GETTING THAT OUT IN THE OPEN.
DO YOU REALLY BELIEVE...
...THAT FAIRIES ENGRAVED THIS?
HUMANS COULD HAVE DONE THIS.
IT DOESN'T PROVE THAT FAIRIES ARE REAL.
YOU DON'T BELIEVE IN FAIRIES, BUT YOU WANT A FAIRY DOCTOR YOU DON'T TRUST...
...TO FIND A LEGENDARY SWORD THAT MIGHT NOT EVEN EXIST?!

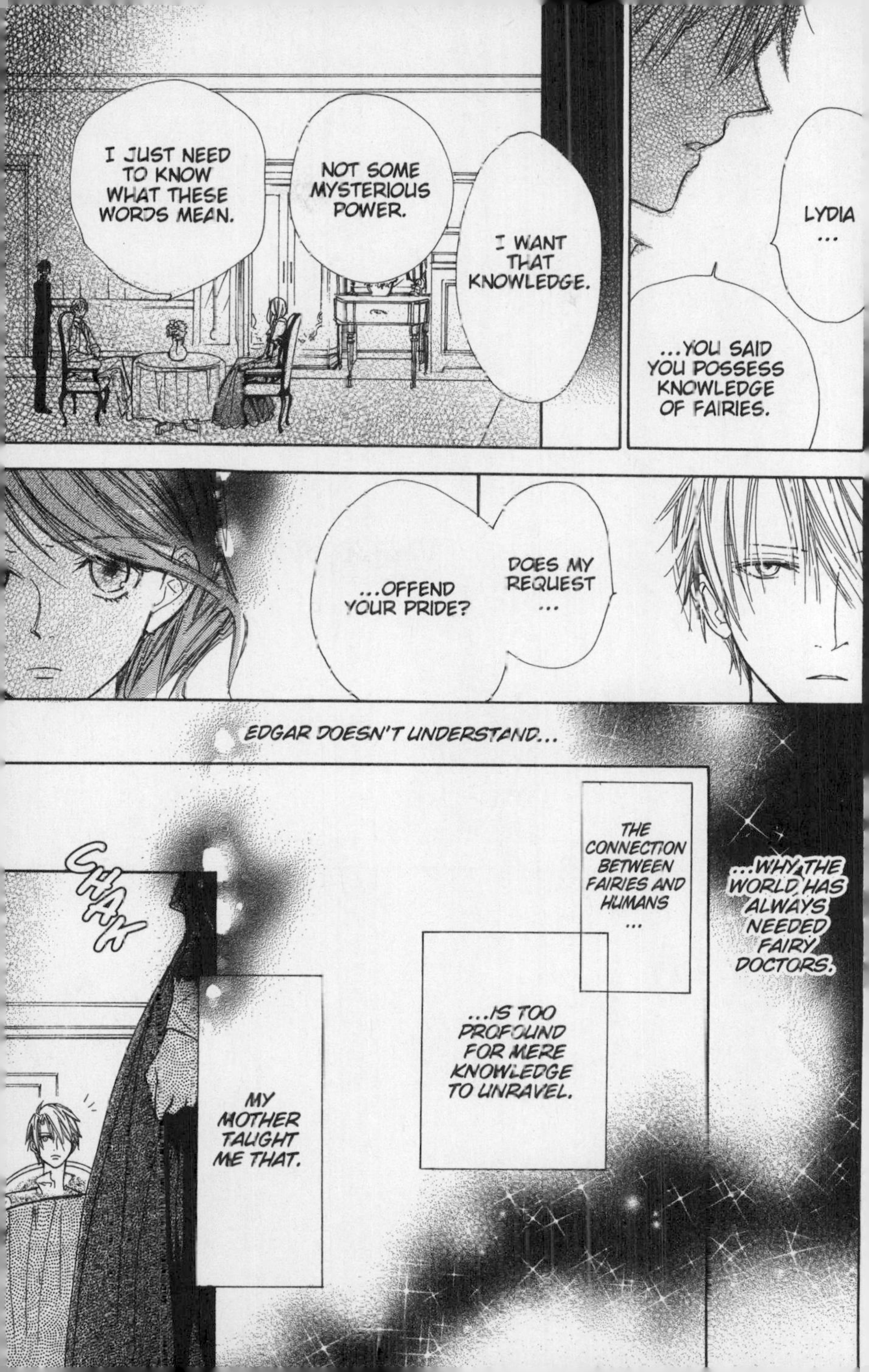
LYDIA ...
...YOU SAID YOU POSSESS KNOWLEDGE OF FAIRIES.
I WANT THAT KNOWLEDGE.
NOT SOME MYSTERIOUS POWER.
I JUST NEED TO KNOW WHAT THESE WORDS MEAN.
DOES MY REQUEST ...
...OFFEND YOUR PRIDE?
EDGAR DOESN'T UNDERSTAND...
...WHY THE WORLD HAS ALWAYS NEEDED FAIRY DOCTORS.
THE CONNECTION BETWEEN FAIRIES AND HUMANS ...
...IS TOO PROFOUND FOR MERE KNOWLEDGE TO UNRAVEL.
CHAK
MY MOTHER TAUGHT ME THAT.

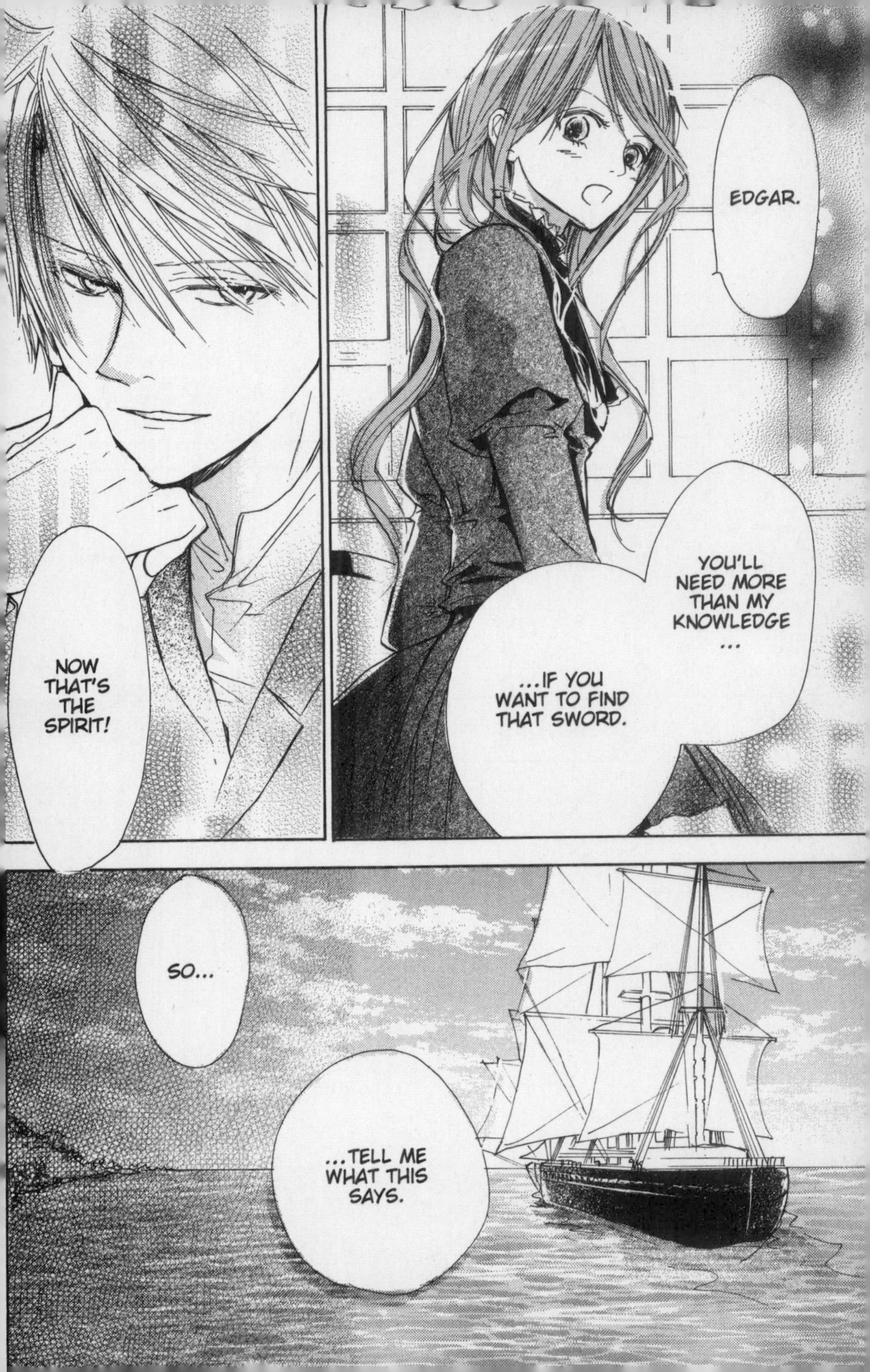
EDGAR.
YOU'LL NEED MORE THAN MY KNOWLEDGE...
...IF YOU WANT TO FIND THAT SWORD.
NOW THAT'S THE SPIRIT!
SO...
...TELL ME WHAT THIS SAYS.

The Earl & the Fairy

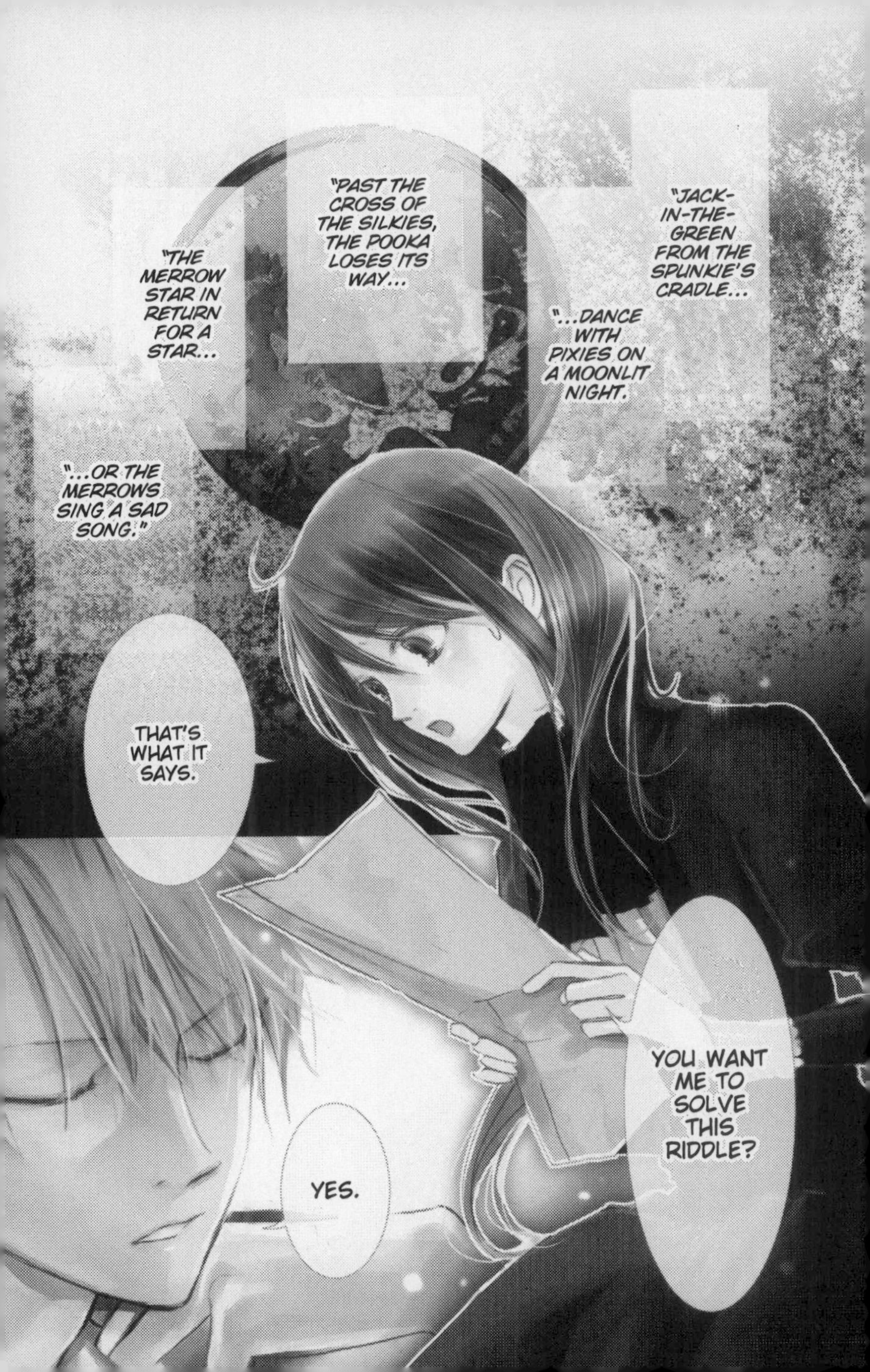
"JACK-IN-THE-GREEN FROM THE SPUNKIE'S CRADLE...
"...DANCE WITH PIXIES ON A MOONLIT NIGHT.
"PAST THE CROSS OF THE SILKIES, THE POOKA LOSES ITS WAY...
"THE MERROW STAR IN RETURN FOR A STAR...
"...OR THE MERROWS SING A SAD SONG."
THAT'S WHAT IT SAYS.
YOU WANT ME TO SOLVE THIS RIDDLE?
YES.

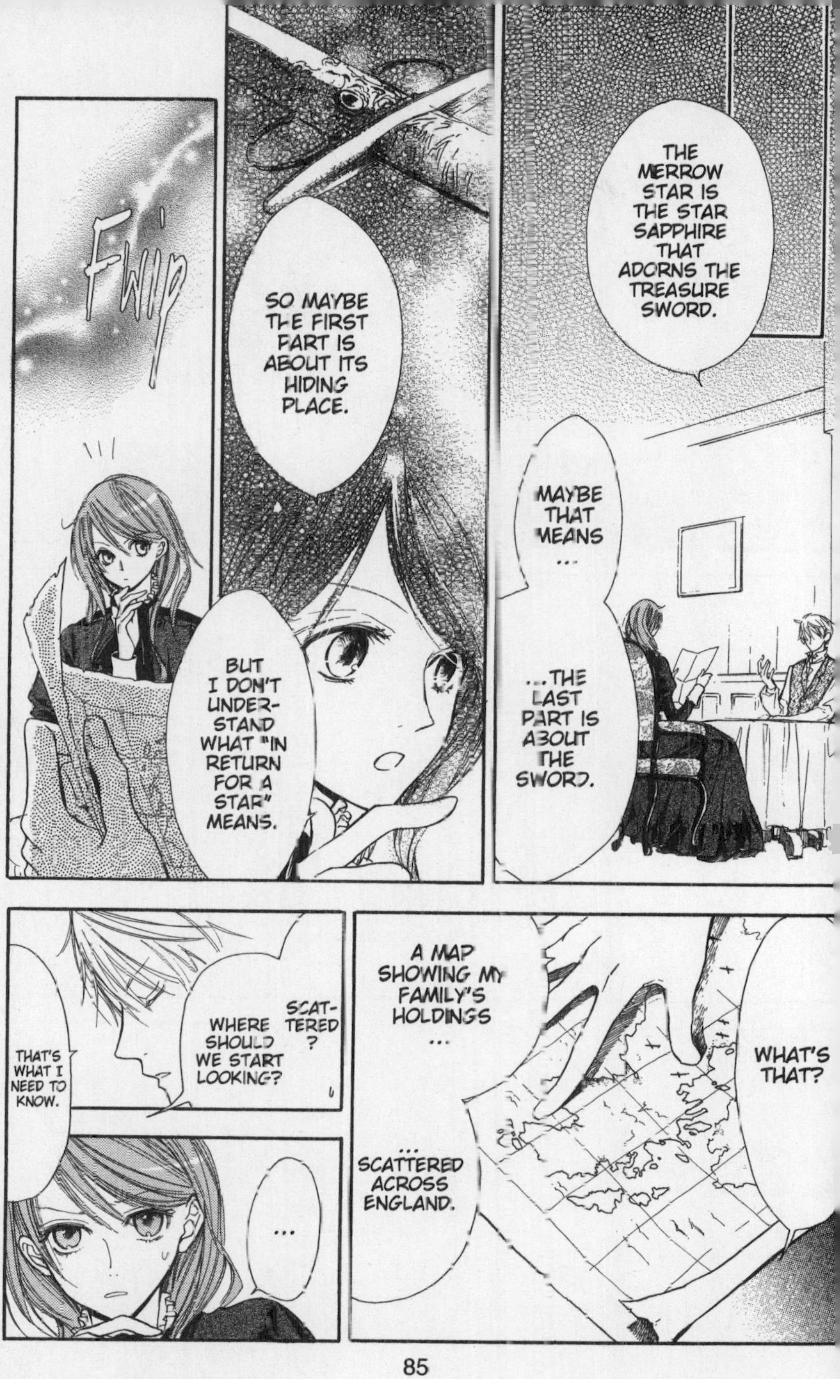
THE MERROW STAR IS THE STAR SAPPHIRE THAT ADORNS THE TREASURE SWORD.
MAYBE THAT MEANS...
...THE LAST PART IS ABOUT THE SWORD.
SO MAYBE THE FIRST PART IS ABOUT ITS HIDING PLACE.
BUT I DON'T UNDERSTAND WHAT "IN RETURN FOR A STAR" MEANS.
Fwip
WHAT'S THAT?
A MAP SHOWING MY FAMILY'S HOLDINGS...
...SCATTERED ACROSS ENGLAND.
SCATTERED?
WHERE SHOULD WE START LOOKING?
THAT'S WHAT I NEED TO KNOW.
...

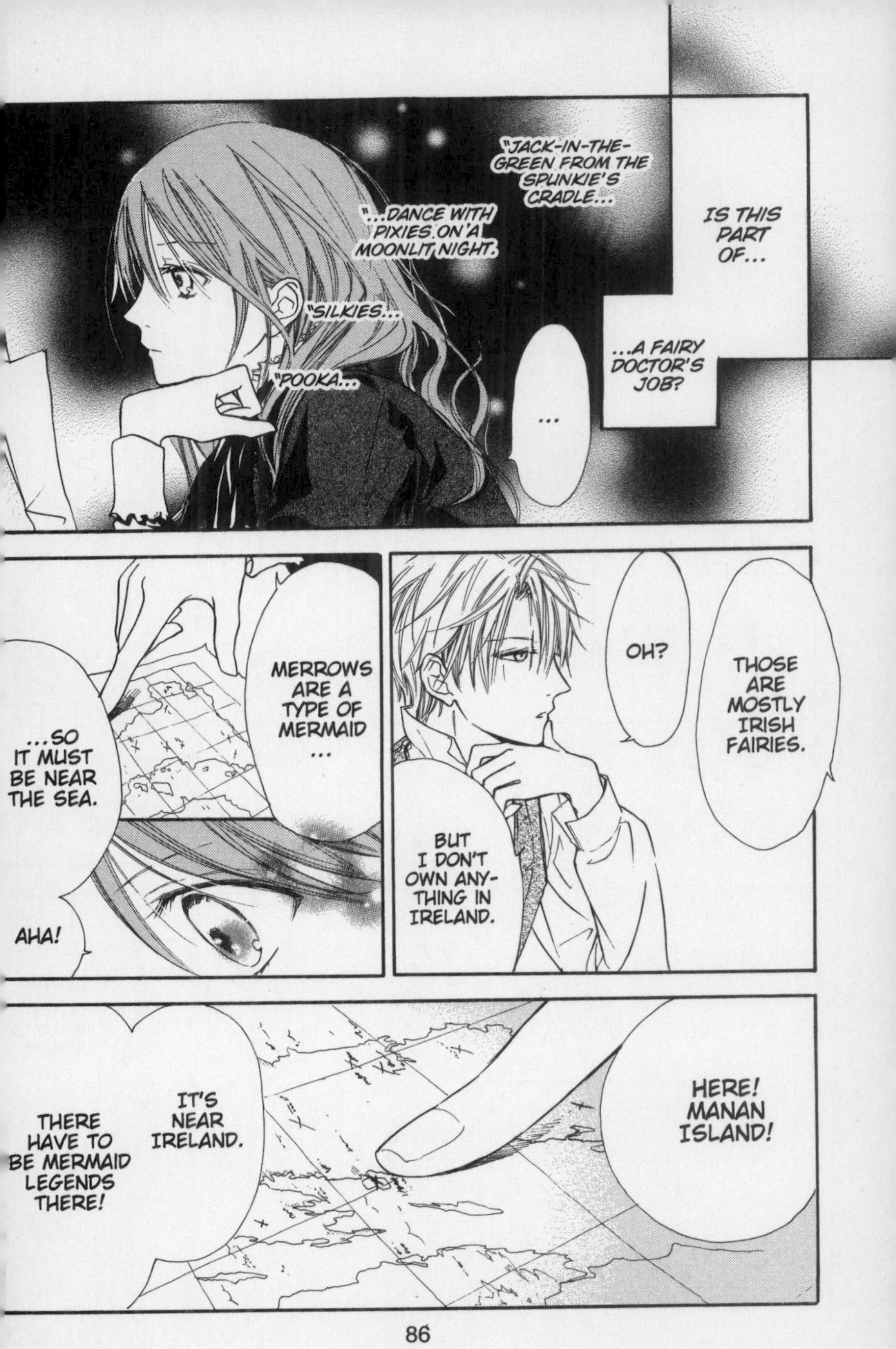
IS THIS PART OF...
...A FAIRY DOCTOR'S JOB?
...
"JACK-IN-THE-GREEN FROM THE SPUNKIE'S CRADLE...
"...DANCE WITH PIXIES ON A MOONLIT NIGHT.
"SILKIES...
"POOKA...
THOSE ARE MOSTLY IRISH FAIRIES.
OH?
BUT I DON'T OWN ANYTHING IN IRELAND.
MERROWS ARE A TYPE OF MERMAID...
...SO IT MUST BE NEAR THE SEA.
AHA!
HERE! MANAN ISLAND!
IT'S NEAR IRELAND.
THERE HAVE TO BE MERMAID LEGENDS THERE!

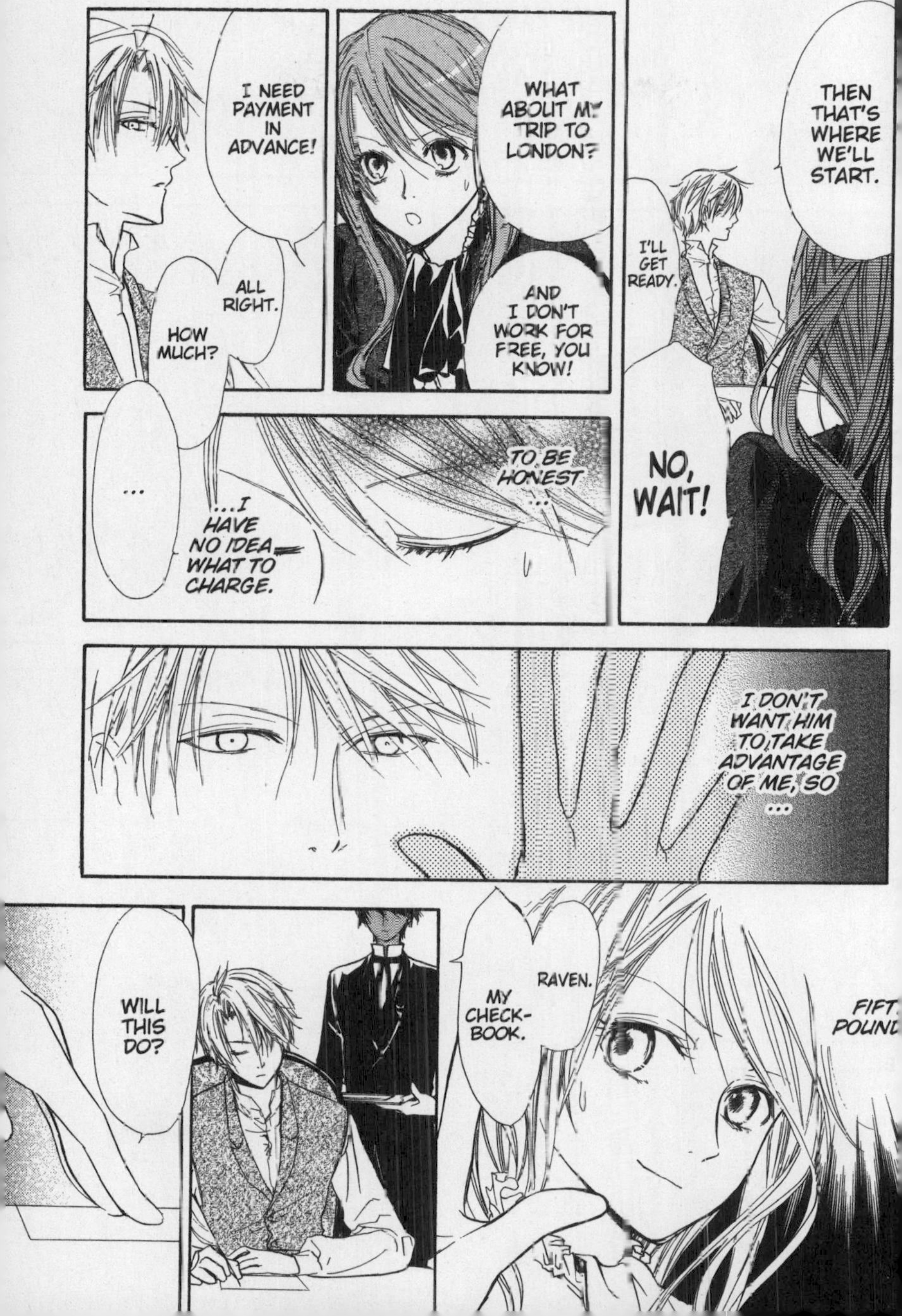
THEN THAT'S WHERE WE'LL START.
I'LL GET READY.
NO, WAIT!
WHAT ABOUT MY TRIP TO LONDON?
AND I DON'T WORK FOR FREE, YOU KNOW!
I NEED PAYMENT IN ADVANCE!
ALL RIGHT.
HOW MUCH?
TO BE HONEST ...
...I HAVE NO IDEA WHAT TO CHARGE.
...
I DON'T WANT HIM TO TAKE ADVANTAGE OF ME, SO ...
FIFT POUND
RAVEN.
MY CHECK-BOOK.
WILL THIS DO?

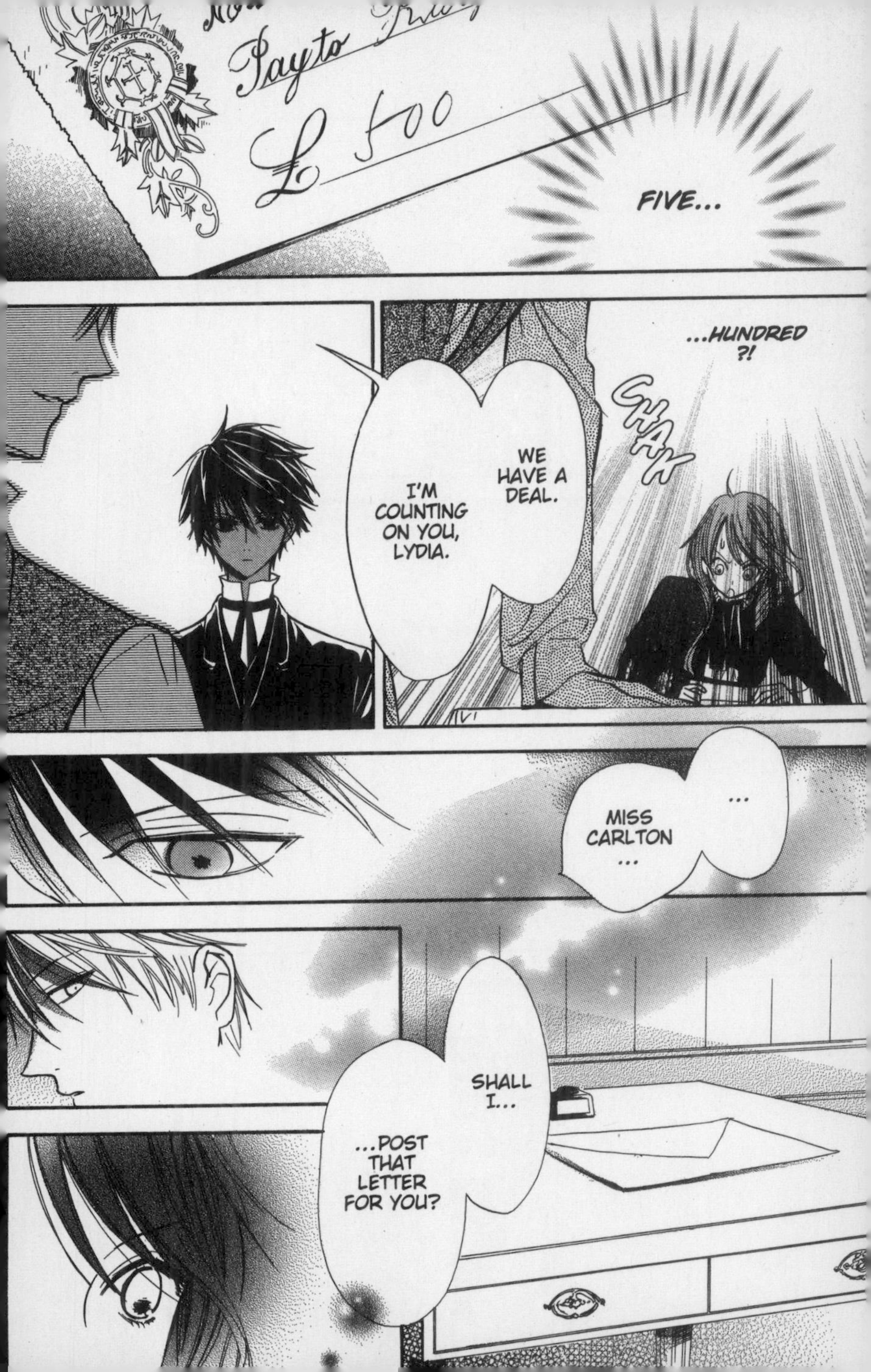
Pay to
£ 500
FIVE...
...HUNDRED ?!
CHAK
WE HAVE A DEAL.
I'M COUNTING ON YOU, LYDIA.
...
MISS CARLTON ...
SHALL I...
...POST THAT LETTER FOR YOU?

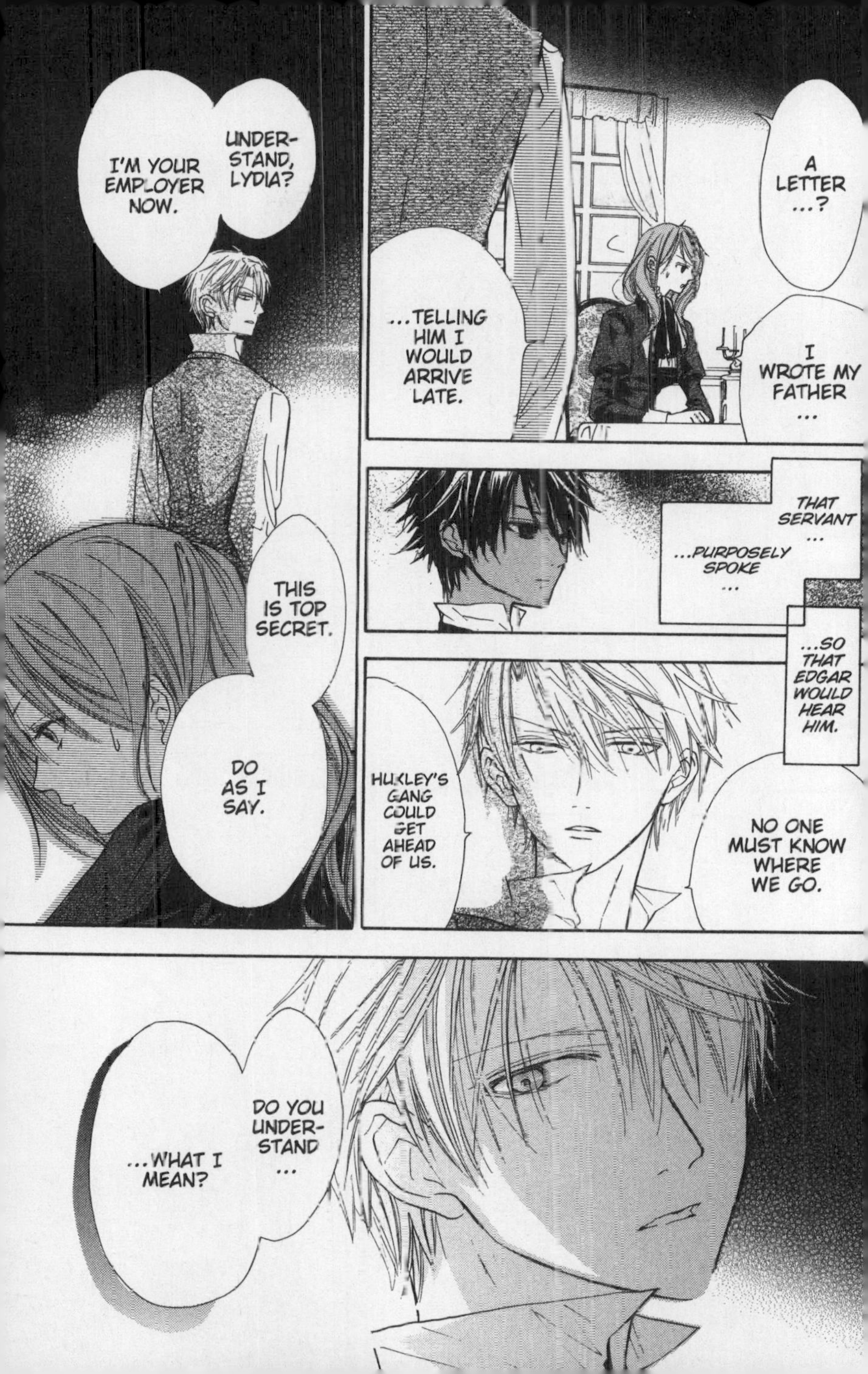
A LETTER ...?
I WROTE MY FATHER ...
...TELLING HIM I WOULD ARRIVE LATE.
THAT SERVANT ...
...PURPOSELY SPOKE ...
...SO THAT EDGAR WOULD HEAR HIM.
NO ONE MUST KNOW WHERE WE GO.
HUXLEY'S GANG COULD GET AHEAD OF US.
UNDER-STAND, LYDIA?
I'M YOUR EMPLOYER NOW.
THIS IS TOP SECRET.
DO AS I SAY.
DO YOU UNDER-STAND ...
...WHAT I MEAN?

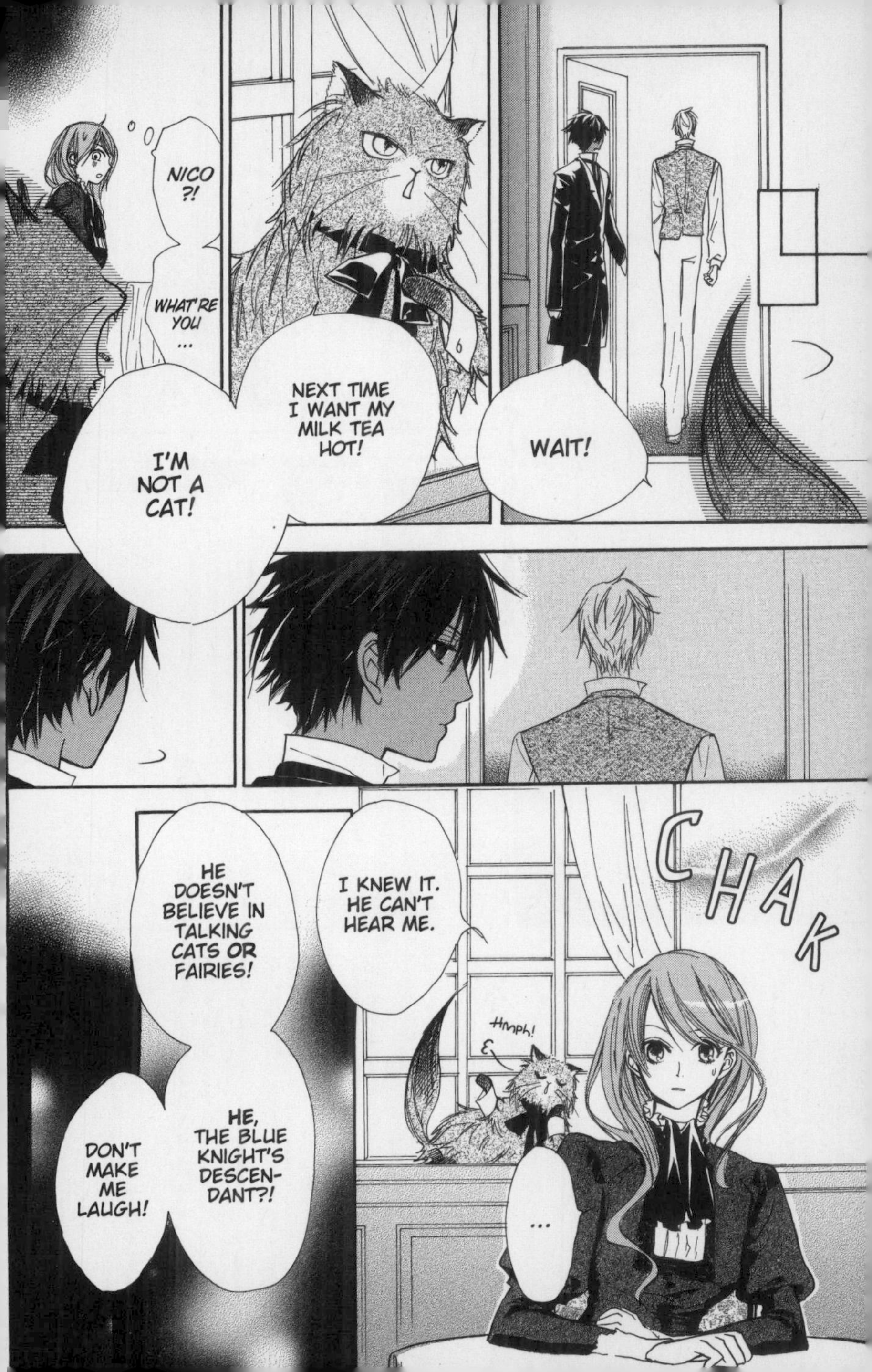
WAIT!
NEXT TIME I WANT MY MILK TEA HOT!
NICO ?!
WHAT'RE YOU ...
I'M NOT A CAT!
CHAK
I KNEW IT. HE CAN'T HEAR ME.
HE DOESN'T BELIEVE IN TALKING CATS OR FAIRIES!
Hmph!
HE, THE BLUE KNIGHT'S DESCEN-DANT?!
DON'T MAKE ME LAUGH!
...

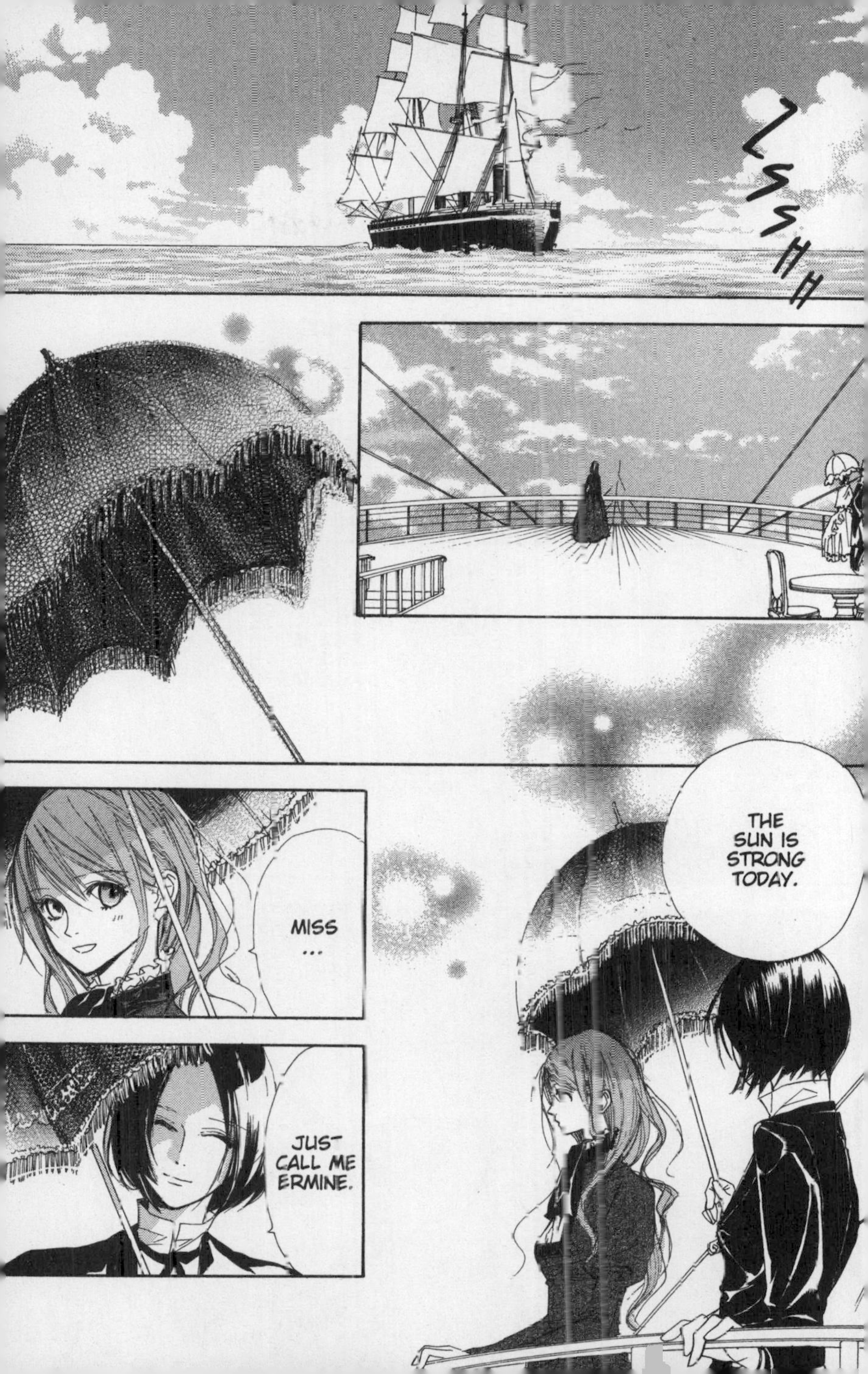
ZSSHH
THE SUN IS STRONG TODAY.
MISS ...
JUS- CALL ME ERMINE.

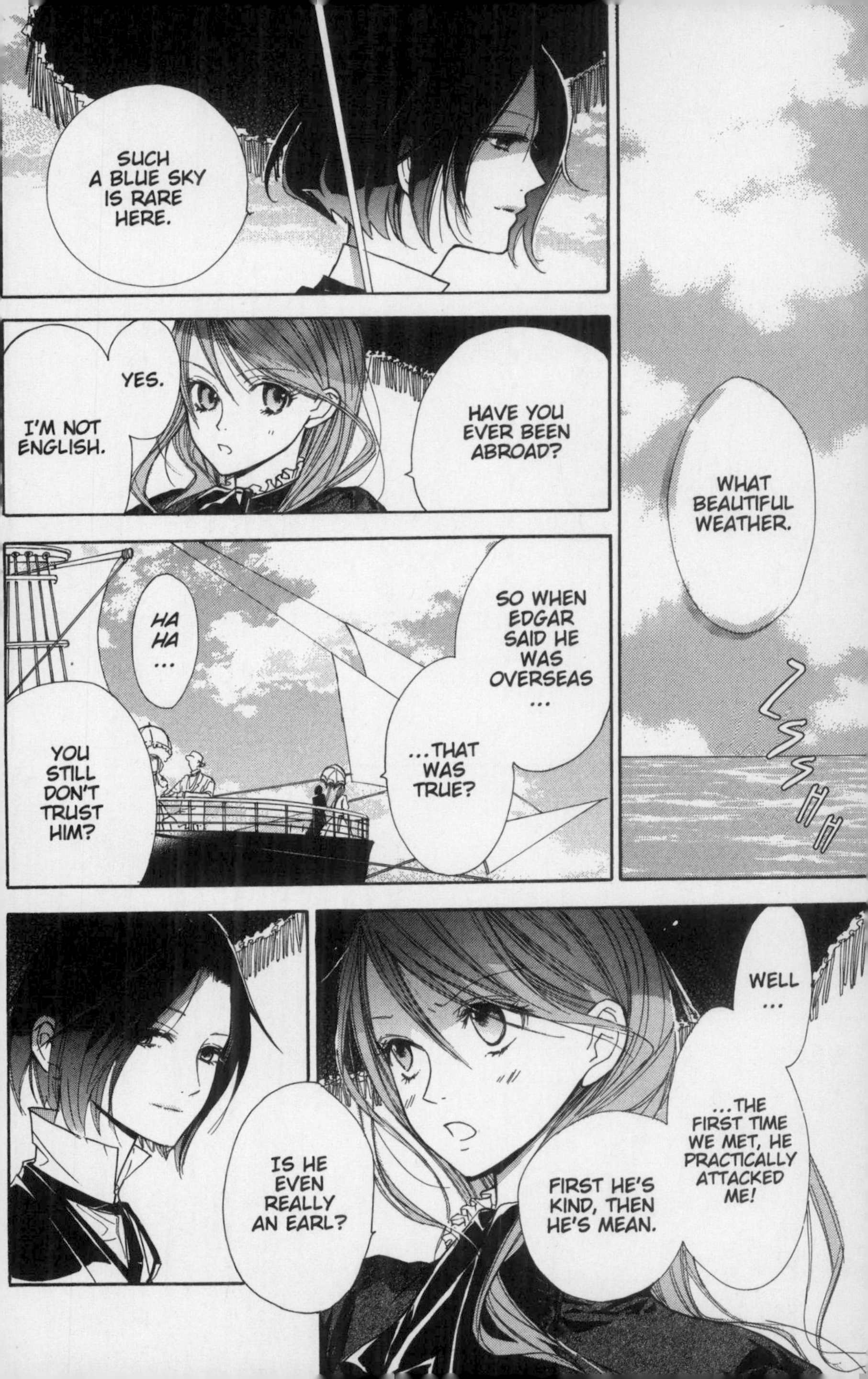
WHAT BEAUTIFUL WEATHER.
ZSSHH
SUCH A BLUE SKY IS RARE HERE.
HAVE YOU EVER BEEN ABROAD?
YES.
I'M NOT ENGLISH.
SO WHEN EDGAR SAID HE WAS OVERSEAS ...
...THAT WAS TRUE?
HA HA ...
YOU STILL DON'T TRUST HIM?
WELL ...
...THE FIRST TIME WE MET, HE PRACTICALLY ATTACKED ME!
FIRST HE'S KIND, THEN HE'S MEAN.
IS HE EVEN REALLY AN EARL?

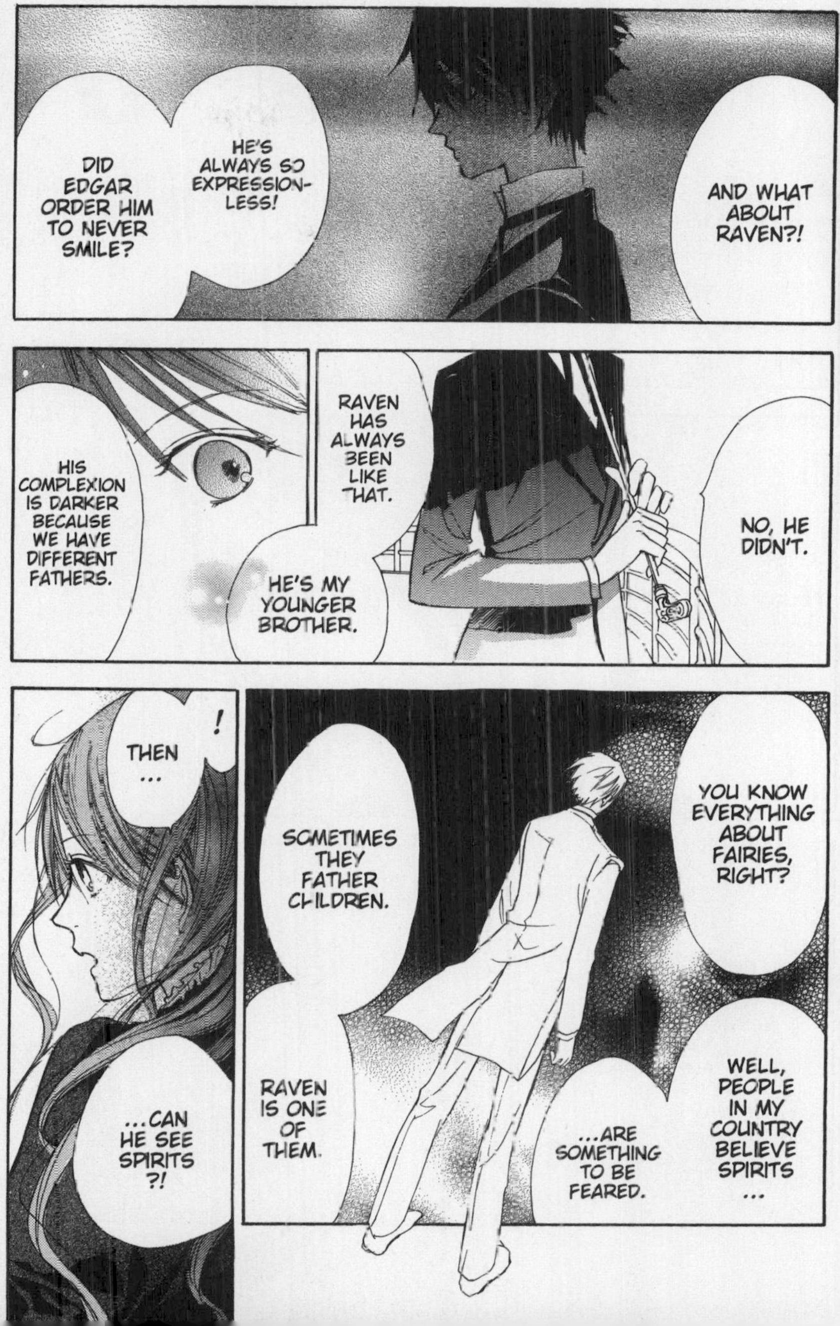
AND WHAT ABOUT RAVEN?!
HE'S ALWAYS SO EXPRESSION-LESS!
DID EDGAR ORDER HIM TO NEVER SMILE?
NO, HE DIDN'T.
RAVEN HAS ALWAYS BEEN LIKE THAT.
HE'S MY YOUNGER BROTHER.
HIS COMPLEXION IS DARKER BECAUSE WE HAVE DIFFERENT FATHERS.
YOU KNOW EVERYTHING ABOUT FAIRIES, RIGHT?
WELL, PEOPLE IN MY COUNTRY BELIEVE SPIRITS ...
...ARE SOMETHING TO BE FEARED.
SOMETIMES THEY FATHER CHILDREN.
RAVEN IS ONE OF THEM.
!
THEN ...
...CAN HE SEE SPIRITS ?!

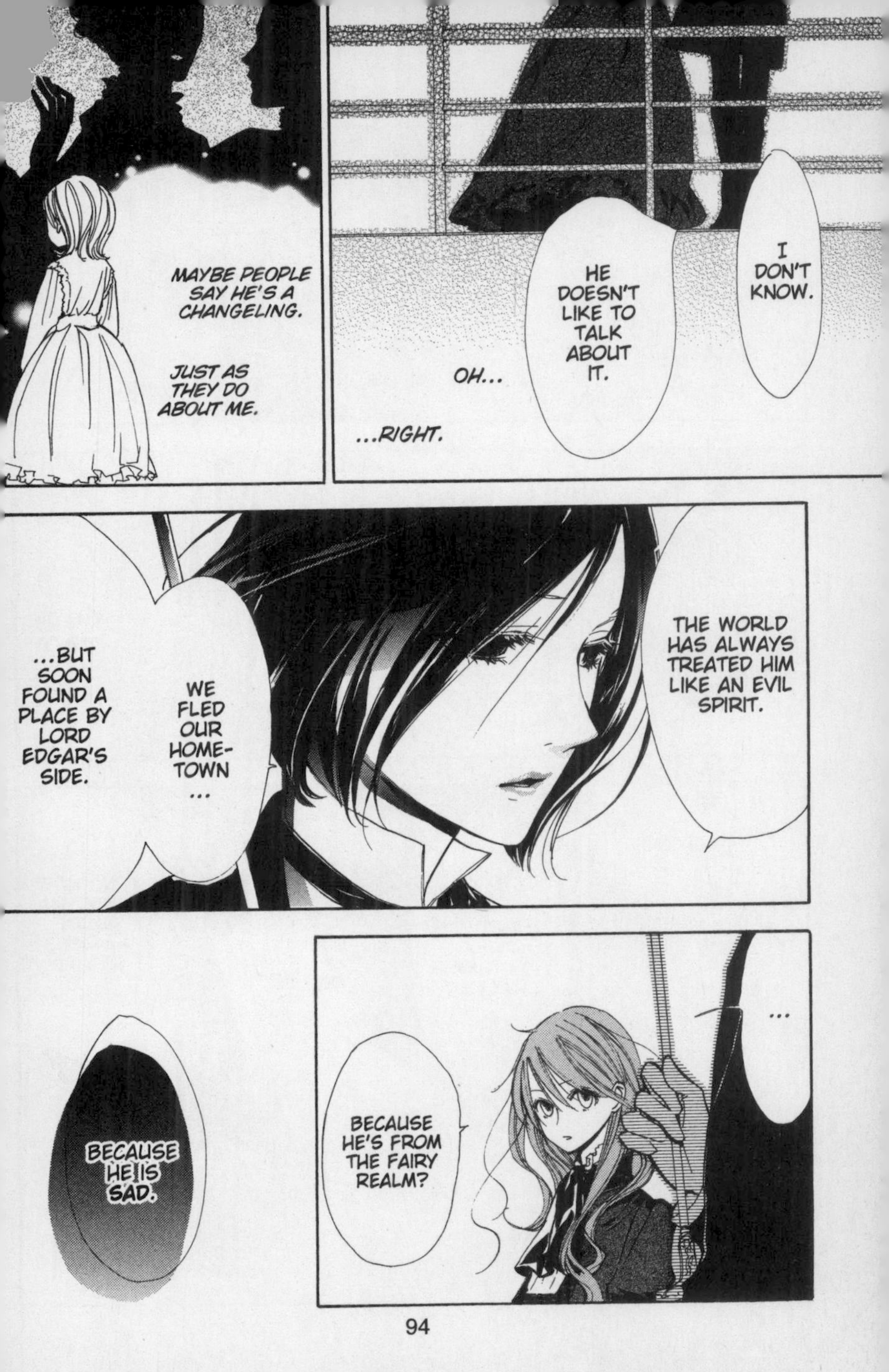
I DON'T KNOW.
HE DOESN'T LIKE TO TALK ABOUT IT.
OH...
...RIGHT.
MAYBE PEOPLE SAY HE'S A CHANGELING.
JUST AS THEY DO ABOUT ME.
THE WORLD HAS ALWAYS TREATED HIM LIKE AN EVIL SPIRIT.
WE FLED OUR HOME-TOWN ...
...BUT SOON FOUND A PLACE BY LORD EDGAR'S SIDE.
...
BECAUSE HE'S FROM THE FAIRY REALM?
BECAUSE HE IS SAD.

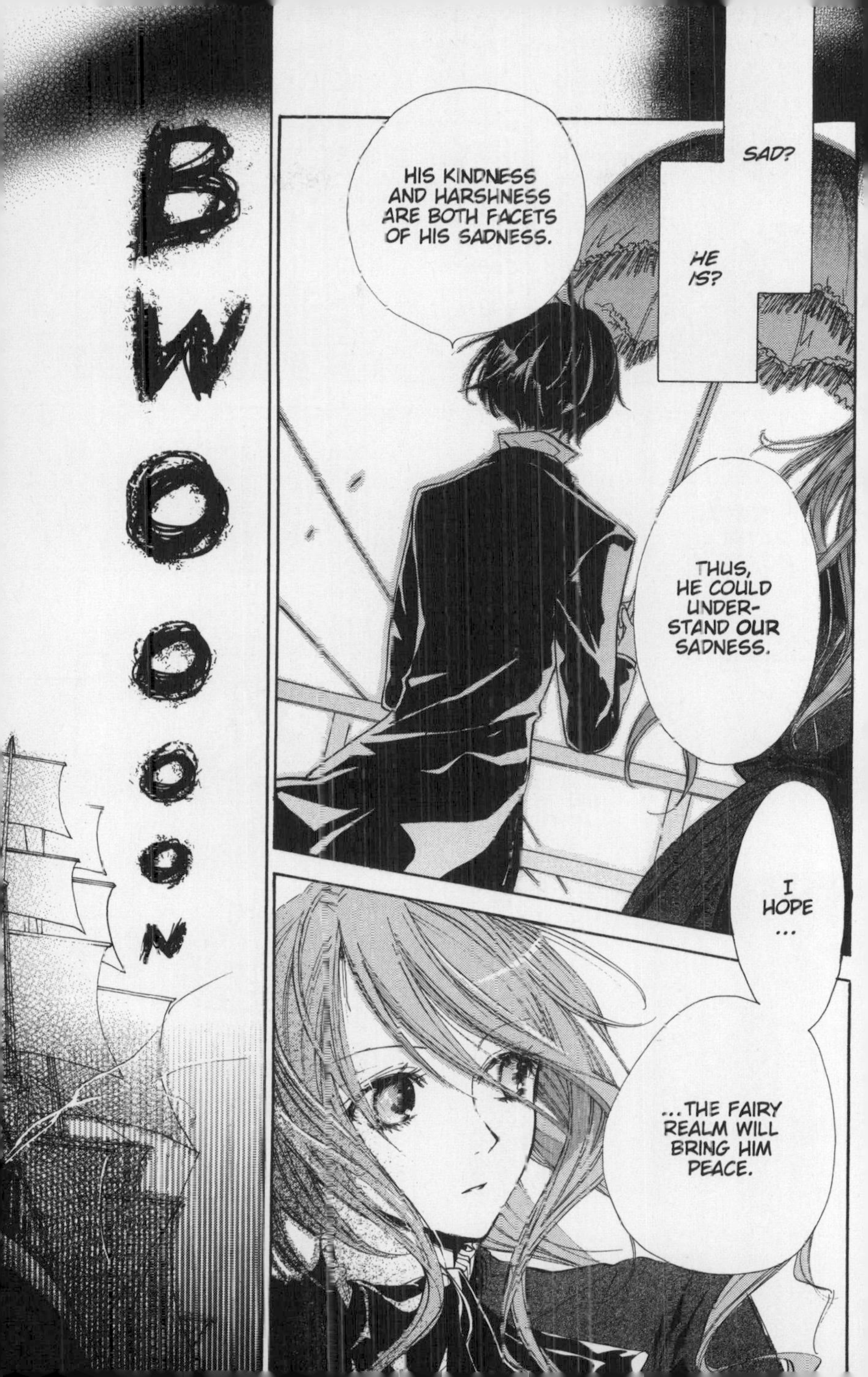
SAD?
HE IS?
HIS KINDNESS AND HARSHNESS ARE BOTH FACETS OF HIS SADNESS.
THUS, HE COULD UNDER-STAND OUR SADNESS.
I HOPE...
...THE FAIRY REALM WILL BRING HIM PEACE.
BWOOOON

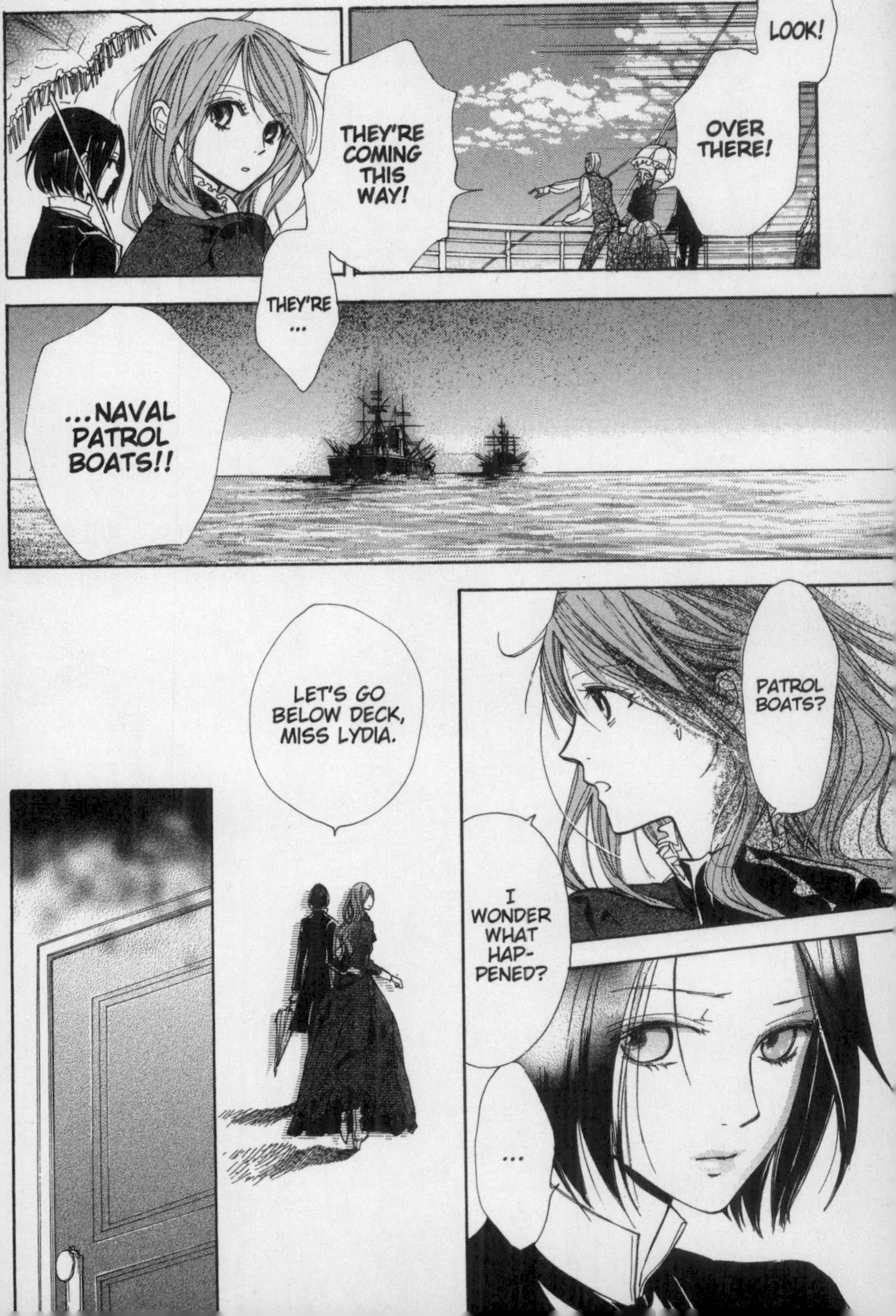
LOOK!
OVER THERE!
THEY'RE COMING THIS WAY!
THEY'RE ...
...NAVAL PATROL BOATS!!
PATROL BOATS?
I WONDER WHAT HAP-PENED?
...
LET'S GO BELOW DECK, MISS LYDIA.

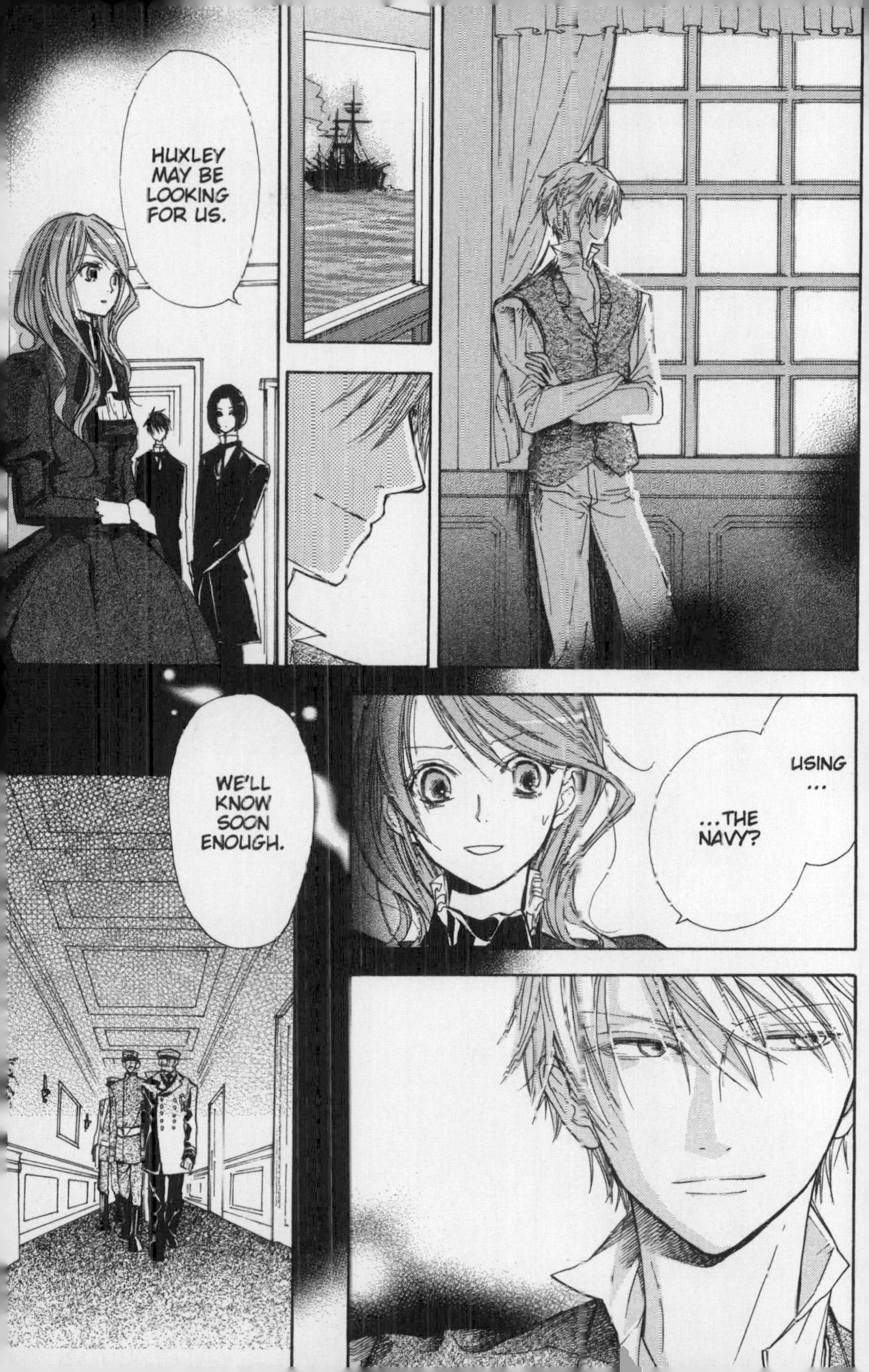
HUXLEY MAY BE LOOKING FOR US.
USING... ...THE NAVY?
WE'LL KNOW SOON ENOUGH.

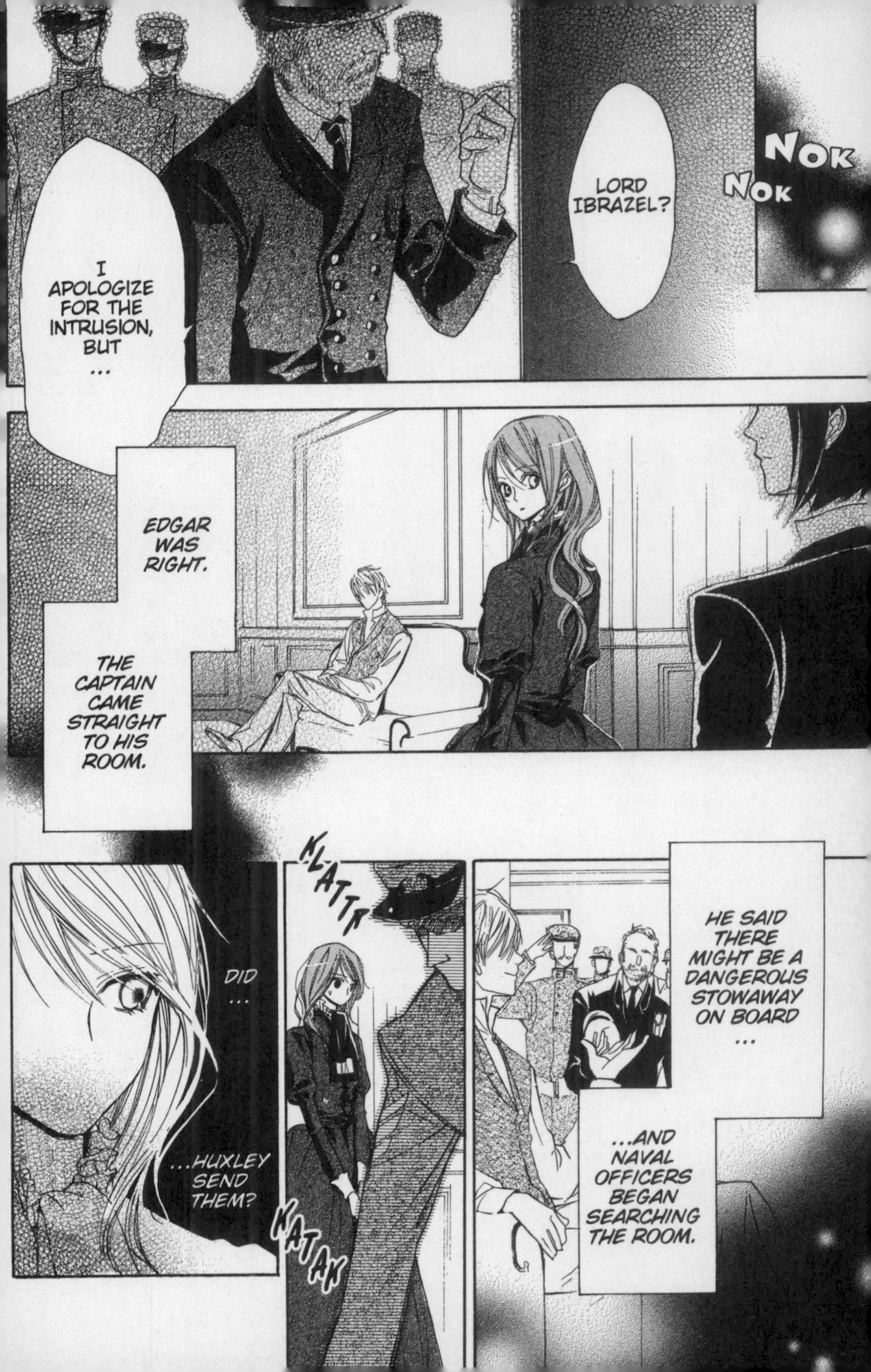
NOK NOK
LORD IBRAZEL?
I APOLOGIZE FOR THE INTRUSION, BUT ...
EDGAR WAS RIGHT.
THE CAPTAIN CAME STRAIGHT TO HIS ROOM.
HE SAID THERE MIGHT BE A DANGEROUS STOWAWAY ON BOARD ...
...AND NAVAL OFFICERS BEGAN SEARCHING THE ROOM.
KLATTR
KATAK
DID ...
...HUXLEY SEND THEM?

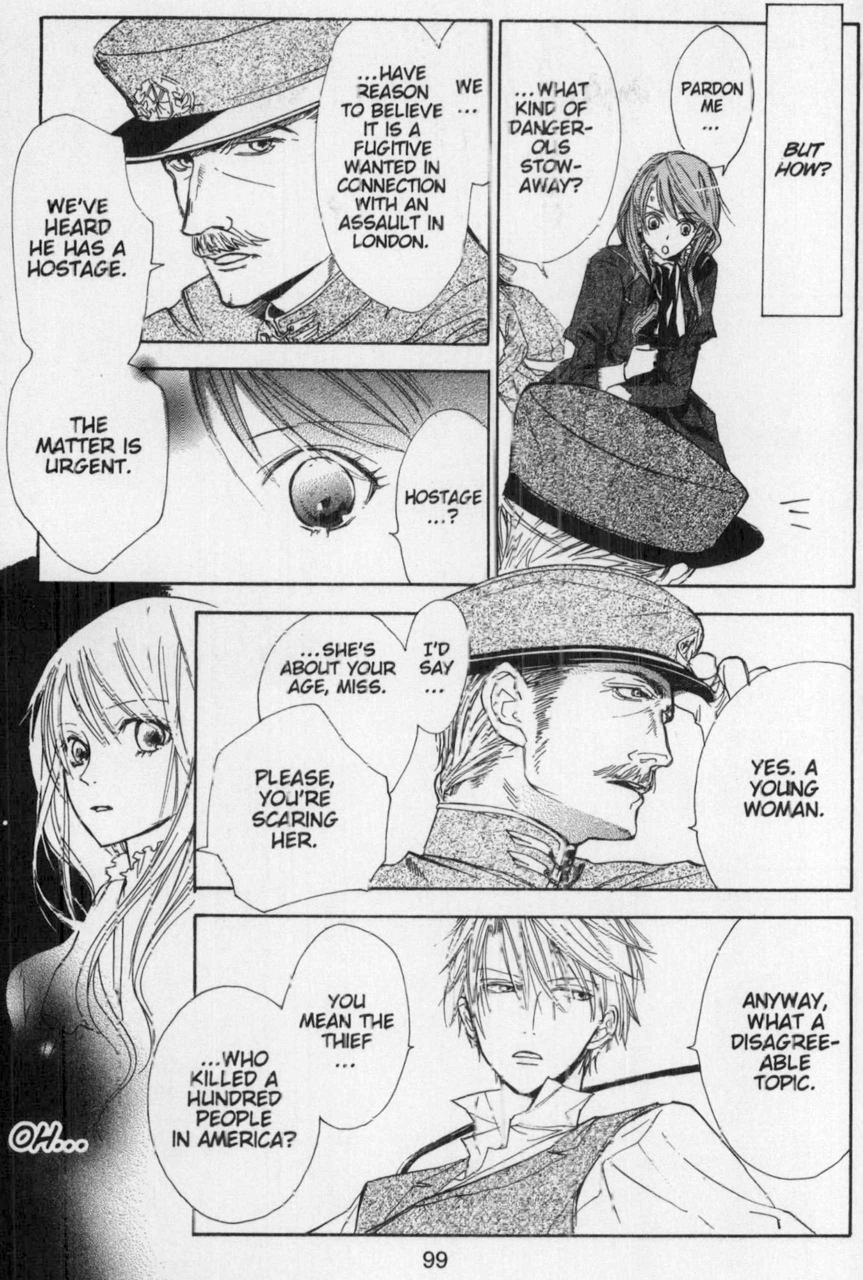

BUT HOW?
PARDON ME ...
...WHAT KIND OF DANGER-OUS STOW-AWAY?
WE ...
...HAVE REASON TO BELIEVE IT IS A FUGITIVE WANTED IN CONNECTION WITH AN ASSAULT IN LONDON.
WE'VE HEARD HE HAS A HOSTAGE.
HOSTAGE ...?
THE MATTER IS URGENT.
YES. A YOUNG WOMAN.
I'D SAY ...
...SHE'S ABOUT YOUR AGE, MISS.
PLEASE, YOU'RE SCARING HER.
ANYWAY, WHAT A DISAGREE-ABLE TOPIC.
YOU MEAN THE THIEF ...
...WHO KILLED A HUNDRED PEOPLE IN AMERICA?
OH...

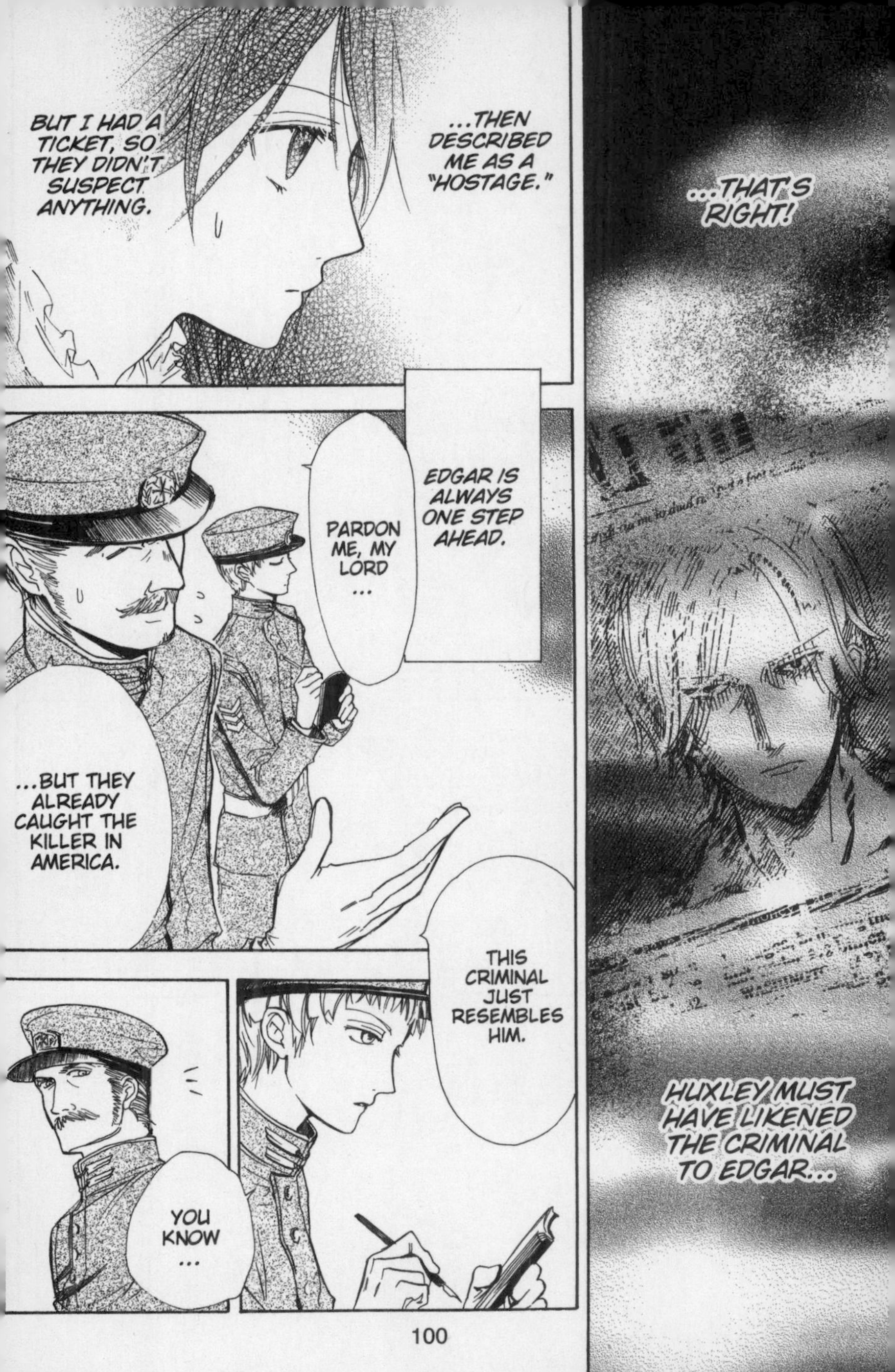
...THAT'S RIGHT!
HUXLEY MUST HAVE LIKENED THE CRIMINAL TO EDGAR...
...THEN DESCRIBED ME AS A "HOSTAGE."
BUT I HAD A TICKET, SO THEY DIDN'T SUSPECT ANYTHING.
EDGAR IS ALWAYS ONE STEP AHEAD.
PARDON ME, MY LORD ...
...BUT THEY ALREADY CAUGHT THE KILLER IN AMERICA.
THIS CRIMINAL JUST RESEMBLES HIM.
YOU KNOW ...

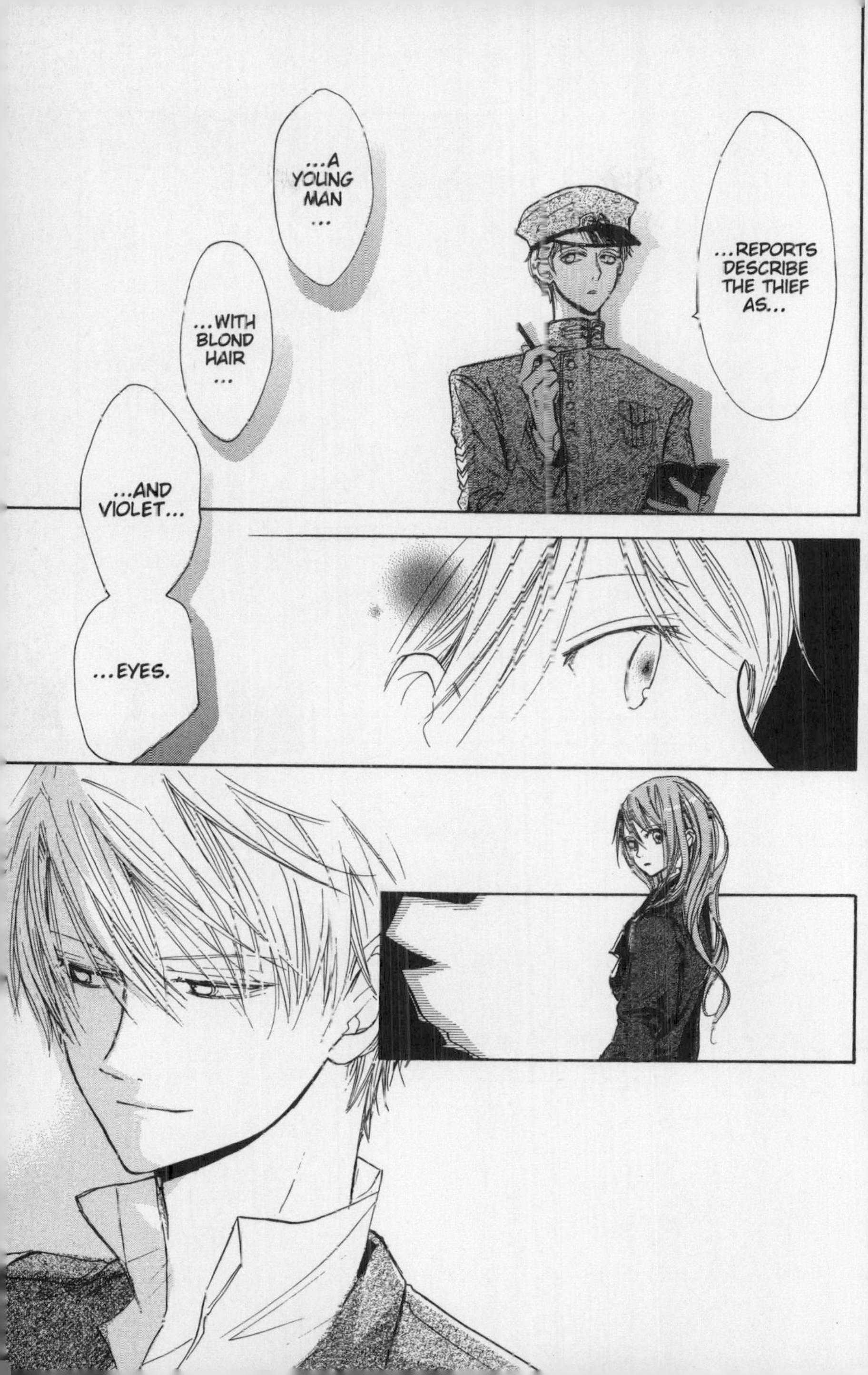
...REPORTS DESCRIBE THE THIEF AS...
...A YOUNG MAN ...
...WITH BLOND HAIR ...
...AND VIOLET...
...EYES.

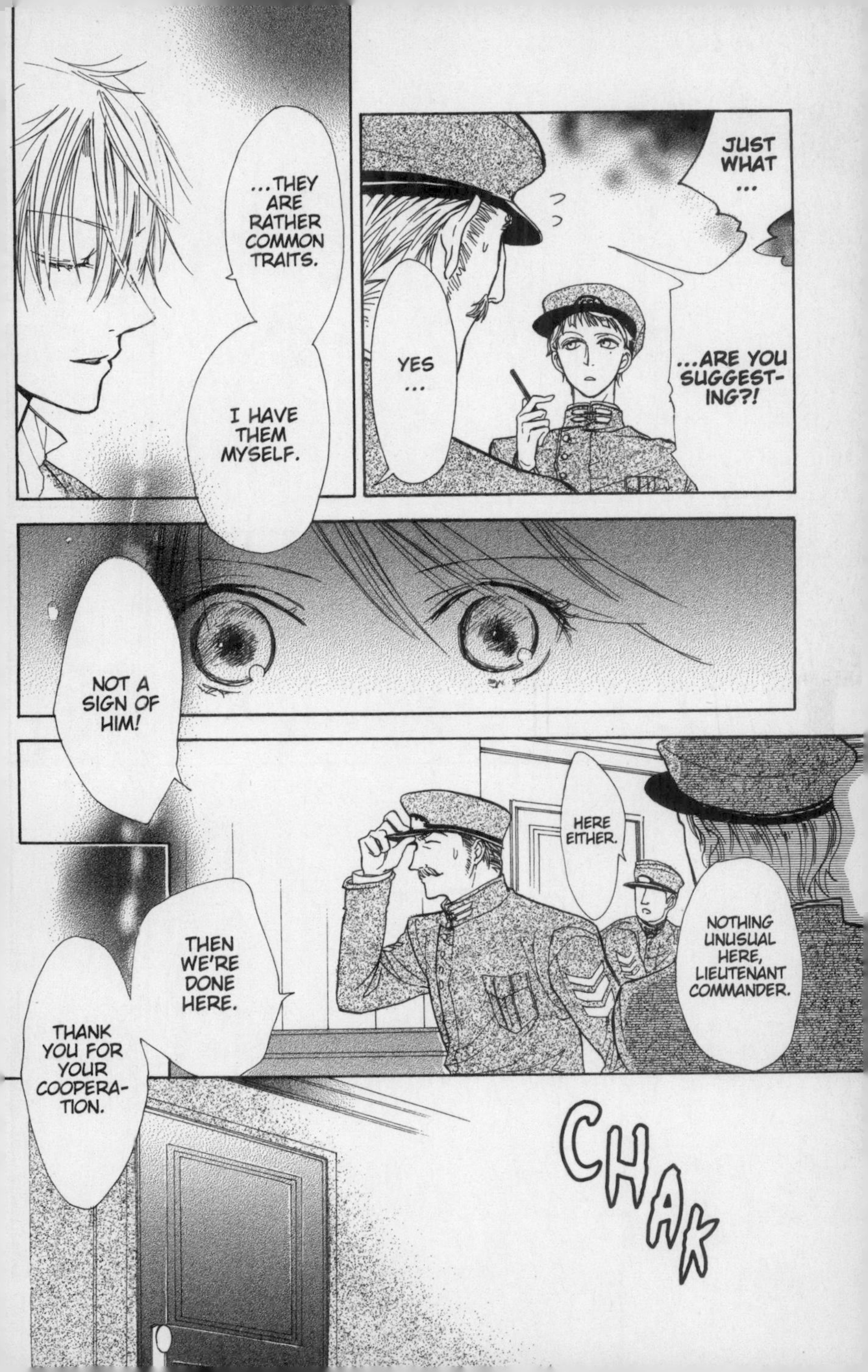
JUST WHAT ...
...ARE YOU SUGGEST-ING?!
YES ...
...THEY ARE RATHER COMMON TRAITS.
I HAVE THEM MYSELF.
NOT A SIGN OF HIM!
NOTHING UNUSUAL HERE, LIEUTENANT COMMANDER.
HERE EITHER.
THEN WE'RE DONE HERE.
THANK YOU FOR YOUR COOPERA-TION.
CHAK

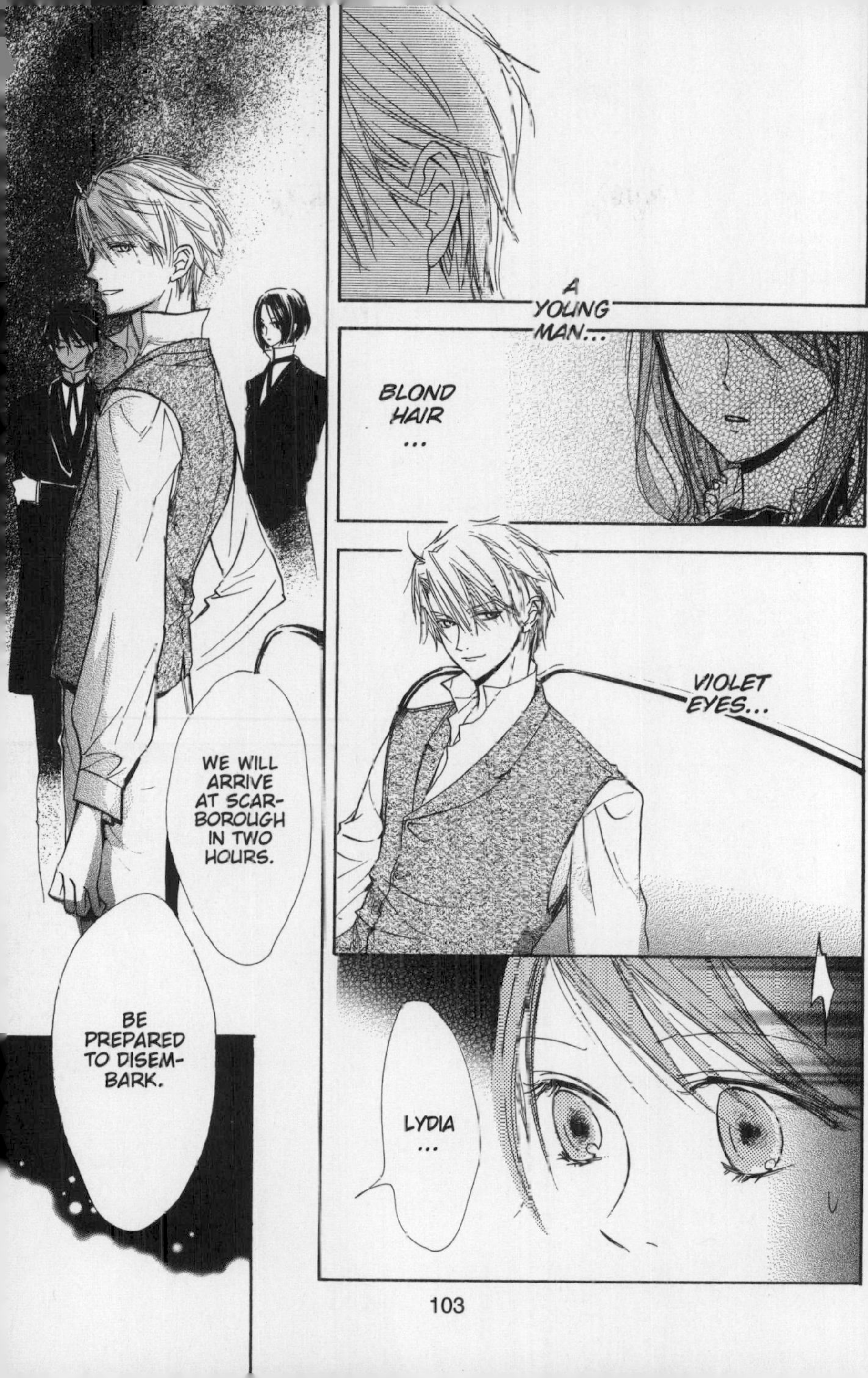
A YOUNG MAN...
BLOND HAIR ...
VIOLET EYES...
LYDIA ...
WE WILL ARRIVE AT SCAR-BOROUGH IN TWO HOURS.
BE PREPARED TO DISEM-BARK.

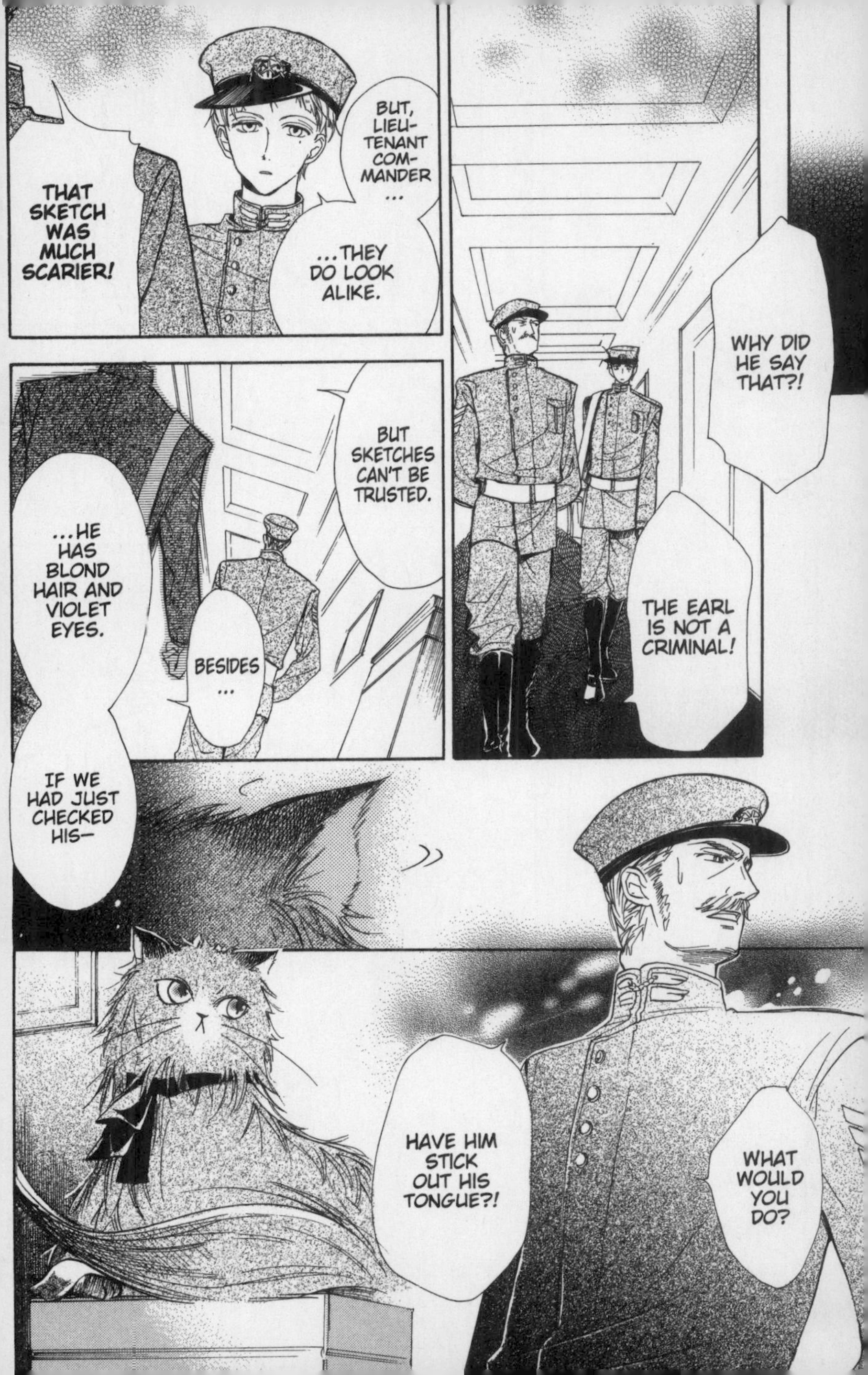
WHY DID HE SAY THAT?!
THE EARL IS NOT A CRIMINAL!
BUT, LIEU-TENANT COM-MANDER...
...THEY DO LOOK ALIKE.
THAT SKETCH WAS MUCH SCARIER!
BUT SKETCHES CAN'T BE TRUSTED.
BESIDES...
...HE HAS BLOND HAIR AND VIOLET EYES.
IF WE HAD JUST CHECKED HIS—
WHAT WOULD YOU DO?
HAVE HIM STICK OUT HIS TONGUE?!

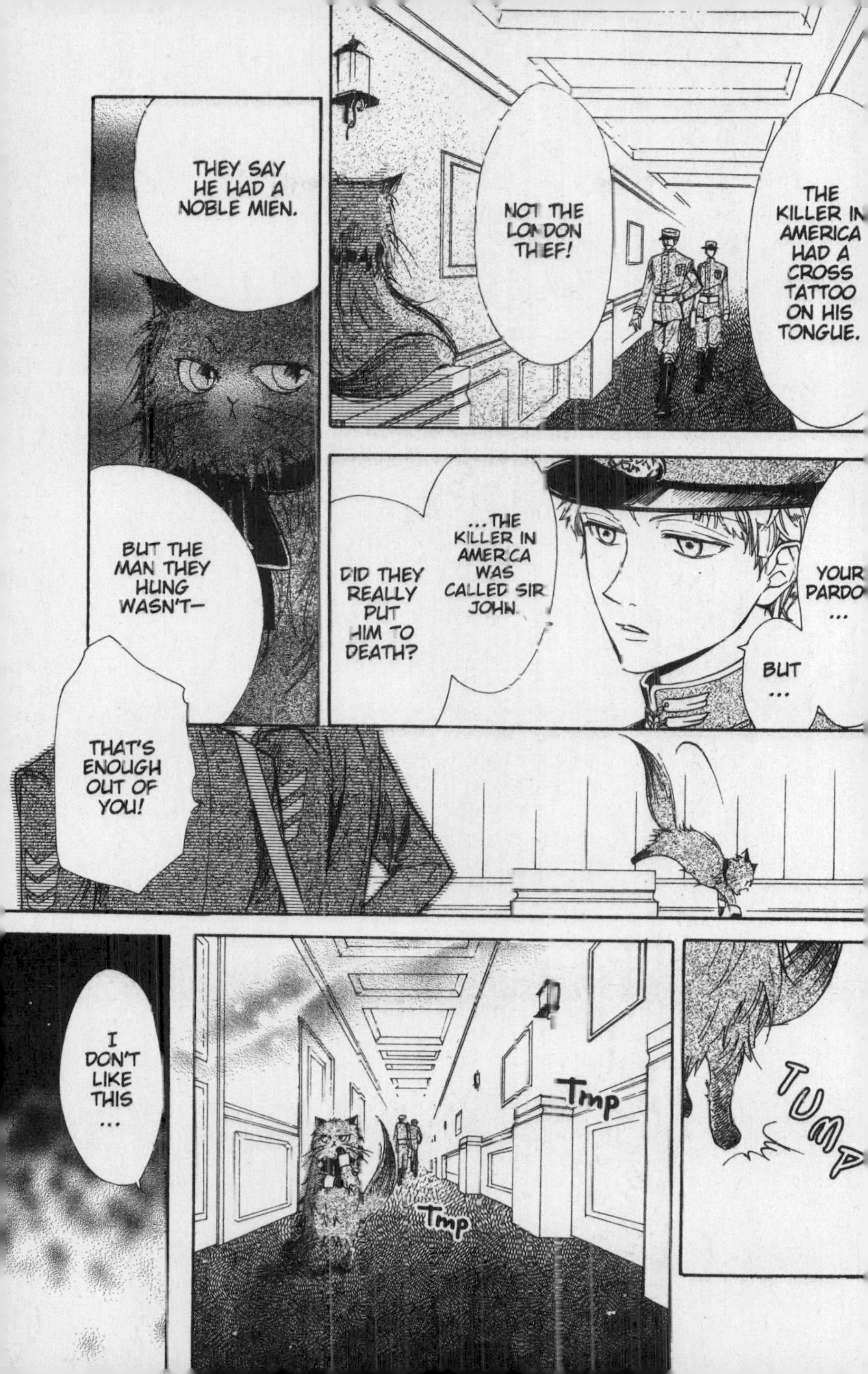
THE KILLER IN AMERICA HAD A CROSS TATTOO ON HIS TONGUE.
NOT THE LONDON THIEF!
THEY SAY HE HAD A NOBLE MIEN.
YOUR PARDO...
BUT...
...THE KILLER IN AMERICA WAS CALLED SIR JOHN.
DID THEY REALLY PUT HIM TO DEATH?
BUT THE MAN THEY HUNG WASN'T—
THAT'S ENOUGH OUT OF YOU!
TUMP
Tmp
Tmp
I DON'T LIKE THIS...

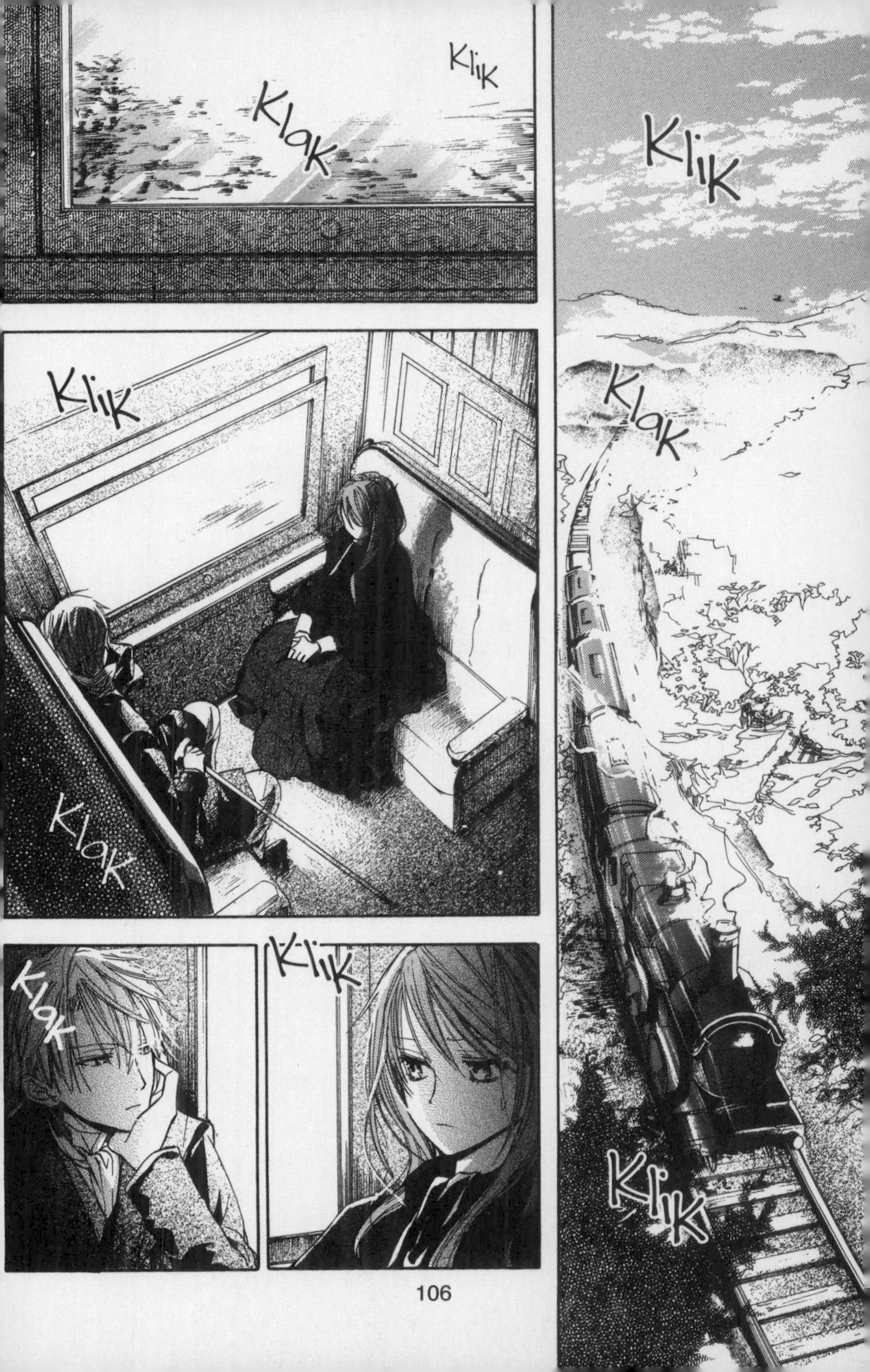
Klik
Klak
Klik
Klik
Klak
Klik
Klak
Klik
Klak

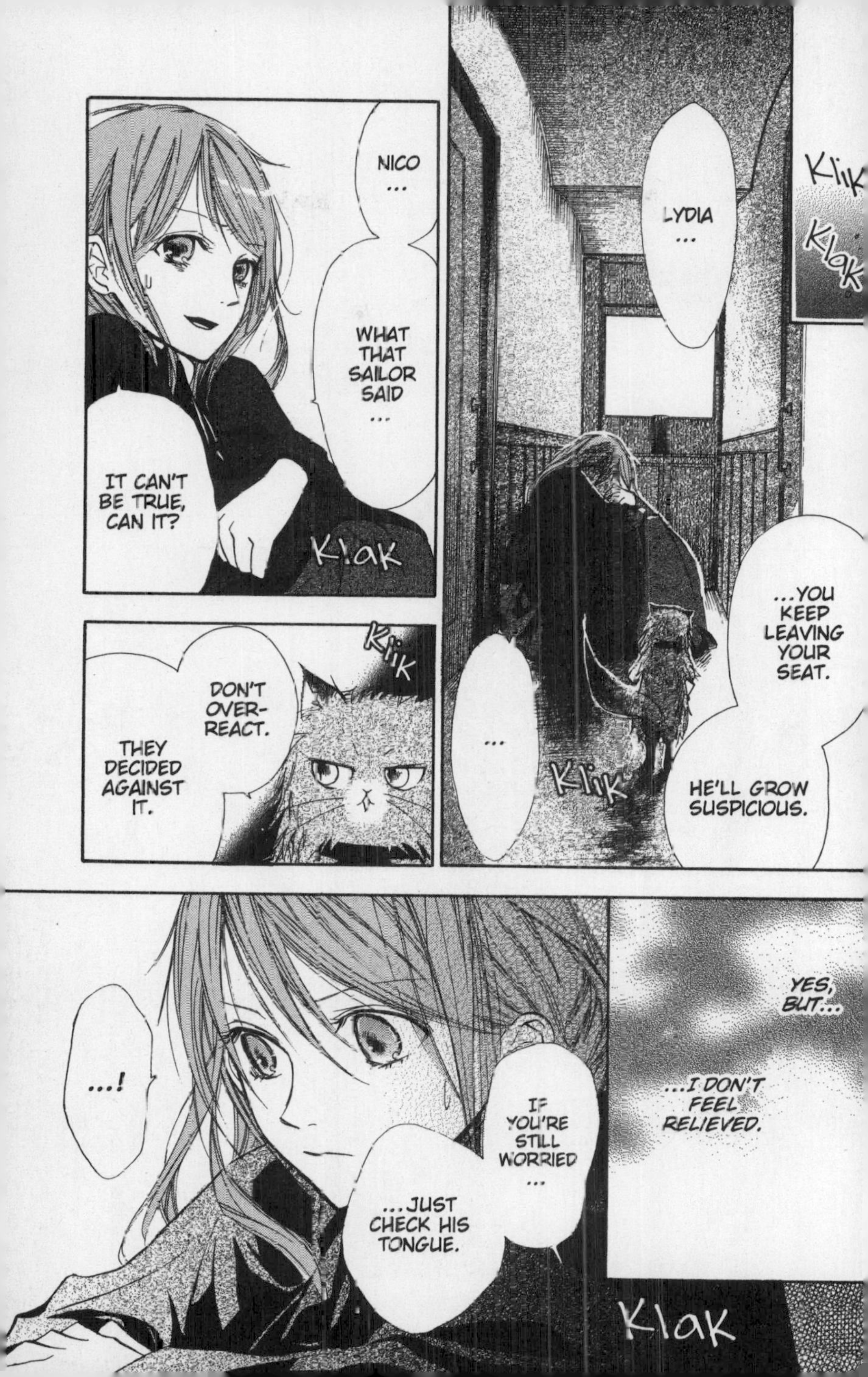
Kliik
Klak
LYDIA ...
...YOU KEEP LEAVING YOUR SEAT.
HE'LL GROW SUSPICIOUS.
...
Kliik
NICO ...
WHAT THAT SAILOR SAID ...
IT CAN'T BE TRUE, CAN IT?
Klak
Kliik
DON'T OVER-REACT.
THEY DECIDED AGAINST IT.
YES, BUT...
...I DON'T FEEL RELIEVED.
IF YOU'RE STILL WORRIED ...
...JUST CHECK HIS TONGUE.
...!
Klak

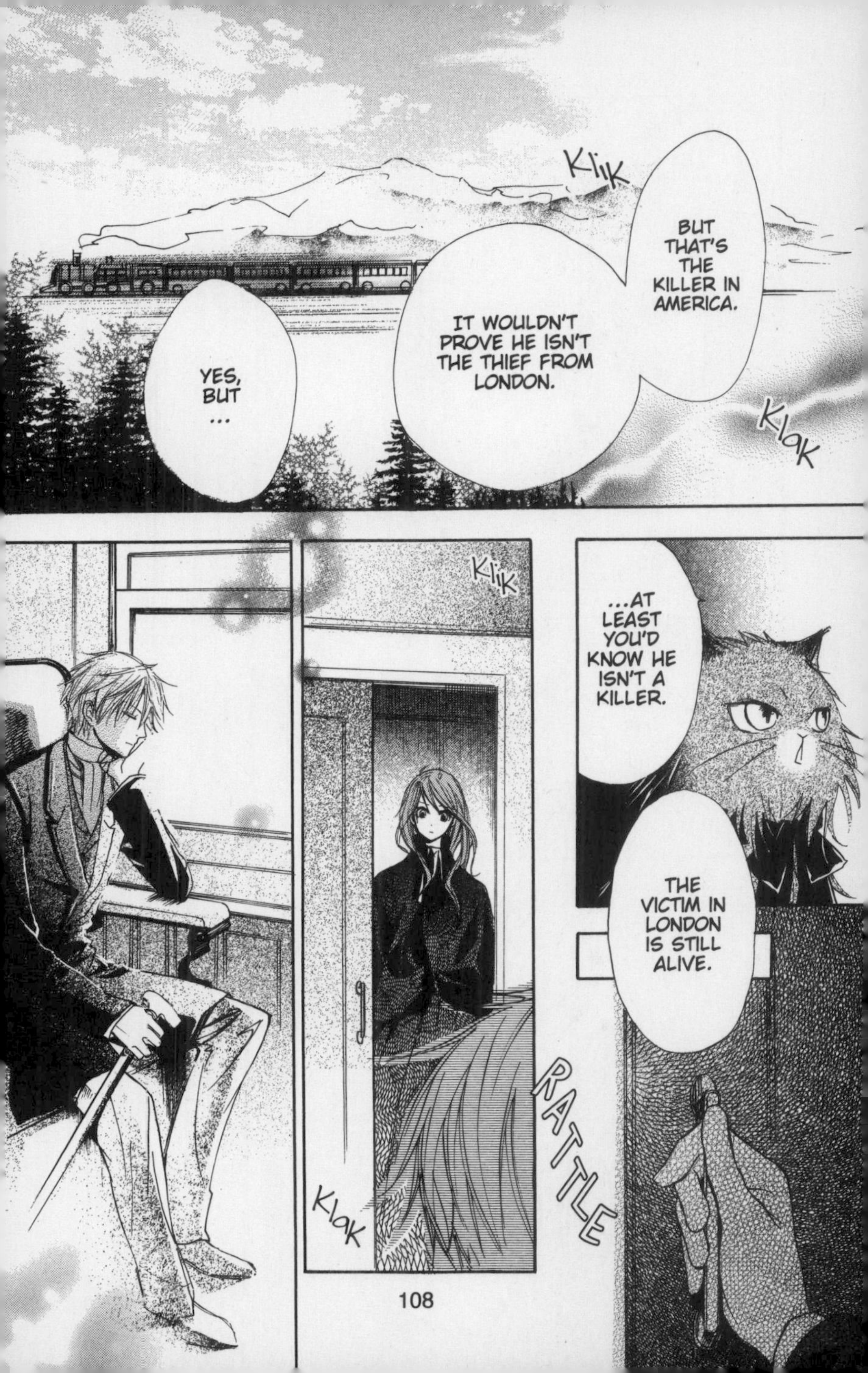
Kliik
BUT THAT'S THE KILLER IN AMERICA.
IT WOULDN'T PROVE HE ISN'T THE THIEF FROM LONDON.
Klak
YES, BUT ...
...AT LEAST YOU'D KNOW HE ISN'T A KILLER.
THE VICTIM IN LONDON IS STILL ALIVE.
RATTLE
Kliik
Klak

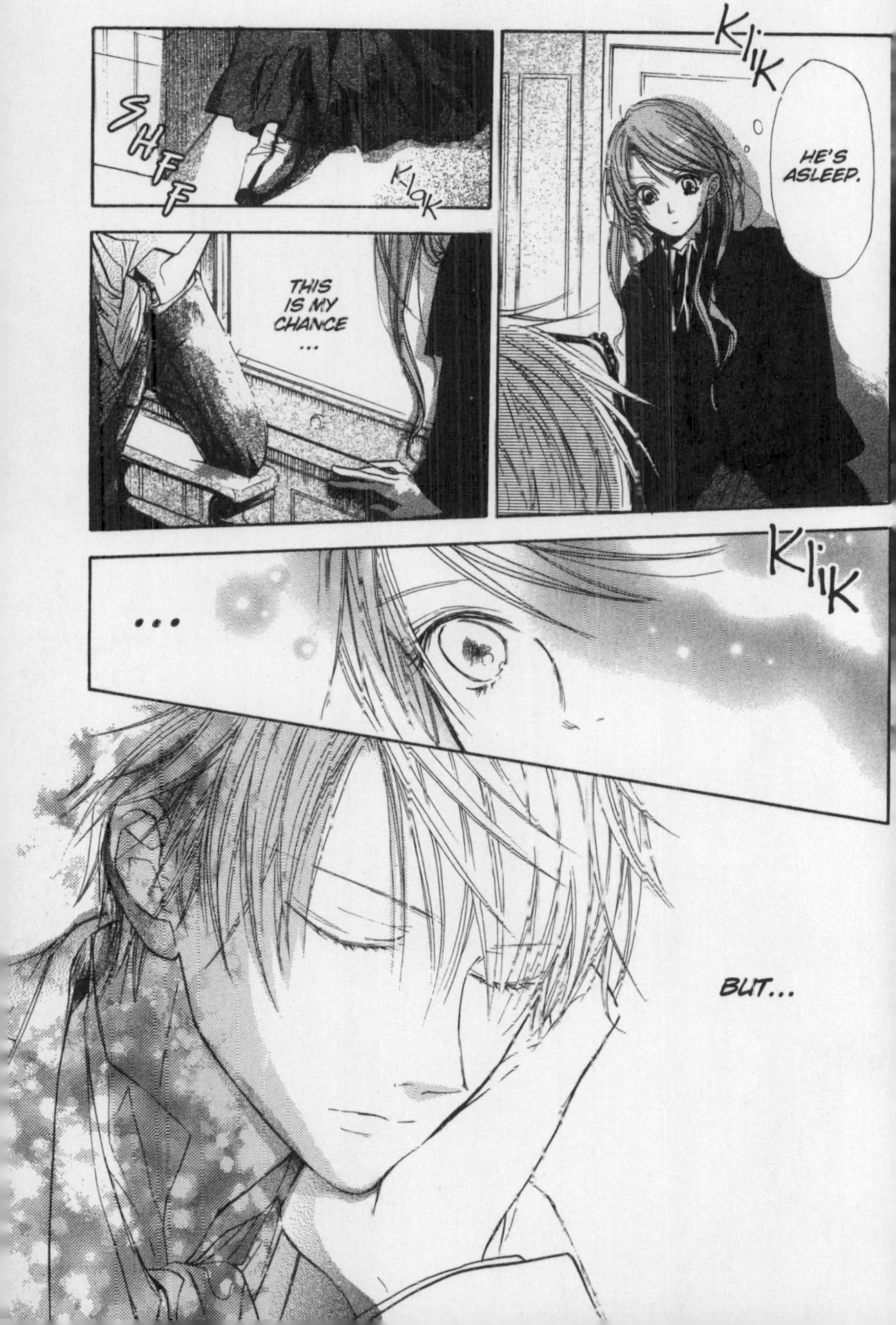
K-lik
HE'S ASLEEP.
SHFF
K-lak
THIS IS MY CHANCE ...
Klik
...
BUT...

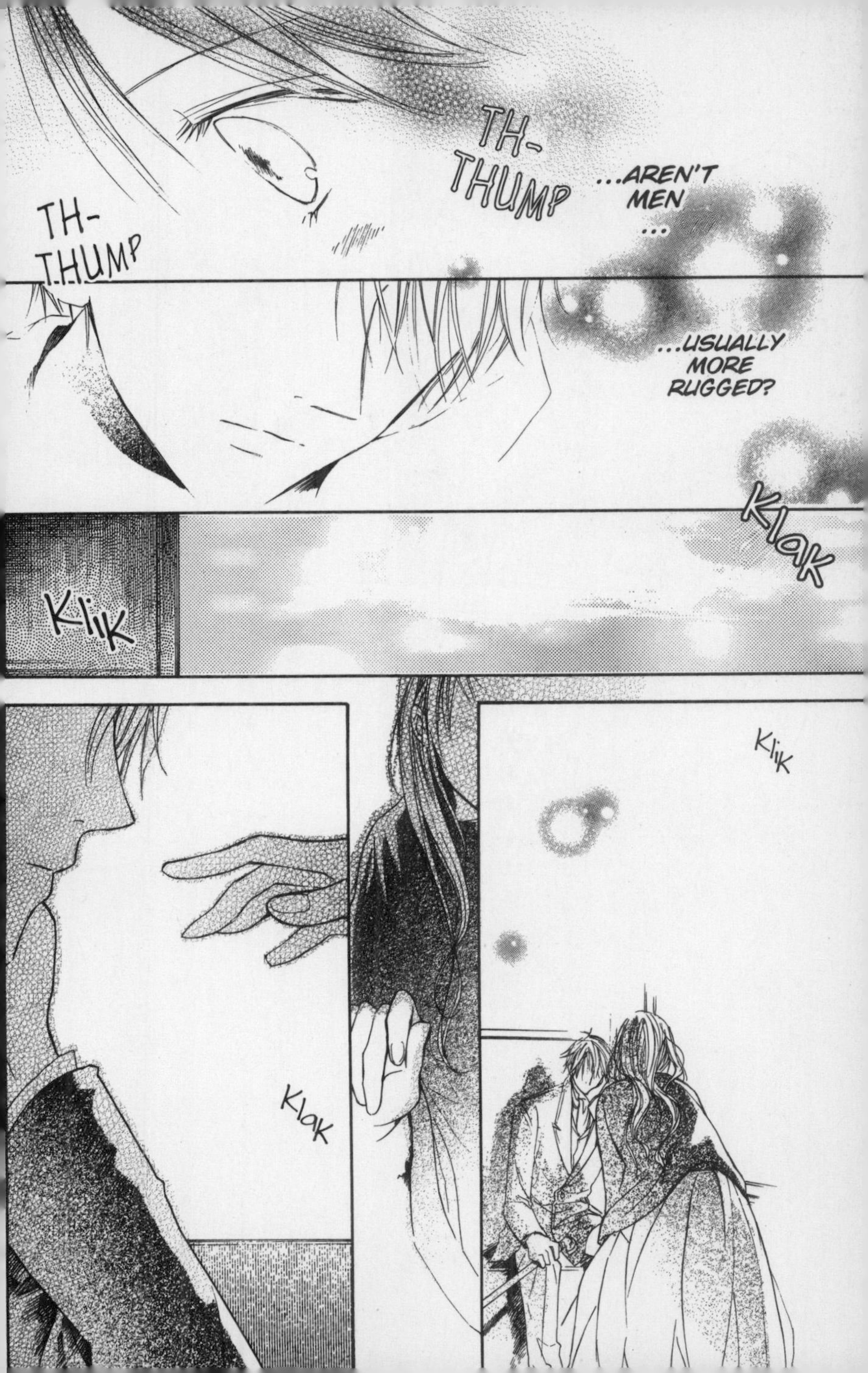
...AREN'T MEN ...
TH-THUMP
TH-THUMP
...USUALLY MORE RUGGED?
Klak
Klik
Klik
Klak

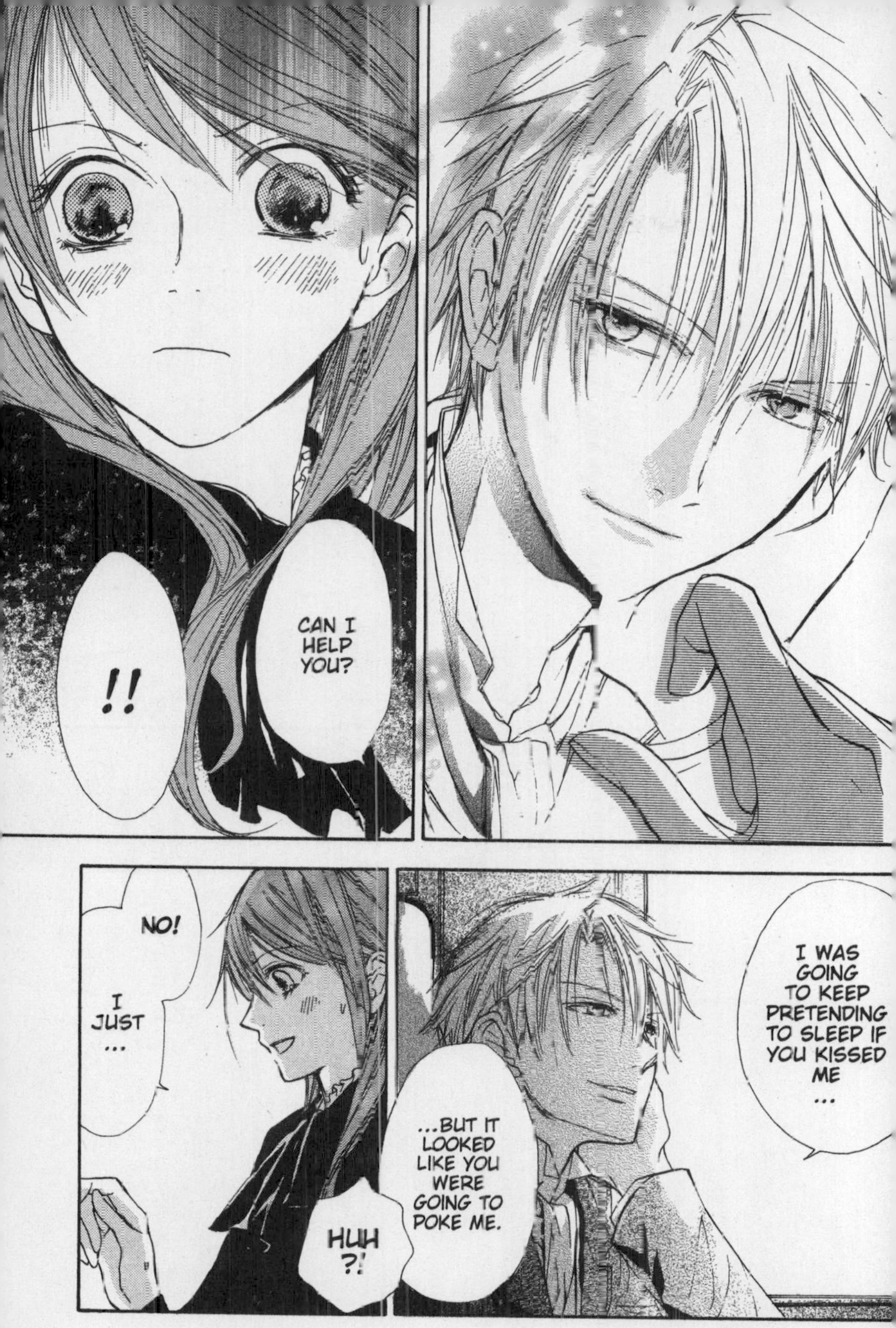
CAN I HELP YOU?
!!
I WAS GOING TO KEEP PRETENDING TO SLEEP IF YOU KISSED ME ...
...BUT IT LOOKED LIKE YOU WERE GOING TO POKE ME.
HUH ?!
NO!
I JUST ...

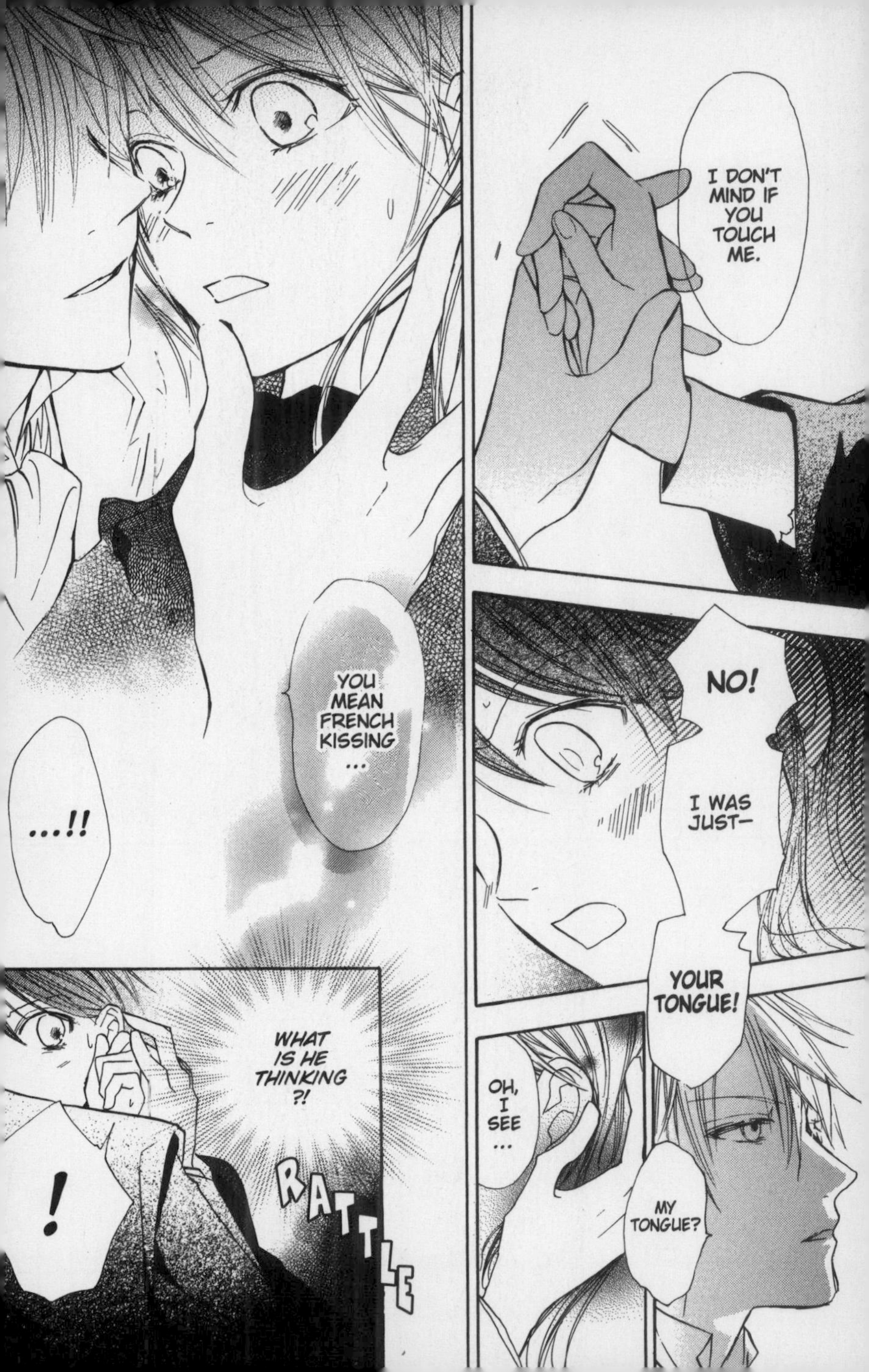
I DON'T MIND IF YOU TOUCH ME.
NO!
I WAS JUST—
YOUR TONGUE!
MY TONGUE?
OH, I SEE ...
YOU MEAN FRENCH KISSING ...
...!!
WHAT IS HE THINKING ?!
RATTLE
!

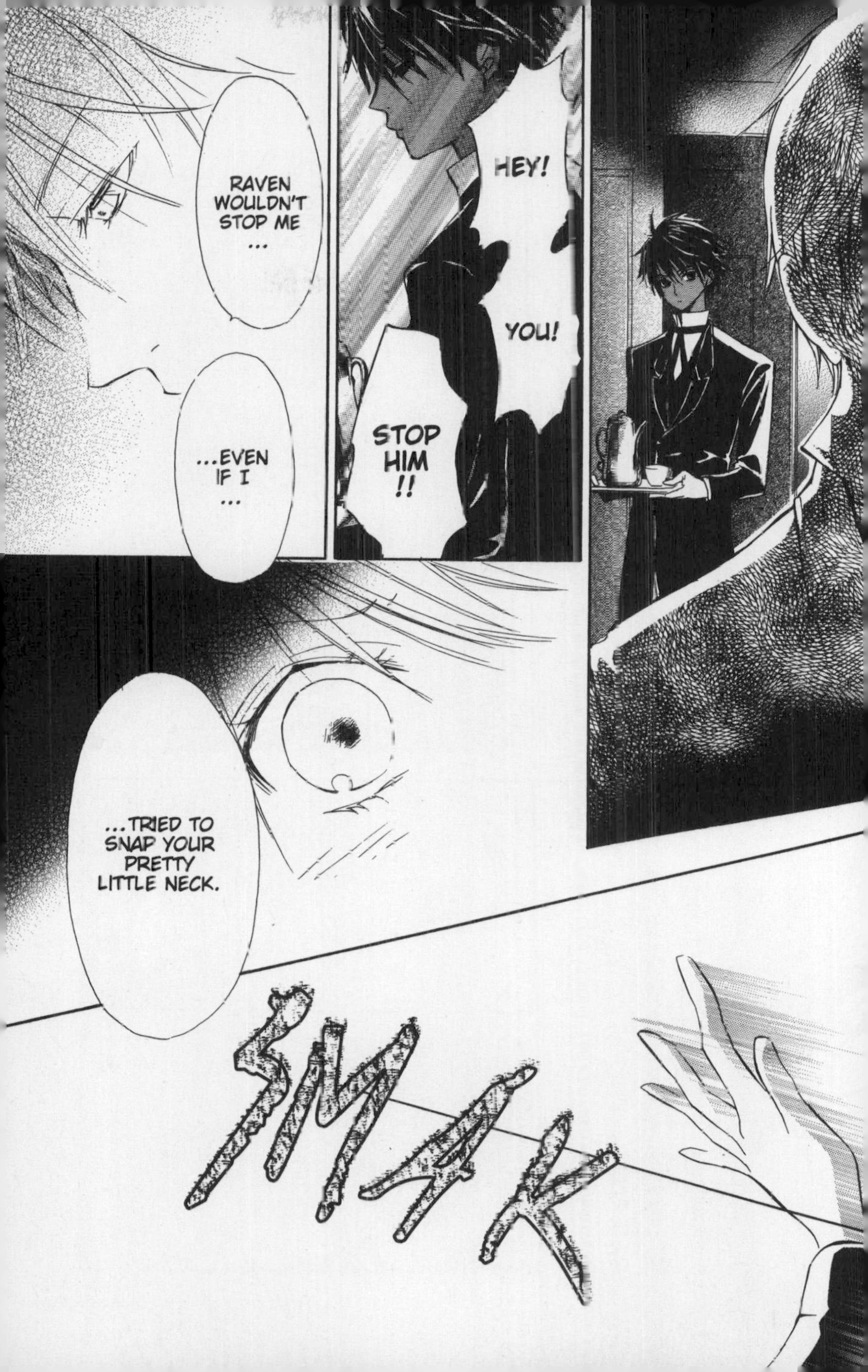
HEY!
YOU!
STOP HIM !!
RAVEN WOULDN'T STOP ME ...
...EVEN IF I ...
...TRIED TO SNAP YOUR PRETTY LITTLE NECK.
SMAK

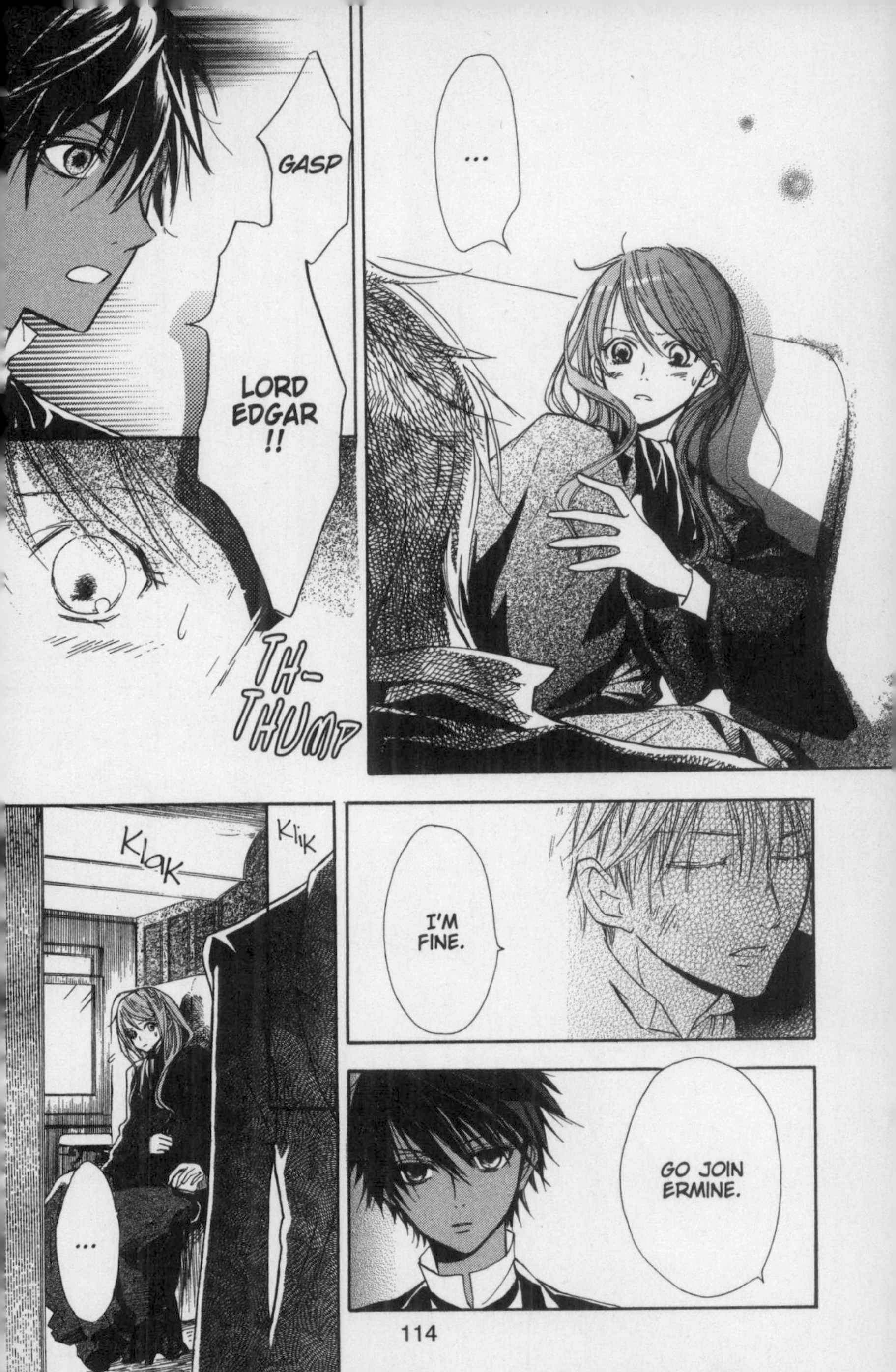
...
GASP
LORD EDGAR !!
TH-THUMP
I'M FINE.
GO JOIN ERMINE.
Klik
Klak
...

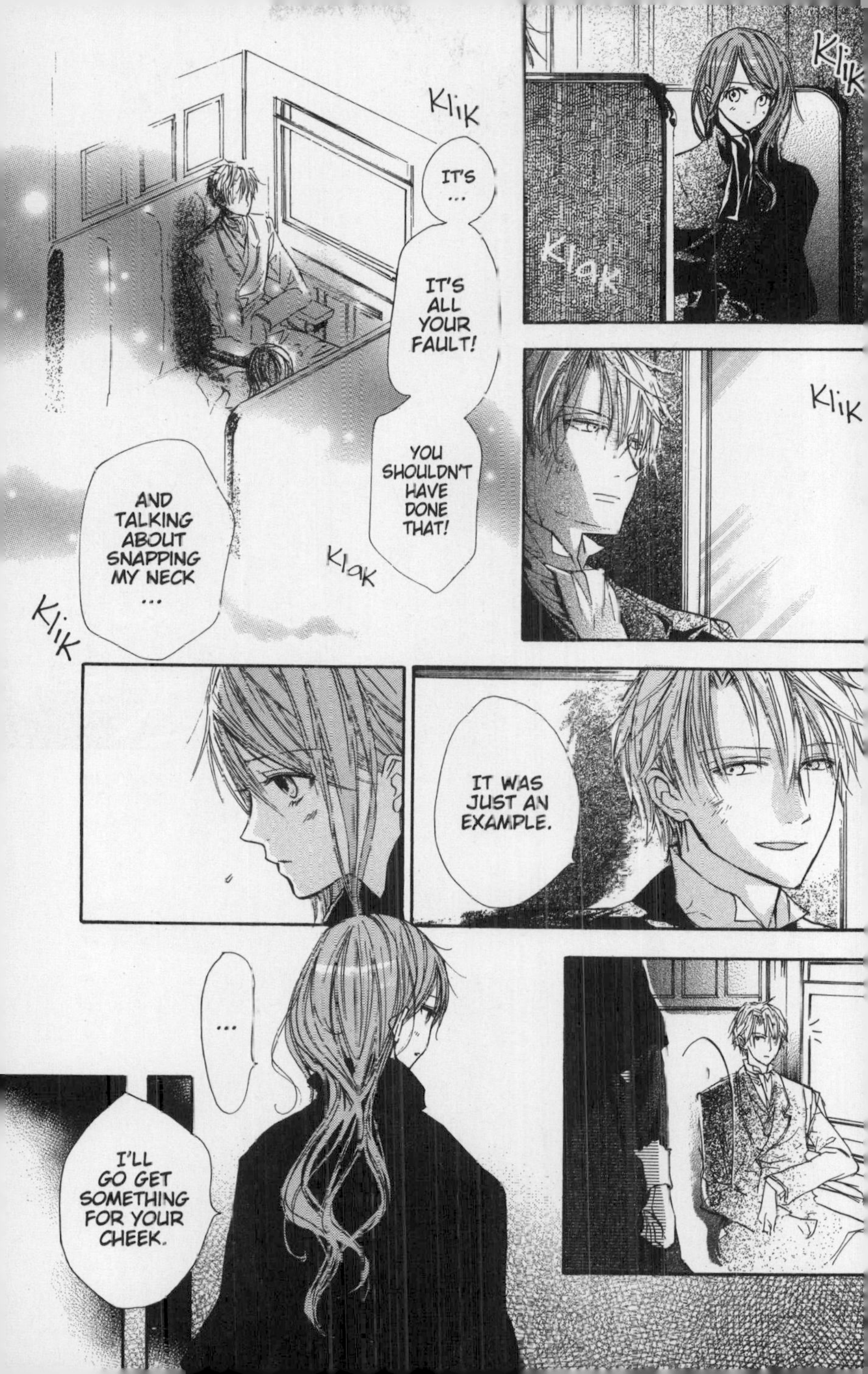
Klik
Klak
Klik
Klik
It's ...
It's all your fault!
You shouldn't have done that!
Klak
And talking about snapping my neck ...
Klik
It was just an example.
...
I'll go get something for your cheek.

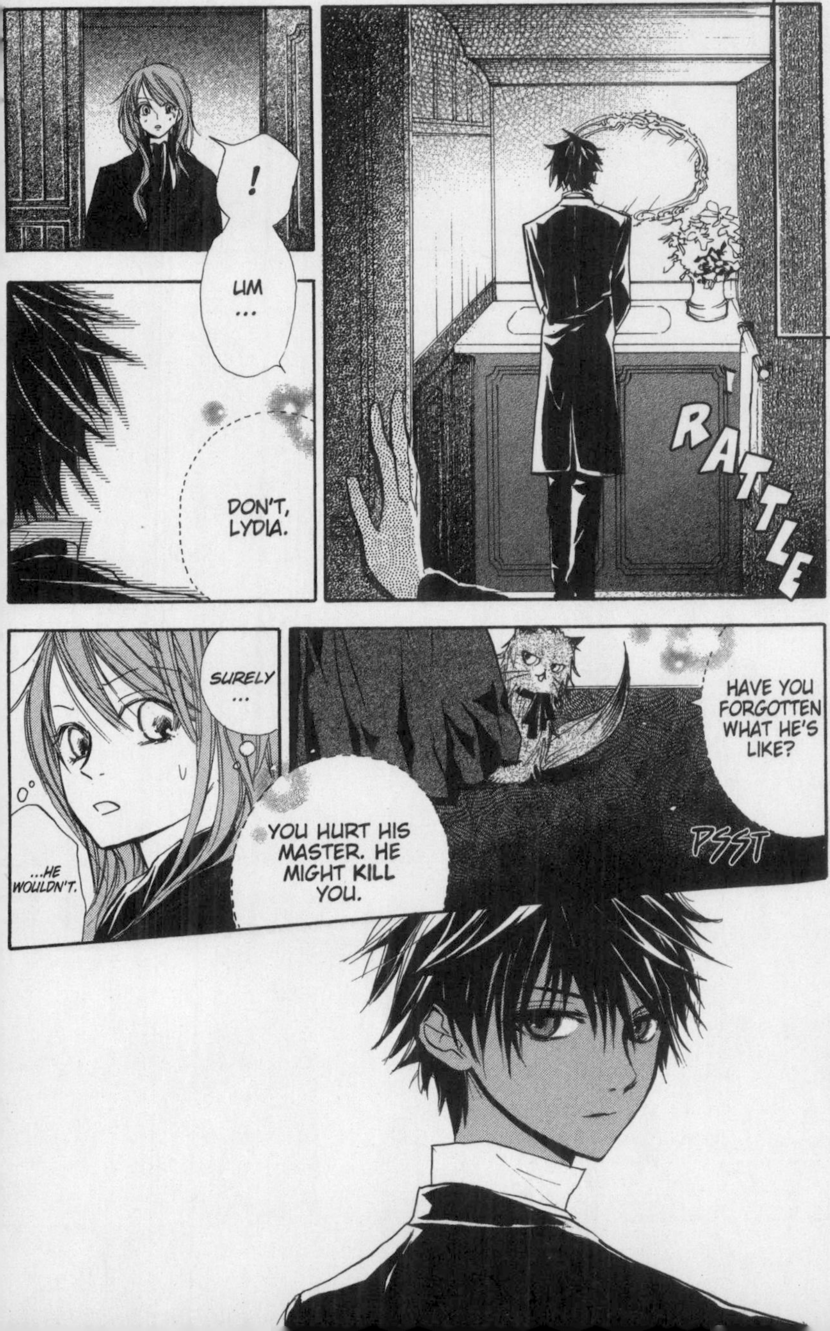
RATTLE
!
UM ...
DON'T, LYDIA.
HAVE YOU FORGOTTEN WHAT HE'S LIKE?
PSST
YOU HURT HIS MASTER. HE MIGHT KILL YOU.
SURELY ...
...HE WOULDN'T.

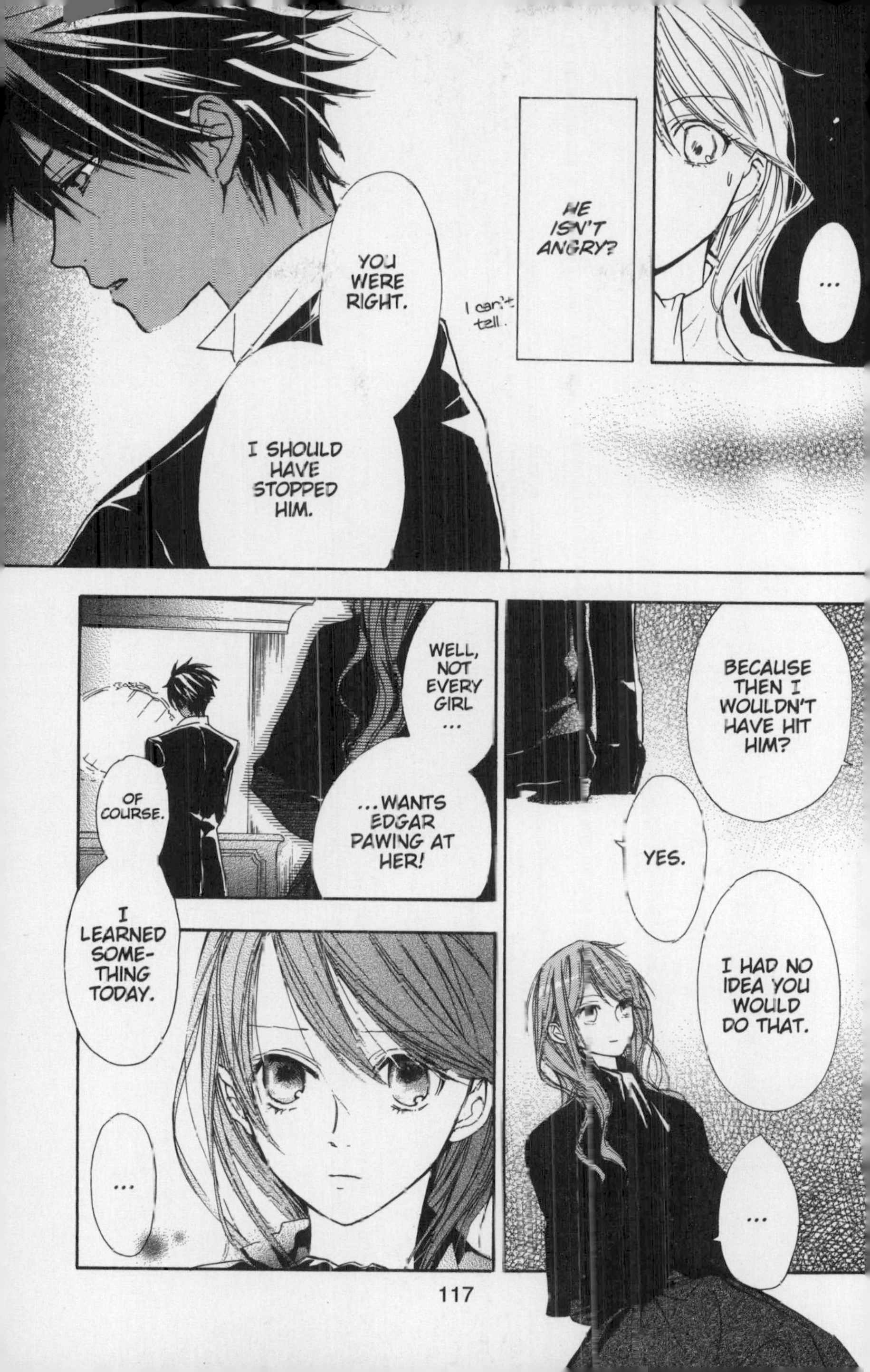
...
HE ISN'T ANGRY?
I can't tell.
YOU WERE RIGHT.
I SHOULD HAVE STOPPED HIM.
BECAUSE THEN I WOULDN'T HAVE HIT HIM?
YES.
I HAD NO IDEA YOU WOULD DO THAT.
...
WELL, NOT EVERY GIRL...
...WANTS EDGAR PAWING AT HER!
OF COURSE.
I LEARNED SOME-THING TODAY.
...

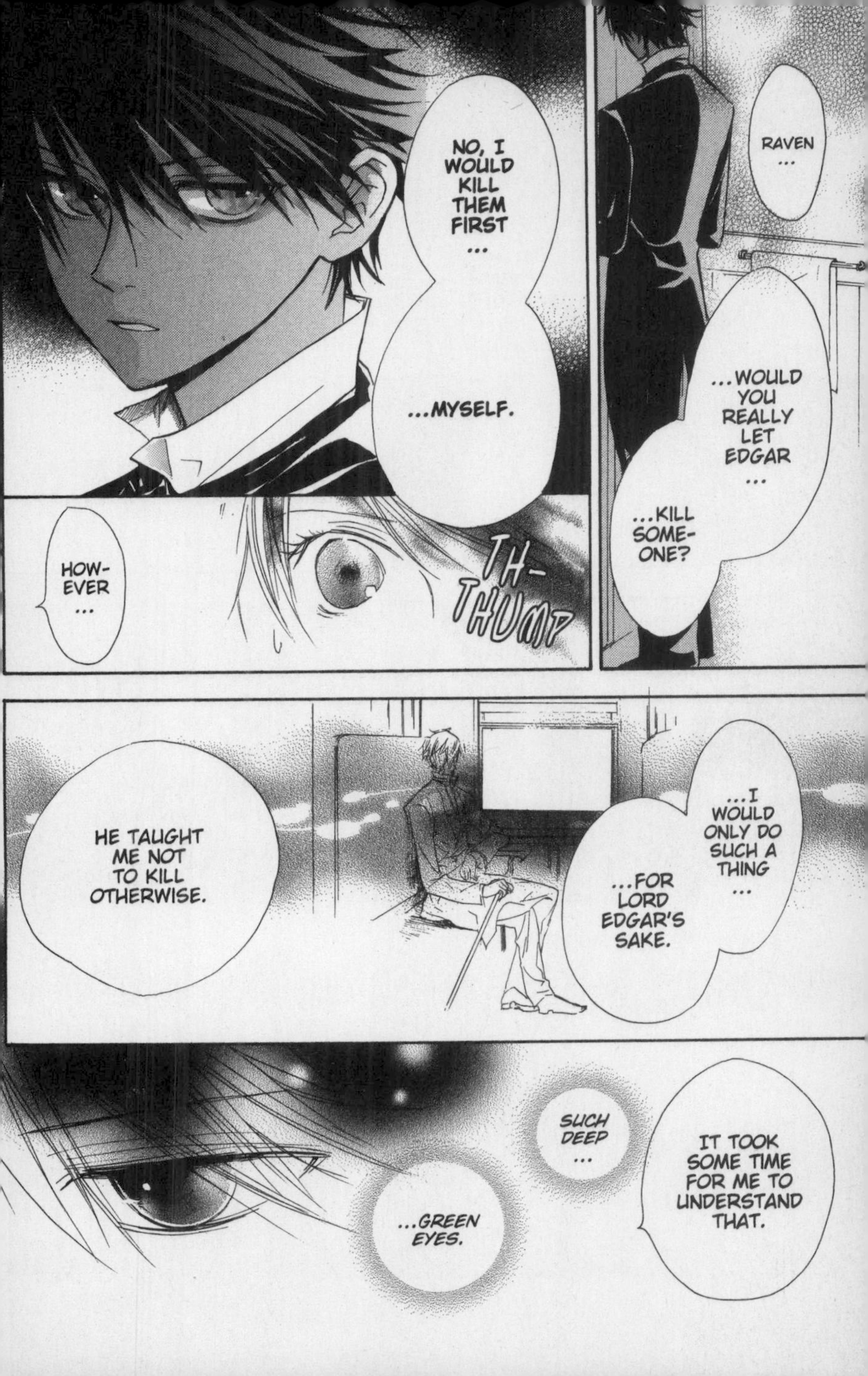
RAVEN ...
...WOULD YOU REALLY LET EDGAR ...
...KILL SOME-ONE?
NO, I WOULD KILL THEM FIRST ...
...MYSELF.
HOW-EVER ...
TH-THUMP
...I WOULD ONLY DO SUCH A THING ...
...FOR LORD EDGAR'S SAKE.
HE TAUGHT ME NOT TO KILL OTHERWISE.
IT TOOK SOME TIME FOR ME TO UNDERSTAND THAT.
SUCH DEEP ...
...GREEN EYES.

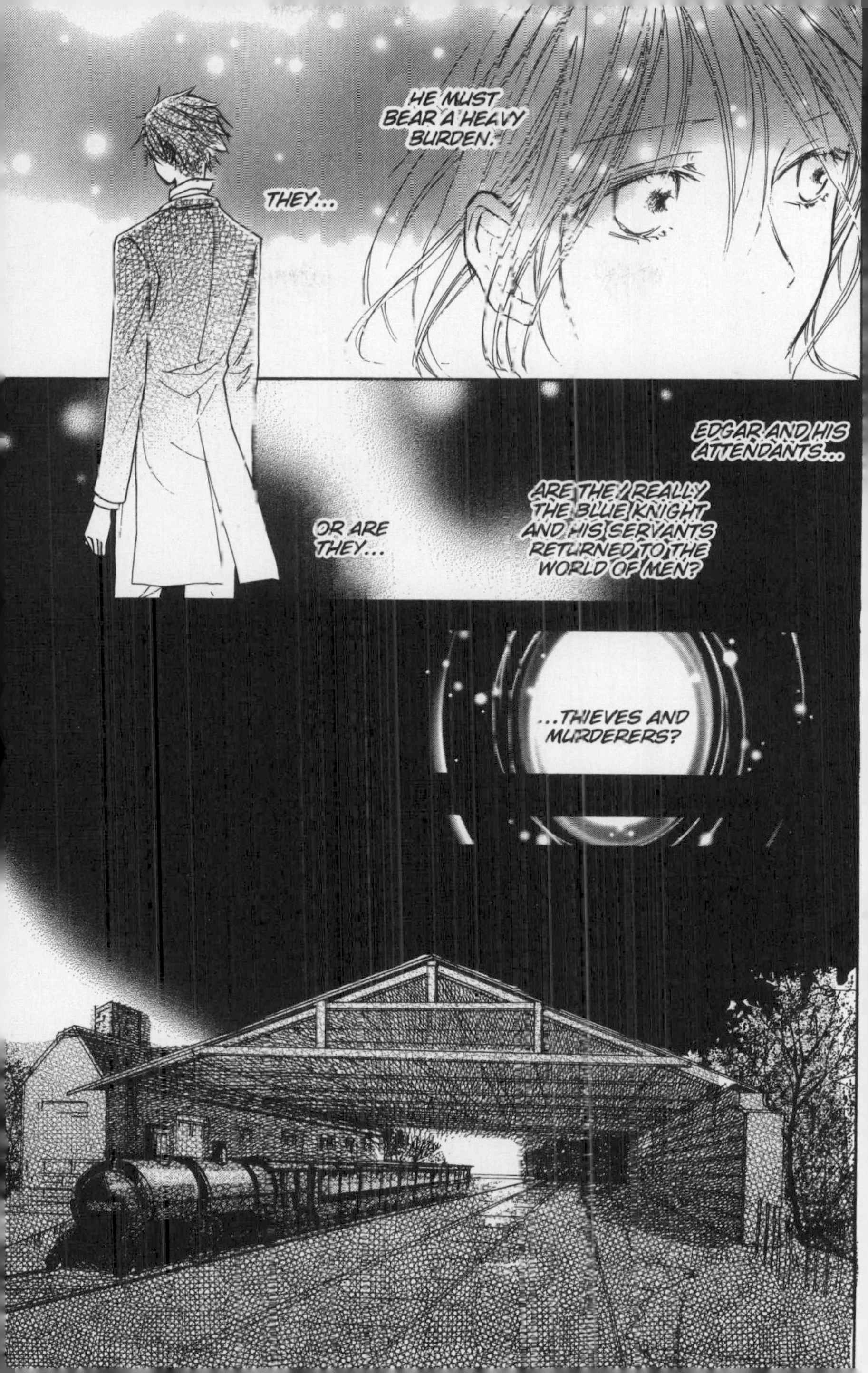
HE MUST BEAR A HEAVY BURDEN.
THEY...
EDGAR AND HIS ATTENDANTS...
ARE THEY REALLY THE BLUE KNIGHT AND HIS SERVANTS RETURNED TO THE WORLD OF MEN?
OR ARE THEY...
...THIEVES AND MURDERERS?

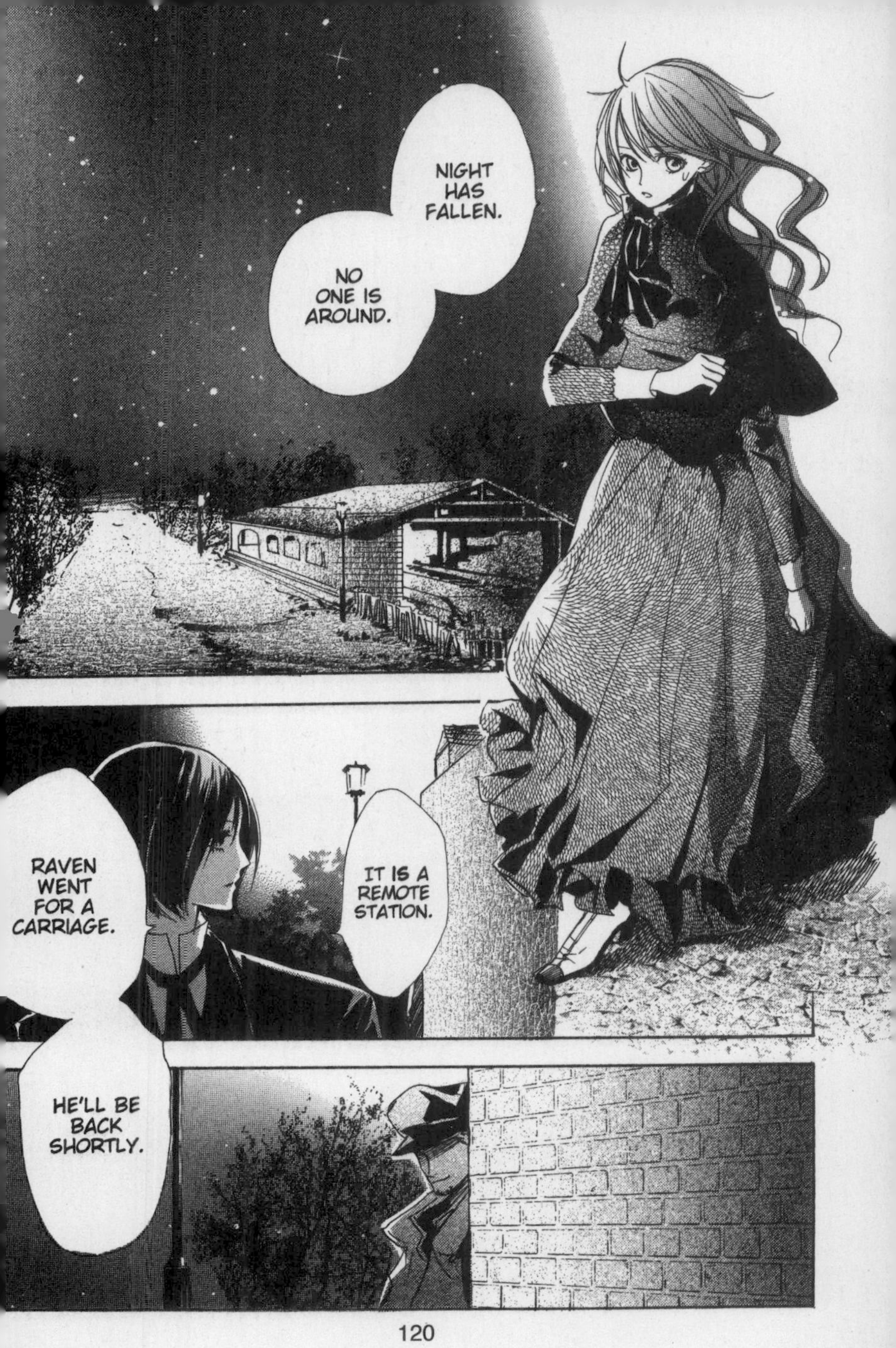
NIGHT HAS FALLEN.
NO ONE IS AROUND.
IT IS A REMOTE STATION.
RAVEN WENT FOR A CARRIAGE.
HE'LL BE BACK SHORTLY.

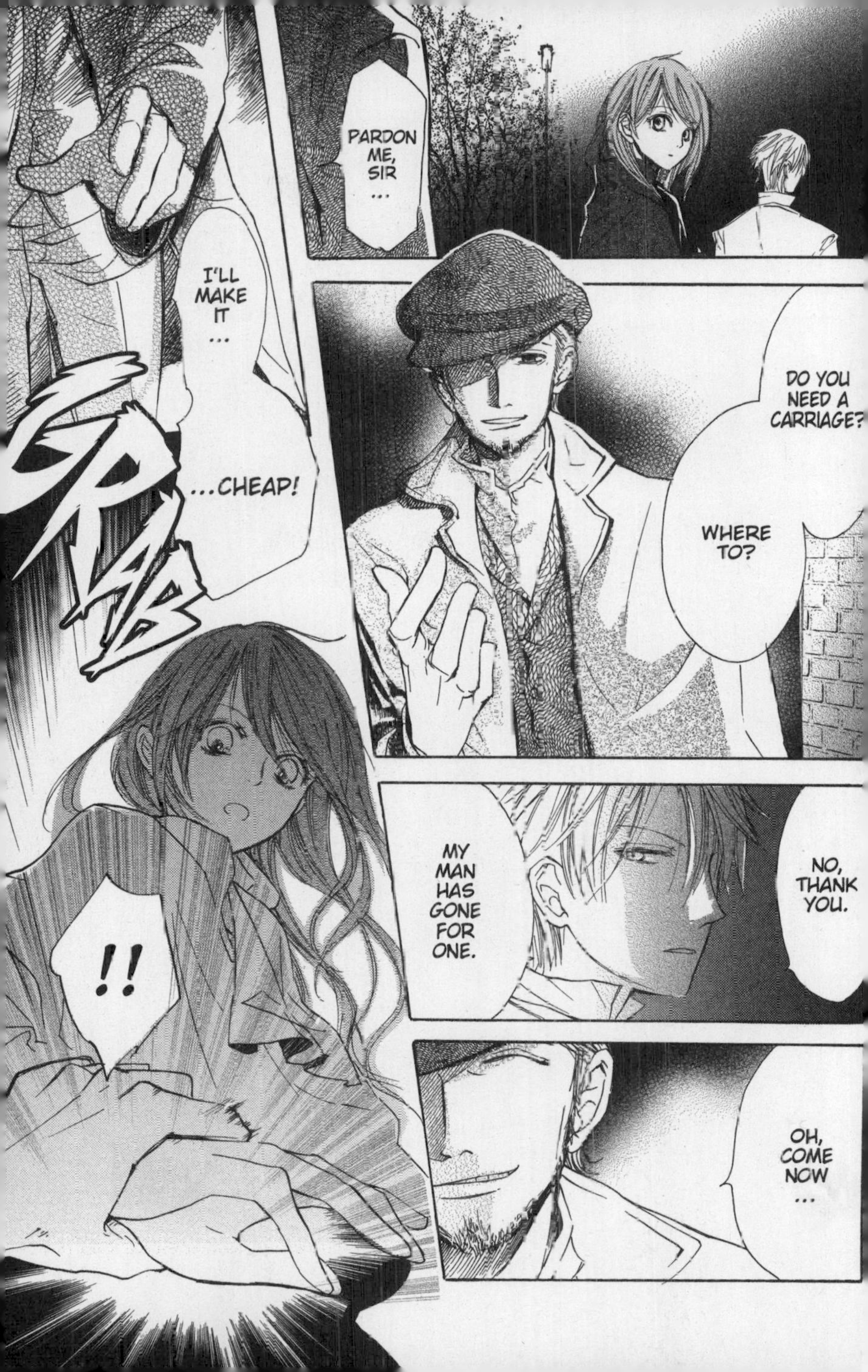
PARDON ME, SIR ...
DO YOU NEED A CARRIAGE?
WHERE TO?
NO, THANK YOU.
MY MAN HAS GONE FOR ONE.
OH, COME NOW ...
I'LL MAKE IT ...
...CHEAP!
GRAB
!!

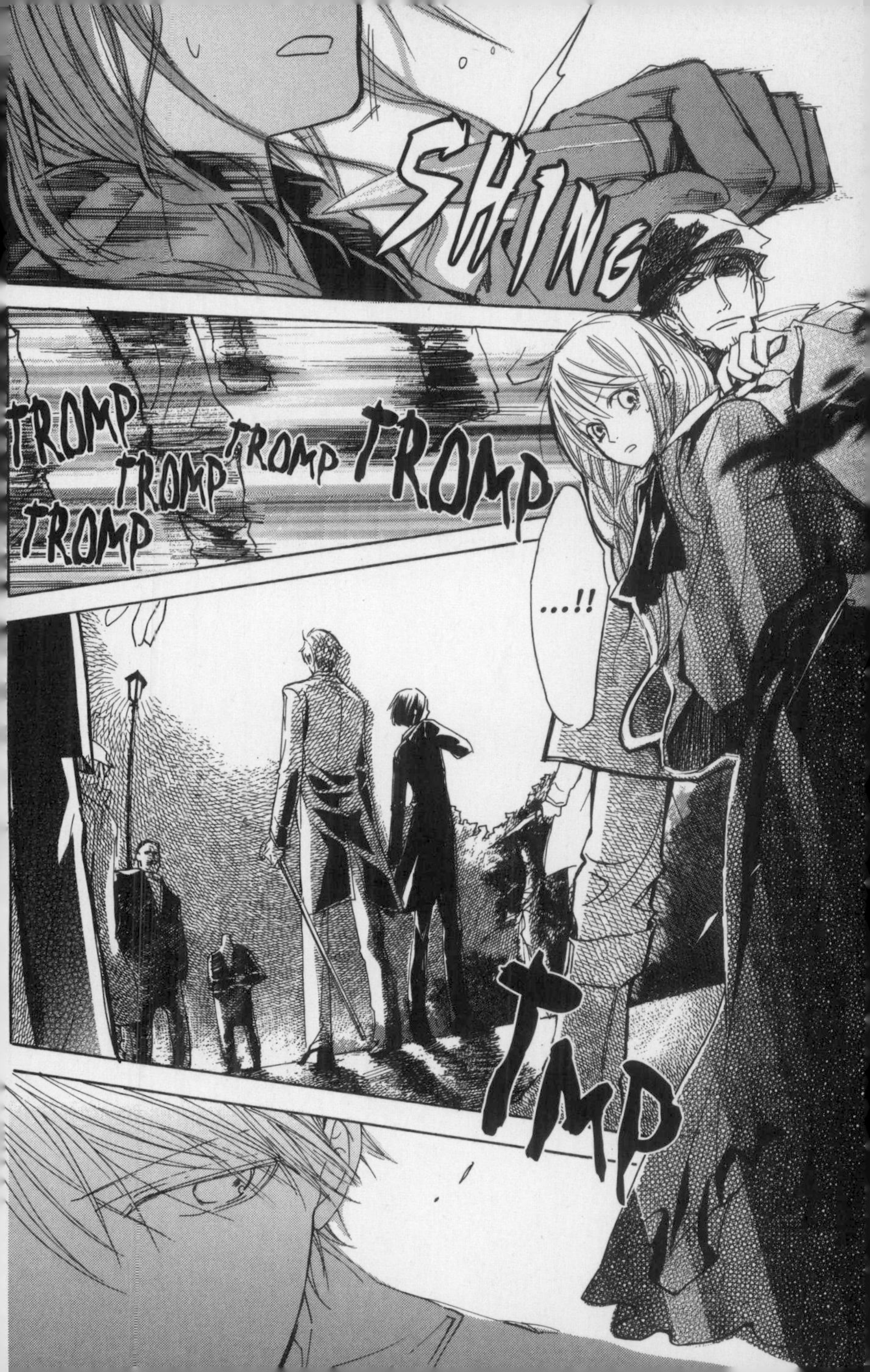
SHING
TROMP
TROMP
TROMP
TROMP
TROMP
...!!
TIMP

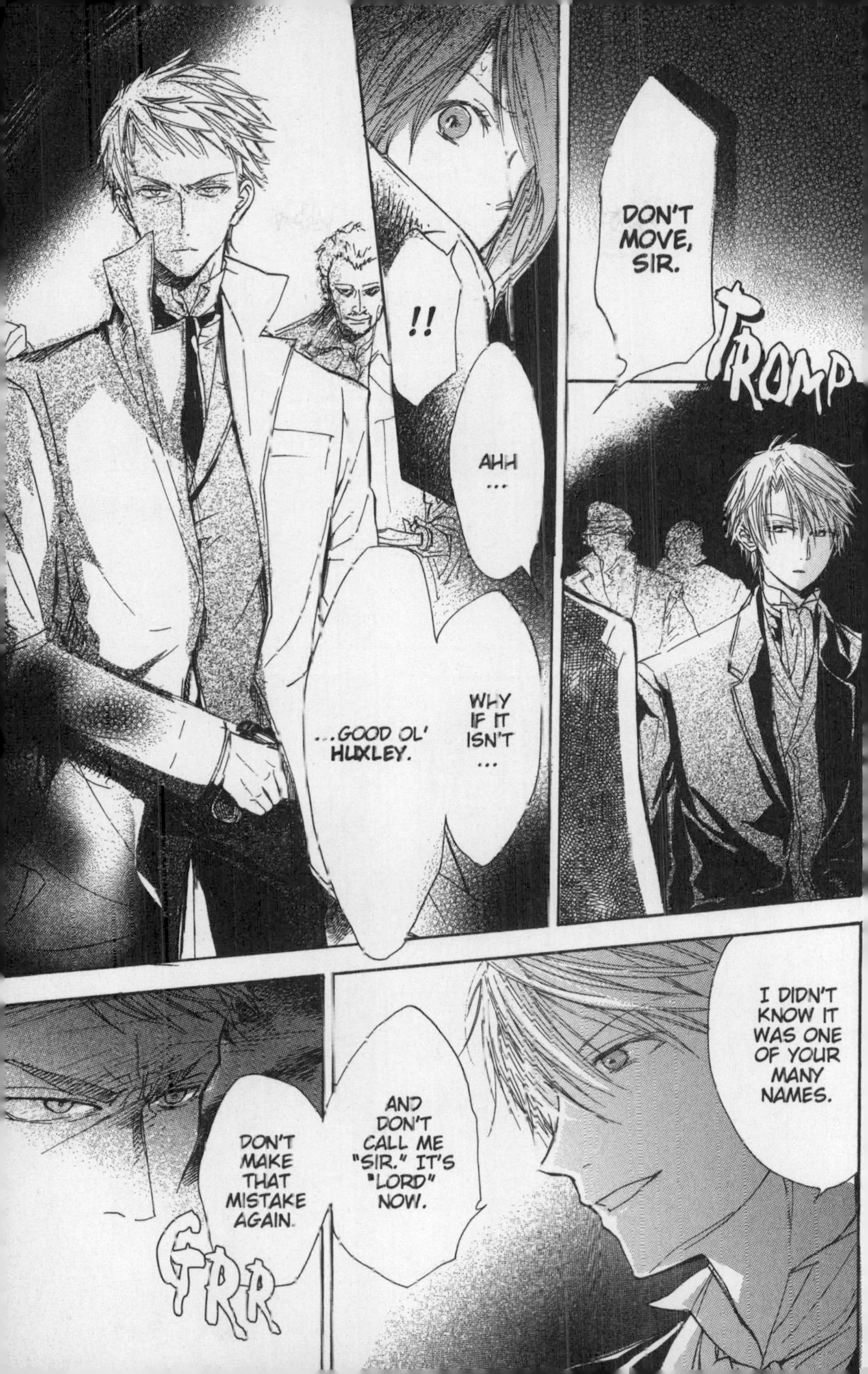
DON'T MOVE, SIR.
TROMP
!!
AHH ...
WHY IF IT ISN'T ...
...GOOD OL' HUXLEY.
I DIDN'T KNOW IT WAS ONE OF YOUR MANY NAMES.
AND DON'T CALL ME "SIR." IT'S "LORD" NOW.
DON'T MAKE THAT MISTAKE AGAIN.
GRR

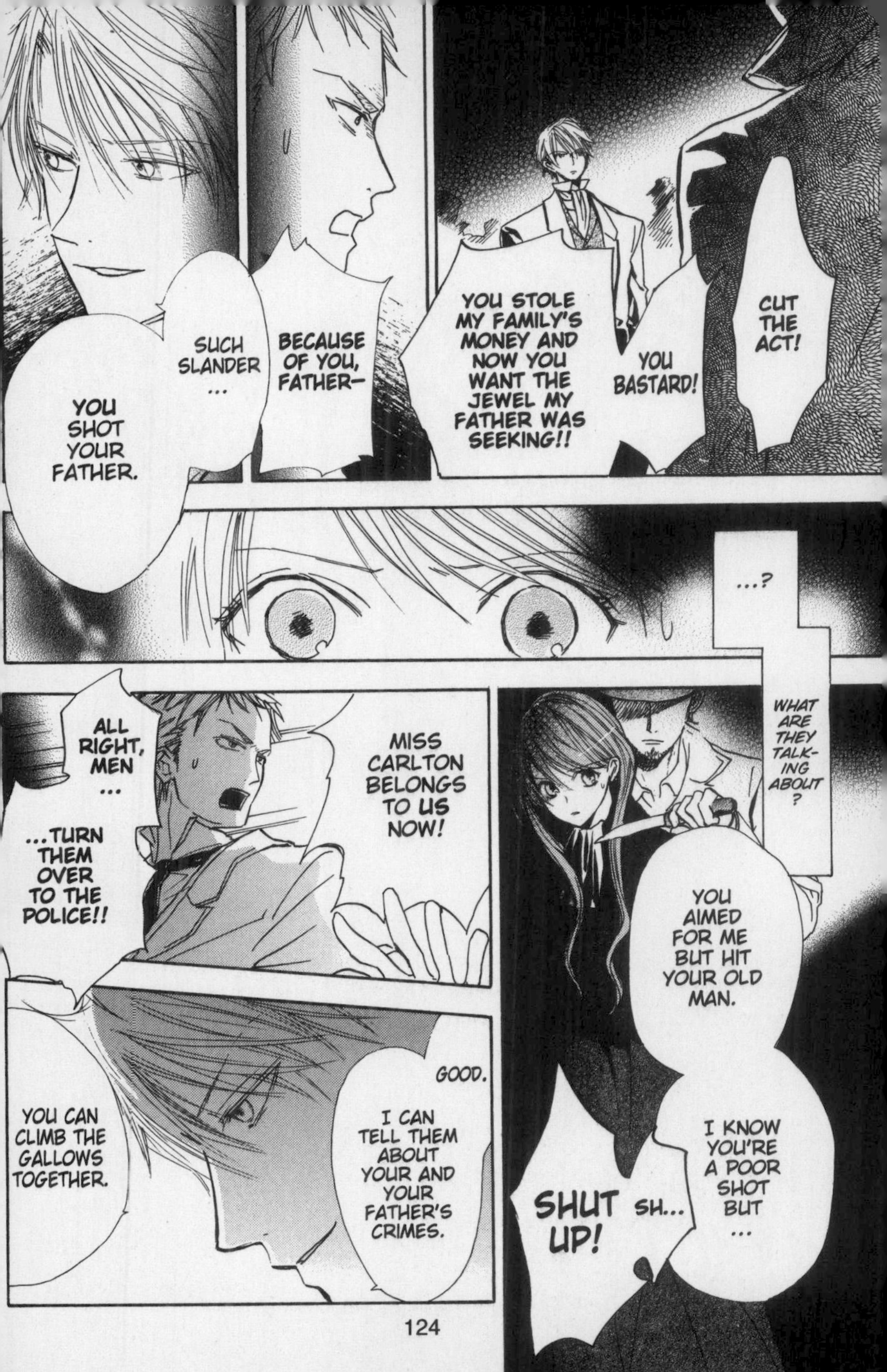
CUT THE ACT!
YOU BASTARD!
YOU STOLE MY FAMILY'S MONEY AND NOW YOU WANT THE JEWEL MY FATHER WAS SEEKING!!
BECAUSE OF YOU, FATHER—
SUCH SLANDER ...
YOU SHOT YOUR FATHER.
...?
WHAT ARE THEY TALKING ABOUT?
YOU AIMED FOR ME BUT HIT YOUR OLD MAN.
I KNOW YOU'RE A POOR SHOT BUT ...
SH...
SHUT UP!
MISS CARLTON BELONGS TO US NOW!
ALL RIGHT, MEN ...
...TURN THEM OVER TO THE POLICE!!
GOOD.
I CAN TELL THEM ABOUT YOUR AND YOUR FATHER'S CRIMES.
YOU CAN CLIMB THE GALLOWS TOGETHER.

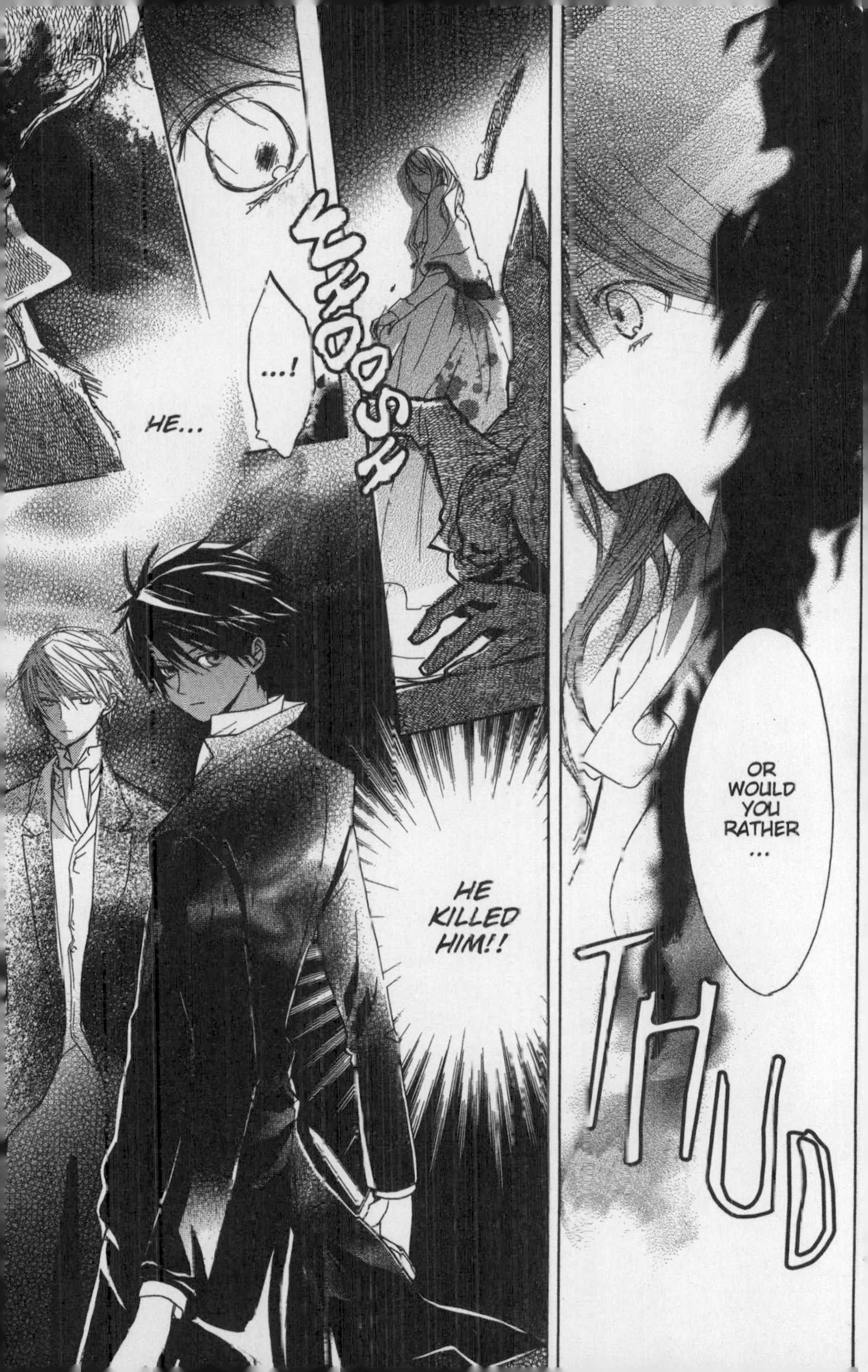
OR WOULD YOU RATHER ...
THUD
WHOOSH
...!
HE...
HE KILLED HIM!!

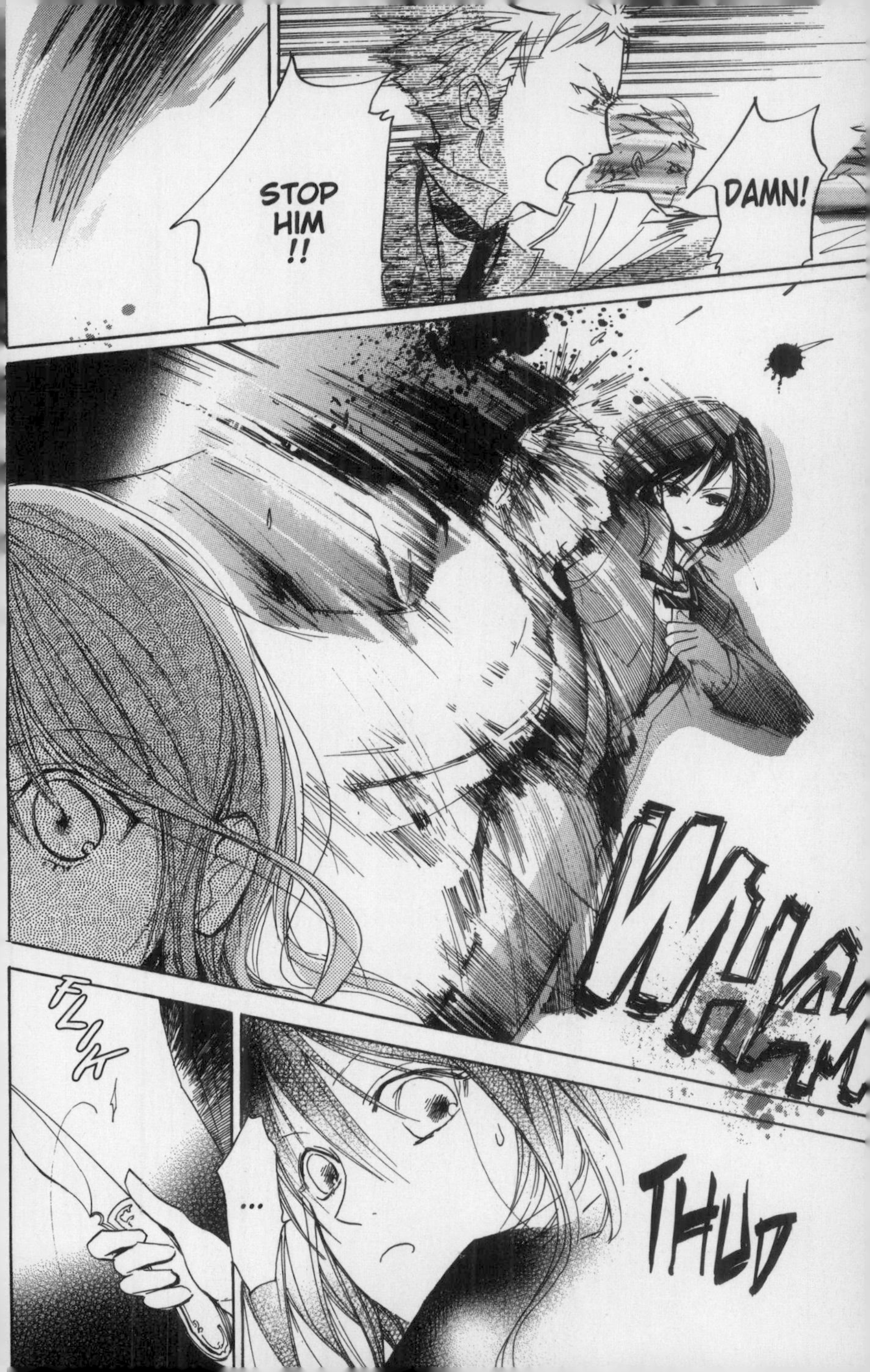
DAMN!
STOP HIM !!
THUD
...
FLIK

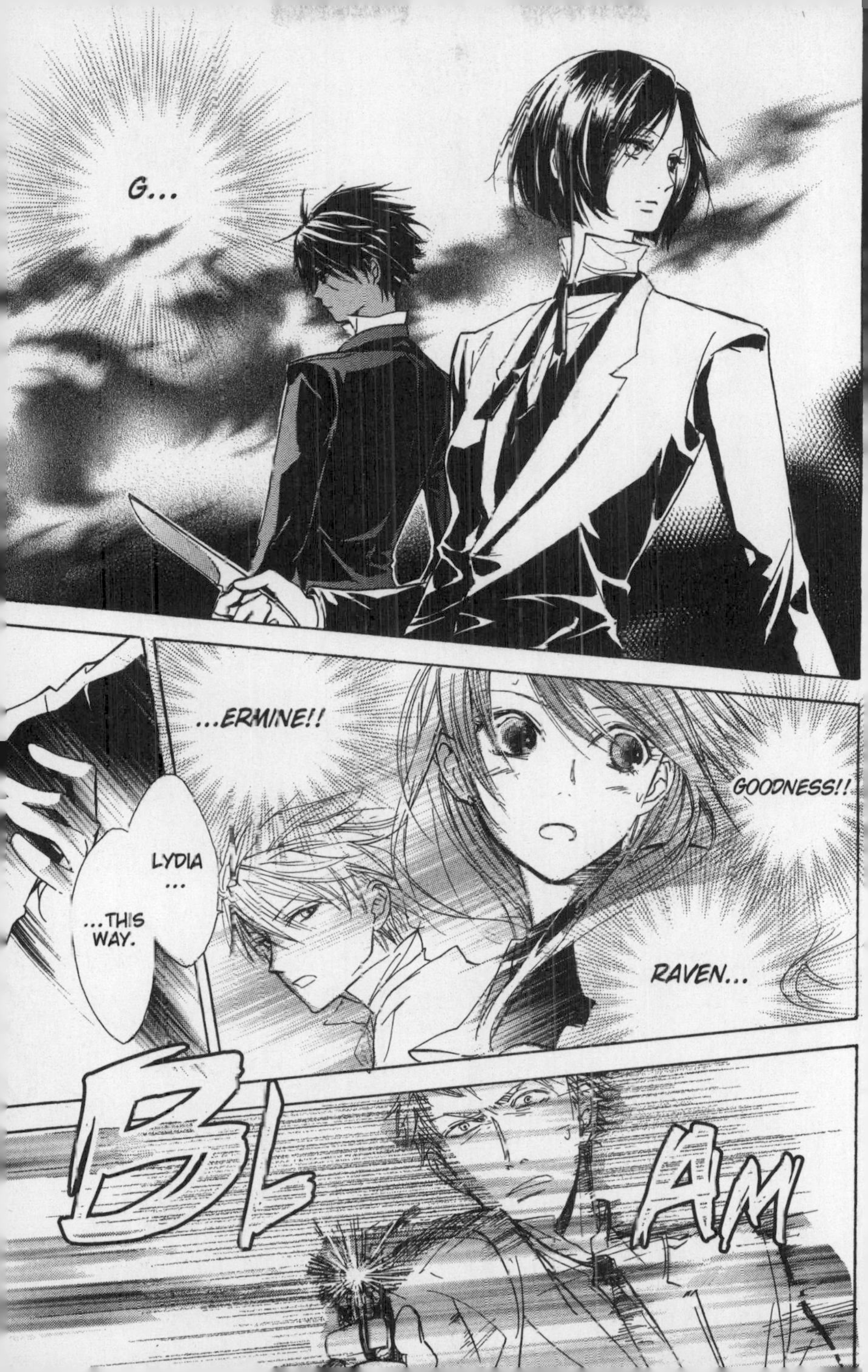
G...
...ERMINE!!
GOODNESS!!
RAVEN...
LYDIA ... ...THIS WAY.
BLAM

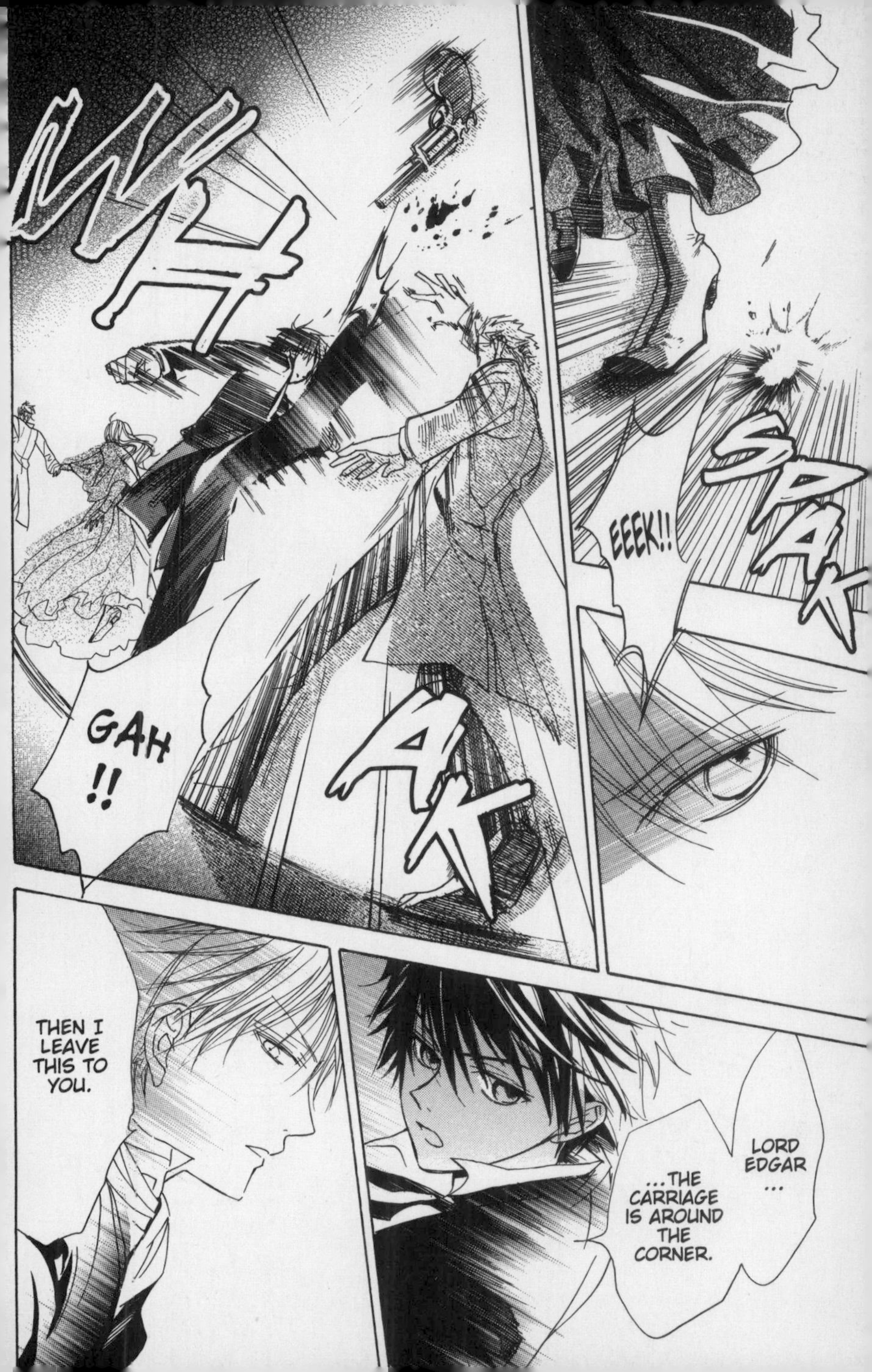
SPAK
EEEK!!
GAH !!
LORD EDGAR ...
...THE CARRIAGE IS AROUND THE CORNER.
THEN I LEAVE THIS TO YOU.

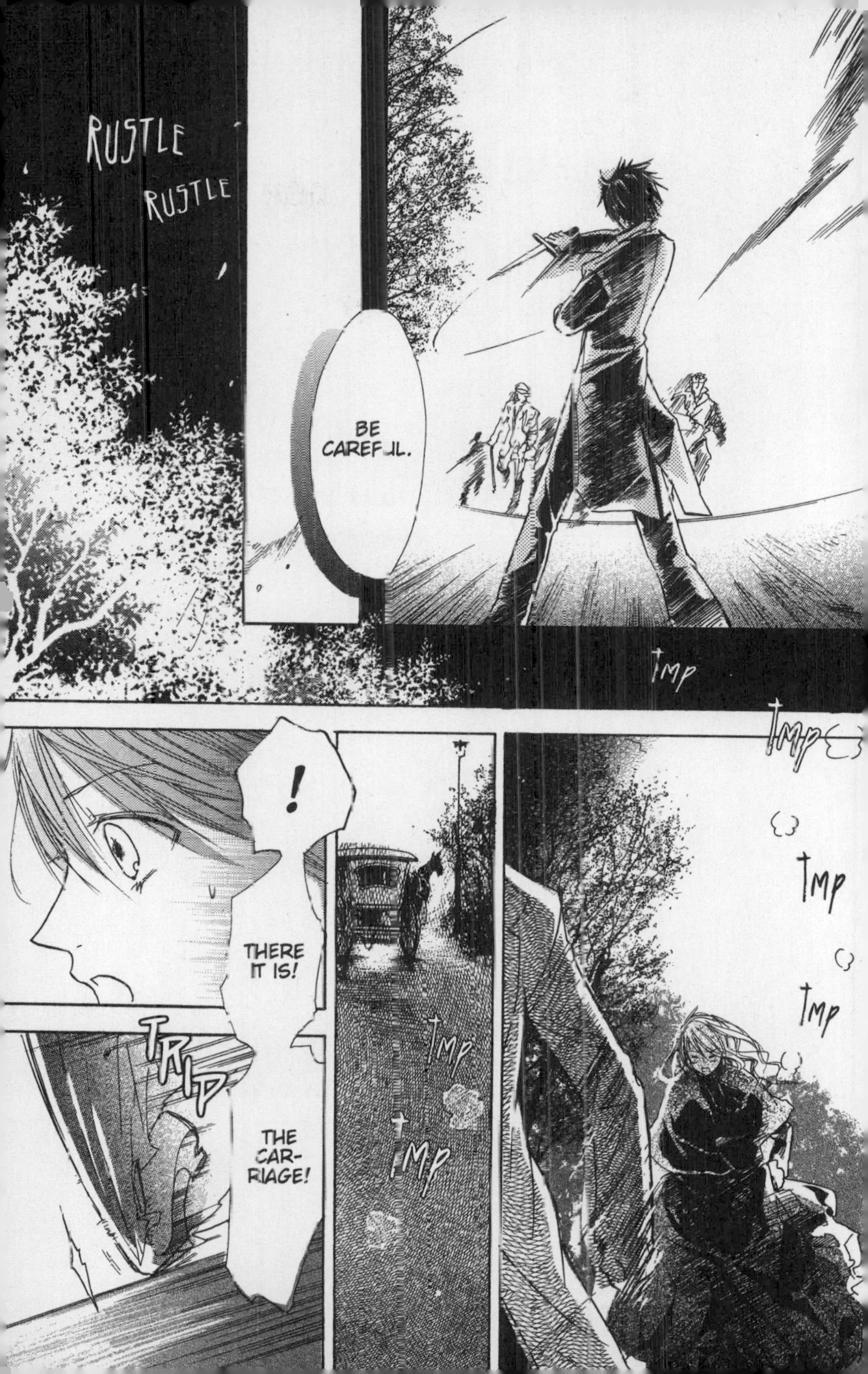
BE CAREFUL.
RUSTLE
RUSTLE
Tmp
Tmp
Tmp
Tmp
Tmp
Tmp
Tmp
!
THERE IT IS!
TRIP
THE CAR-RIAGE!

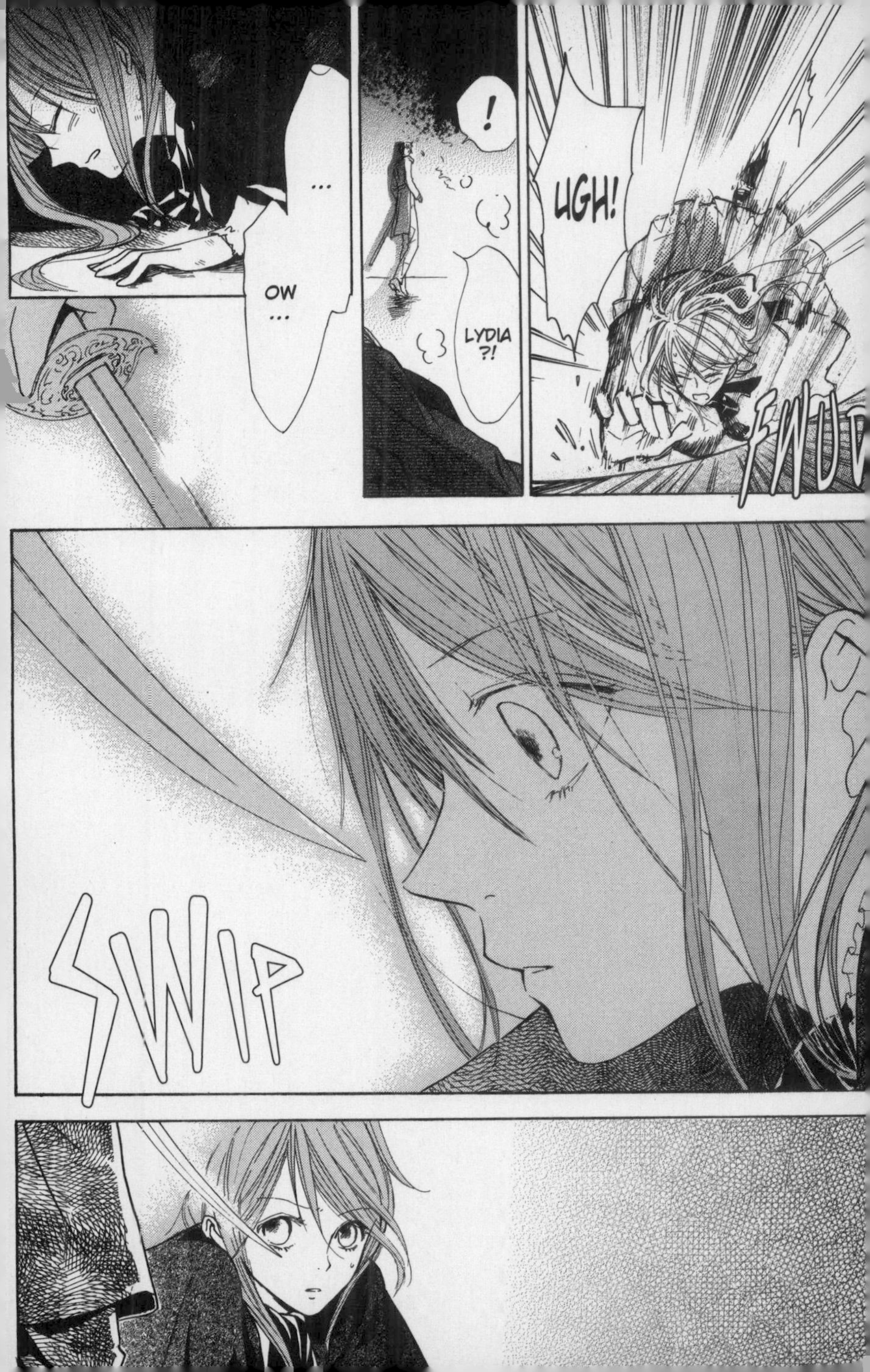
UGH!
FWUD
!
LYDIA ?!
...
OW ...
SWIP

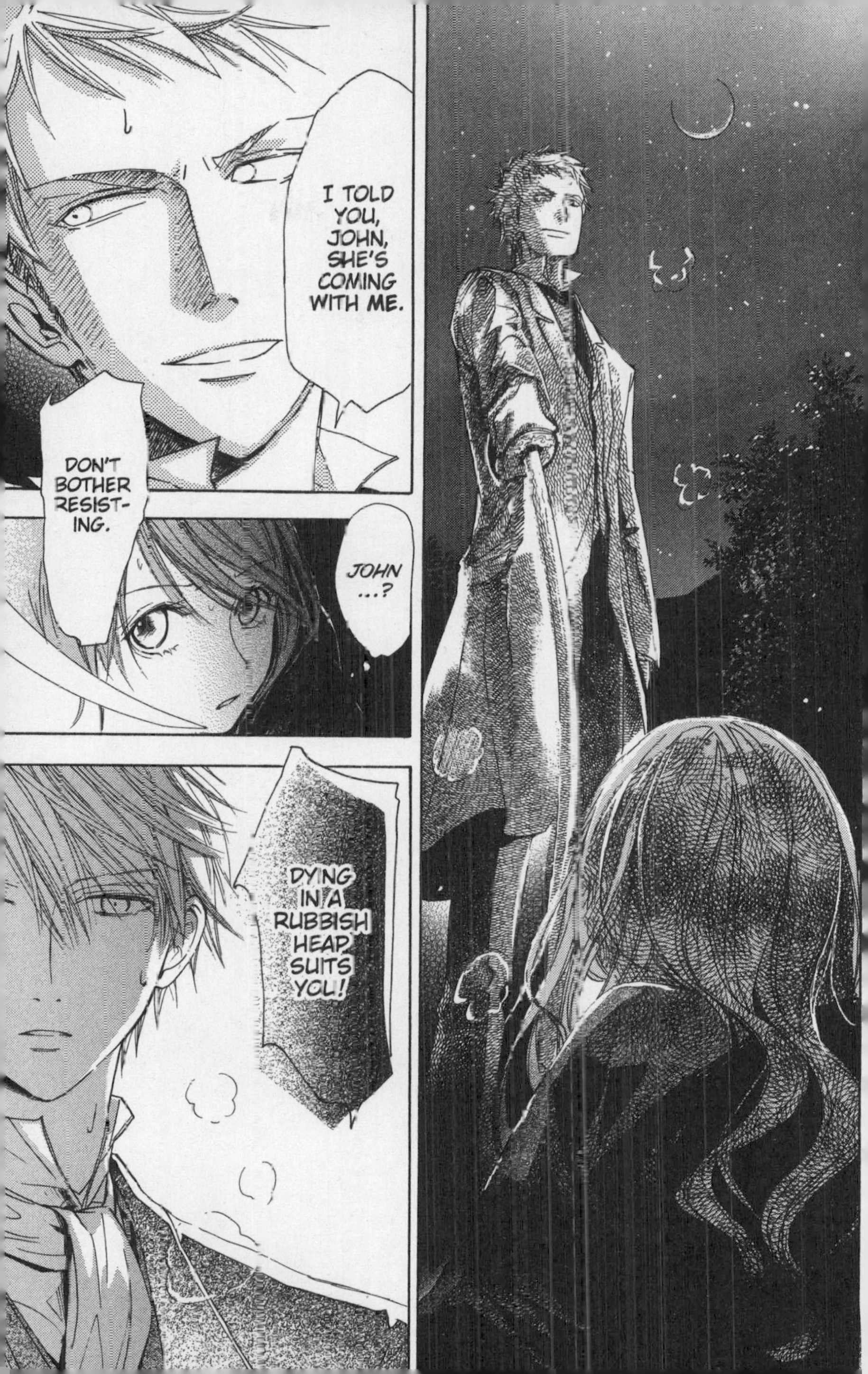
I TOLD YOU, JOHN, SHE'S COMING WITH ME.
DON'T BOTHER RESIST-ING.
JOHN ...?
DYING IN A RUBBISH HEAP SUITS YOU!

The Earl & the Fairy

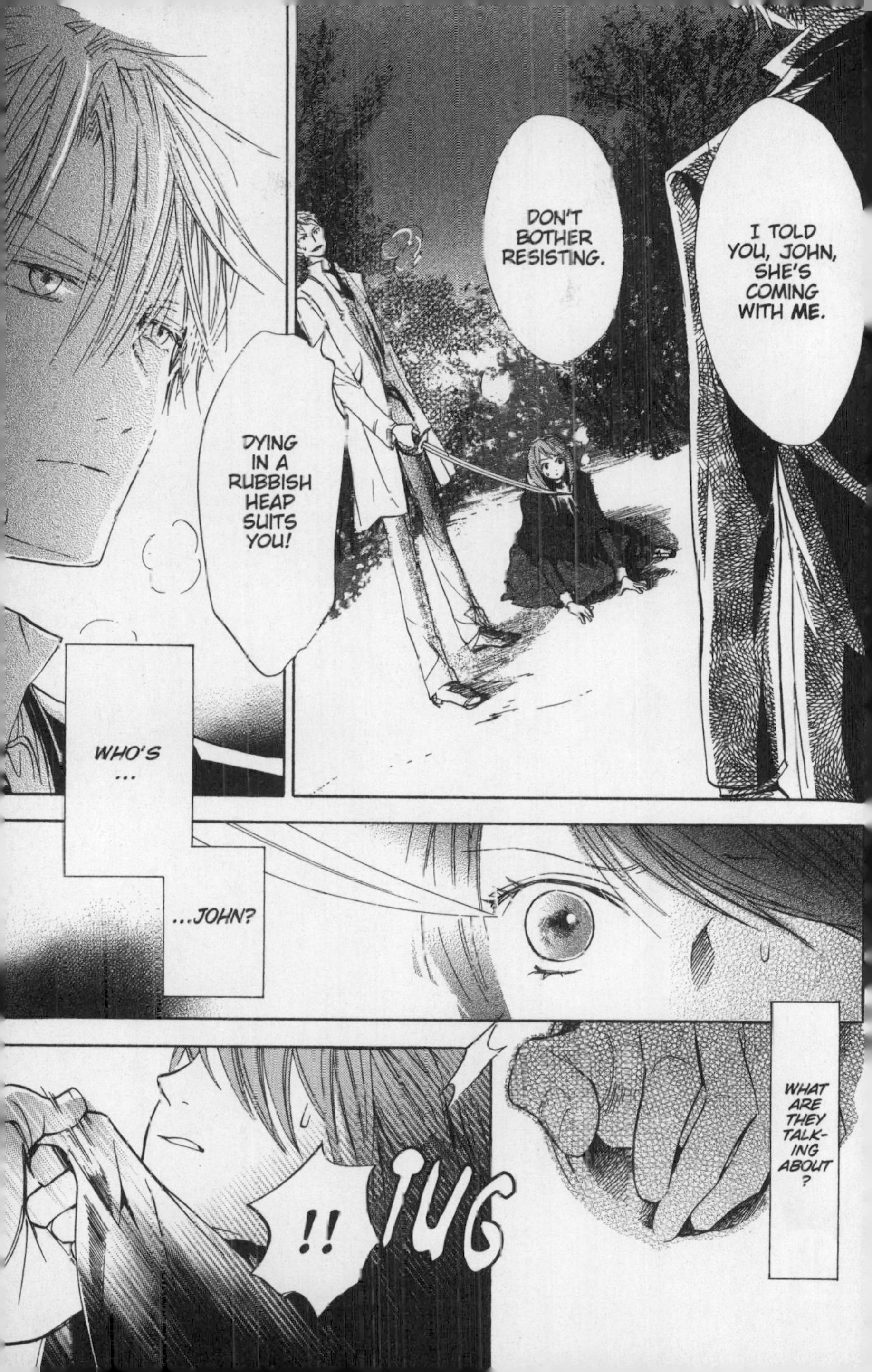

I TOLD YOU, JOHN, SHE'S COMING WITH ME.
DON'T BOTHER RESISTING.
DYING IN A RUBBISH HEAP SUITS YOU!
WHO'S ...
...JOHN?
WHAT ARE THEY TALKING ABOUT?
!!
TUG

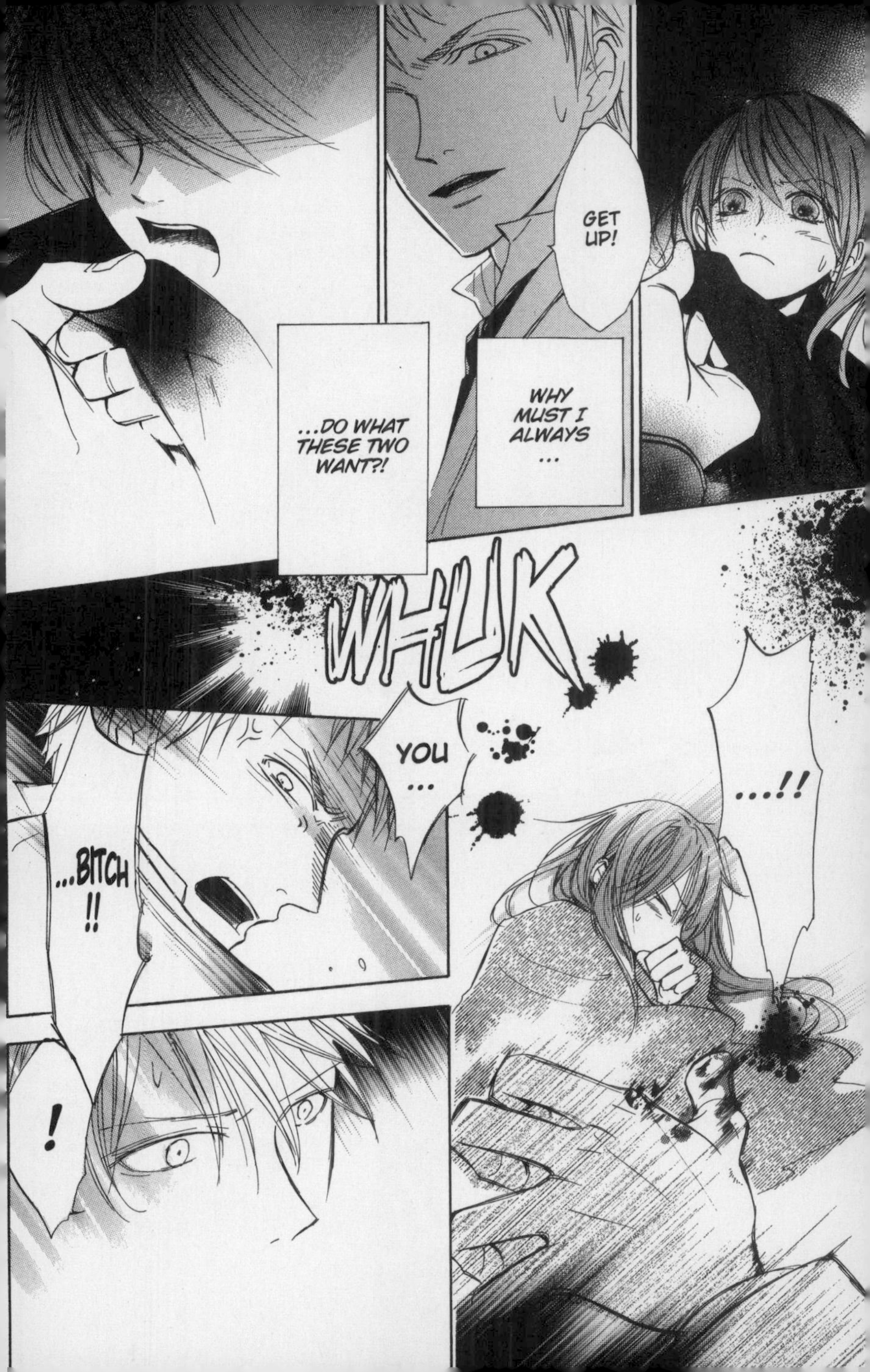
GET UP!
WHY MUST I ALWAYS ...
...DO WHAT THESE TWO WANT?!
WHUK
...!!
YOU ...
...BITCH !!
!

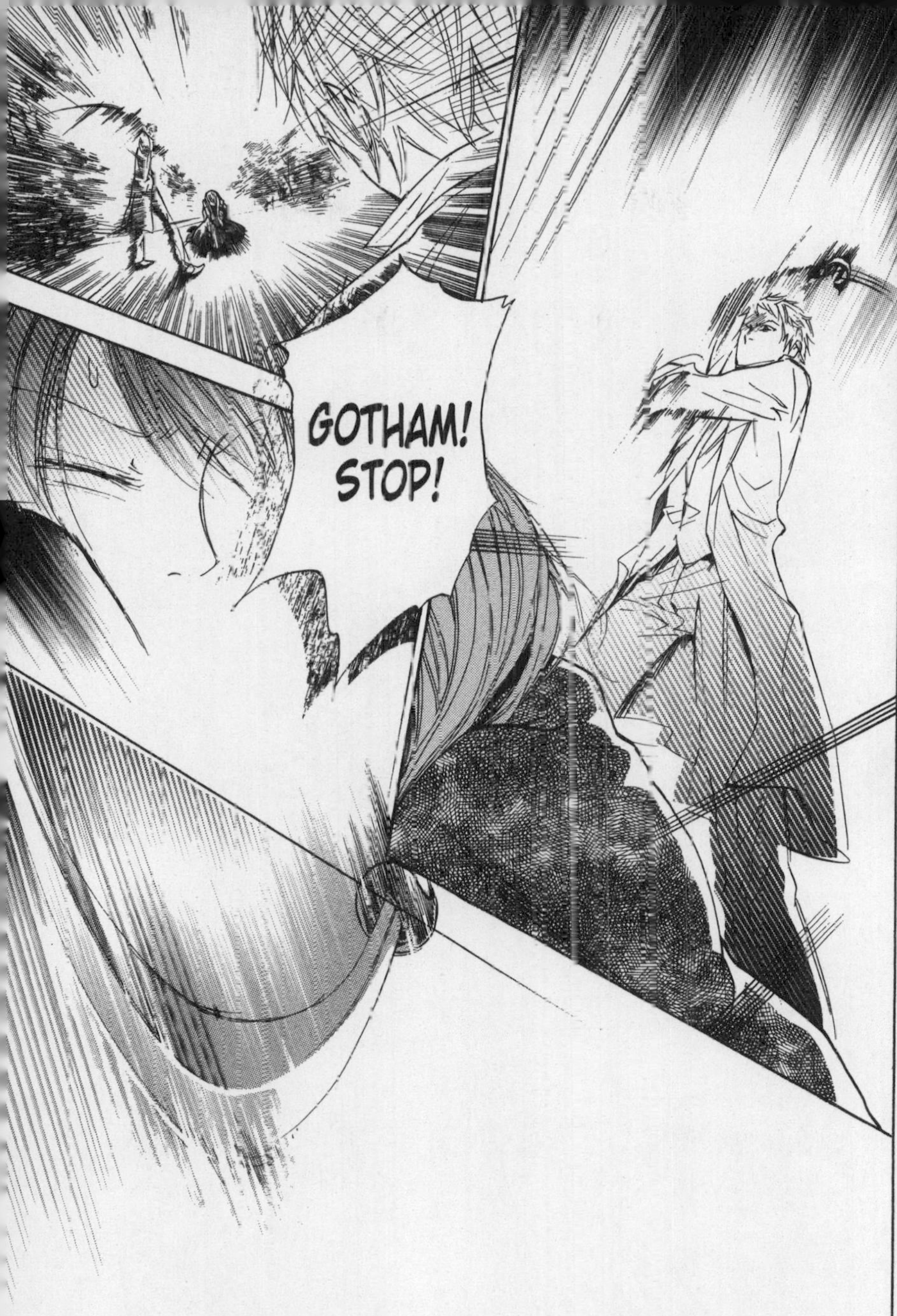
GOTHAM! STOP!

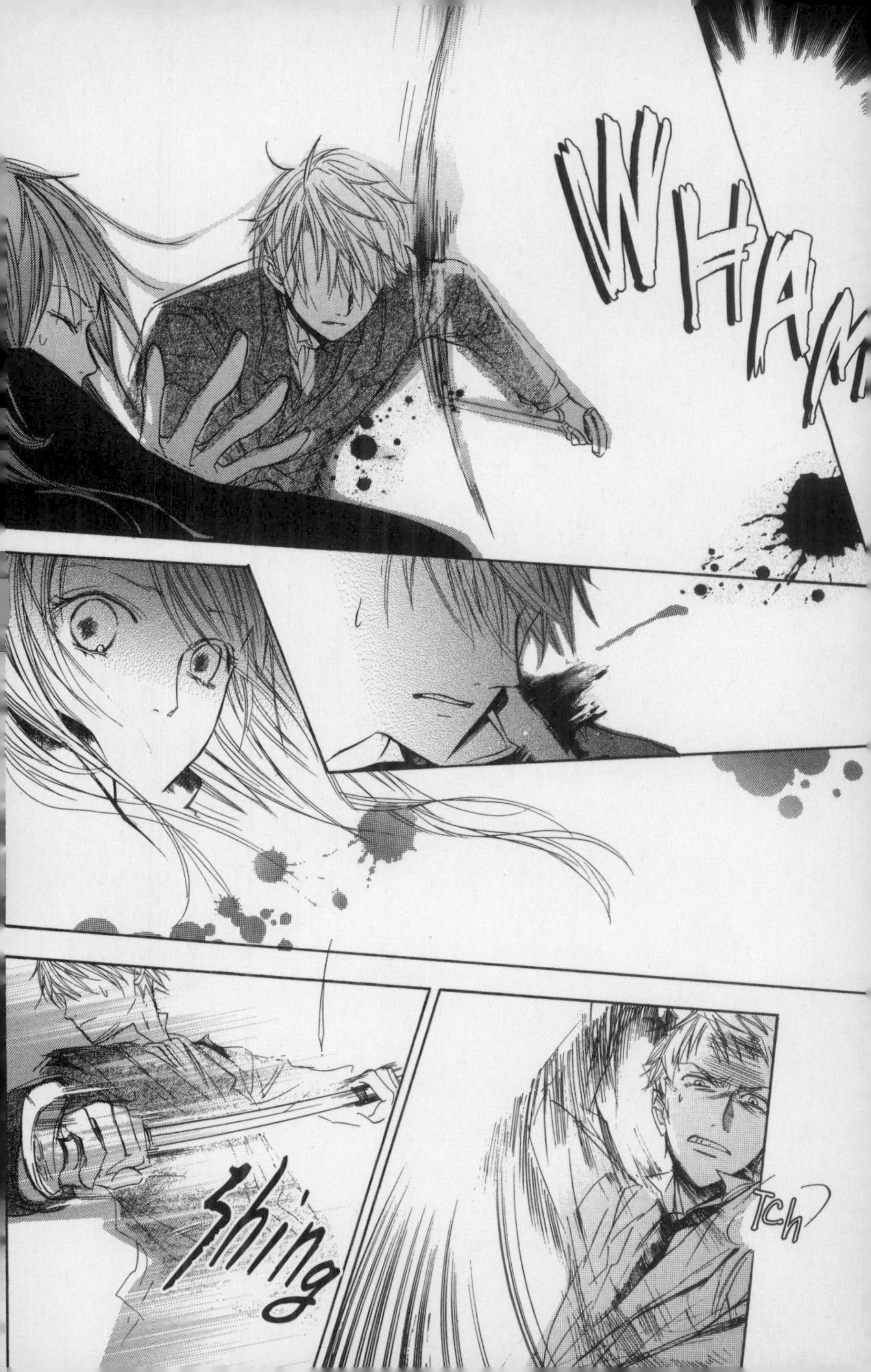
WHAM
Tch
Shing

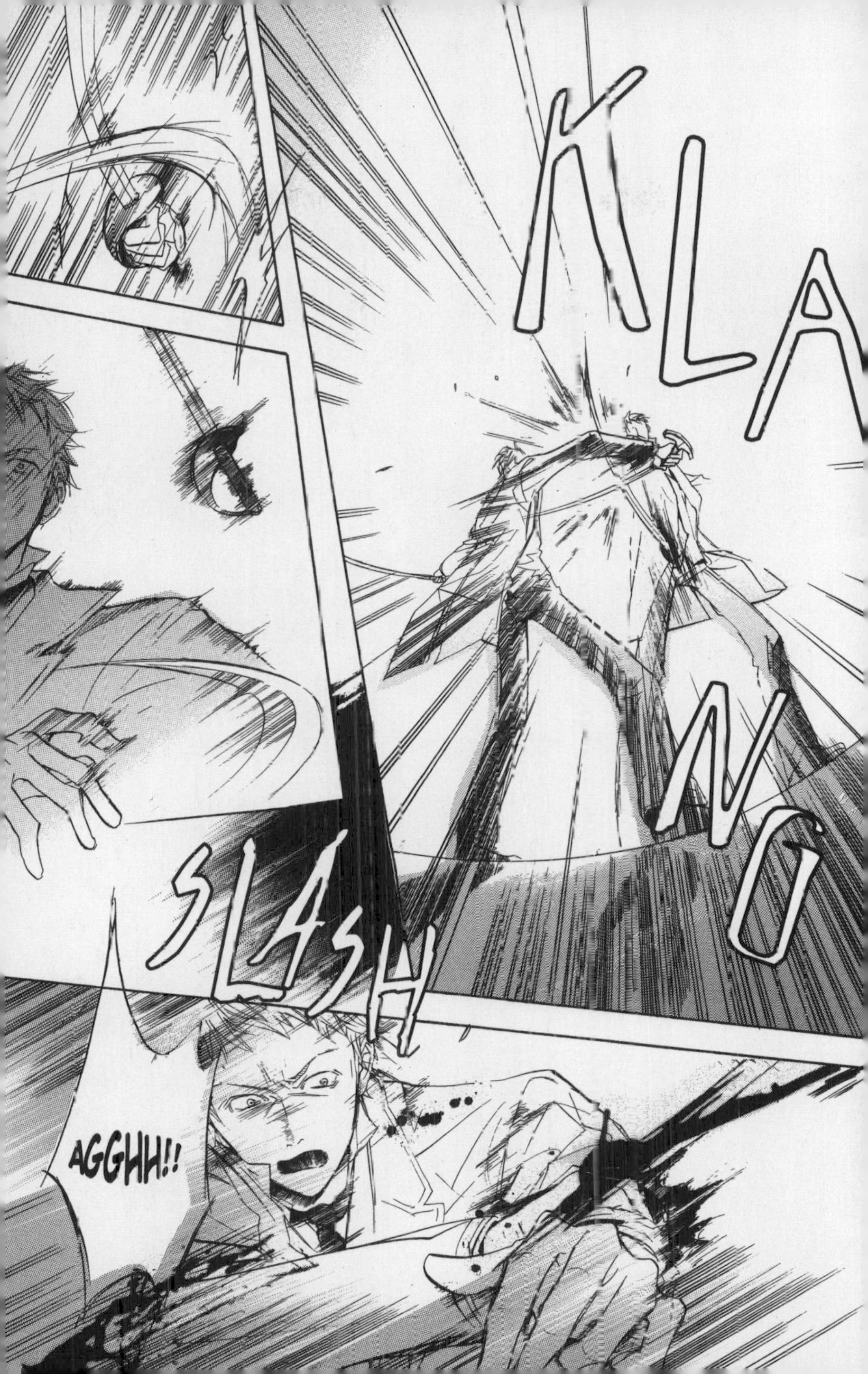
KLANG
SLASH
AGGHH!!

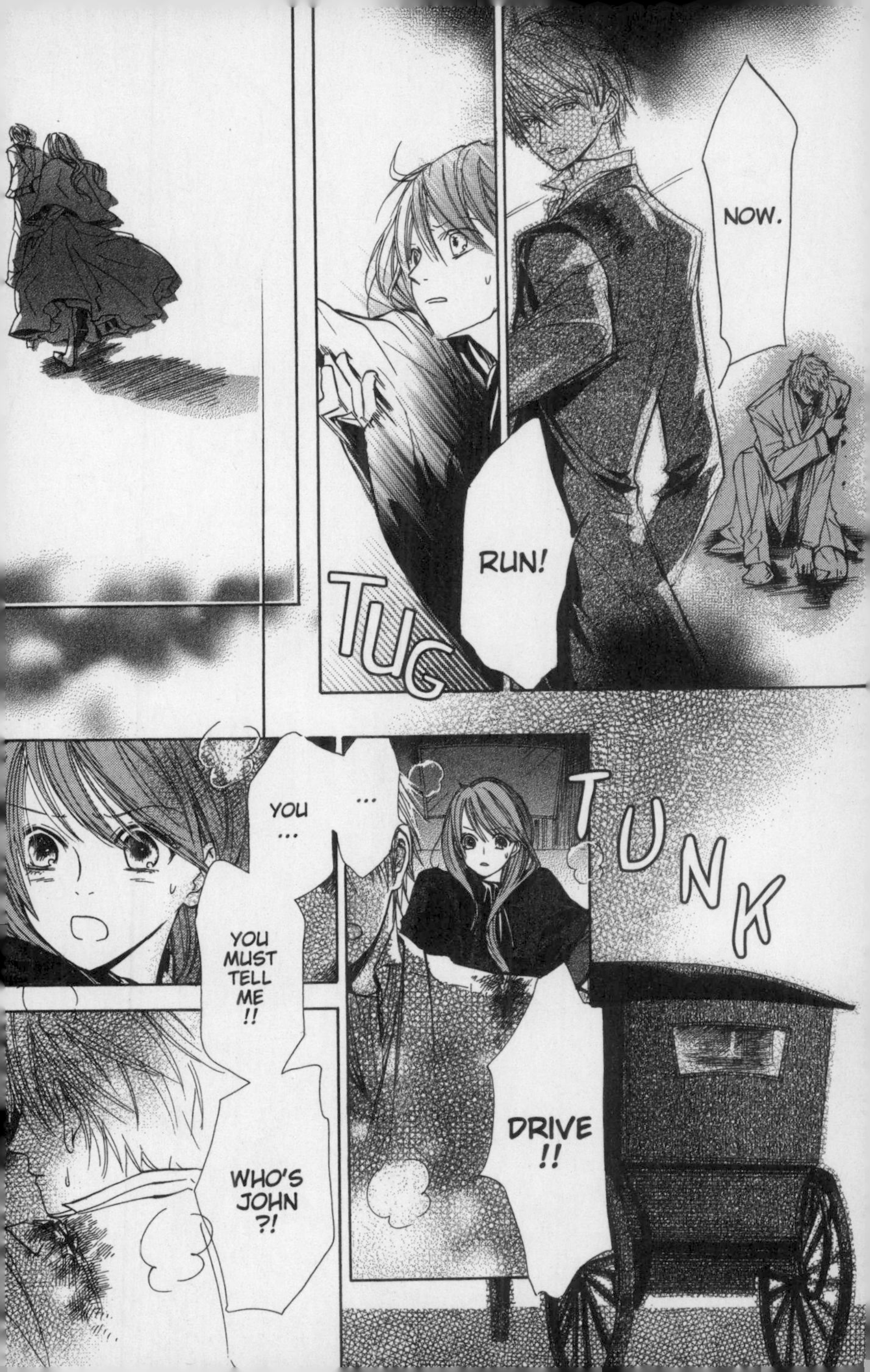

NOW.
RUN!
TUG
TUNK
...
DRIVE!!
YOU ...
YOU MUST TELL ME!!
WHO'S JOHN?!

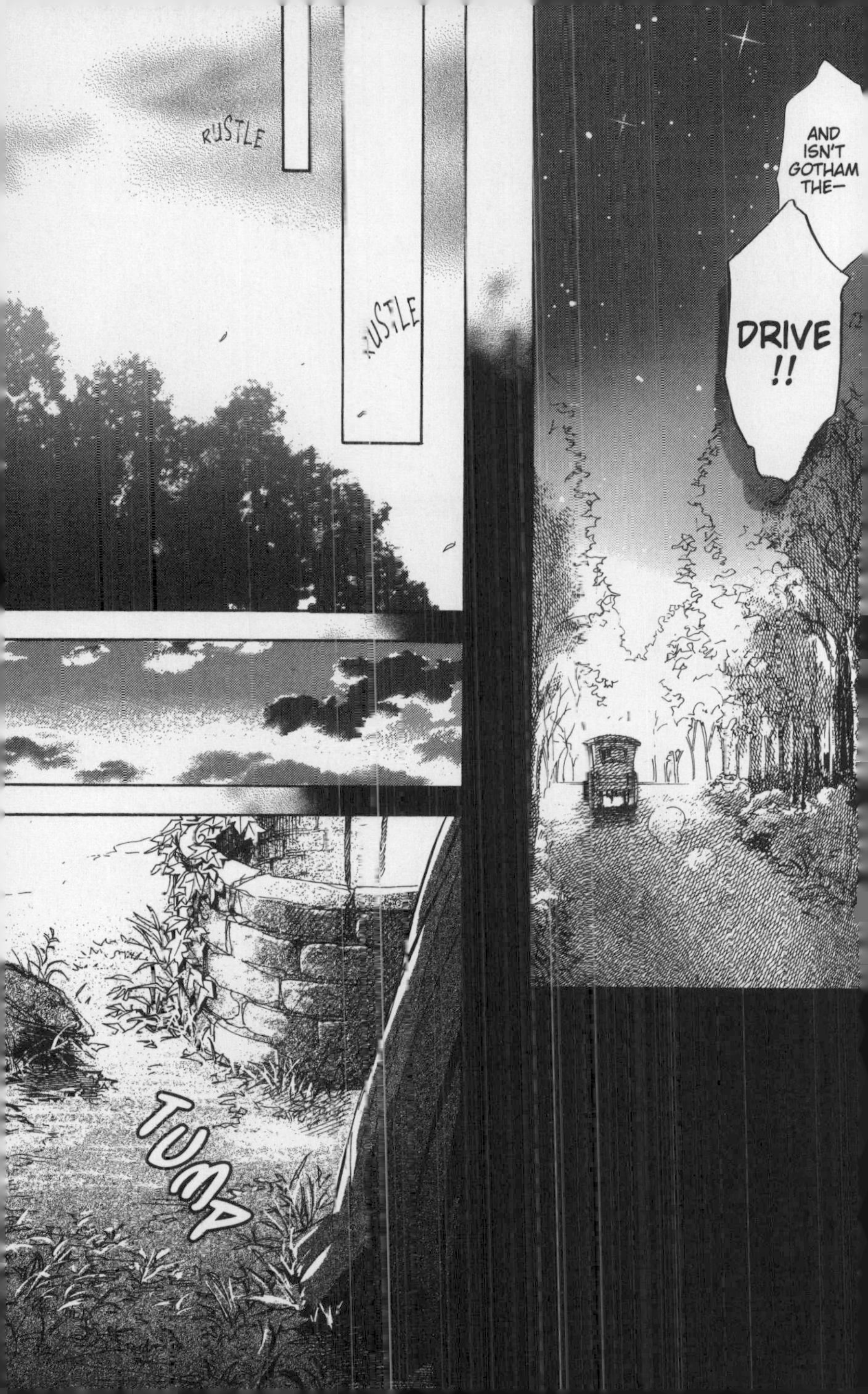
AND ISN'T GOTHAM THE—
DRIVE !!
RUSTLE
RUSTLE
TUMP

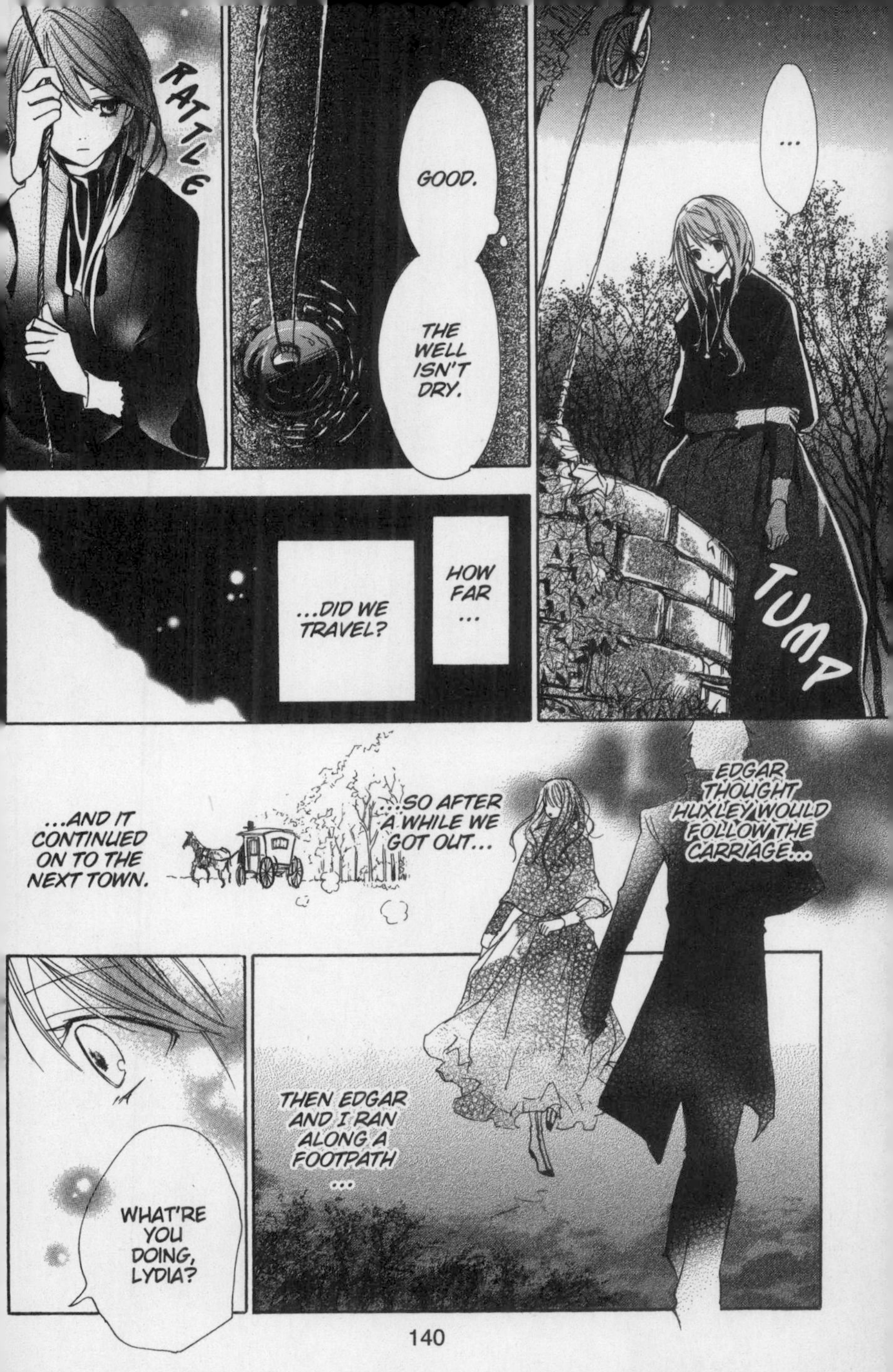
...
TUMP
GOOD.
THE WELL ISN'T DRY.
RATTLE
HOW FAR...
...DID WE TRAVEL?
EDGAR THOUGHT HUXLEY WOULD FOLLOW THE CARRIAGE...
...SO AFTER A WHILE WE GOT OUT...
...AND IT CONTINUED ON TO THE NEXT TOWN.
THEN EDGAR AND I RAN ALONG A FOOTPATH...
WHAT'RE YOU DOING, LYDIA?

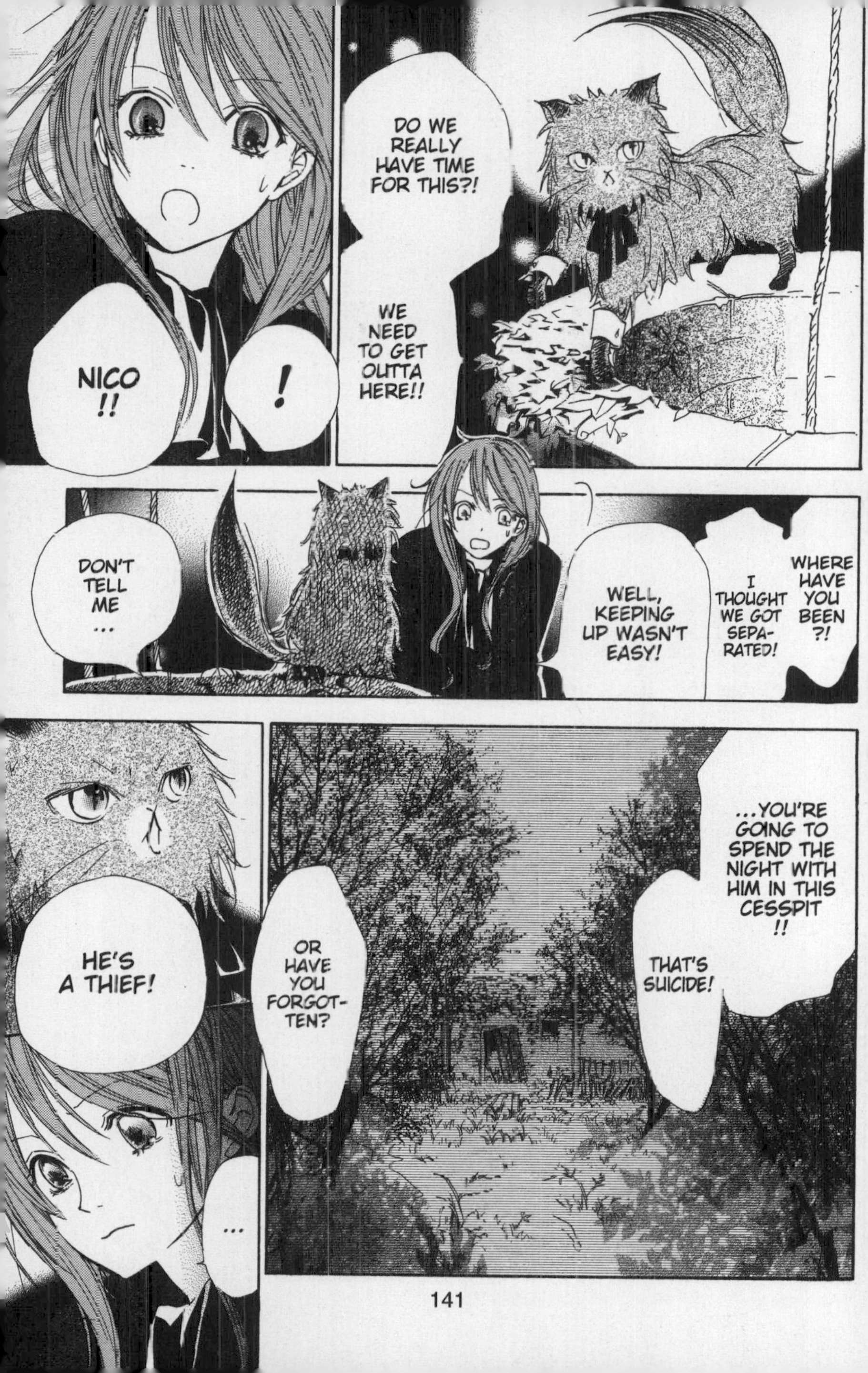
DO WE REALLY HAVE TIME FOR THIS?!
WE NEED TO GET OUTTA HERE!!
!
NICO!!
WHERE HAVE YOU BEEN?!
I THOUGHT WE GOT SEPA-RATED!
WELL, KEEPING UP WASN'T EASY!
DON'T TELL ME ...
...YOU'RE GOING TO SPEND THE NIGHT WITH HIM IN THIS CESSPIT!!
THAT'S SUICIDE!
OR HAVE YOU FORGOT-TEN?
HE'S A THIEF!
...

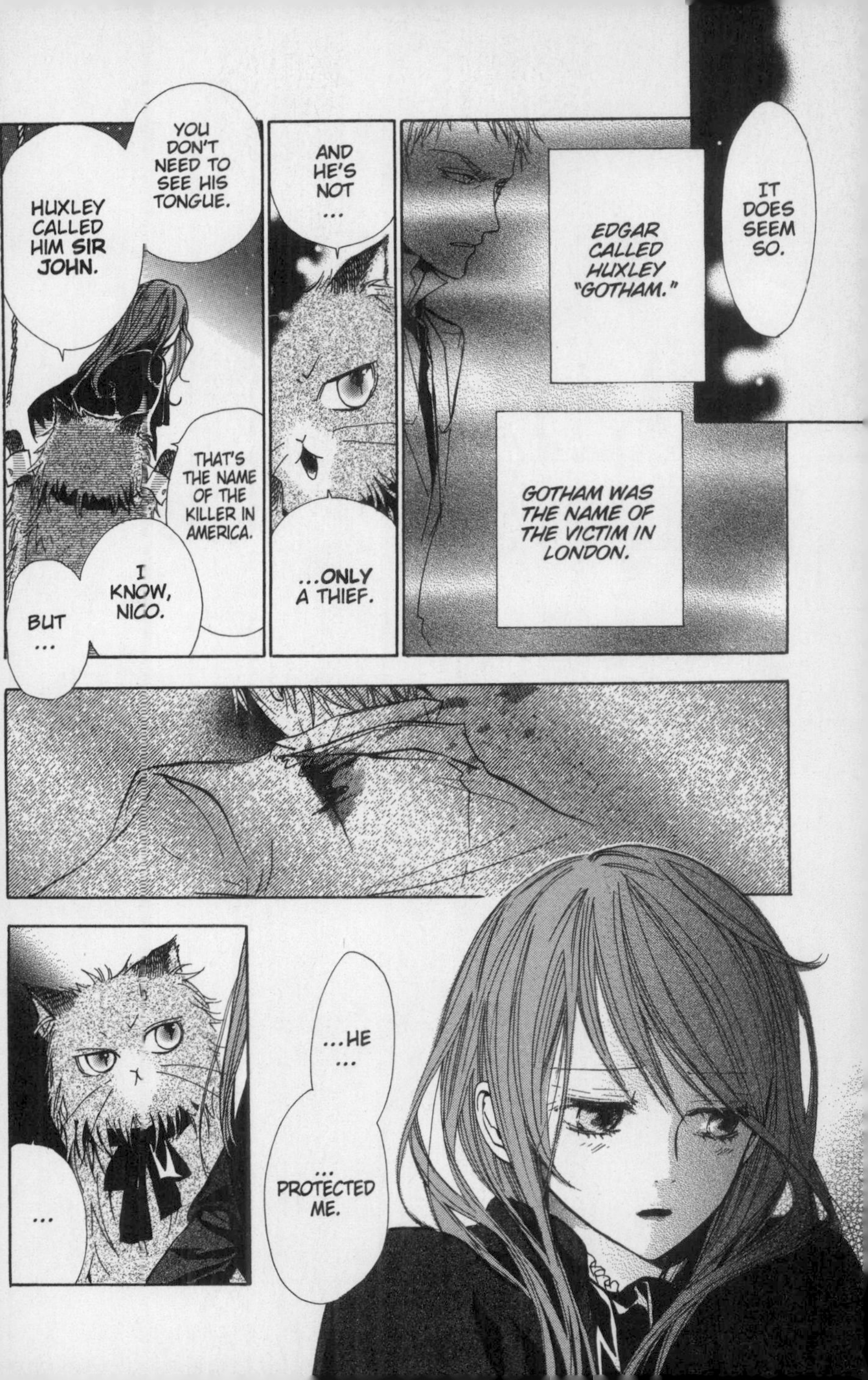
IT DOES SEEM SO.
EDGAR CALLED HUXLEY "GOTHAM."
GOTHAM WAS THE NAME OF THE VICTIM IN LONDON.
AND HE'S NOT ...
...ONLY A THIEF.
YOU DON'T NEED TO SEE HIS TONGUE.
HUXLEY CALLED HIM SIR JOHN.
THAT'S THE NAME OF THE KILLER IN AMERICA.
I KNOW, NICO.
BUT ...
...HE ...
... PROTECTED ME.
...

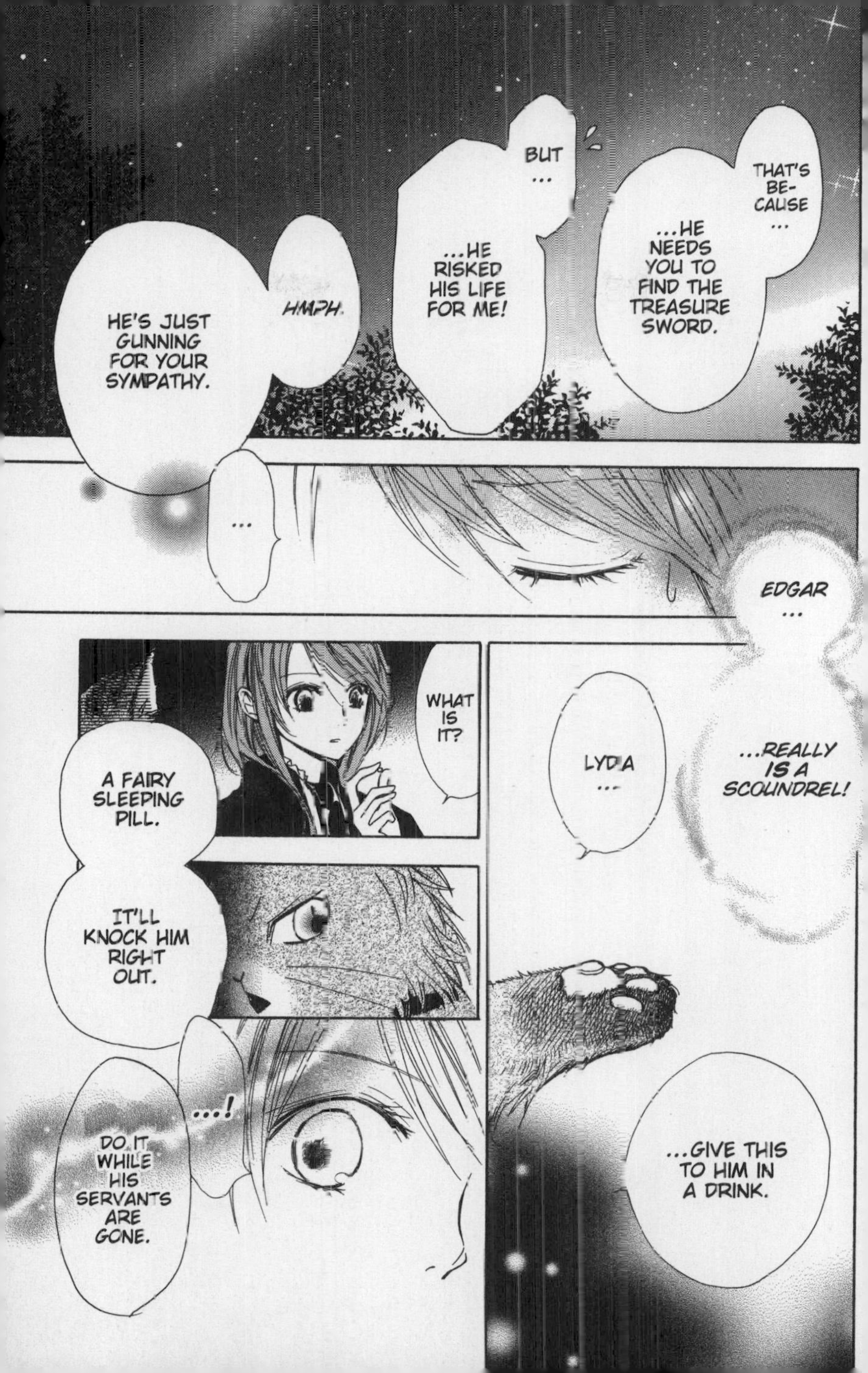
THAT'S BE-CAUSE ...
...HE NEEDS YOU TO FIND THE TREASURE SWORD.
BUT ...
...HE RISKED HIS LIFE FOR ME!
HMPH.
HE'S JUST GUNNING FOR YOUR SYMPATHY.
EDGAR ...
...
...REALLY IS A SCOUNDREL!
LYDIA ...
WHAT IS IT?
A FAIRY SLEEPING PILL.
IT'LL KNOCK HIM RIGHT OUT.
...GIVE THIS TO HIM IN A DRINK.
...!
DO IT WHILE HIS SERVANTS ARE GONE.

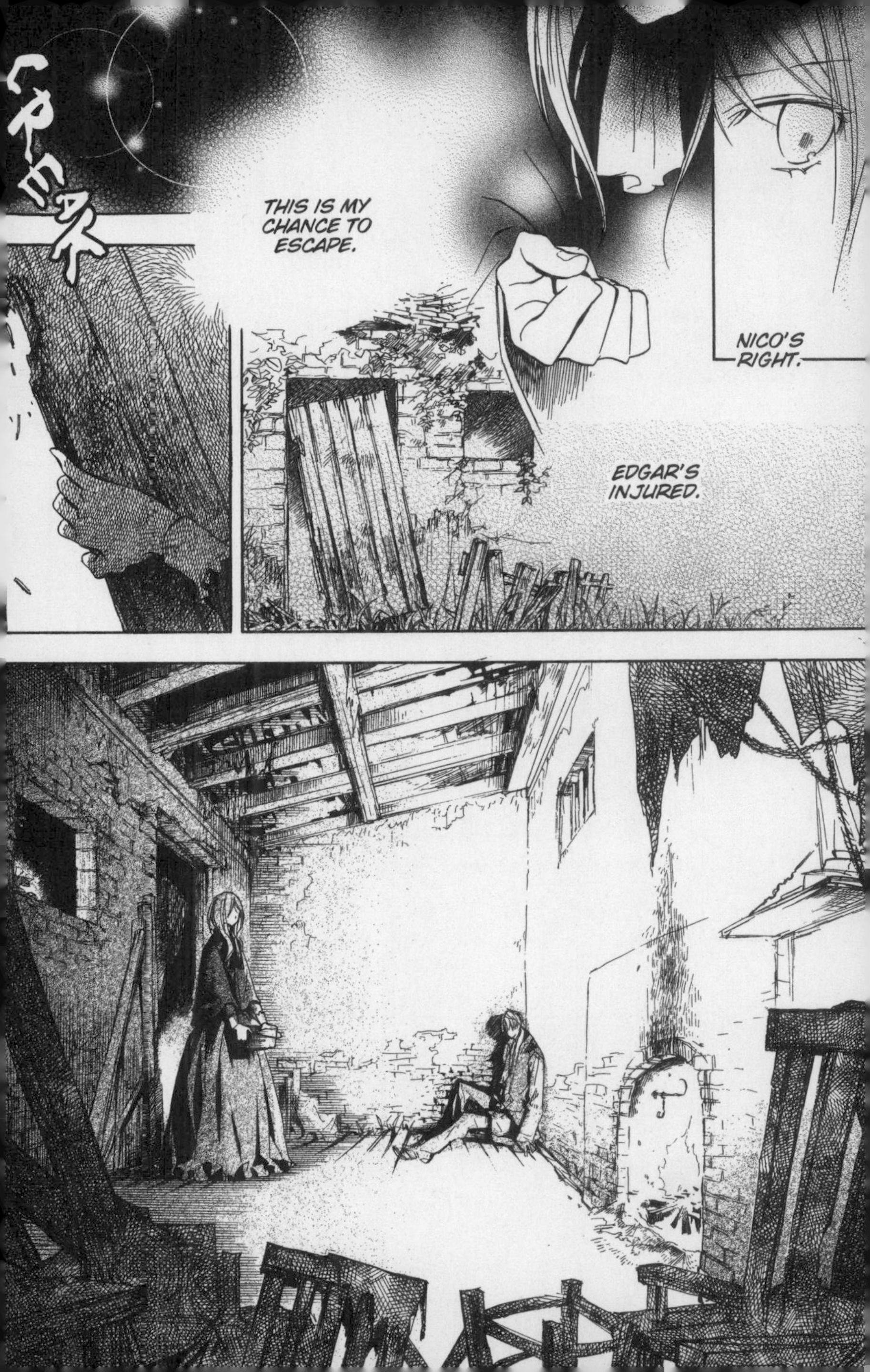
NICO'S RIGHT.
THIS IS MY CHANCE TO ESCAPE.
EDGAR'S INJURED.
CREAK

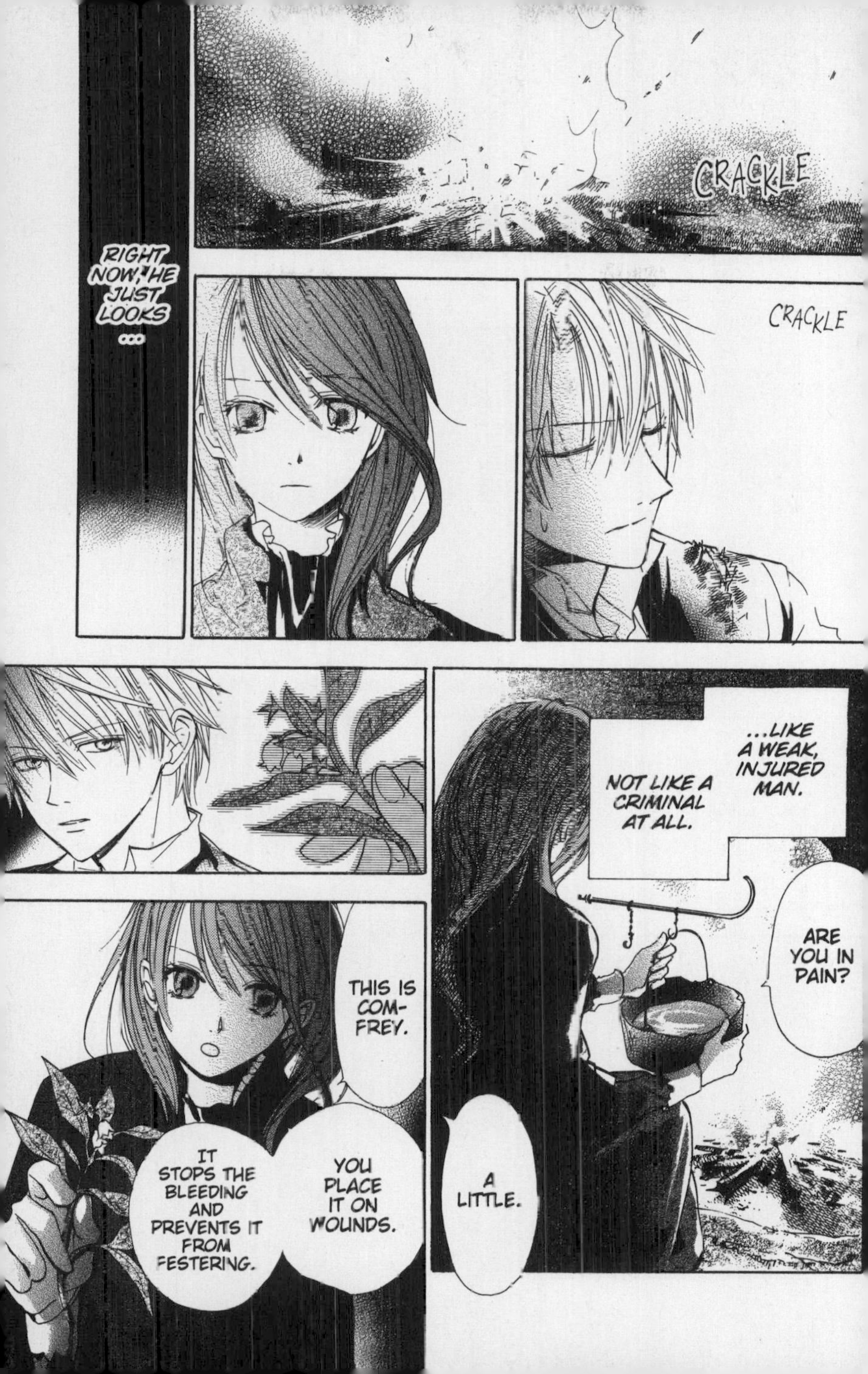
CRACKLE
CRACKLE
RIGHT NOW, HE JUST LOOKS...
NOT LIKE A CRIMINAL AT ALL.
...LIKE A WEAK, INJURED MAN.
ARE YOU IN PAIN?
A LITTLE.
THIS IS COM-FREY.
YOU PLACE IT ON WOUNDS.
IT STOPS THE BLEEDING AND PREVENTS IT FROM FESTERING.

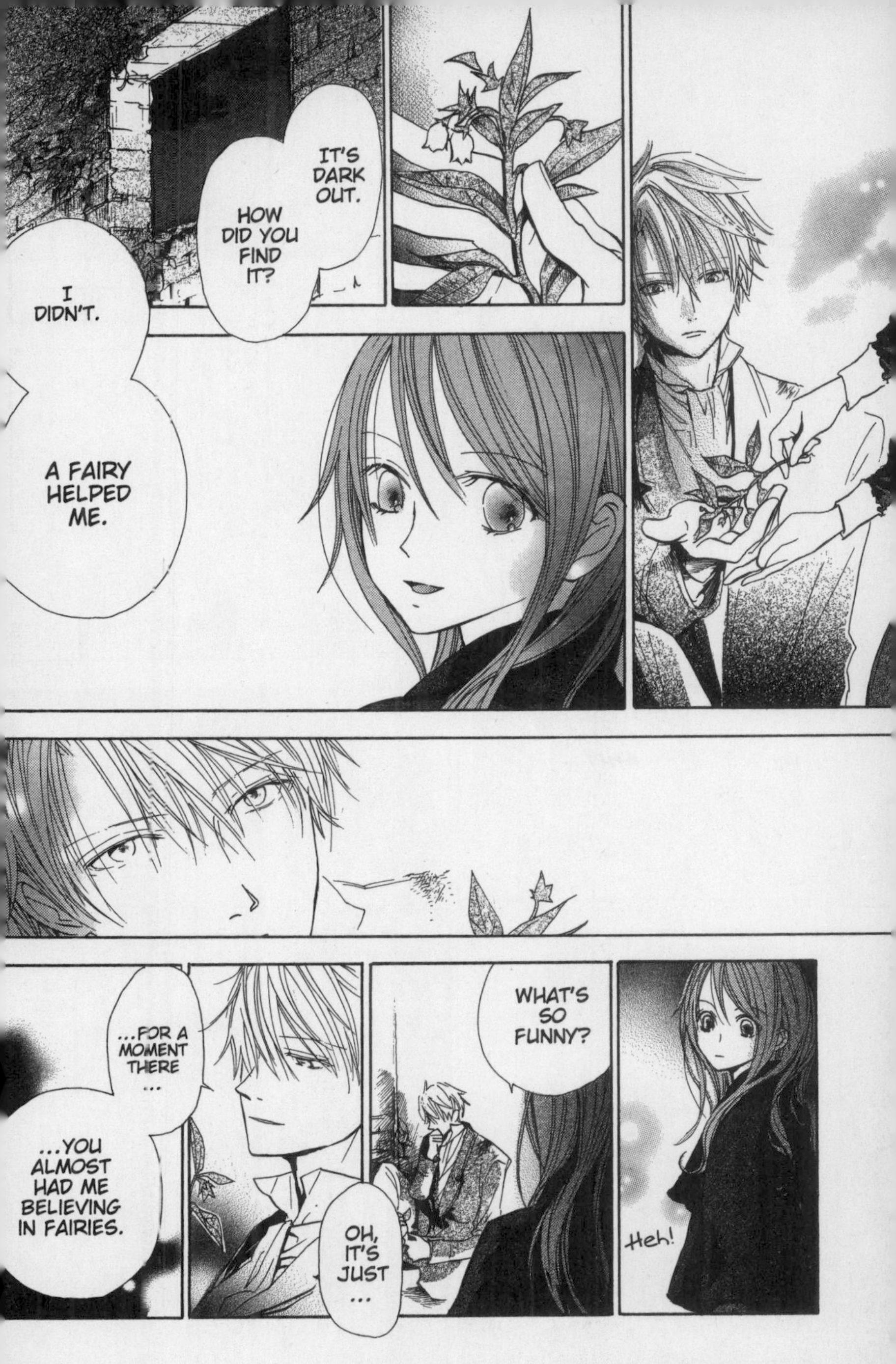
IT'S DARK OUT.
HOW DID YOU FIND IT?
I DIDN'T.
A FAIRY HELPED ME.
Heh!
WHAT'S SO FUNNY?
OH, IT'S JUST ...
...FOR A MOMENT THERE ...
...YOU ALMOST HAD ME BELIEVING IN FAIRIES.

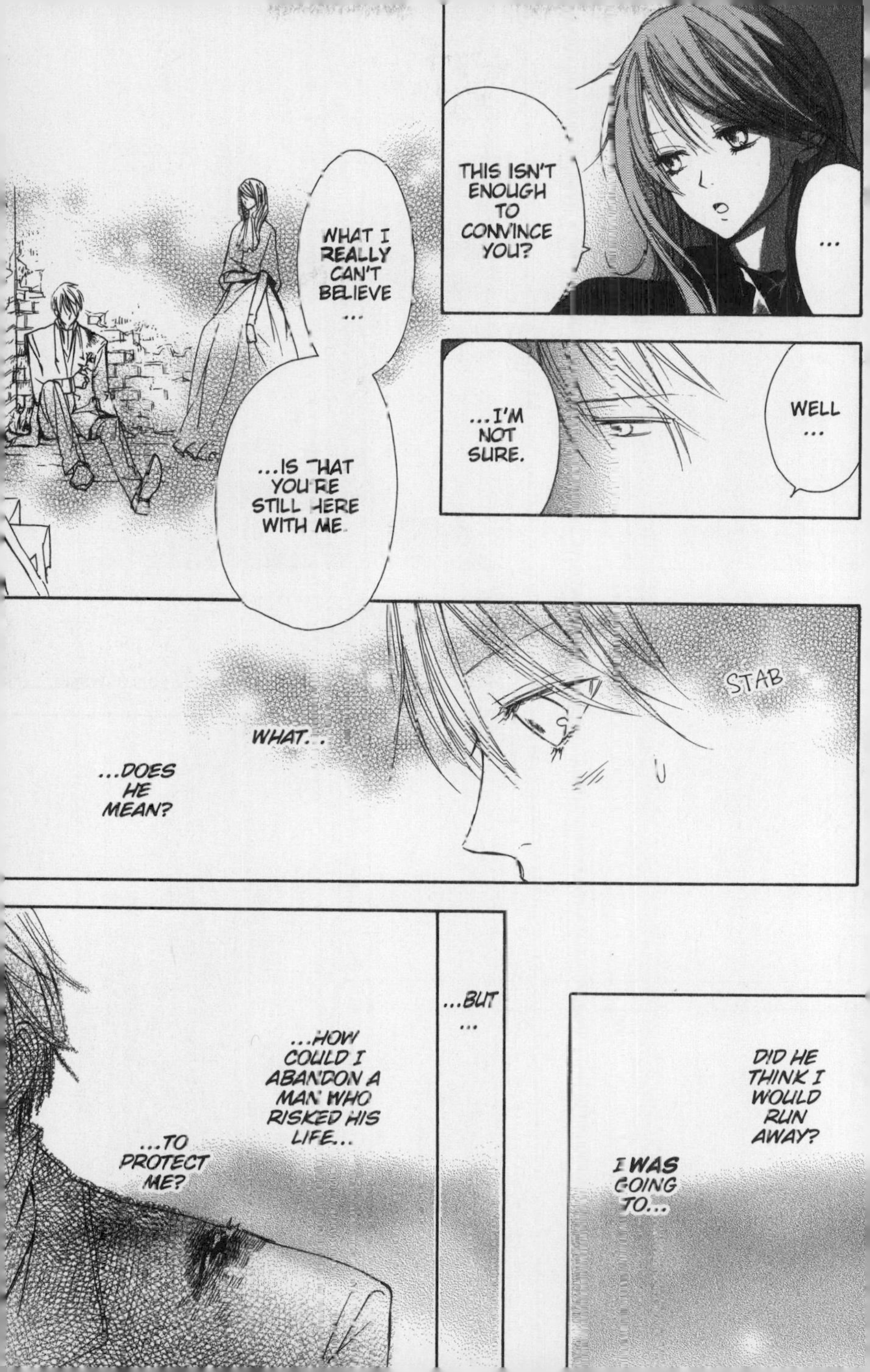
THIS ISN'T ENOUGH TO CONVINCE YOU?
...
WELL ...
...I'M NOT SURE.
WHAT I REALLY CAN'T BELIEVE ...
...IS THAT YOU'RE STILL HERE WITH ME.
STAB
WHAT...
...DOES HE MEAN?
DID HE THINK I WOULD RUN AWAY?
I WAS GOING TO...
...BUT ...
...HOW COULD I ABANDON A MAN WHO RISKED HIS LIFE...
...TO PROTECT ME?

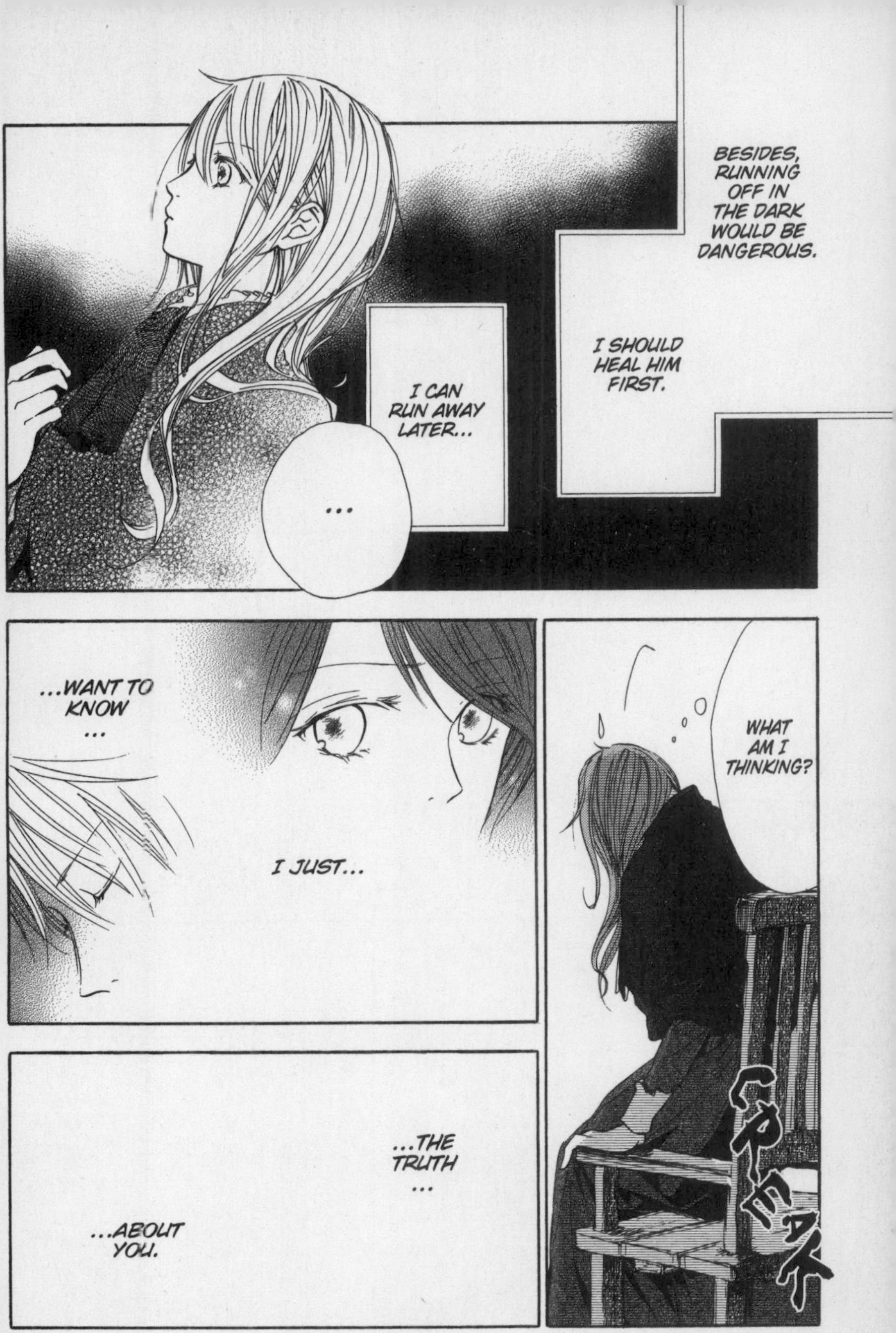
BESIDES, RUNNING OFF IN THE DARK WOULD BE DANGEROUS.
I SHOULD HEAL HIM FIRST.
I CAN RUN AWAY LATER...
...
WHAT AM I THINKING?
CREAK
I JUST...
...WANT TO KNOW ...
...THE TRUTH ...
...ABOUT YOU.

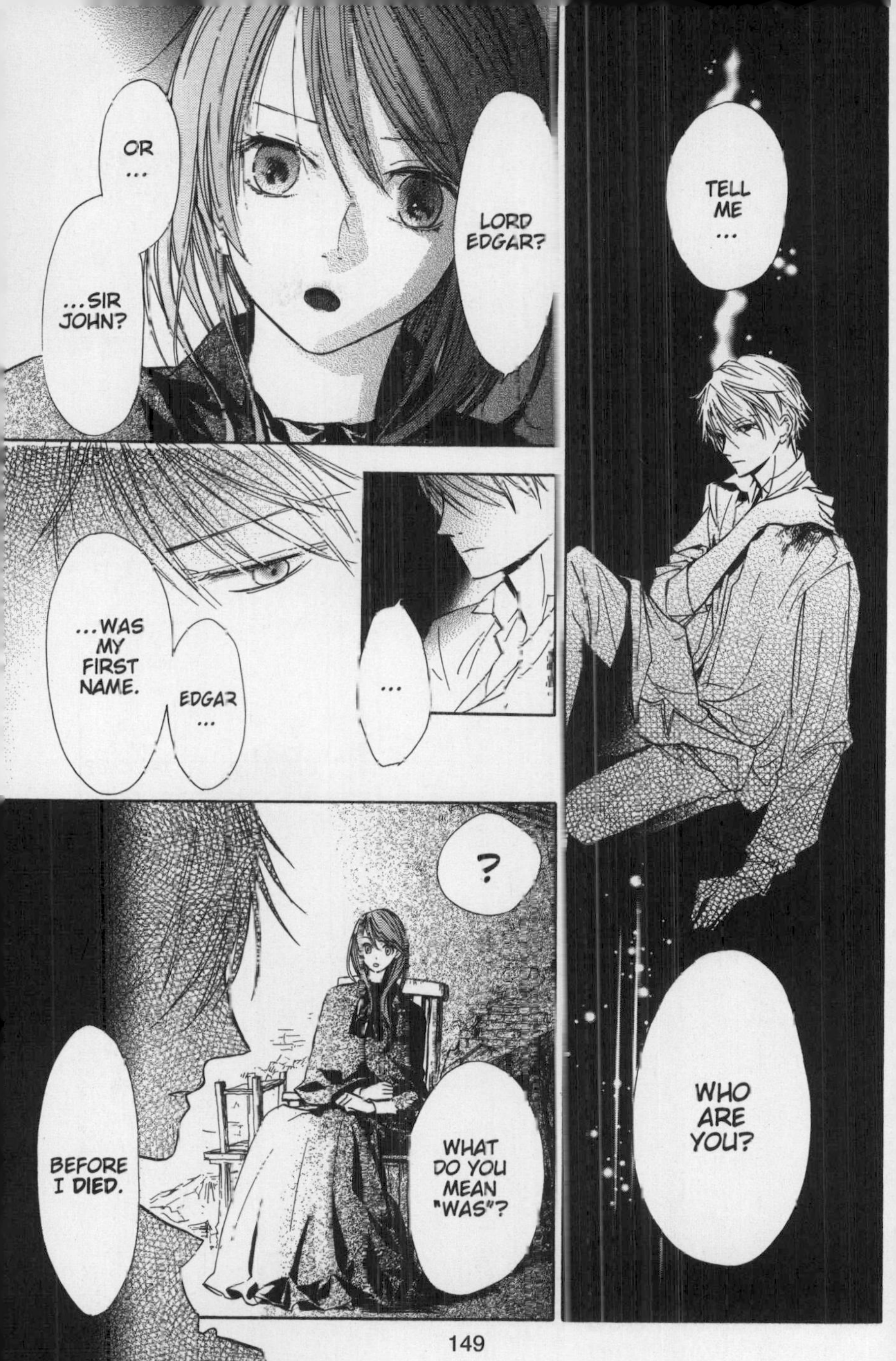
TELL ME ...
WHO ARE YOU?
LORD EDGAR?
OR ...
...SIR JOHN?
...
EDGAR ...
...WAS MY FIRST NAME.
?
WHAT DO YOU MEAN "WAS"?
BEFORE I DIED.

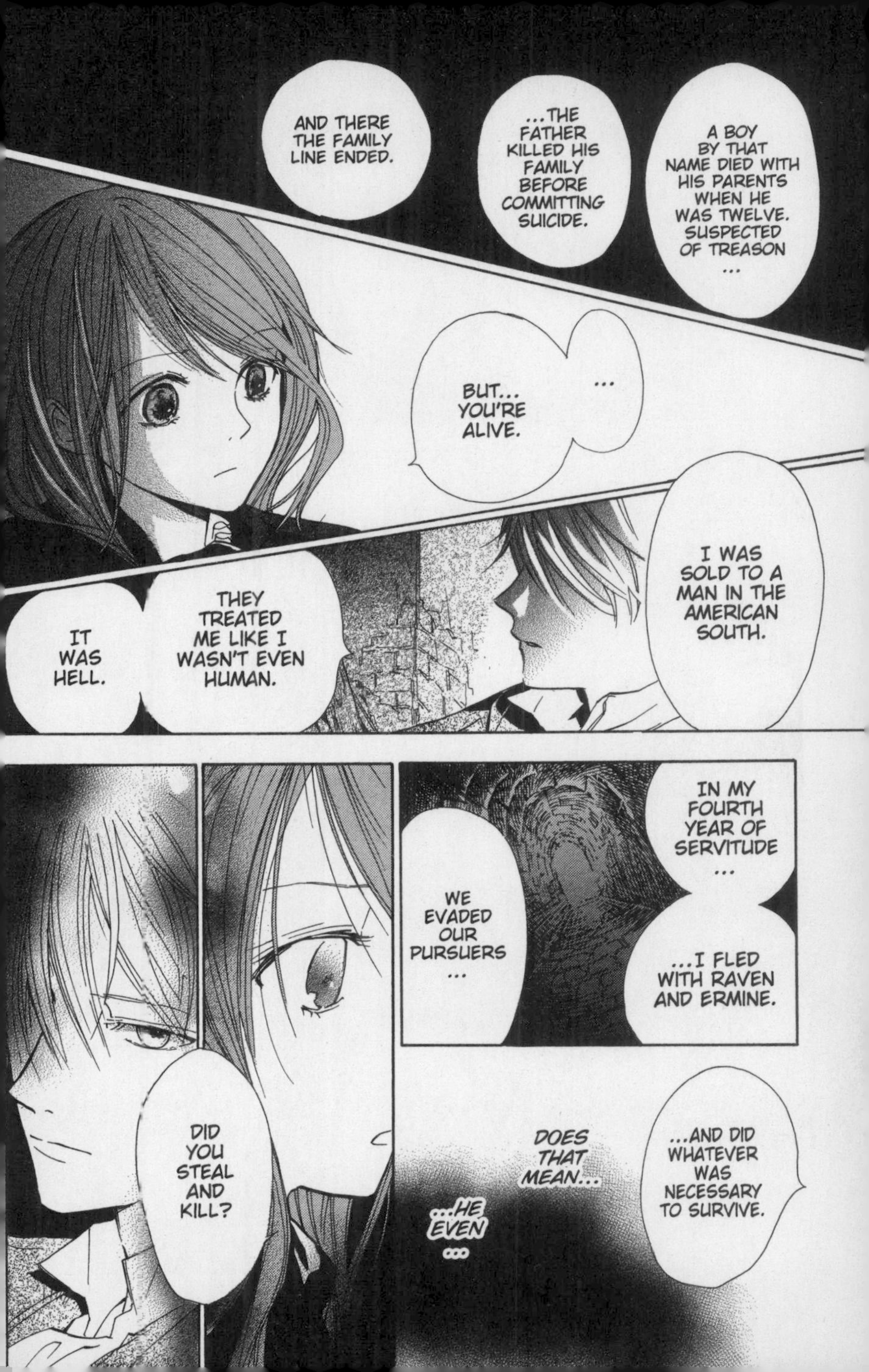
A BOY BY THAT NAME DIED WITH HIS PARENTS WHEN HE WAS TWELVE. SUSPECTED OF TREASON ...
...THE FATHER KILLED HIS FAMILY BEFORE COMMITTING SUICIDE.
AND THERE THE FAMILY LINE ENDED.
...
BUT... YOU'RE ALIVE.
I WAS SOLD TO A MAN IN THE AMERICAN SOUTH.
THEY TREATED ME LIKE I WASN'T EVEN HUMAN.
IT WAS HELL.
IN MY FOURTH YEAR OF SERVITUDE ...
...I FLED WITH RAVEN AND ERMINE.
WE EVADED OUR PURSUERS ...
...AND DID WHATEVER WAS NECESSARY TO SURVIVE.
DOES THAT MEAN...
...HE EVEN ...
DID YOU STEAL AND KILL?

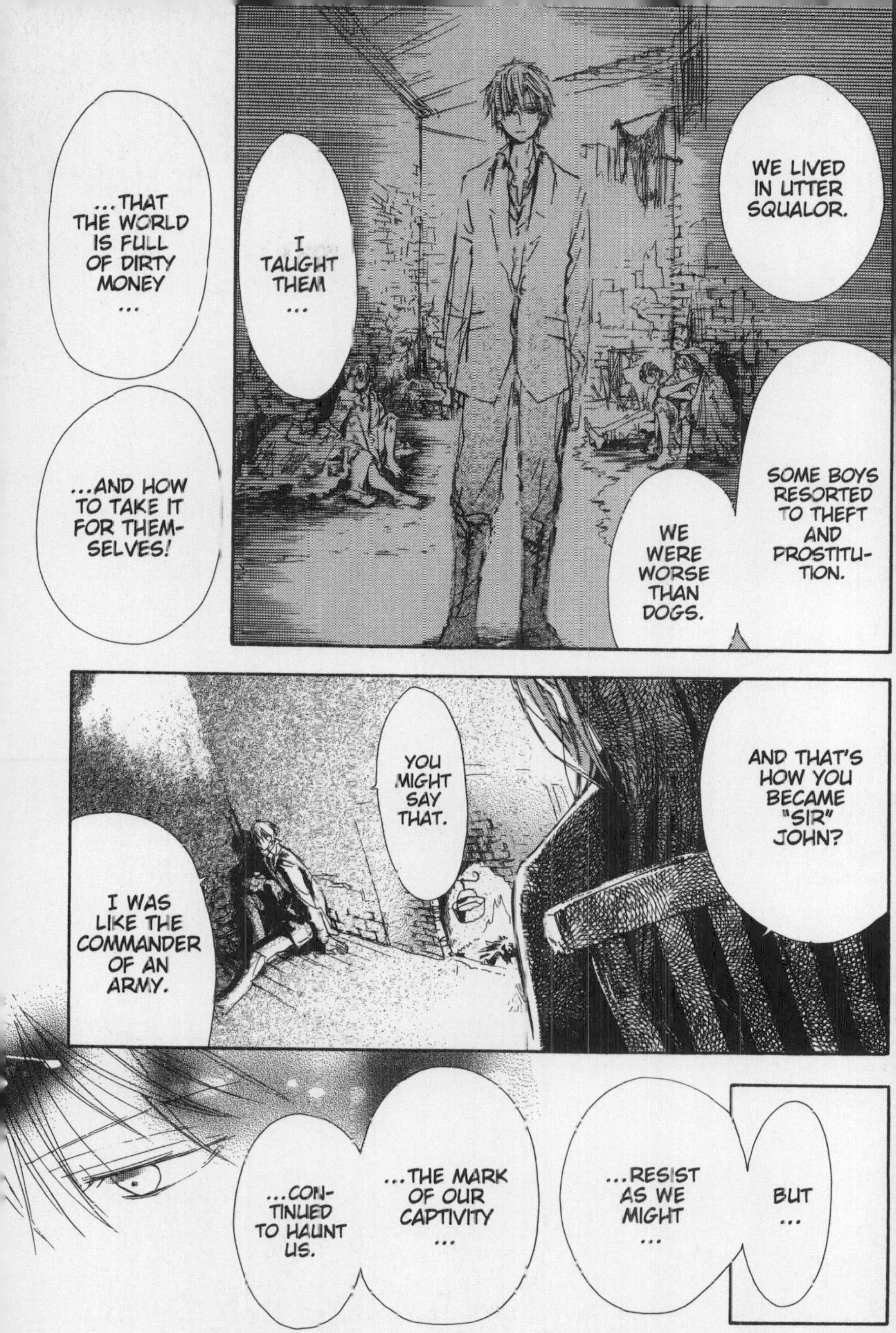
WE LIVED IN UTTER SQUALOR.
SOME BOYS RESORTED TO THEFT AND PROSTITU-TION.
WE WERE WORSE THAN DOGS.
I TAUGHT THEM ...
...THAT THE WORLD IS FULL OF DIRTY MONEY ...
...AND HOW TO TAKE IT FOR THEM-SELVES!
AND THAT'S HOW YOU BECAME "SIR" JOHN?
YOU MIGHT SAY THAT.
I WAS LIKE THE COMMANDER OF AN ARMY.
BUT ...
...RESIST AS WE MIGHT ...
...THE MARK OF OUR CAPTIVITY ...
...CON-TINUED TO HAUNT US.

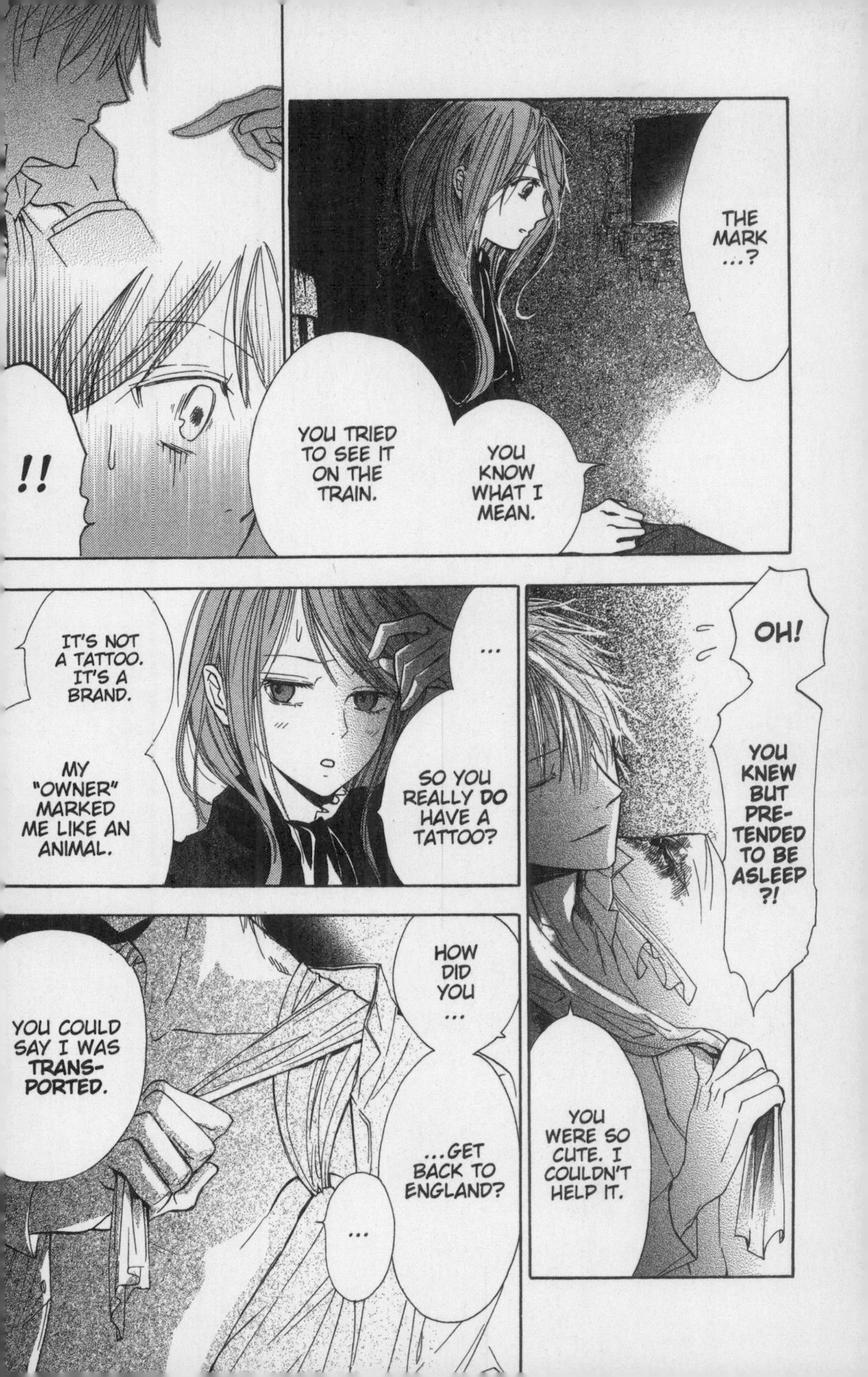
THE MARK ...?
YOU KNOW WHAT I MEAN.
YOU TRIED TO SEE IT ON THE TRAIN.
!!
OH!
YOU KNEW BUT PRE-TENDED TO BE ASLEEP?!
YOU WERE SO CUTE. I COULDN'T HELP IT.
...
SO YOU REALLY DO HAVE A TATTOO?
IT'S NOT A TATTOO. IT'S A BRAND.
MY "OWNER" MARKED ME LIKE AN ANIMAL.
HOW DID YOU ...
...GET BACK TO ENGLAND?
...
YOU COULD SAY I WAS TRANS-PORTED.

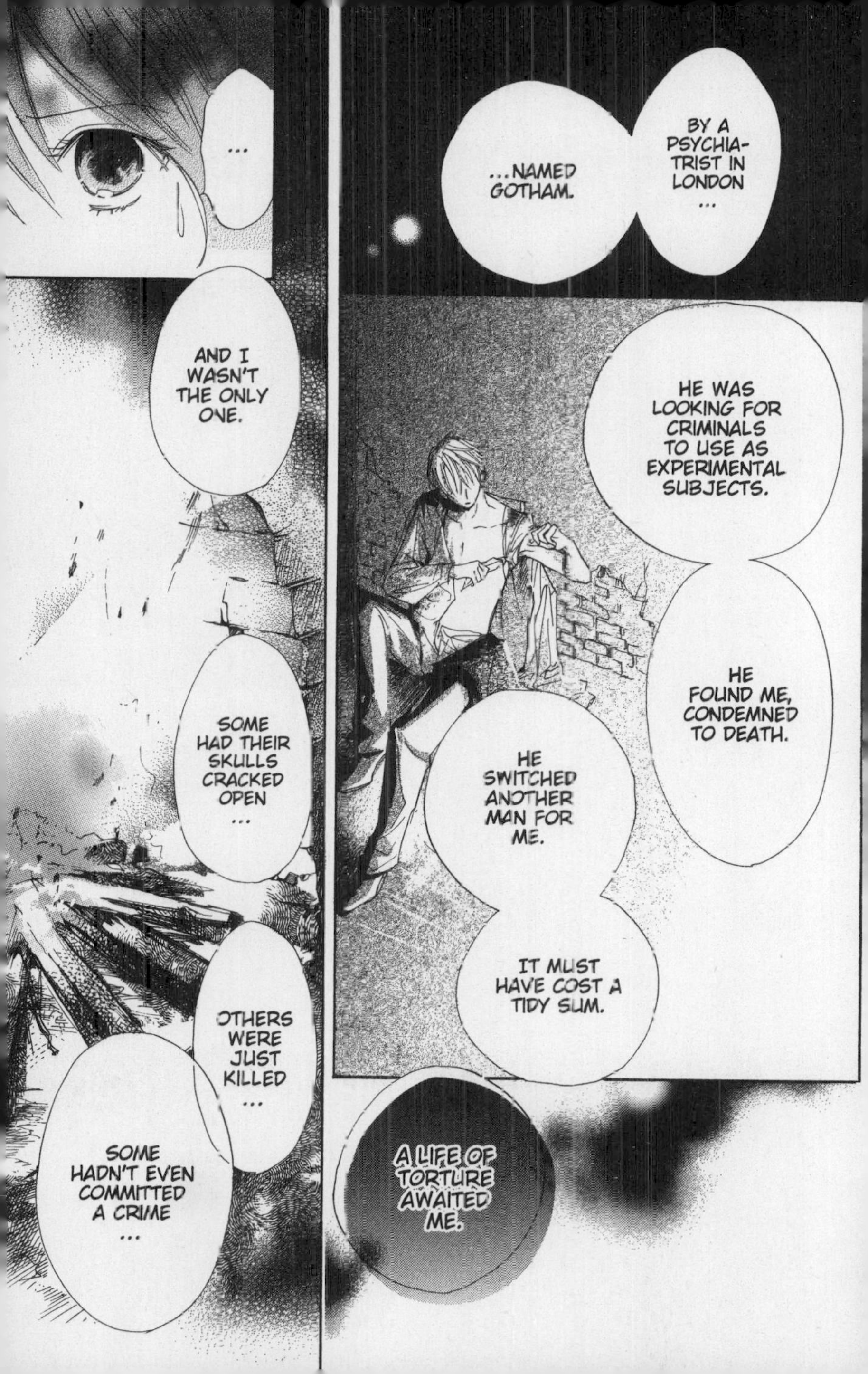
BY A PSYCHIA-TRIST IN LONDON ...
...NAMED GOTHAM.
HE WAS LOOKING FOR CRIMINALS TO USE AS EXPERIMENTAL SUBJECTS.
HE FOUND ME, CONDEMNED TO DEATH.
HE SWITCHED ANOTHER MAN FOR ME.
IT MUST HAVE COST A TIDY SUM.
A LIFE OF TORTURE AWAITED ME.
...
AND I WASN'T THE ONLY ONE.
SOME HAD THEIR SKULLS CRACKED OPEN ...
OTHERS WERE JUST KILLED ...
SOME HADN'T EVEN COMMITTED A CRIME ...

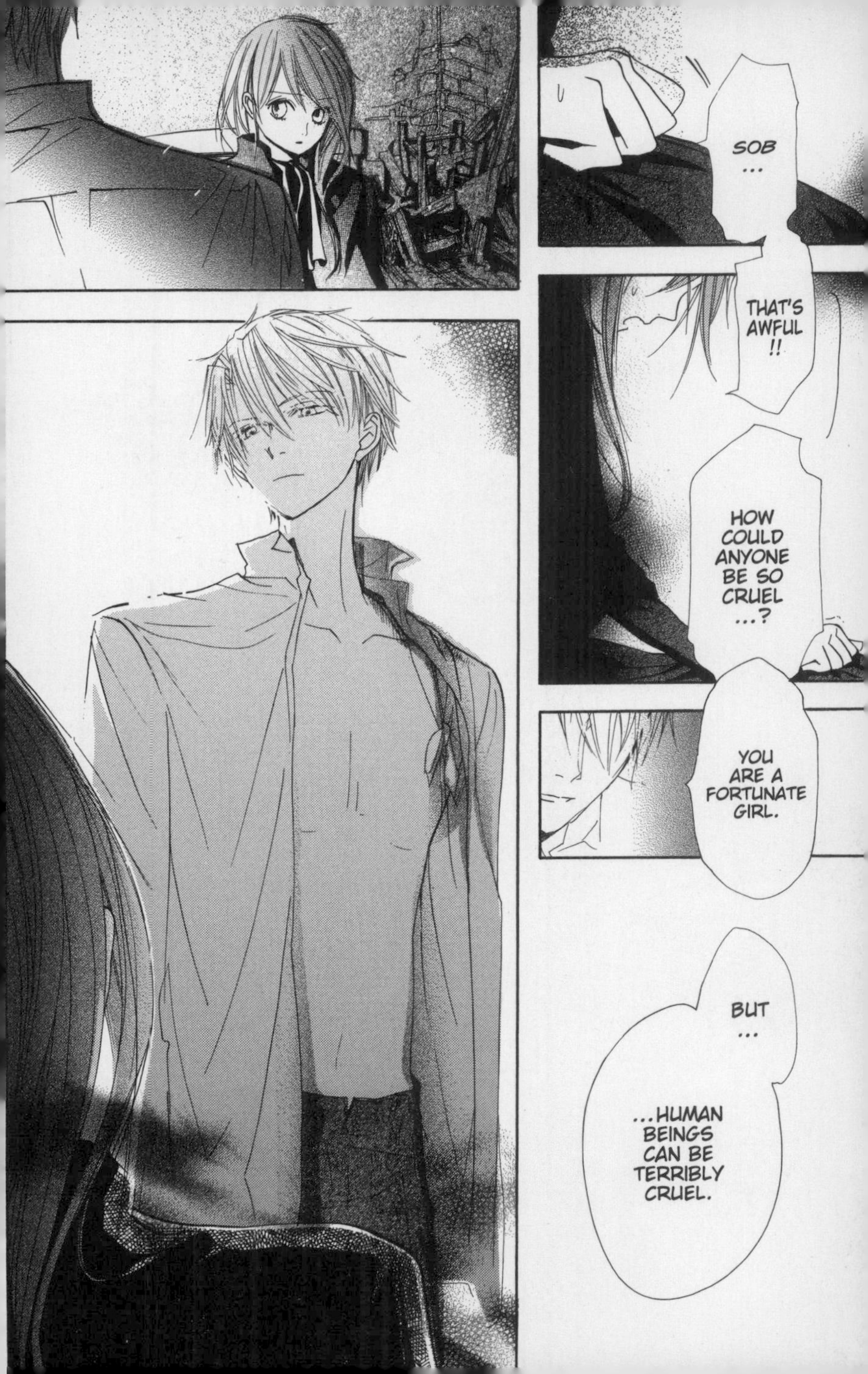
SOB ...
THAT'S AWFUL !!
HOW COULD ANYONE BE SO CRUEL ...?
YOU ARE A FORTUNATE GIRL.
BUT ...
...HUMAN BEINGS CAN BE TERRIBLY CRUEL.

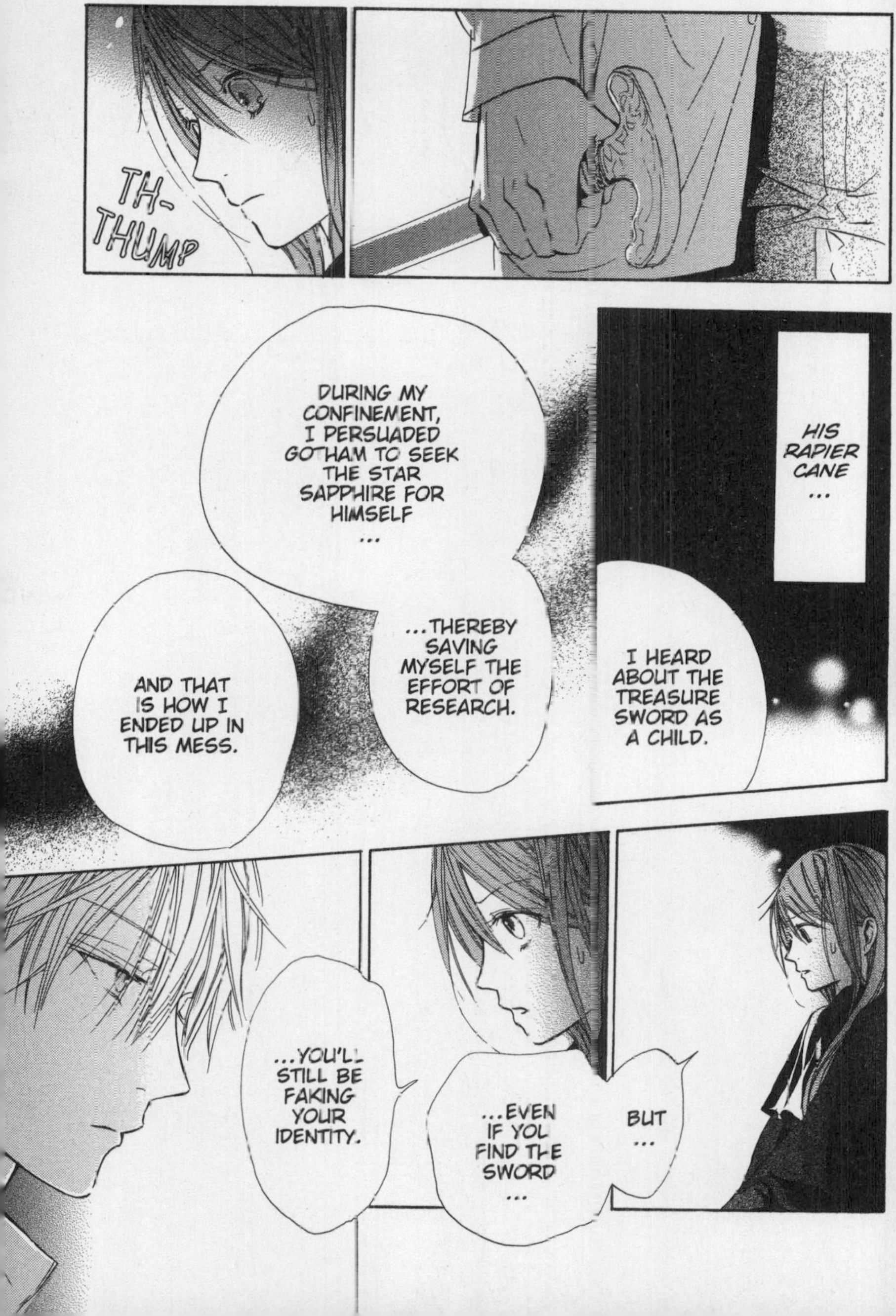
TH-THUMP
HIS RAPIER CANE ...
I HEARD ABOUT THE TREASURE SWORD AS A CHILD.
DURING MY CONFINEMENT, I PERSUADED GOTHAM TO SEEK THE STAR SAPPHIRE FOR HIMSELF ...
...THEREBY SAVING MYSELF THE EFFORT OF RESEARCH.
AND THAT IS HOW I ENDED UP IN THIS MESS.
BUT ...
...EVEN IF YOU FIND THE SWORD ...
...YOU'LL STILL BE FAKING YOUR IDENTITY.

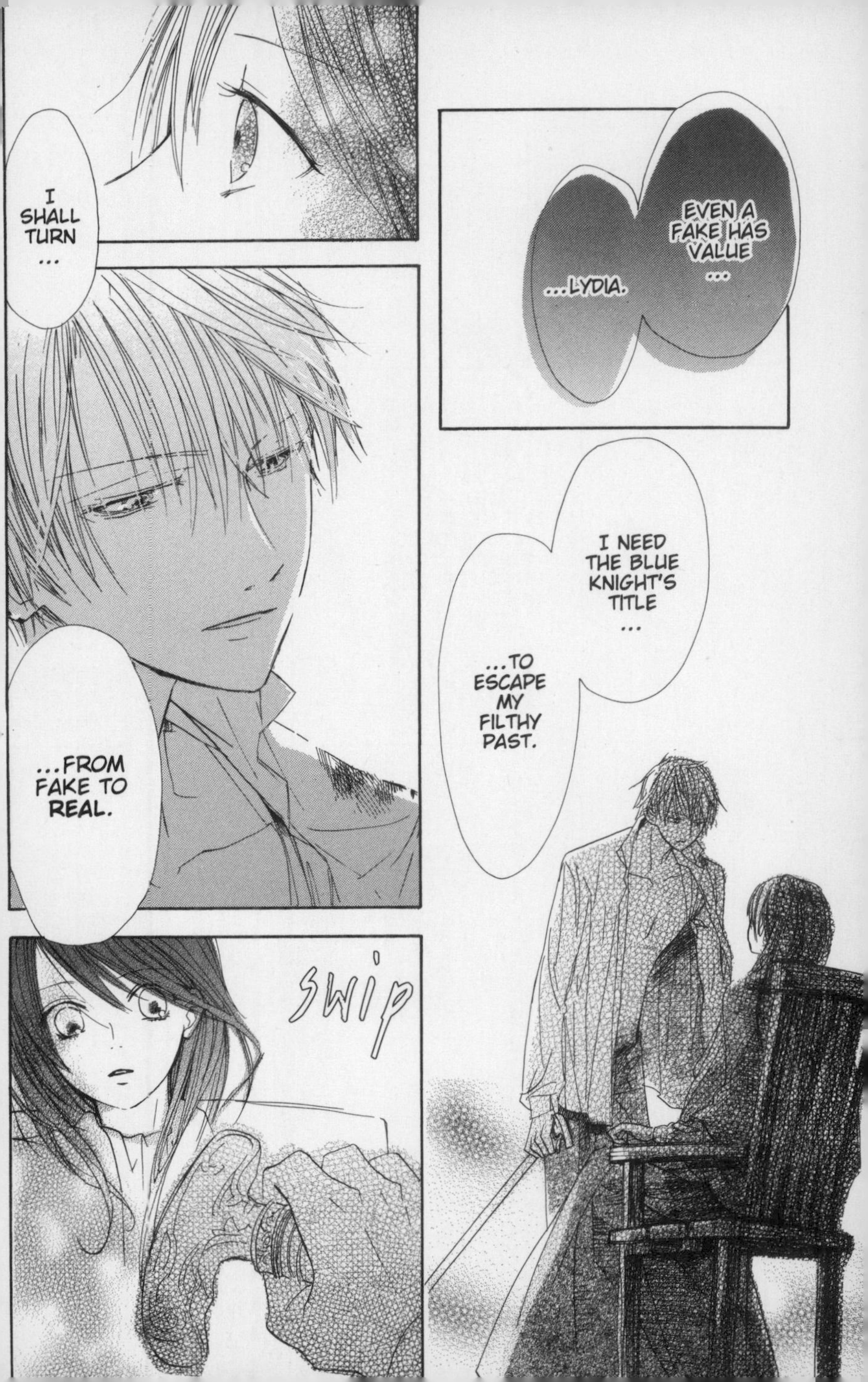
EVEN A FAKE HAS VALUE ...
...LYDIA.
I SHALL TURN ...
...FROM FAKE TO REAL.
I NEED THE BLUE KNIGHT'S TITLE ...
...TO ESCAPE MY FILTHY PAST.
SWIP

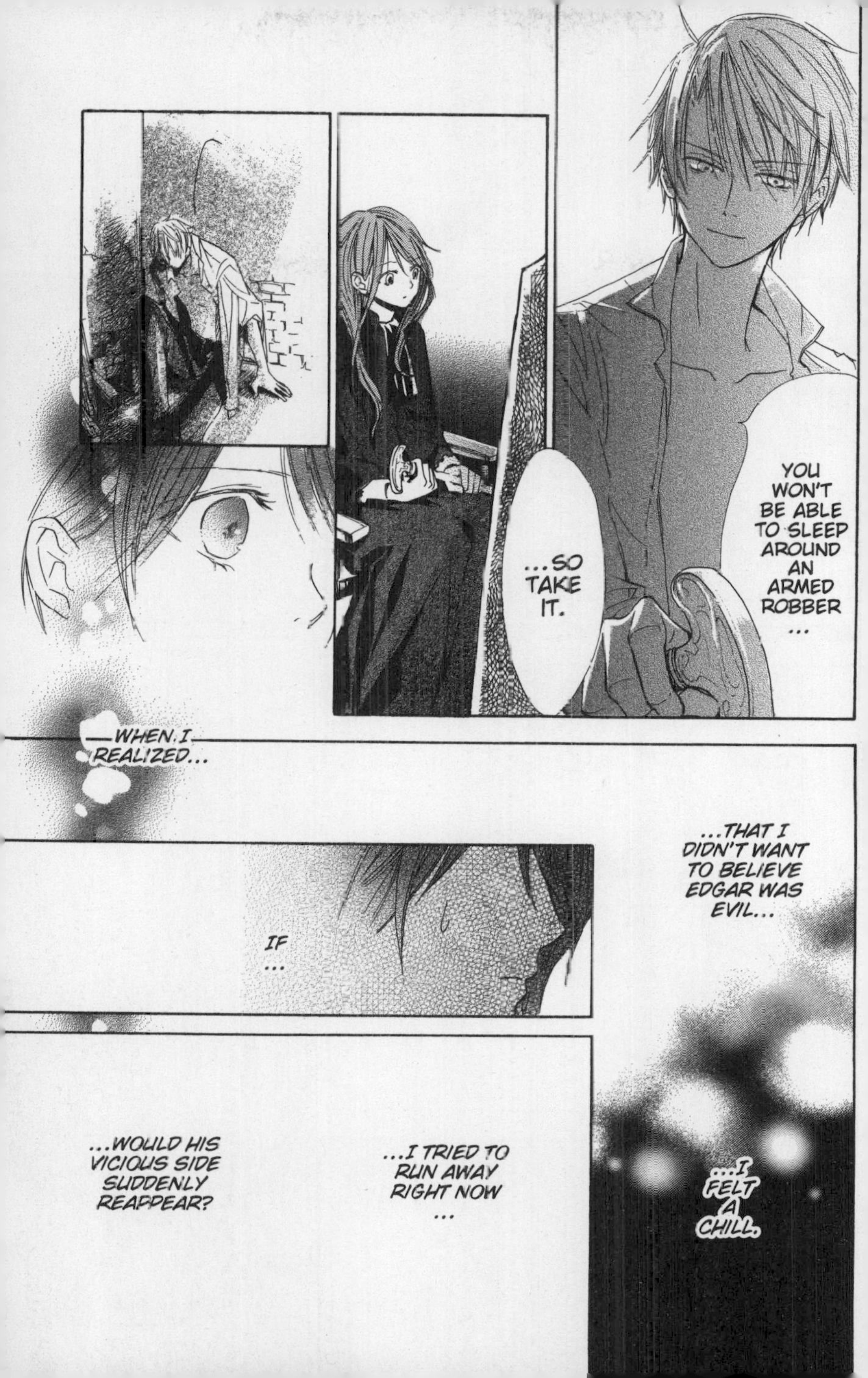
YOU WON'T BE ABLE TO SLEEP AROUND AN ARMED ROBBER ...
...SO TAKE IT.
—WHEN I REALIZED...
...THAT I DIDN'T WANT TO BELIEVE EDGAR WAS EVIL...
...I FELT A CHILL.
IF ...
...I TRIED TO RUN AWAY RIGHT NOW ...
...WOULD HIS VICIOUS SIDE SUDDENLY REAPPEAR?

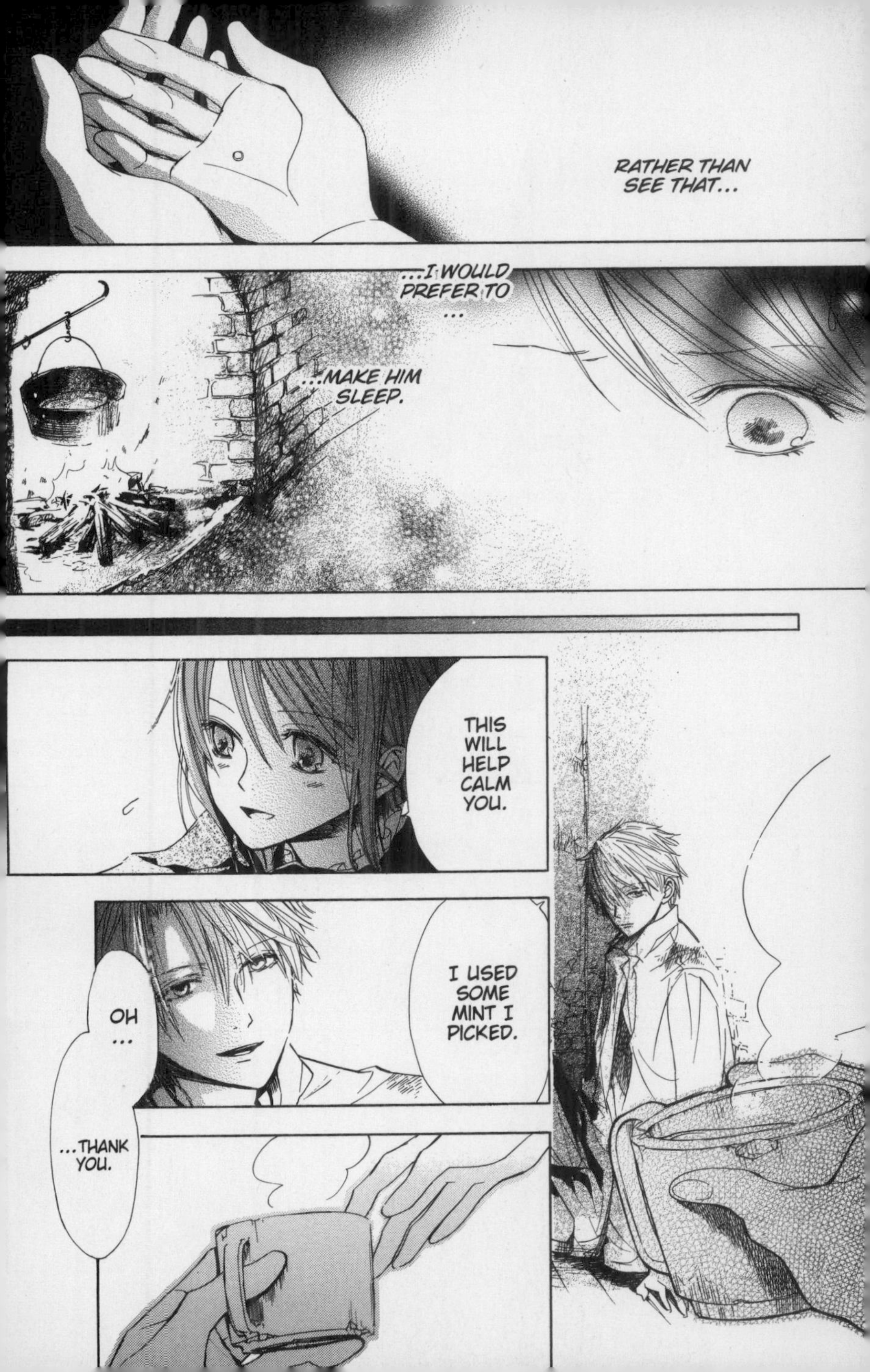
RATHER THAN SEE THAT...
...I WOULD PREFER TO ...
...MAKE HIM SLEEP.
THIS WILL HELP CALM YOU.
I USED SOME MINT I PICKED.
OH ...
...THANK YOU.

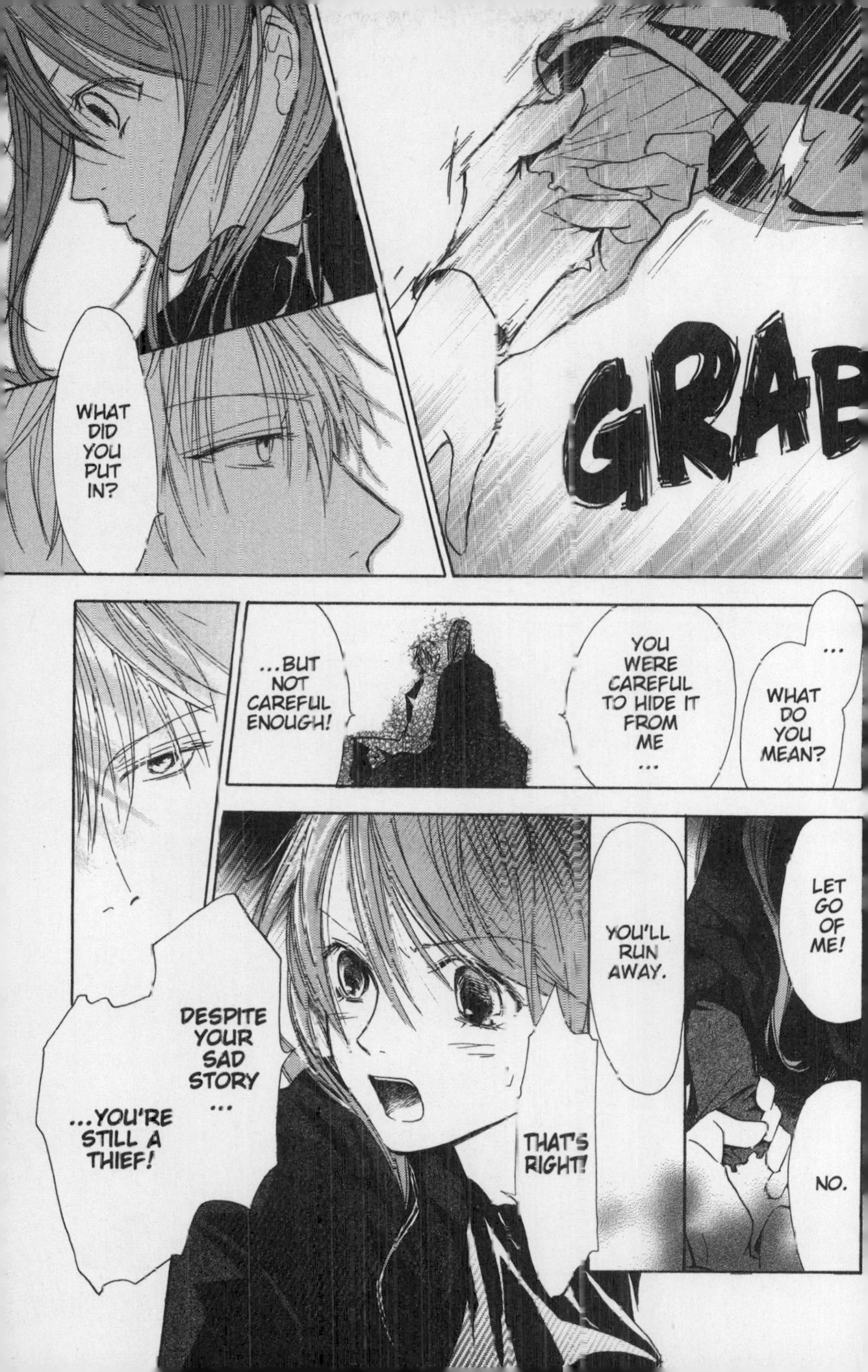
GRAB
WHAT DID YOU PUT IN?
... WHAT DO YOU MEAN?
YOU WERE CAREFUL TO HIDE IT FROM ME ...
...BUT NOT CAREFUL ENOUGH!
LET GO OF ME!
NO.
YOU'LL RUN AWAY.
THAT'S RIGHT!
DESPITE YOUR SAD STORY ...
...YOU'RE STILL A THIEF!

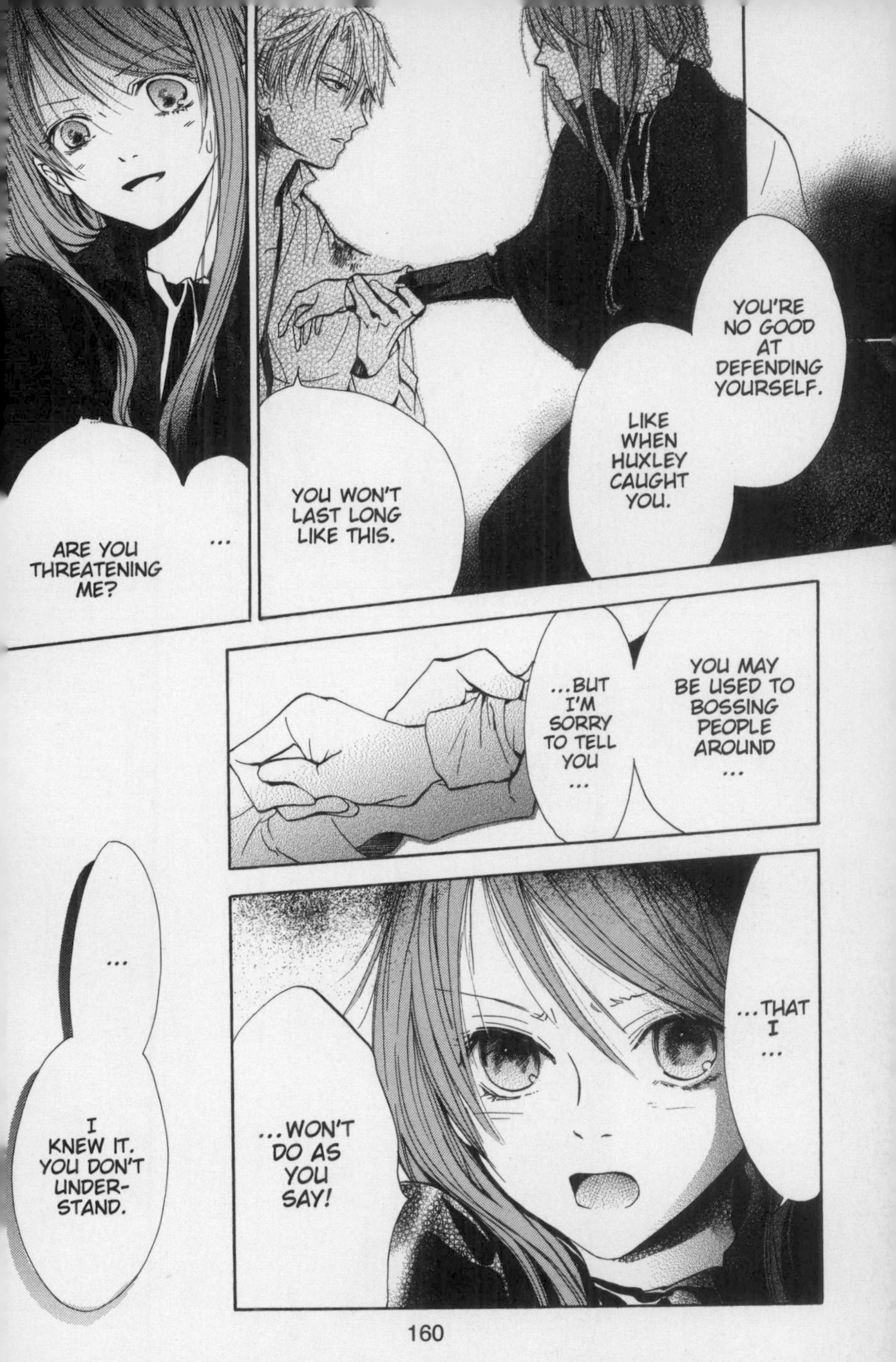
YOU'RE NO GOOD AT DEFENDING YOURSELF.
LIKE WHEN HUXLEY CAUGHT YOU.
YOU WON'T LAST LONG LIKE THIS.
...
ARE YOU THREATENING ME?
YOU MAY BE USED TO BOSSING PEOPLE AROUND ...
...BUT I'M SORRY TO TELL YOU ...
...THAT I ...
...WON'T DO AS YOU SAY!
...
I KNEW IT. YOU DON'T UNDER-STAND.

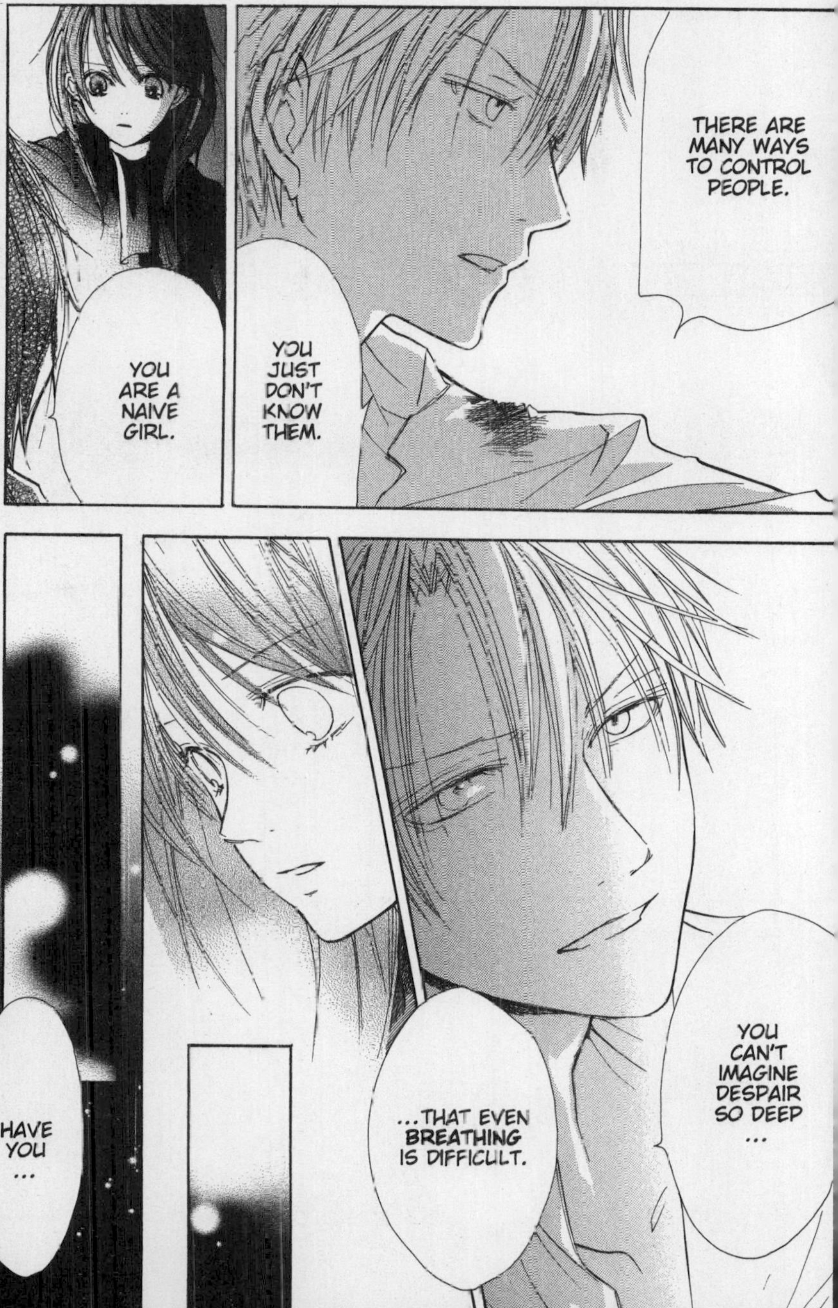
THERE ARE MANY WAYS TO CONTROL PEOPLE.
YOU JUST DON'T KNOW THEM.
YOU ARE A NAIVE GIRL.
YOU CAN'T IMAGINE DESPAIR SO DEEP ...
...THAT EVEN BREATHING IS DIFFICULT.
HAVE YOU ...

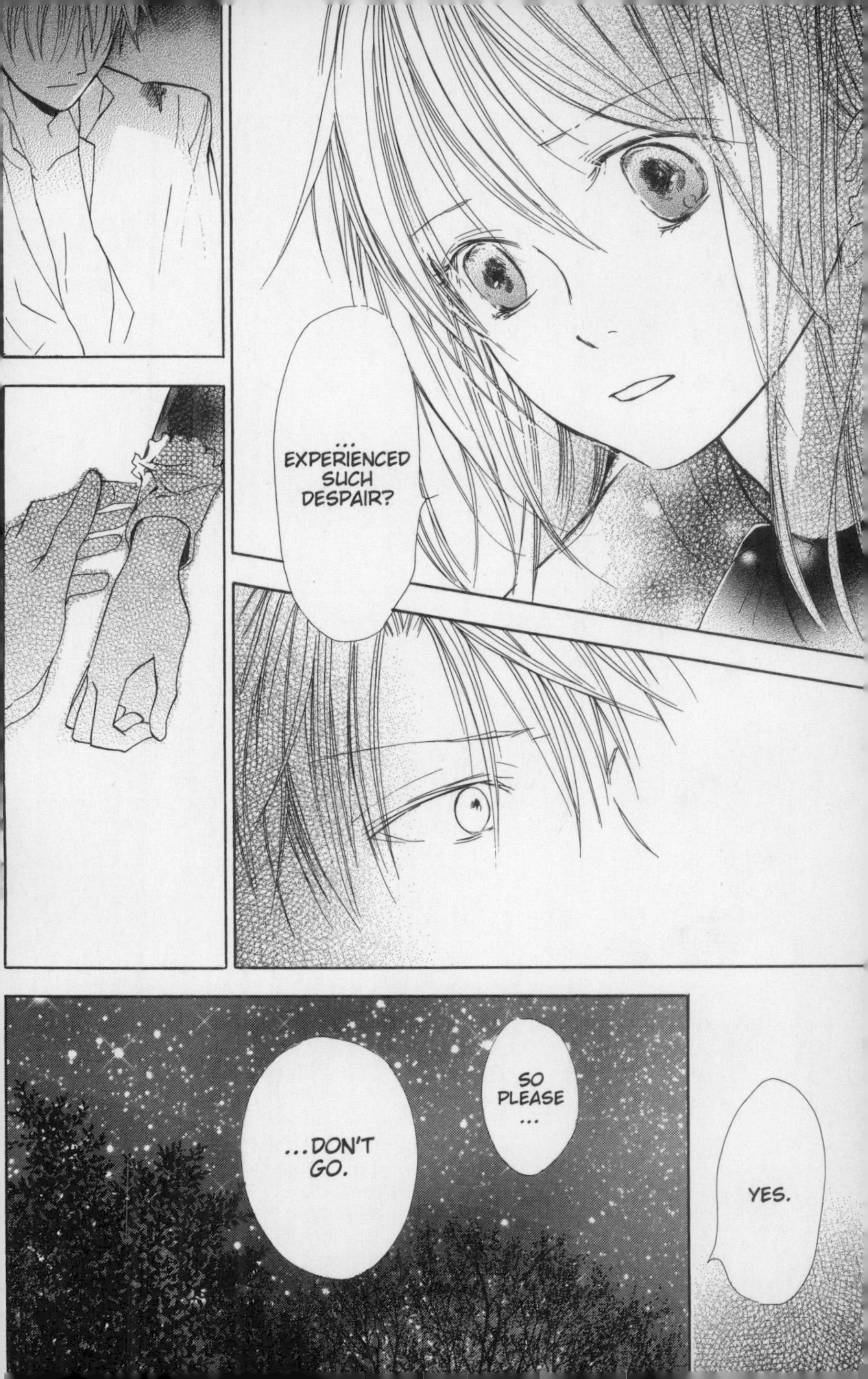
...EXPERIENCED SUCH DESPAIR?
YES.
SO PLEASE ...
...DON'T GO.

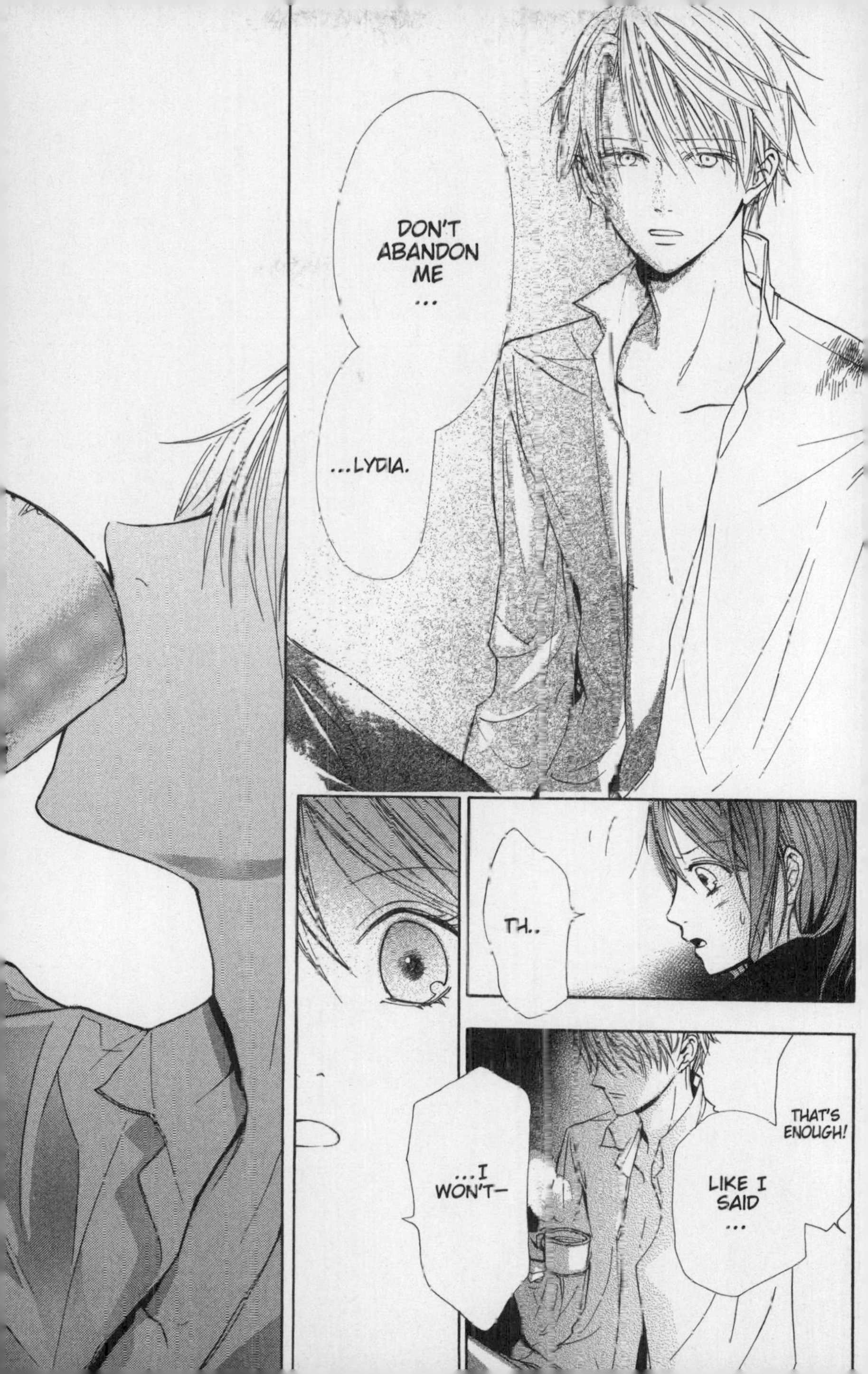
DON'T ABANDON ME ...
...LYDIA.
TH..
THAT'S ENOUGH!
LIKE I SAID ...
...I WON'T—

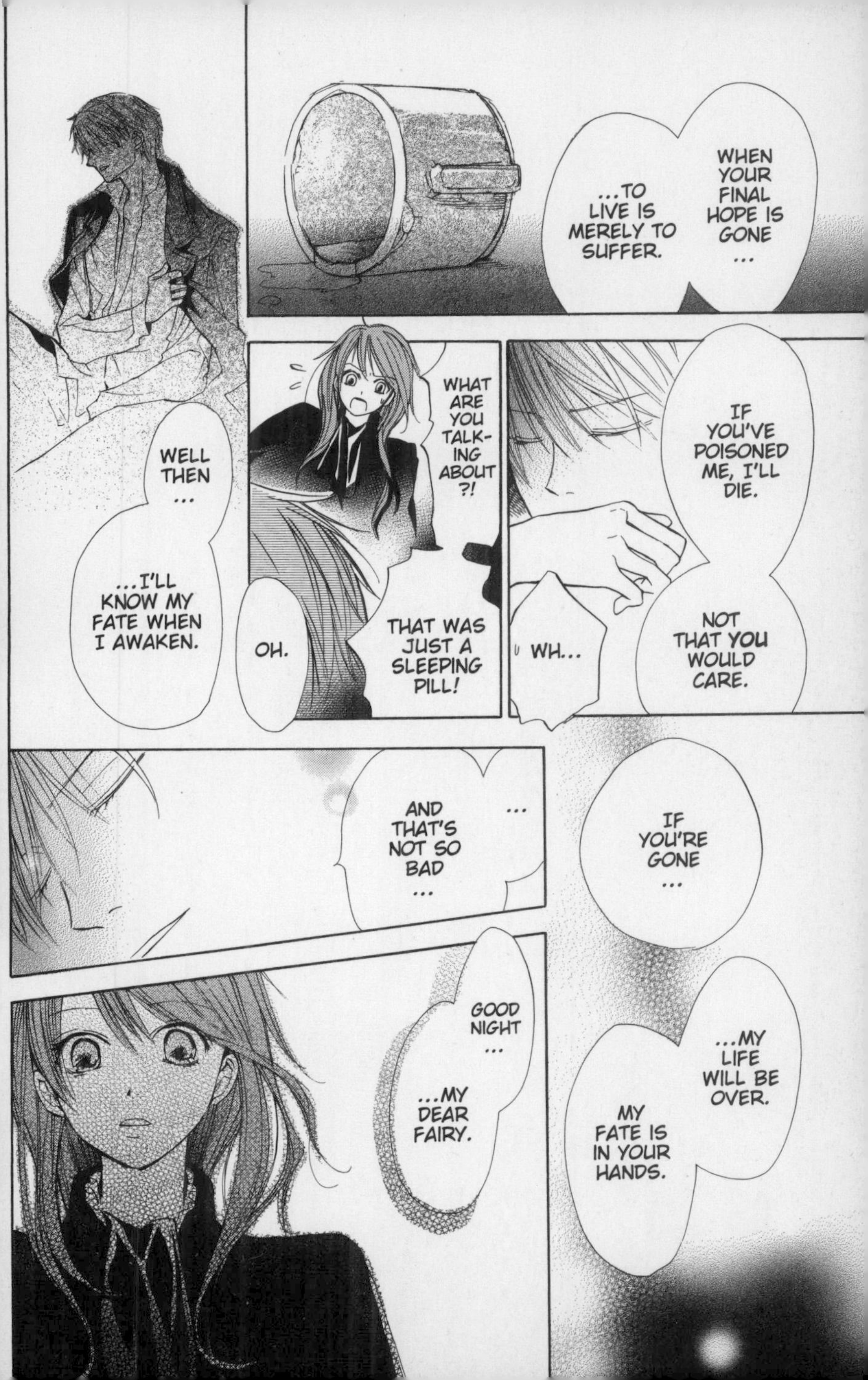
WHEN YOUR FINAL HOPE IS GONE...
...TO LIVE IS MERELY TO SUFFER.
IF YOU'VE POISONED ME, I'LL DIE.
NOT THAT YOU WOULD CARE.
WH...
WHAT ARE YOU TALK-ING ABOUT?!
THAT WAS JUST A SLEEPING PILL!
OH.
WELL THEN...
...I'LL KNOW MY FATE WHEN I AWAKEN.
IF YOU'RE GONE...
AND THAT'S NOT SO BAD... ...
...MY LIFE WILL BE OVER.
MY FATE IS IN YOUR HANDS.
GOOD NIGHT...
...MY DEAR FAIRY.

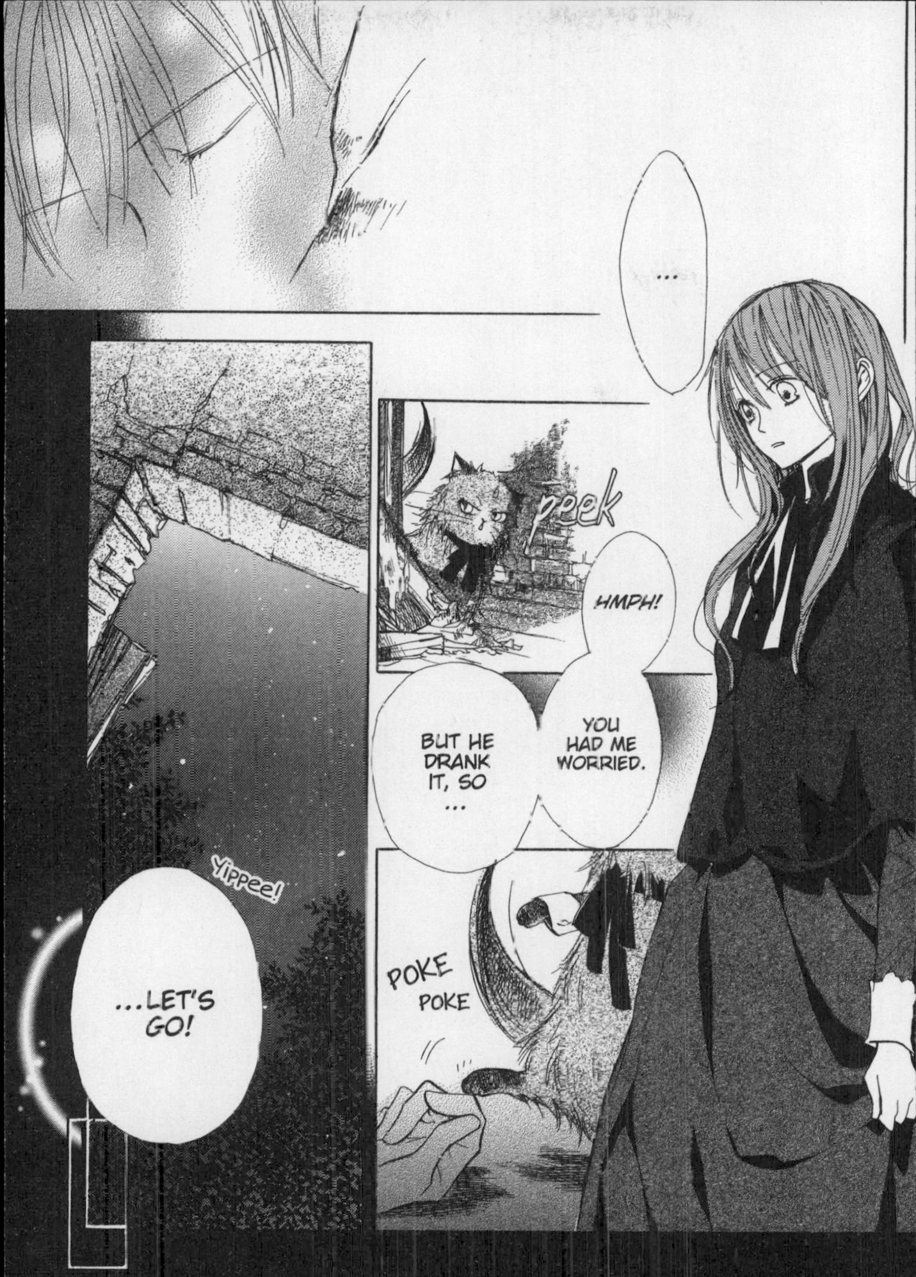
...
peek
HMPH!
YOU HAD ME WORRIED.
BUT HE DRANK IT, SO ...
POKE POKE
Yippee!
...LET'S GO!

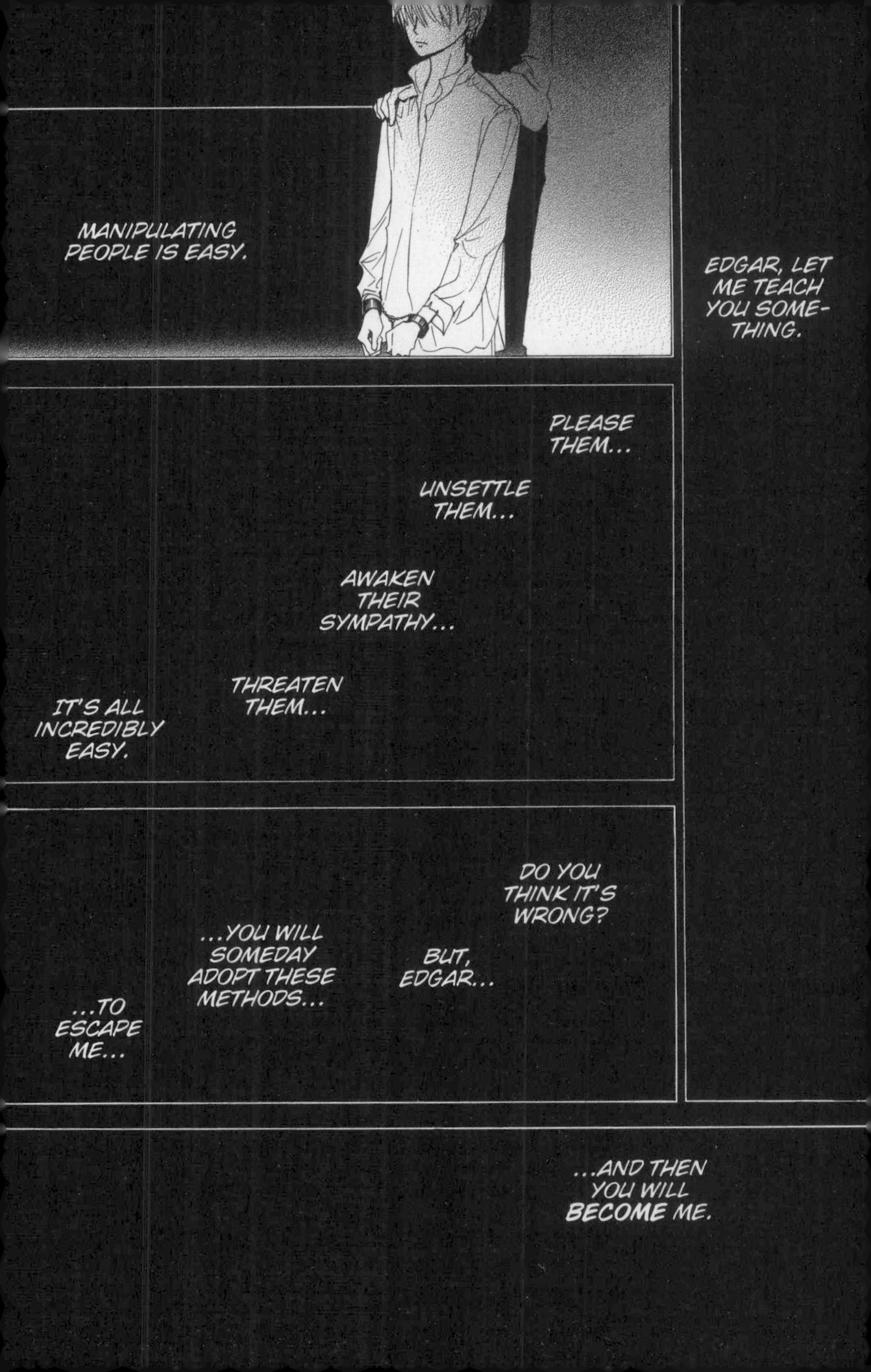
EDGAR, LET ME TEACH YOU SOME-THING.
MANIPULATING PEOPLE IS EASY.
PLEASE THEM...
UNSETTLE THEM...
AWAKEN THEIR SYMPATHY...
THREATEN THEM...
IT'S ALL INCREDIBLY EASY.
DO YOU THINK IT'S WRONG?
BUT, EDGAR...
...YOU WILL SOMEDAY ADOPT THESE METHODS...
...TO ESCAPE ME...
...AND THEN YOU WILL **BECOME** ME.

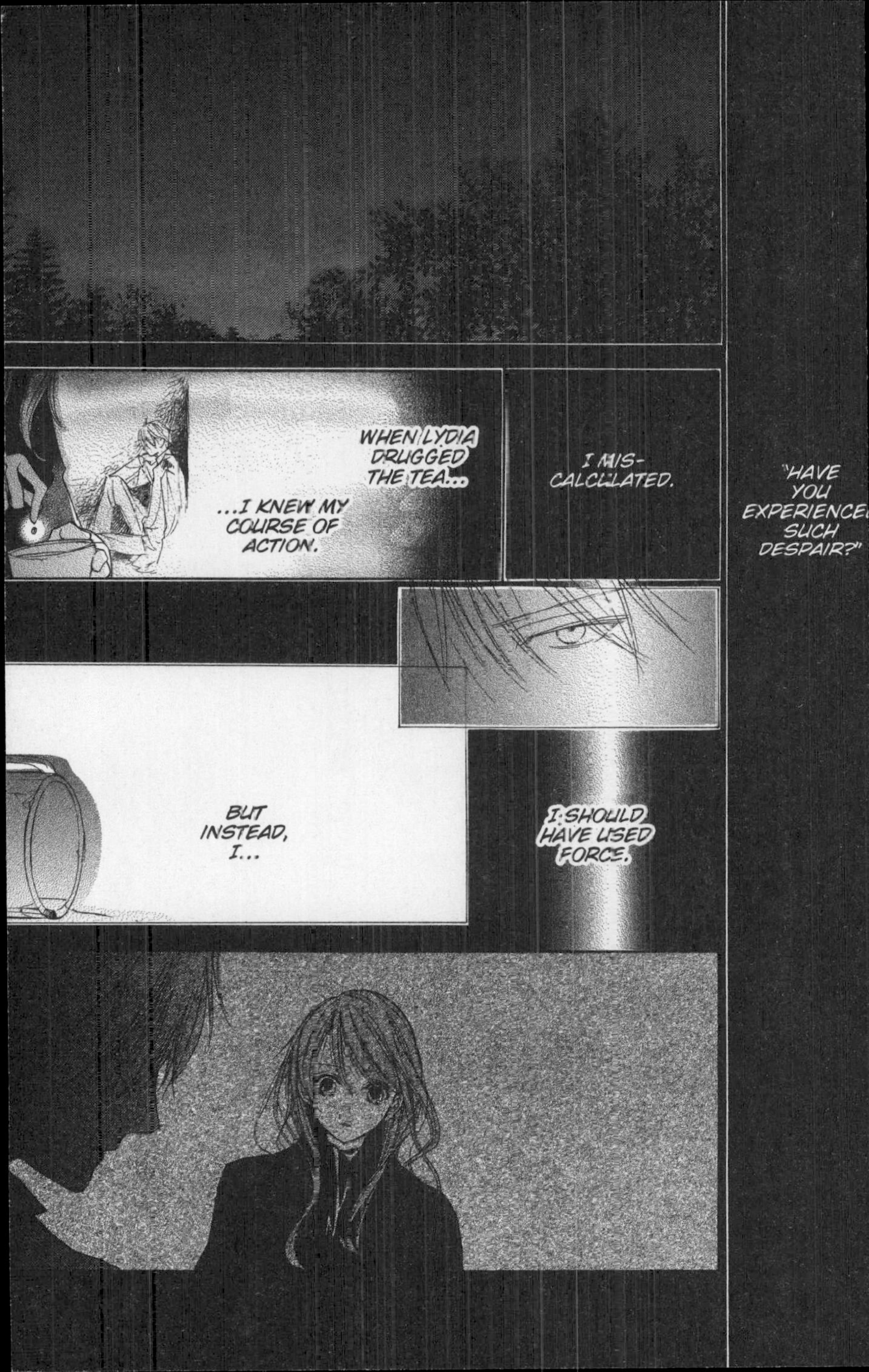
"HAVE YOU EXPERIENCED SUCH DESPAIR?"
I MIS-CALCULATED.
WHEN LYDIA DRUGGED THE TEA...
...I KNEW MY COURSE OF ACTION.
I SHOULD HAVE USED FORCE.
BUT INSTEAD, I...

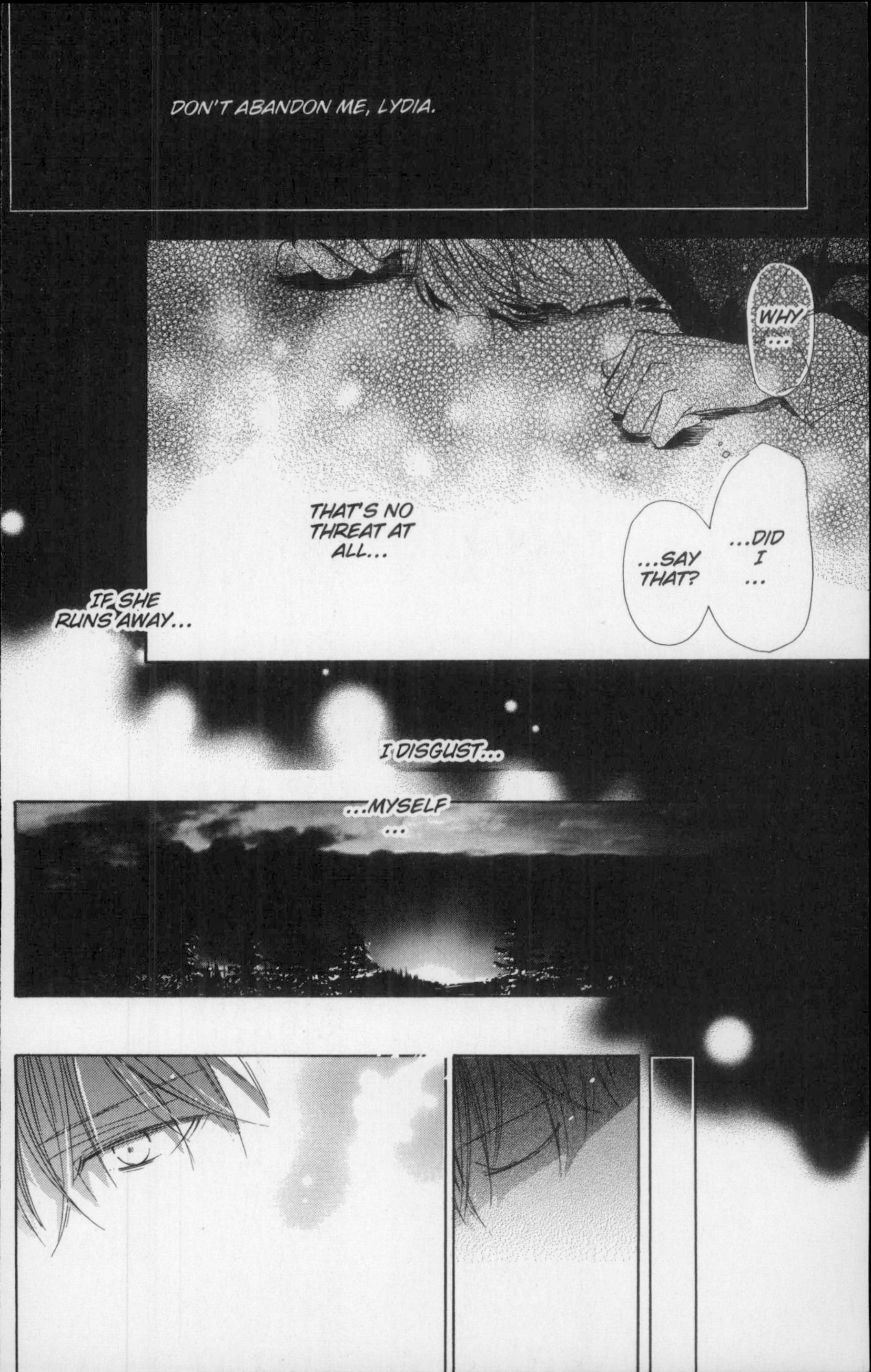
DON'T ABANDON ME, LYDIA.
WHY ...
...DID I ...
...SAY THAT?
THAT'S NO THREAT AT ALL...
IF SHE RUNS AWAY...
I DISGUST...
...MYSELF ...

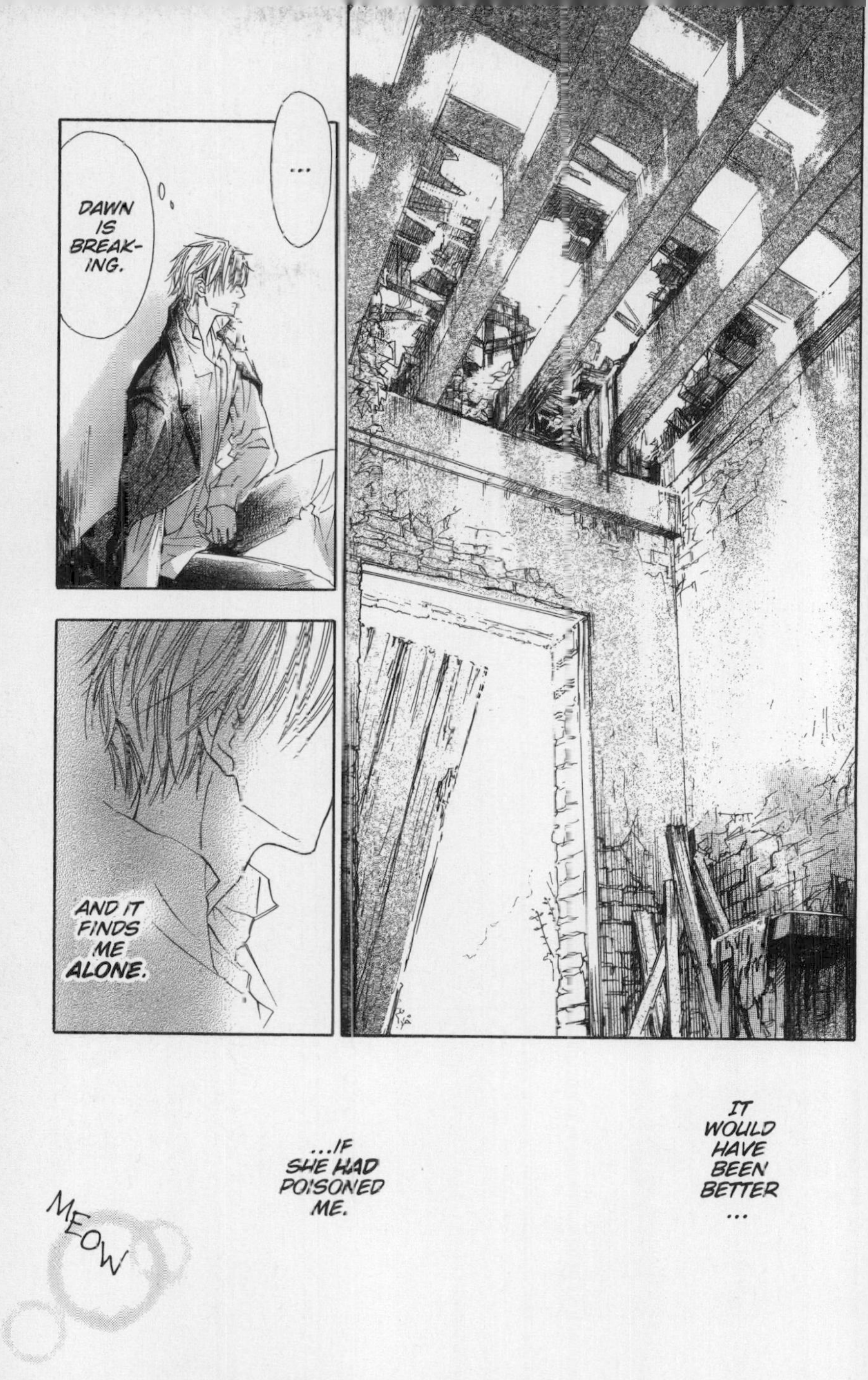
...
DAWN IS BREAKING.
AND IT FINDS ME ALONE.
IT WOULD HAVE BEEN BETTER ...
...IF SHE HAD POISONED ME.
MEOW

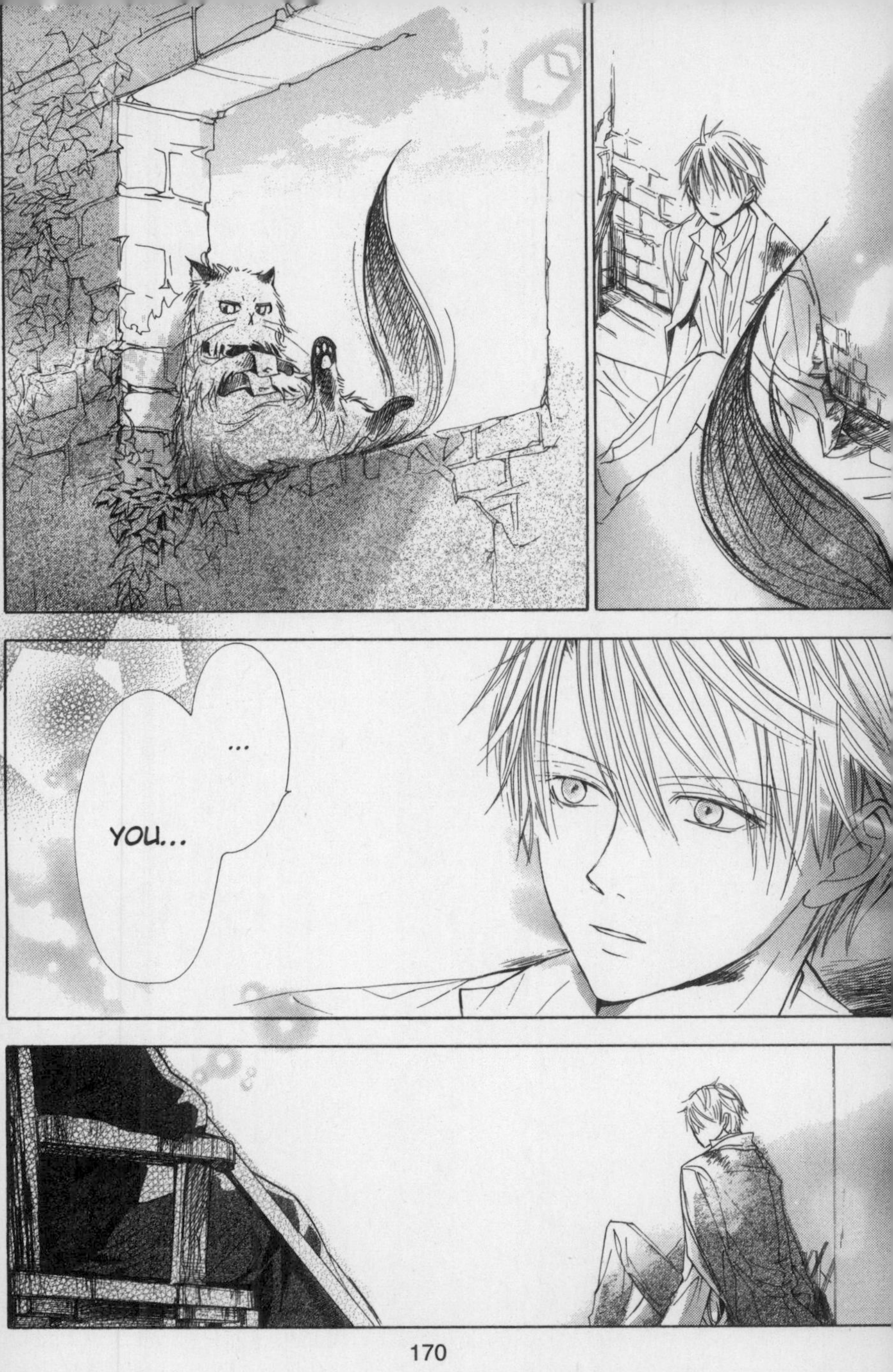
...
YOU...

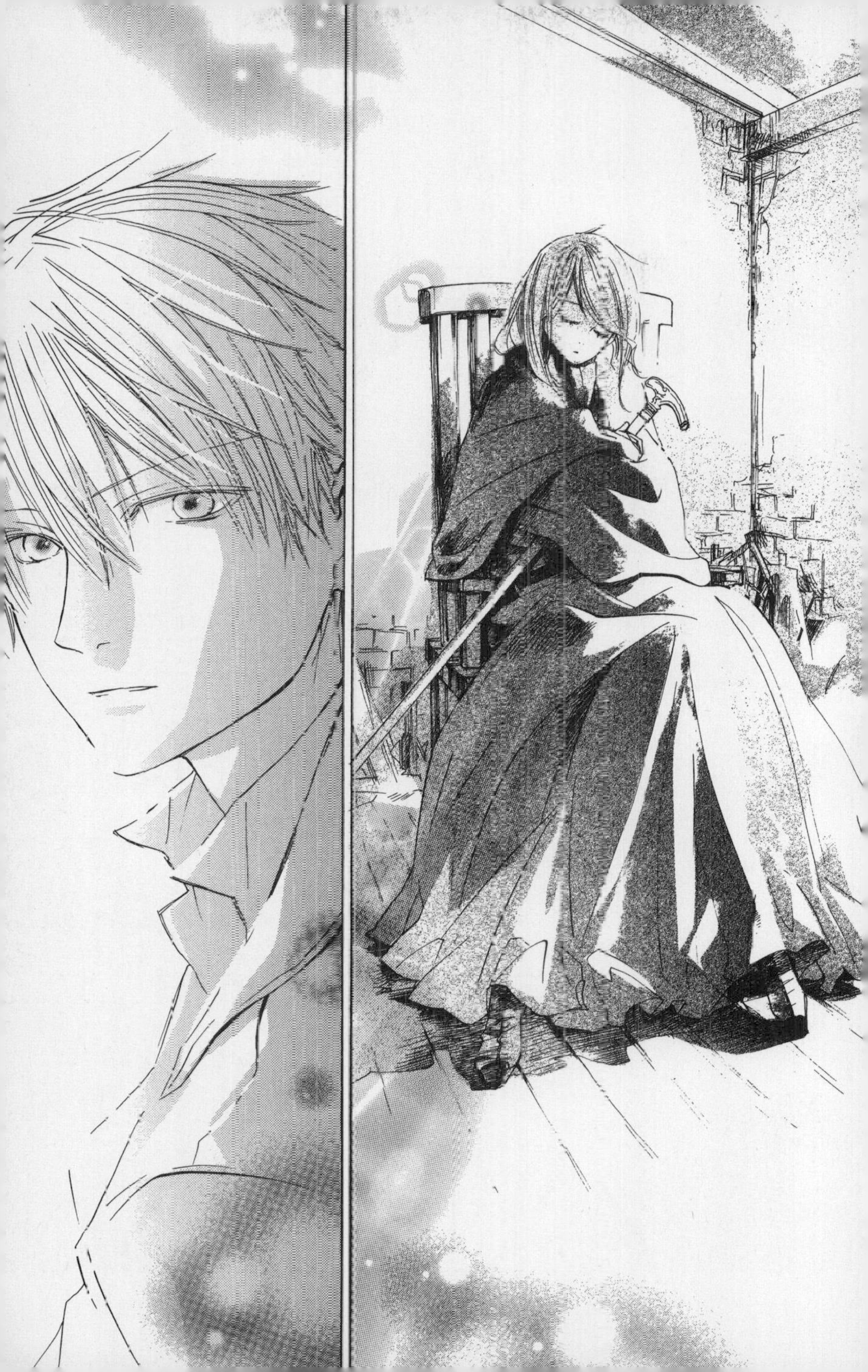

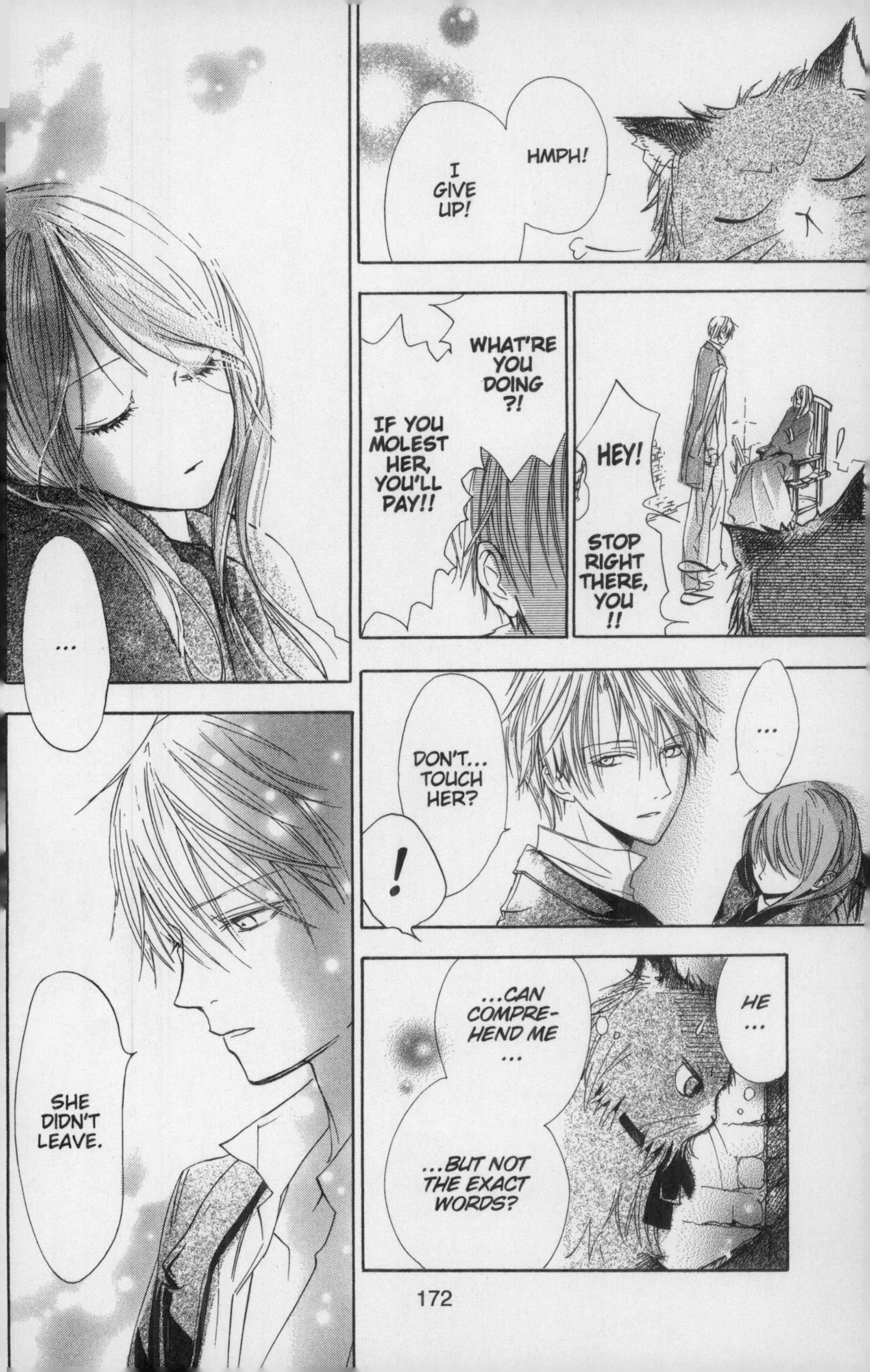
HMPH! I GIVE UP!
HEY!
STOP RIGHT THERE, YOU!!
WHAT'RE YOU DOING?!
IF YOU MOLEST HER, YOU'LL PAY!!
...
DON'T... TOUCH HER?
!
HE...
...CAN COMPREHEND ME...
...BUT NOT THE EXACT WORDS?
...
SHE DIDN'T LEAVE.

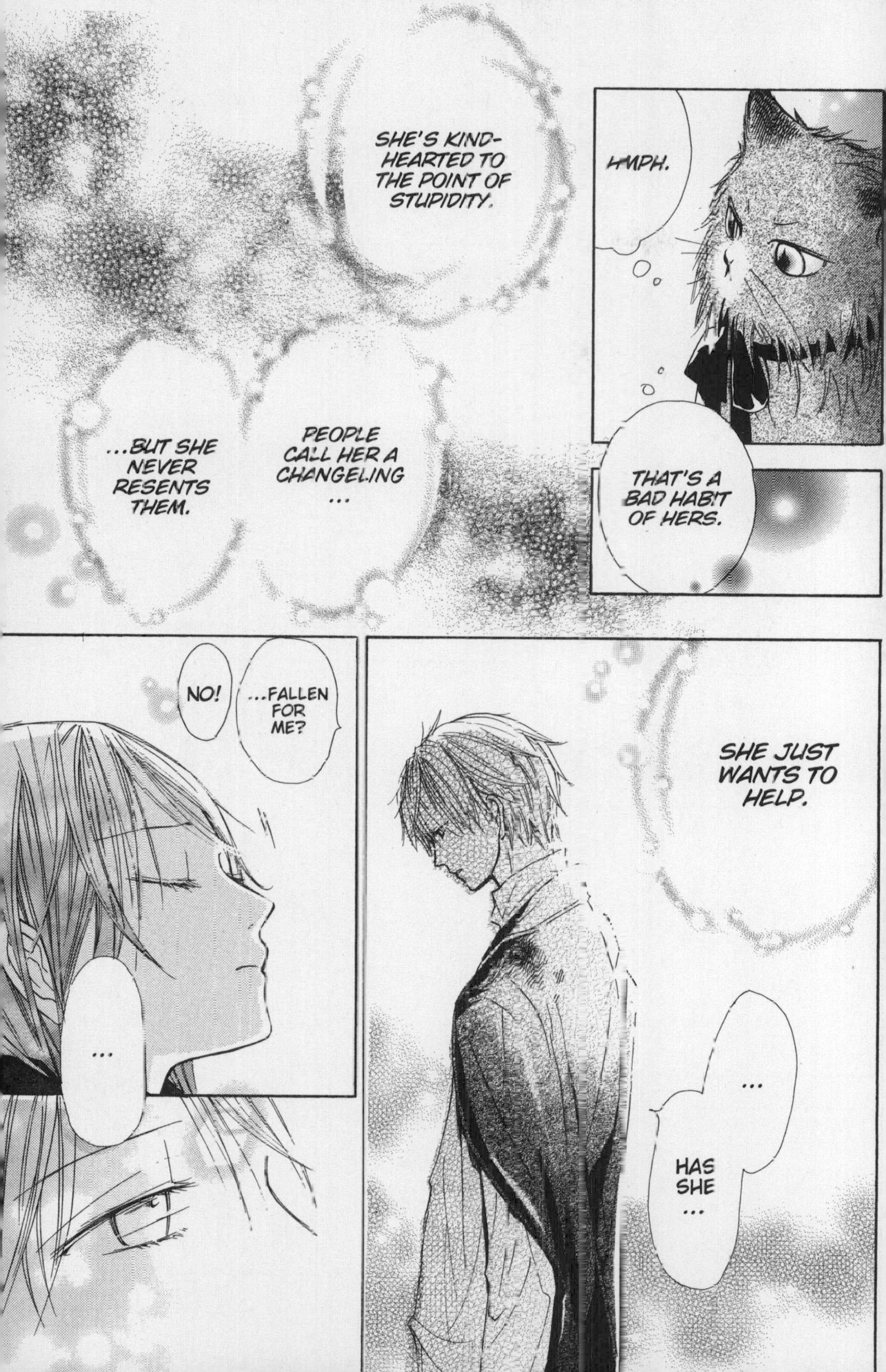
HMPH.
THAT'S A BAD HABIT OF HERS.
SHE'S KIND-HEARTED TO THE POINT OF STUPIDITY.
PEOPLE CALL HER A CHANGELING ...
...BUT SHE NEVER RESENTS THEM.
SHE JUST WANTS TO HELP.
...
HAS SHE ...
...FALLEN FOR ME?
NO!
...

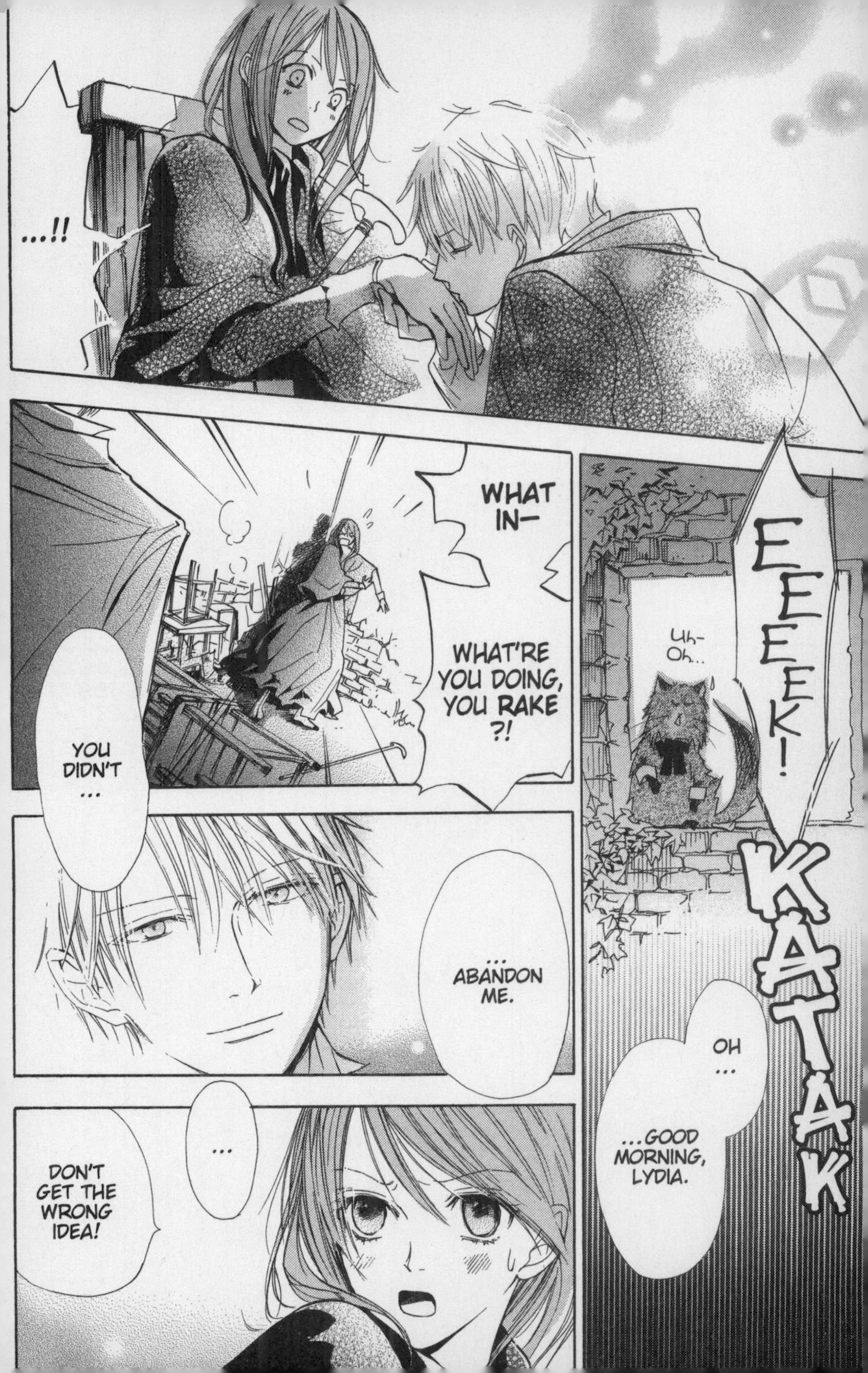

...!!
EEEEK!
Uh-Oh...
KATAK
OH ...
...GOOD MORNING, LYDIA.
WHAT IN—
WHAT'RE YOU DOING, YOU RAKE ?!
YOU DIDN'T ...
... ABANDON ME.
...
DON'T GET THE WRONG IDEA!

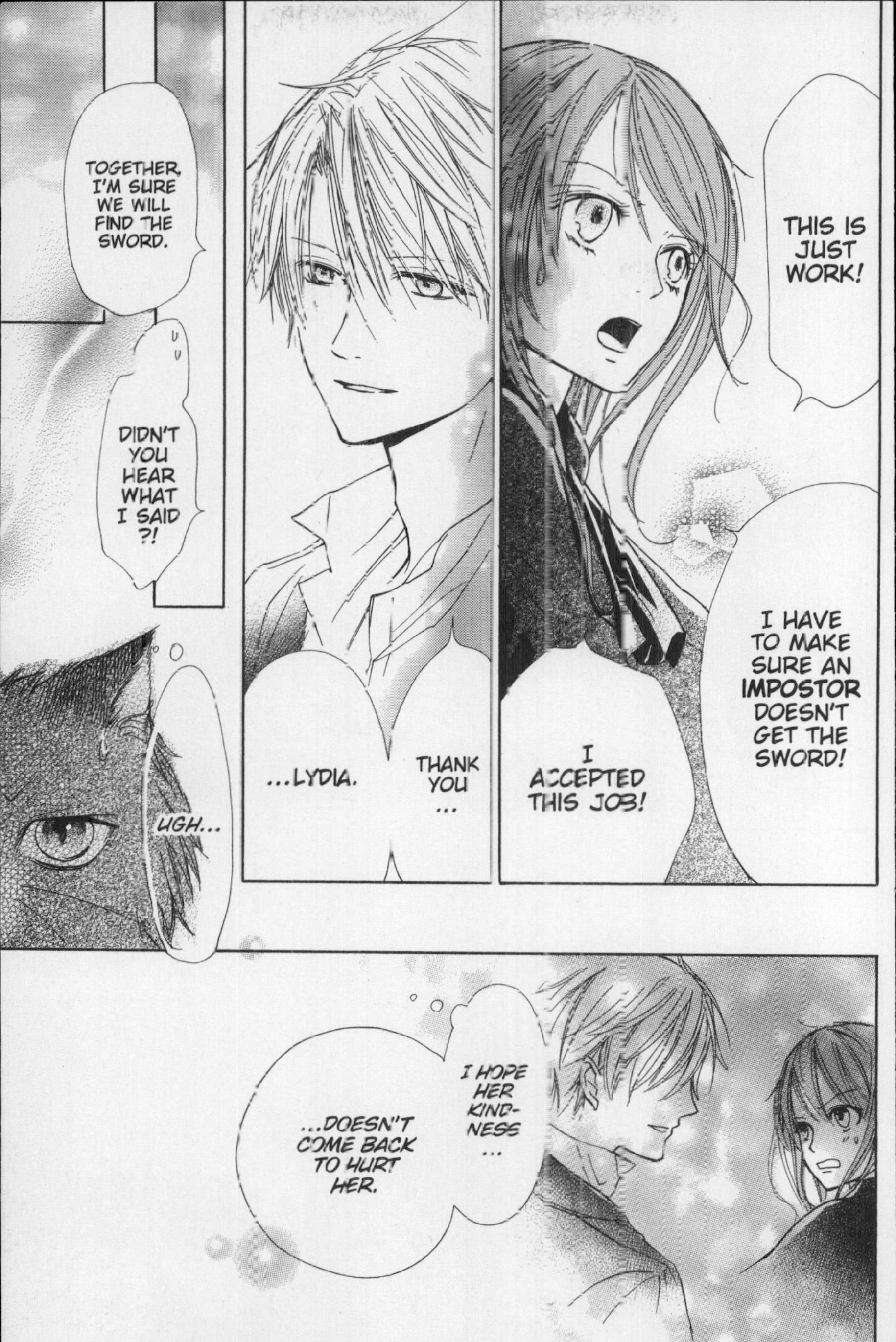
THIS IS JUST WORK!
I HAVE TO MAKE SURE AN IMPOSTOR DOESN'T GET THE SWORD!
I ACCEPTED THIS JOB!
THANK YOU ...
...LYDIA.
TOGETHER, I'M SURE WE WILL FIND THE SWORD.
DIDN'T YOU HEAR WHAT I SAID ?!
UGH...
I HOPE HER KIND-NESS ...
...DOESN'T COME BACK TO HURT HER.

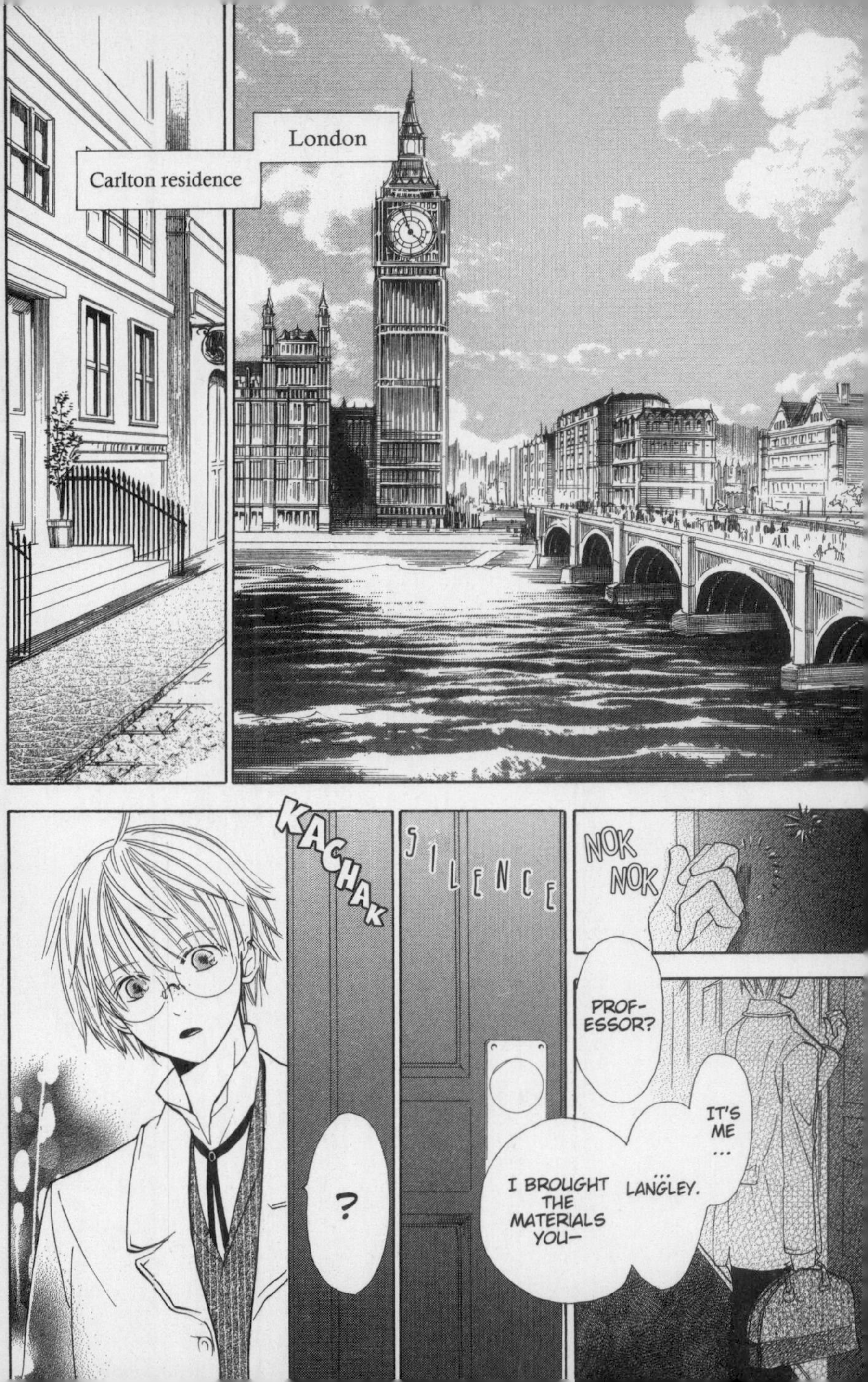
London
Carlton residence
NOK NOK
PROF-ESSOR?
IT'S ME...
...LANGLEY.
I BROUGHT THE MATERIALS YOU—
SILENCE
KACHAK
?

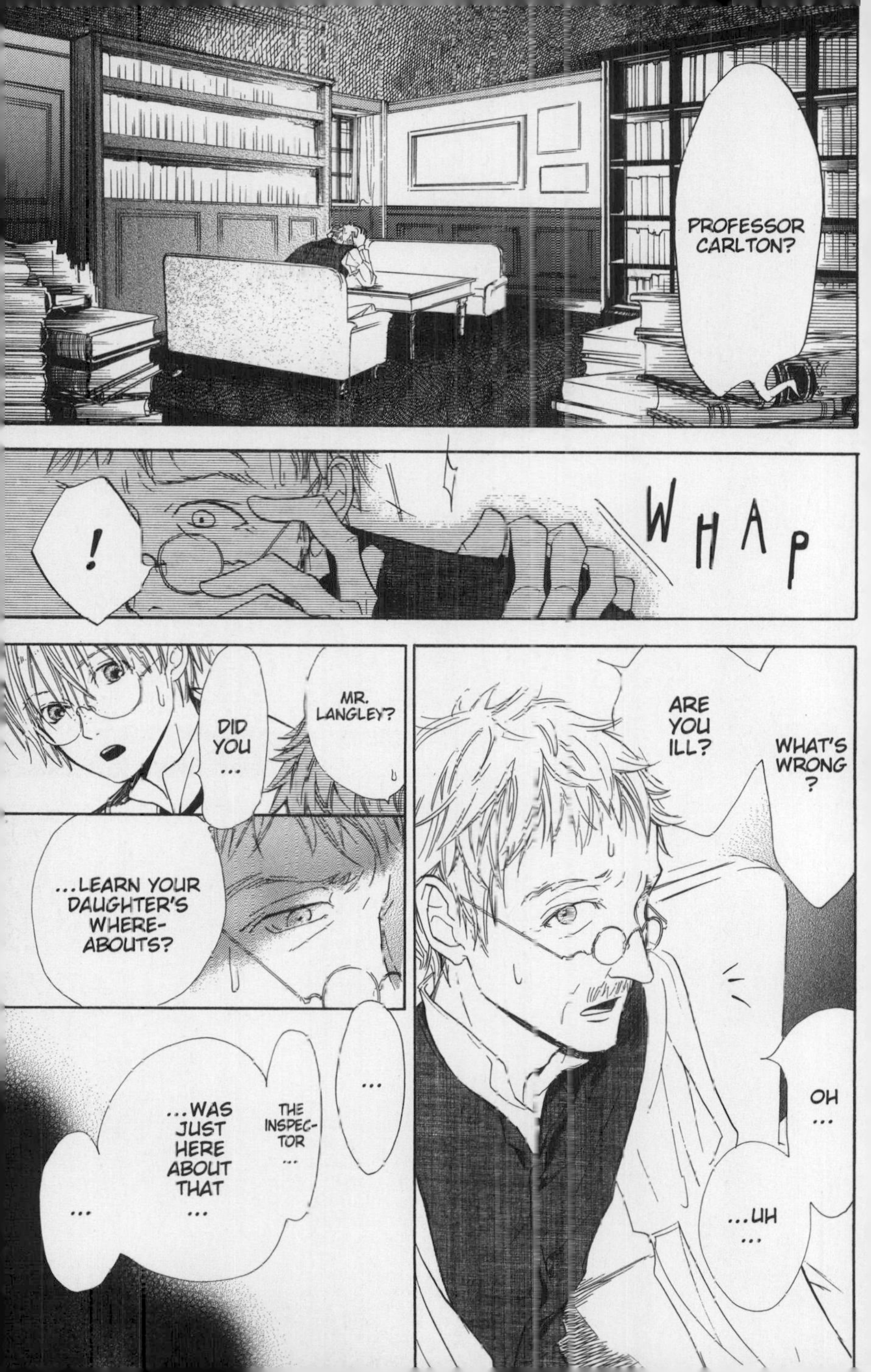
PROFESSOR CARLTON?
WHAP
!
WHAT'S WRONG?
ARE YOU ILL?
OH...
...UH...
MR. LANGLEY?
DID YOU...
...LEARN YOUR DAUGHTER'S WHERE-ABOUTS?
...
THE INSPECTOR...
...WAS JUST HERE ABOUT THAT...
...

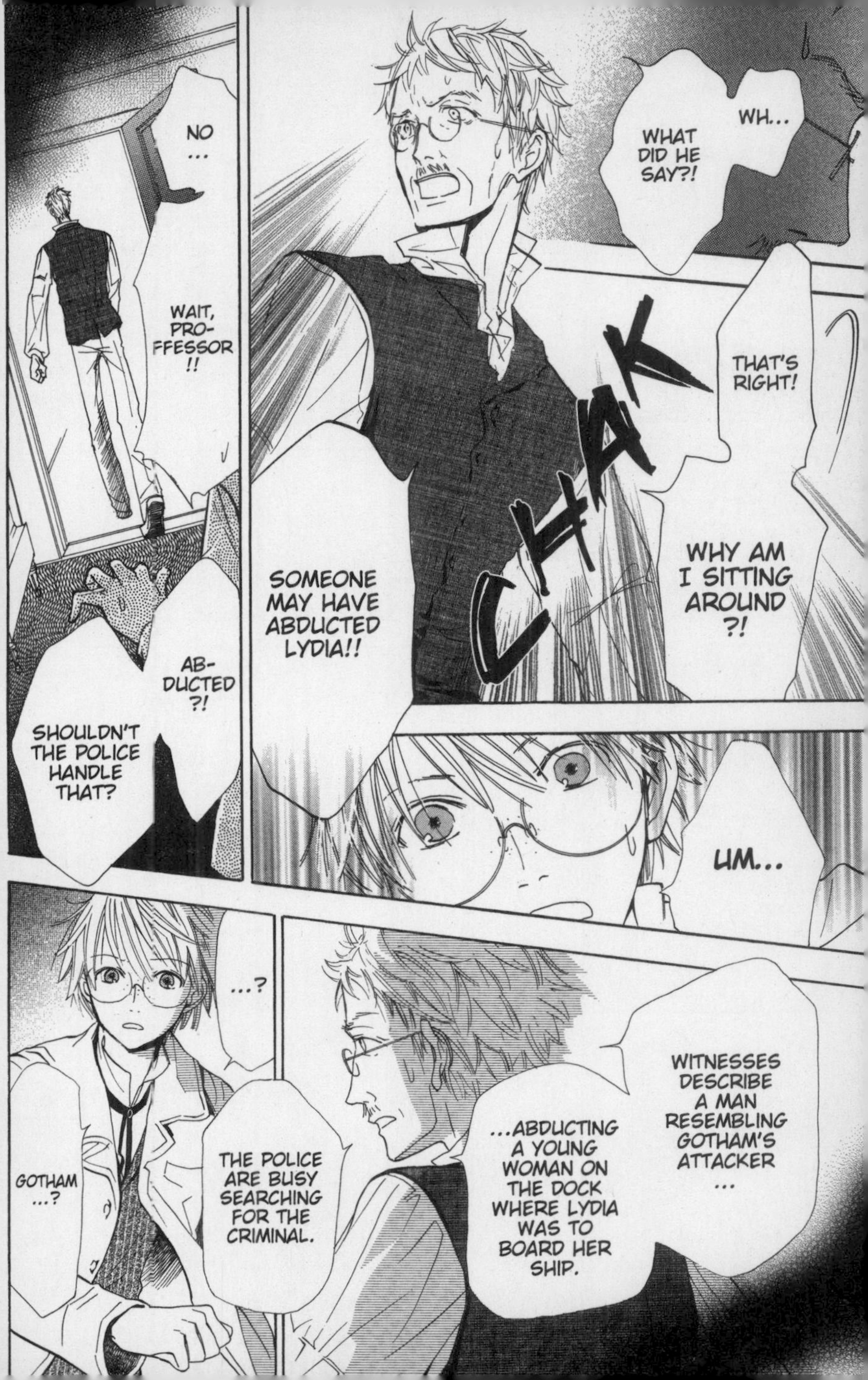
WH...
WHAT DID HE SAY?!
THAT'S RIGHT!
WHY AM I SITTING AROUND ?!
CHAK
SOMEONE MAY HAVE ABDUCTED LYDIA!!
UM...
NO ...
WAIT, PRO-FFESSOR !!
AB-DUCTED ?!
SHOULDN'T THE POLICE HANDLE THAT?
WITNESSES DESCRIBE A MAN RESEMBLING GOTHAM'S ATTACKER ...
...ABDUCTING A YOUNG WOMAN ON THE DOCK WHERE LYDIA WAS TO BOARD HER SHIP.
THE POLICE ARE BUSY SEARCHING FOR THE CRIMINAL.
...?
GOTHAM ...?

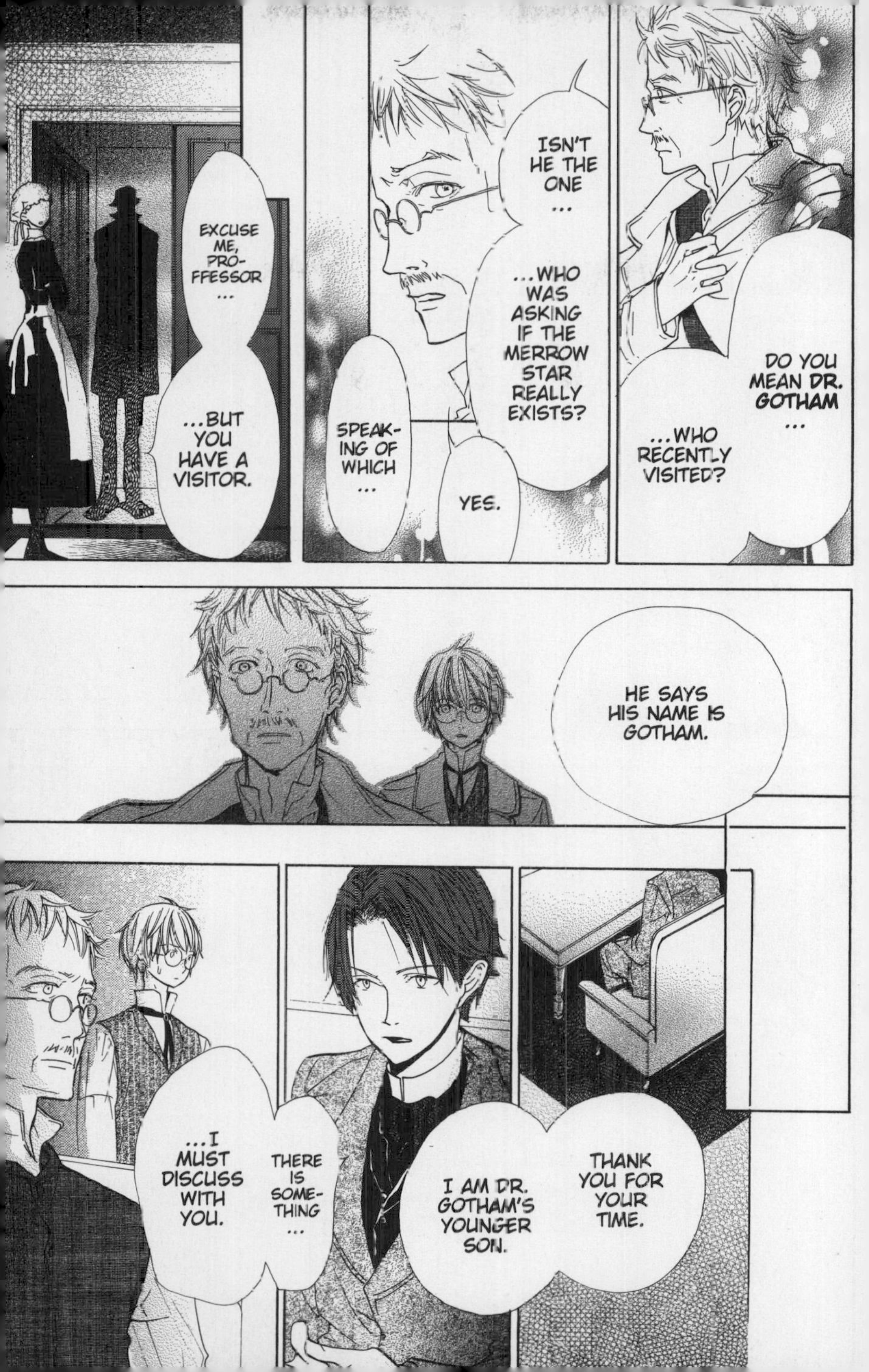
DO YOU MEAN DR. GOTHAM ...
...WHO RECENTLY VISITED?
ISN'T HE THE ONE ...
...WHO WAS ASKING IF THE MERROW STAR REALLY EXISTS?
YES.
SPEAKING OF WHICH ...
EXCUSE ME, PROFFESSOR ...
...BUT YOU HAVE A VISITOR.
HE SAYS HIS NAME IS GOTHAM.
THANK YOU FOR YOUR TIME.
I AM DR. GOTHAM'S YOUNGER SON.
THERE IS SOMETHING ...
...I MUST DISCUSS WITH YOU.

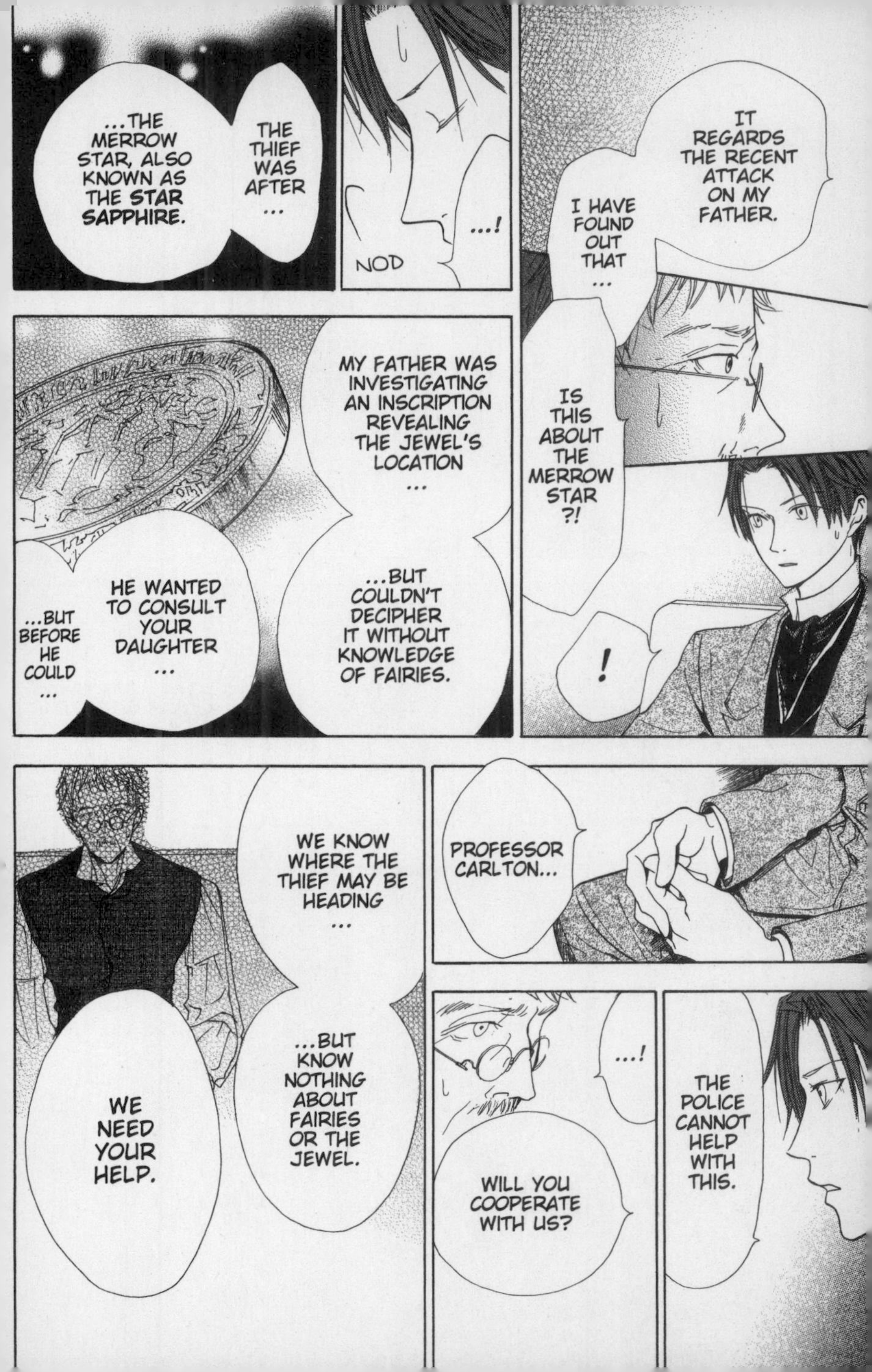
IT REGARDS THE RECENT ATTACK ON MY FATHER.
I HAVE FOUND OUT THAT...
...!
NOD
THE THIEF WAS AFTER...
...THE MERROW STAR, ALSO KNOWN AS THE STAR SAPPHIRE.
IS THIS ABOUT THE MERROW STAR?!
!
MY FATHER WAS INVESTIGATING AN INSCRIPTION REVEALING THE JEWEL'S LOCATION...
...BUT COULDN'T DECIPHER IT WITHOUT KNOWLEDGE OF FAIRIES.
HE WANTED TO CONSULT YOUR DAUGHTER...
...BUT BEFORE HE COULD...
PROFESSOR CARLTON...
THE POLICE CANNOT HELP WITH THIS.
...!
WILL YOU COOPERATE WITH US?
WE KNOW WHERE THE THIEF MAY BE HEADING...
...BUT KNOW NOTHING ABOUT FAIRIES OR THE JEWEL.
WE NEED YOUR HELP.

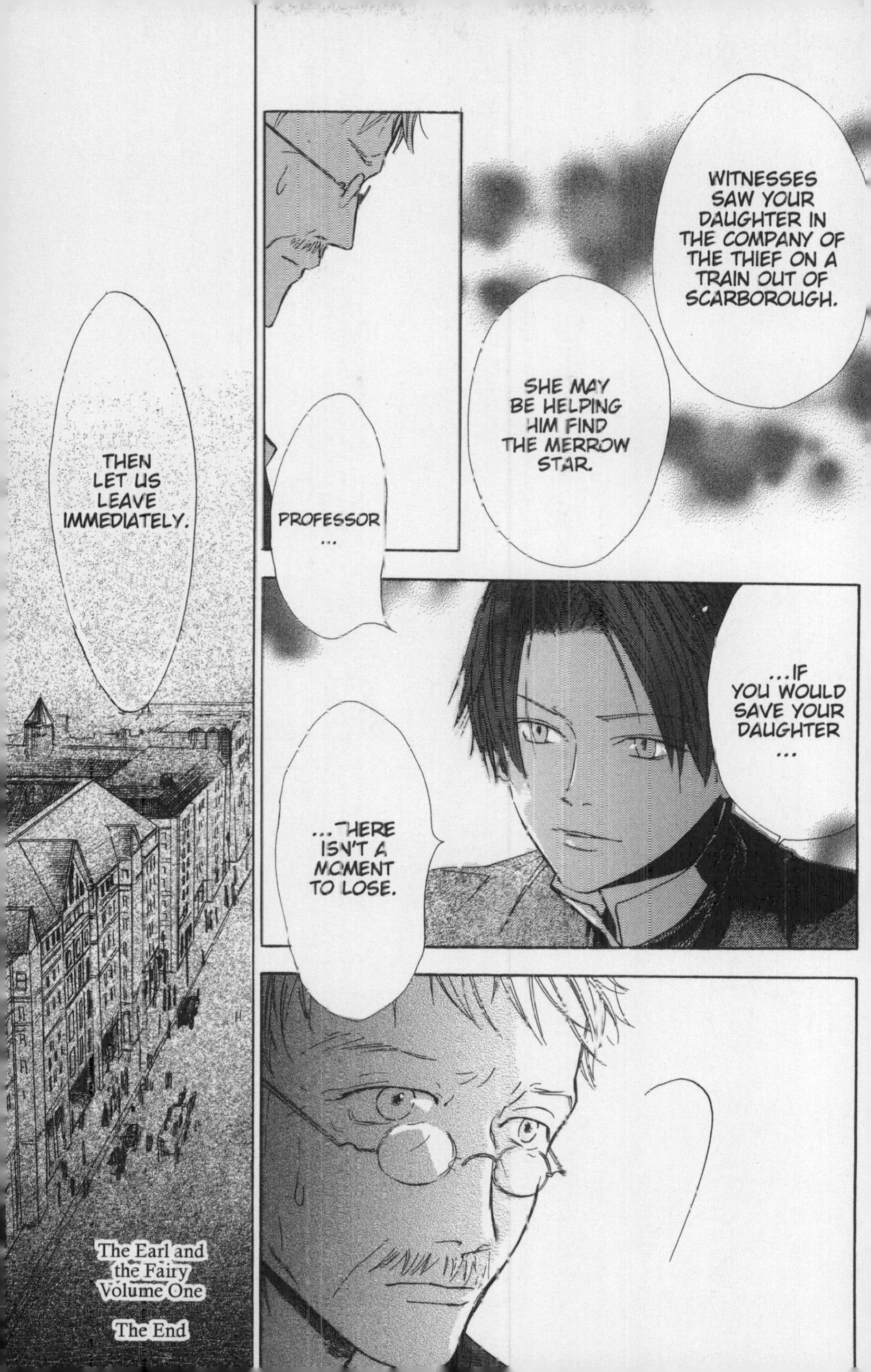
WITNESSES SAW YOUR DAUGHTER IN THE COMPANY OF THE THIEF ON A TRAIN OUT OF SCARBOROUGH.
SHE MAY BE HELPING HIM FIND THE MERROW STAR.
PROFESSOR ...
...IF YOU WOULD SAVE YOUR DAUGHTER ...
...THERE ISN'T A MOMENT TO LOSE.
THEN LET US LEAVE IMMEDIATELY.
The Earl and the Fairy Volume One
The End

The Earl & the Fairy

Will fans of the novels like this? Will I be able to convey the magic of the original series to those encountering the world of *The Earl and the Fairy* for the first time? There were times when I would worry, and there were times I would set aside my worries; that is how I drew this series.

-Ayuko

Ayuko debuted with the story "Us, You and Me" in *Bessatsu Margaret* magazine and has gone on to publish several manga titles in addition to *The Earl and the Fairy*. Born in Kumamoto Prefecture, she's a Leo and loves drawing girl characters.

Mizue Tani is the author of several fantasy novel series and in 1997 received an honorable mention in the Shueisha Roman Taisho awards. Aside from *The Earl and the Fairy*, her other major series is *Majo no Kekkon* (The Witch's Marriage).

The Earl and the Fairy
Volume 1
Shojo Beat Edition

Story and Art by
Ayuko

Original Concept by
Mizue Tani

English Translation & Adaptation/John Werry
Touch-up Art & Lettering/Joanna Estep
Design/Izumi Evers
Editor/Pancha Diaz

Printed in the U.S.A.

Published by VIZ Media, LLC
P.O. Box 77010
San Francisco, CA 94107

10 9 8 7 6 5 4 3 2 1
First printing, March 2012

www.viz.com   www.shojobeat.com